LEAH HENNEL

ALONE TOGETHER

A PANDEMIC PHOTO ESSAY

FOREWORD BY SHELLEY BOETTCHER

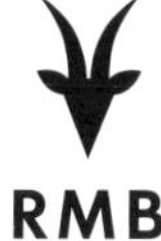

RMB

This book is dedicated to the tireless healthcare workers,
to the patients and their families who shared their stories,
to everyone who allowed themselves to be photographed
in their daily, pandemic-altered lives.

Thank you.

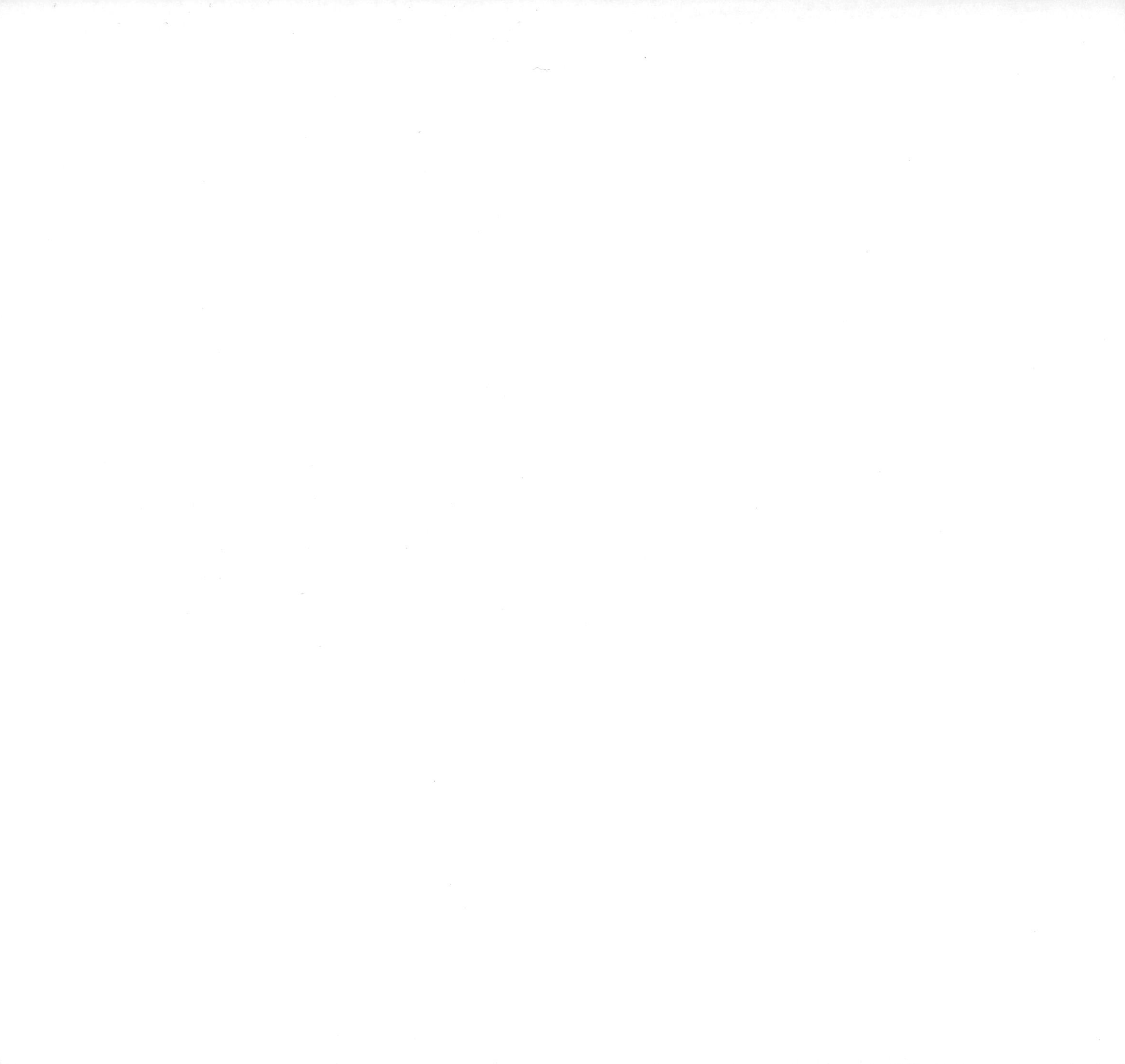

FOREWORD

SHELLEY BOETTCHER

It has been a time of fear and uncertainty and, for millions of people around the world, a time of grief, loss and change.

The COVID-19 pandemic of 2020 and 2021, the greatest health crisis in more than a century, has been unforgettable, an event that will live in history.

Every country in the world, every society, has been affected by the pandemic, and Alberta has been no exception.

As of November 2021, more than 3,200 Albertans have died of COVID-19.

Thousands more have been sick, and of them, many are now long-haul COVID-19 patients with health issues that have lingered for weeks or months. Some patients are still suffering even now, long after their original diagnosis.

Throughout it all, Alberta Health Services staff photographer Leah Hennel has been documenting our province's frontline workers and the COVID-19 patients they care for, showcasing the lives of the Albertans who refused to give up in the face of adversity. Her photographs show how people have adapted and found safe new ways to celebrate special occasions and accomplishments both major and minor. But they also show how Albertans have dealt with the tragedies that the pandemic has brought.

The team at Alberta Health Services has been at the front lines of the global battle against the deadly coronavirus, researching the SARS-CoV-2 virus and treating the Albertans who become sick and need medical attention. They've traced the virus's path through communities in every corner of the province, and, now that vaccines against the virus have become available, they have been working long hours to ensure that any Albertan who wants a vaccine can get one.

A multi-award-winning photographer whose work continues to appear in print publications and online around the world, Leah sees those moments that make us human and, using that skill, she has captured the vulnerability, beauty and strength of those affected by the pandemic and its ongoing legacy of hardship and fear.

It has been a long year and more since the COVID-19 crisis first reared its head, and the world is now full of stories like those presented here. Stories of resilience and courage, of grief, suffering and celebration. They are everywhere.

The COVID-19 pandemic has been a watershed moment in world history. It has reshaped the way we live our lives, and many of its effects will live on, likely for generations to come. Yet, as time goes by, the memory of these past months will start to fade, and life will ease back into normalcy.

Life does that. Life goes on.

But these photographs and stories will always be here, a permanent record of this historical event and a reminder that, at a moment's notice, life can change forever.

INTRODUCTION

LEAH HENNEL

The past year and a half has changed me.

As a photojournalist for more than 20 years, I've covered a lot in my career. But never anything this heavy, this important. The pandemic caused by the SARS-CoV-2 virus has touched the lives of everybody, not just here in Alberta and Canada but throughout the whole world.

Over the past 18 months I've borne witness to a lot of death and sadness, and a lot of grief, but I have also witnessed plenty of happy moments and got to experience first-hand the goodness in people.

Other stories I've followed have been brief – a day or two, maybe a week. I cover them, then move on to the next assignment. This one, though, has been unrelenting.

I am documenting something historic, but I'm also going home and dealing with the same thing as everyone else who's worried about COVID-19, who's worried about passing it on to their family.

Then again, everyone is affected by COVID-19. Maybe you have it. Or know someone who has it. Or have lost a job because of it.

In March 2019, when I was hired by Alberta Health Services to be its Calgary-based staff photographer, my mission was to chronicle, among other things, the different roles within the healthcare system.

And the last couple of years – the height of the pandemic – has revealed the incredible work being done behind the scenes.

For my part, I wanted to capture Albertans – those who are members of the healthcare team, those who are patients, those who are adapting to life outside of healthcare.

Away from medical facilities, too, there was plenty to focus on.

The way people adjusted to fear, to lockdowns, to unknowns. The way they continued to carry on. Visiting with family through a window. Holding socially distanced baby showers. Staging drive-through religious celebrations, drive-through grads, drive-by birthday parties, drive-in movie theatres and drive-in musical recitals.

More than anything, I wanted to portray – and I hope I did – patients and staff with dignity. In many cases, these occasions were literally the worst moments of their lives. When anyone goes to the hospital, they're not feeling their best, so to have a photographer right there, too? Those can be hard conversations. That's why taking the photos of the patients and capturing their stories was more of a collaborative process – I'm not a fly on the wall, and I want to make sure they're comfortable with my camera.

As a photographer, I feel it's important to show that those who died are not just numbers. Rather, these are real people with loved ones and families and friends. Photographs have the power to put human faces on tragedy.

I've learned about the different jobs in a hospital, from porters to healthcare aides to housekeeping to food services. They are there to make a difference. They really do care. And it hurts: they're affected by deaths; they're affected by struggling loved ones.

Through it all, I did see hope. Literally, once. The mural in which a teenaged girl simply spelled out the word "hope" on the wall of a vaccine clinic that was about to open.

This is authentic, truthful storytelling about what I saw. It's not everything – it's just what I happened to be present for. This is what I saw – a small but representative sliver of the pandemic in Alberta.

I want to thank my colleagues at Alberta Health Services, healthcare workers everywhere and, most importantly, the patients and their loved ones for courageously sharing their stories.

THE PHOTOGRAPHS

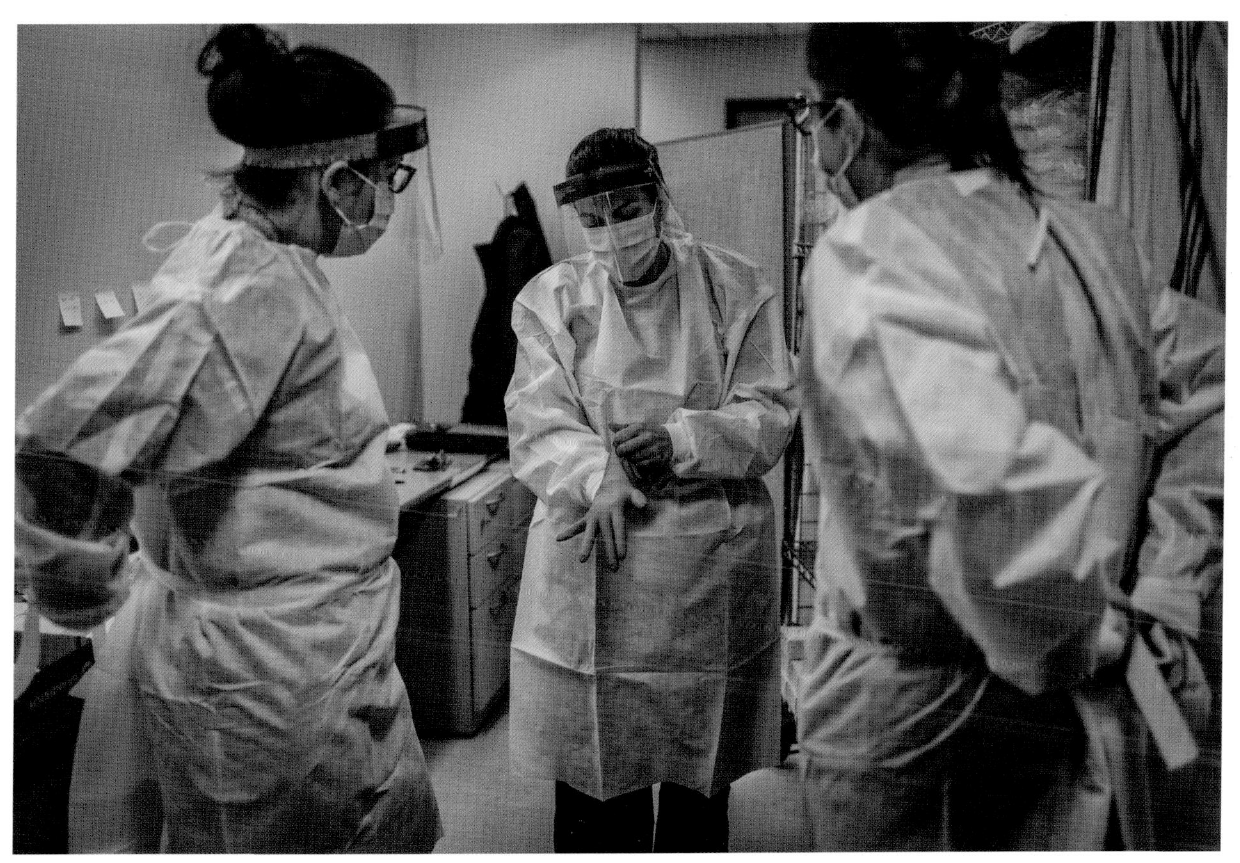

Vanessa Babiuk, middle, and colleagues get ready to swab patients for COVID-19 at one of the drive-through testing sites in Calgary, Alberta, in March 2020.

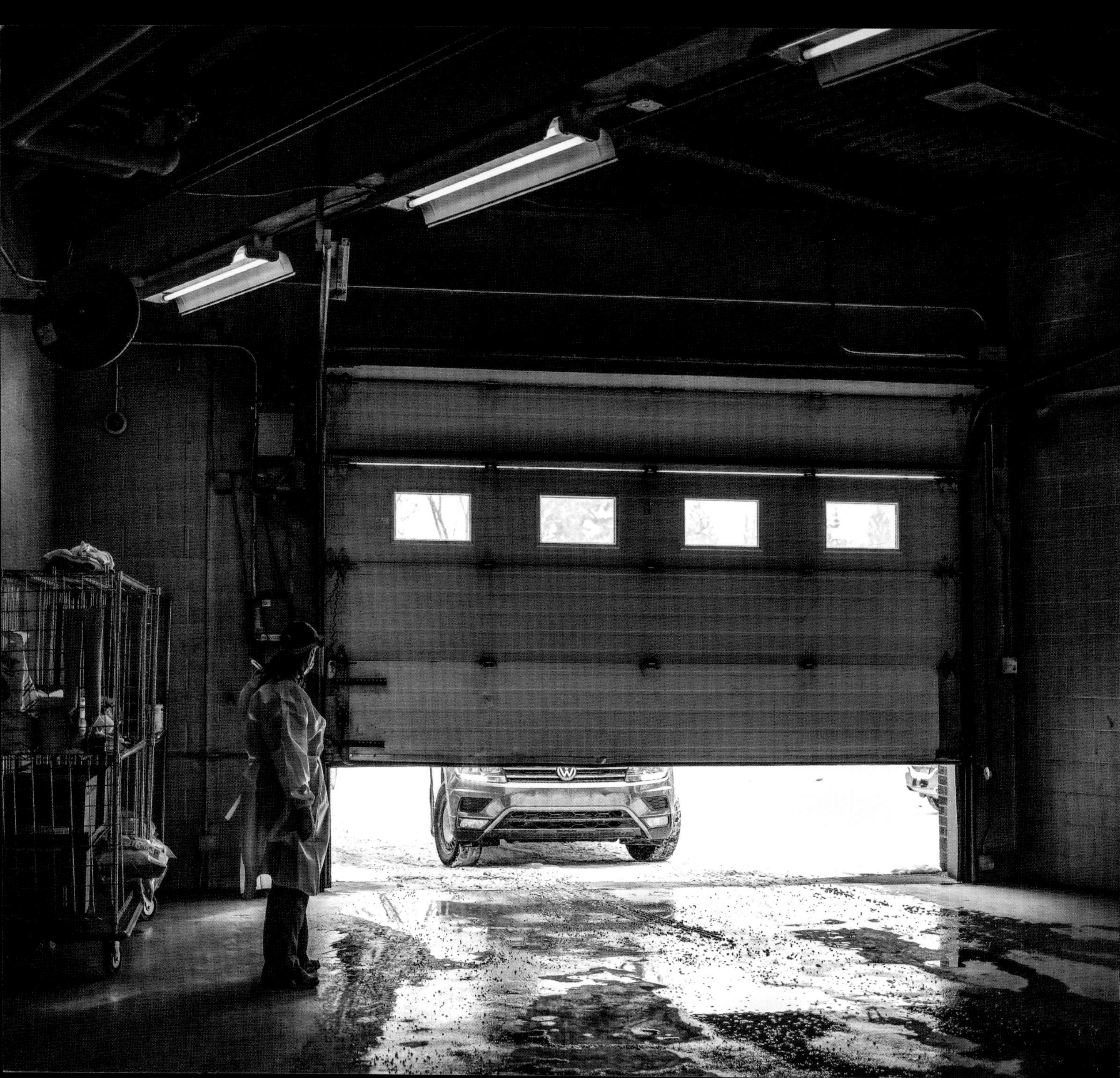

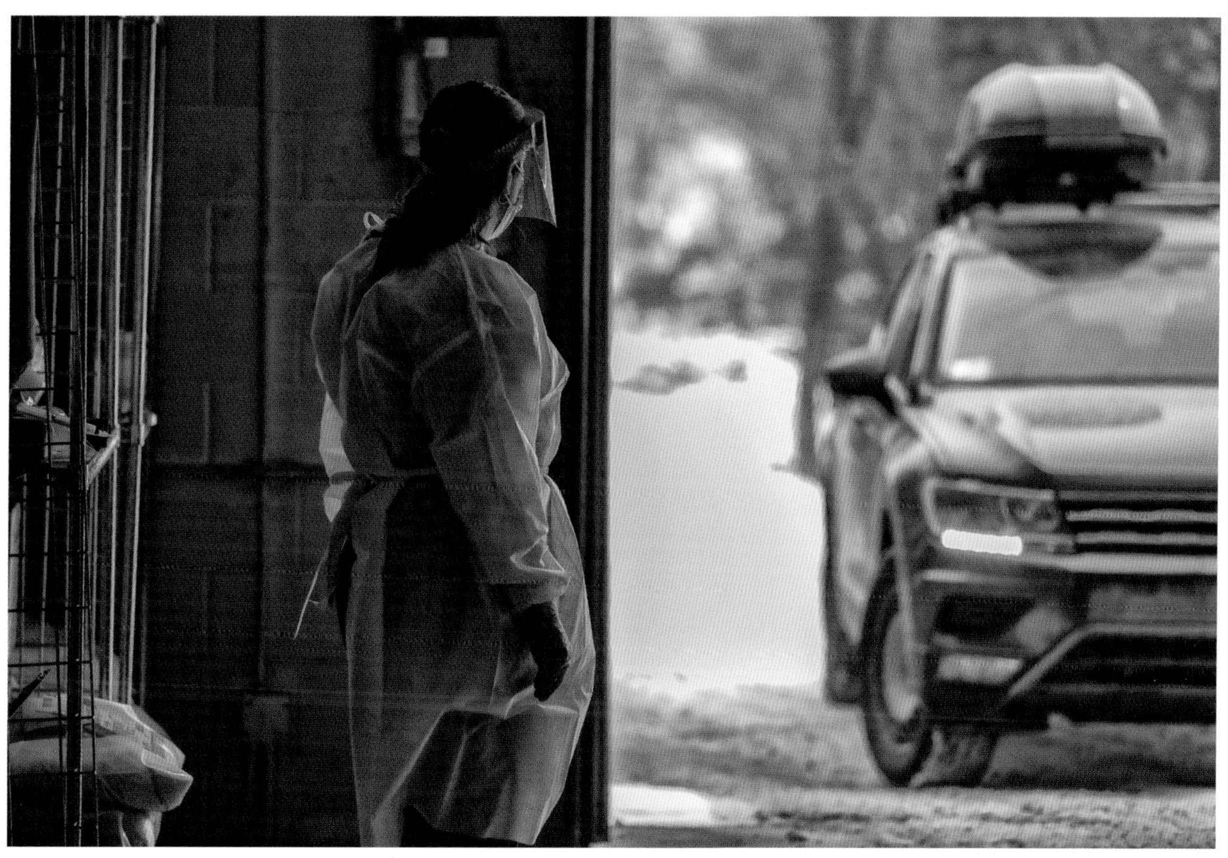

Vanessa Babiuk waits for a car at the one of the drive-through COVID-19 testing sites in Calgary, Alberta, in March 2020.

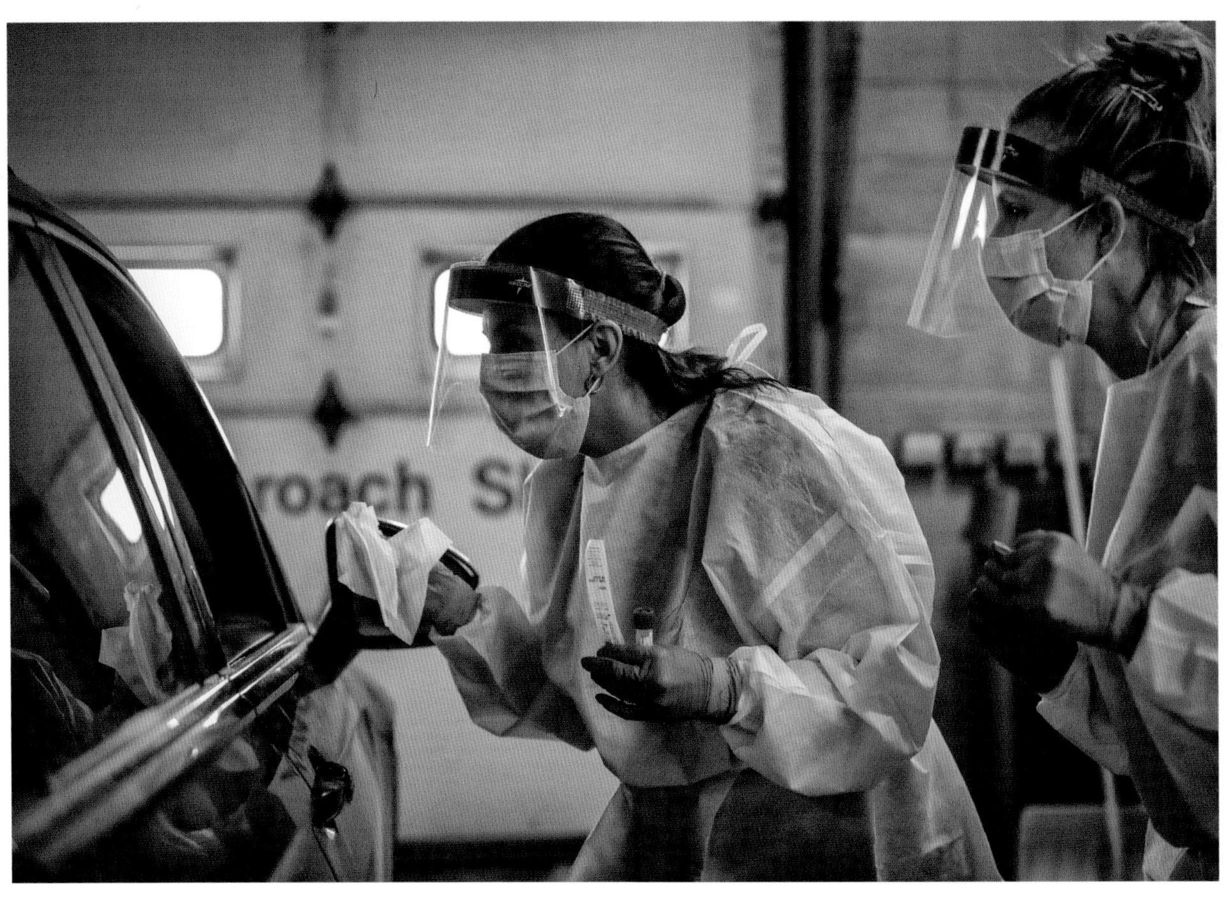

Vanessa Babiuk, left, asks questions before administering a COVID-19 swab.

Lacey Johnson administers a nasal test at a drive-through facility in Calgary, Alberta. March 2020.

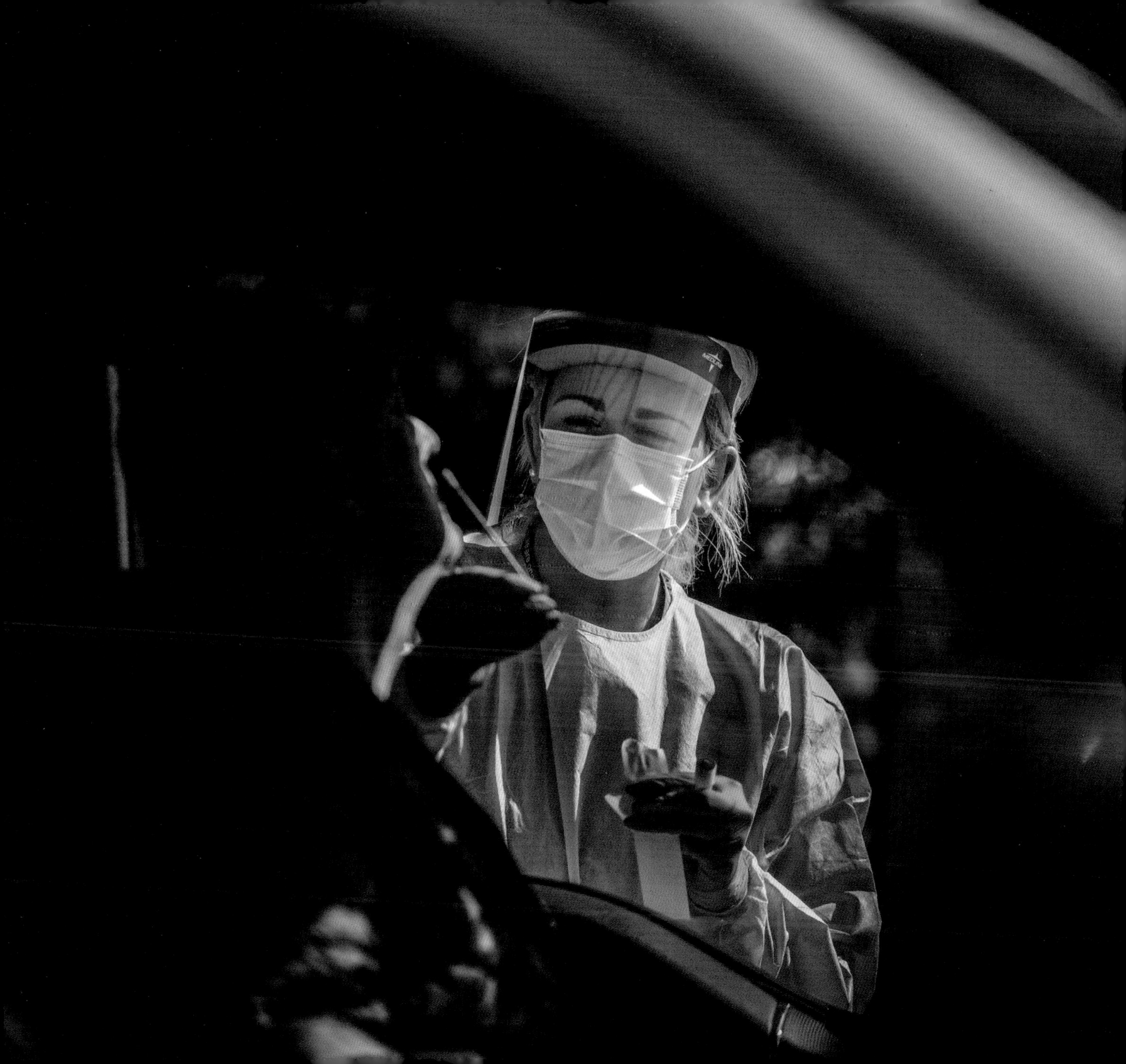

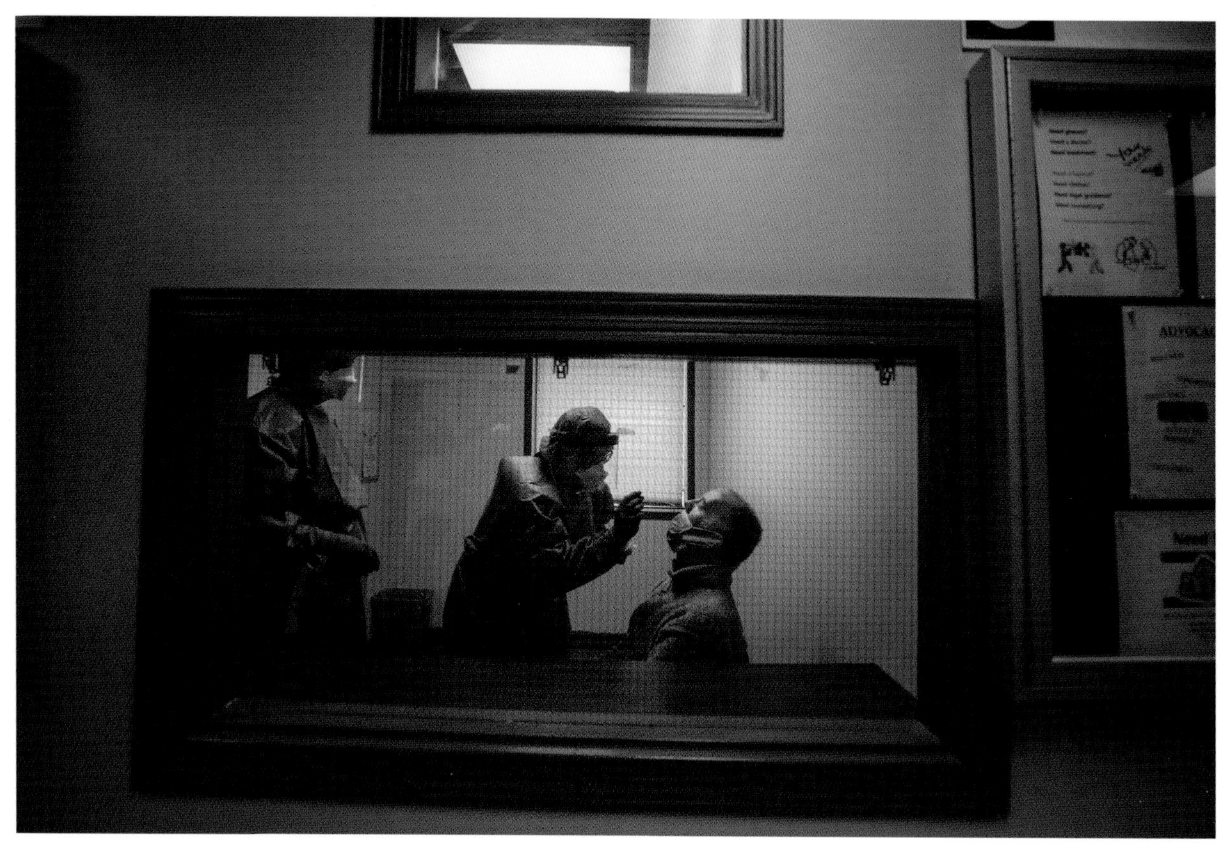

Advanced care paramedic Timothy Chung, centre,
and colleague Lou LaBrash take a COVID-19 swab
from a resident at The Mustard Seed shelter in
Calgary, Alberta, in March 2020.

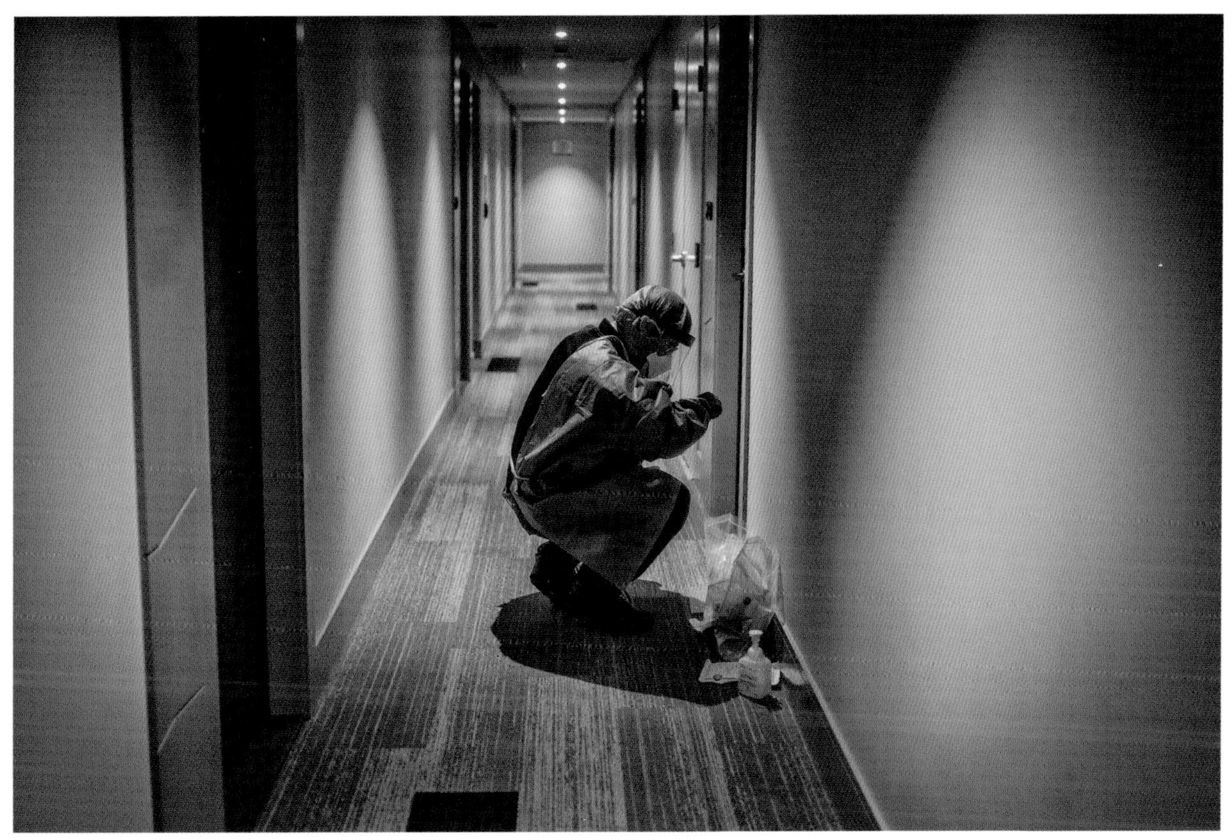

Timothy Chung, advanced care paramedic,
gets ready to go into a home to administer a
COVID-19 swab on March 18, 2020.

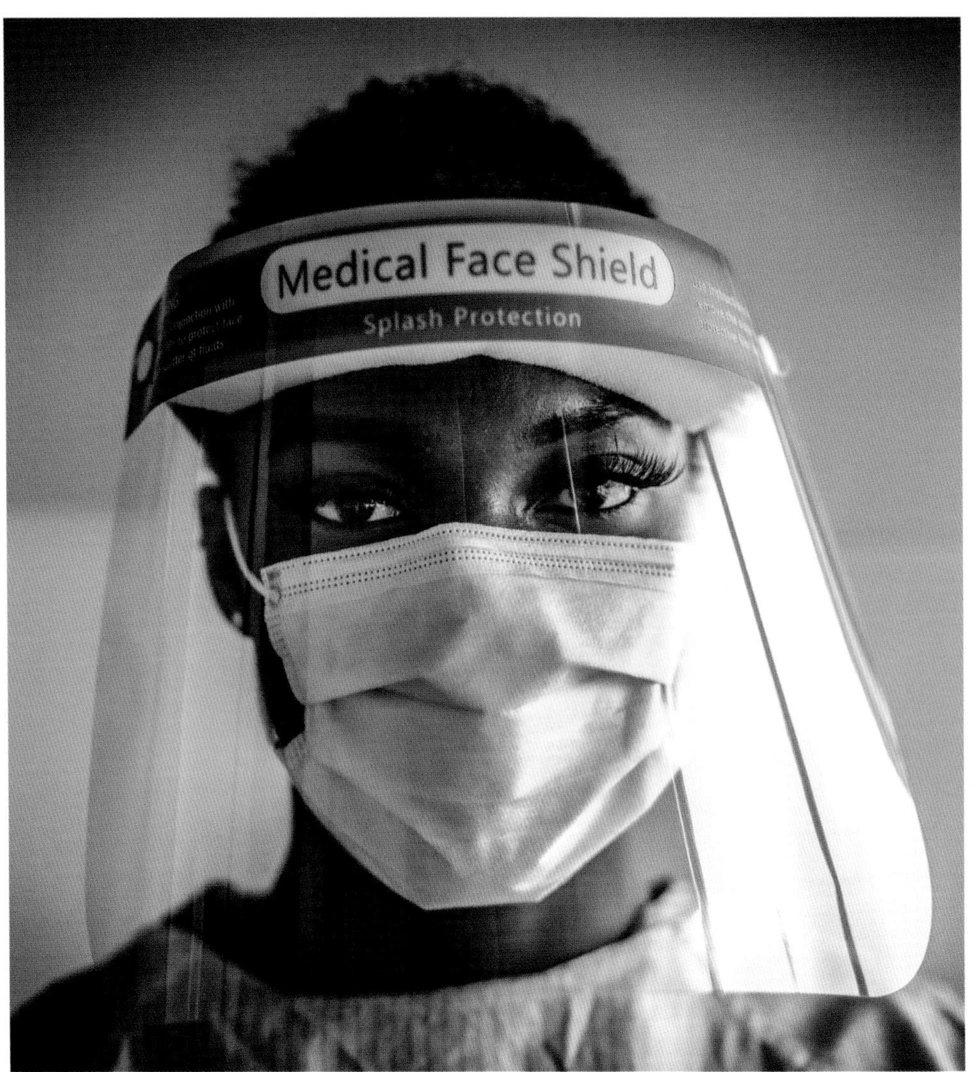

Registered nurse Amaka Ashiofu — at the Richmond Road Diagnostic and Treatment Centre in Calgary, Alberta, on November 27, 2020 — is part of a team that administers COVID-19 tests to Albertans.

Shauna May holds her daughter Izzy May, 2, as she gets a COVID-19 swab from registered nurse Amaka Ashiofu at the Richmond Road Diagnostic and Treatment Centre in Calgary, Alberta, on November 27, 2020

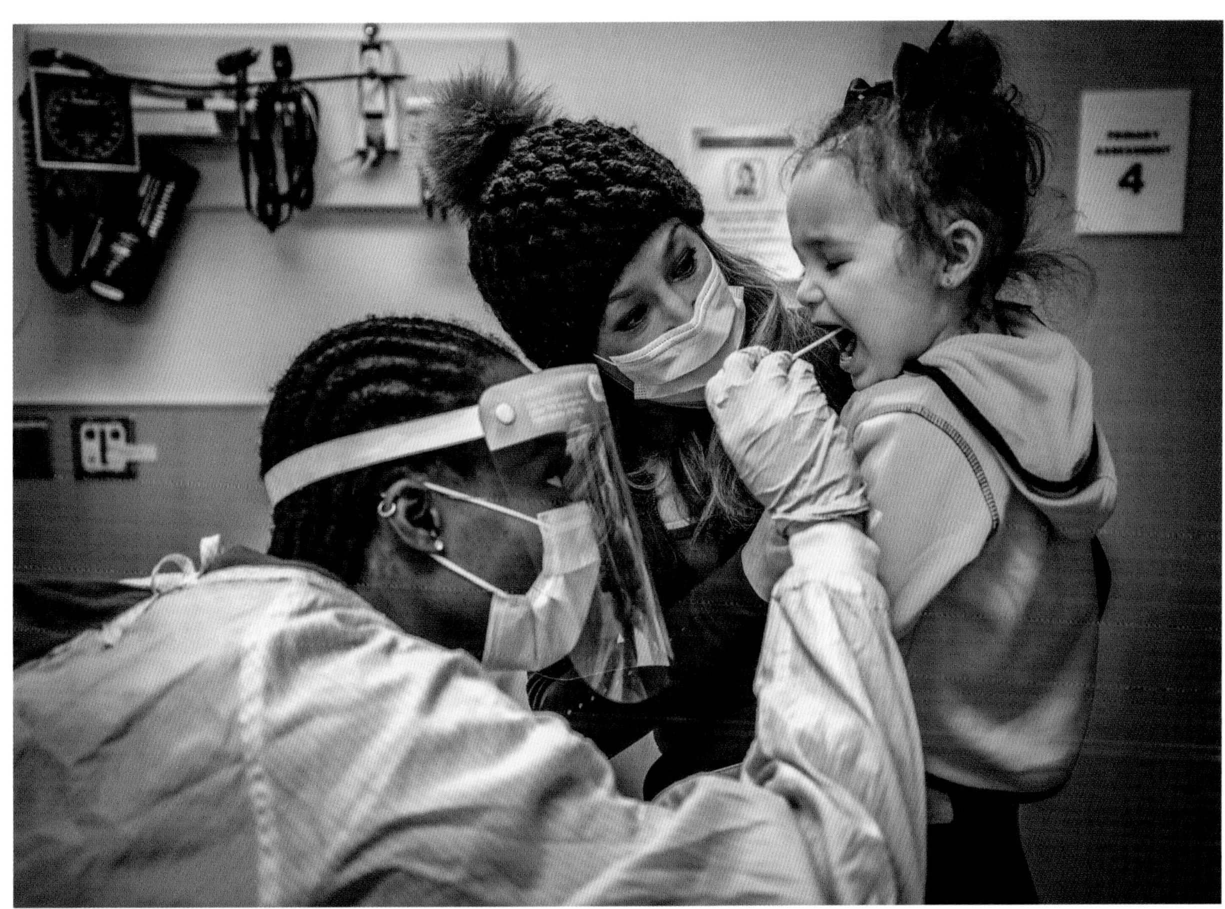

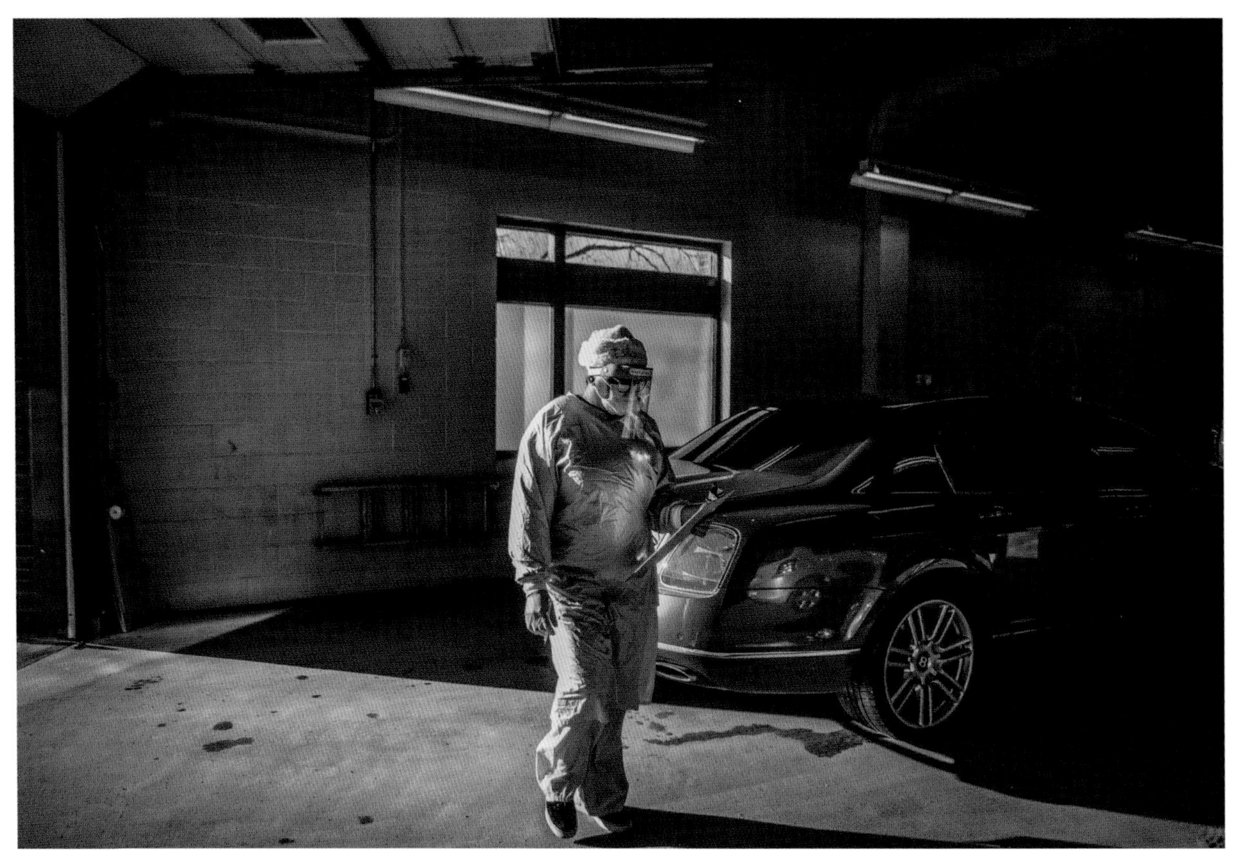

Odiri Orungbemi, licensed practical nurse, works
at the fast track assessment centre for COVID-19
swabs in Calgary, Alberta, on December 11, 2020.

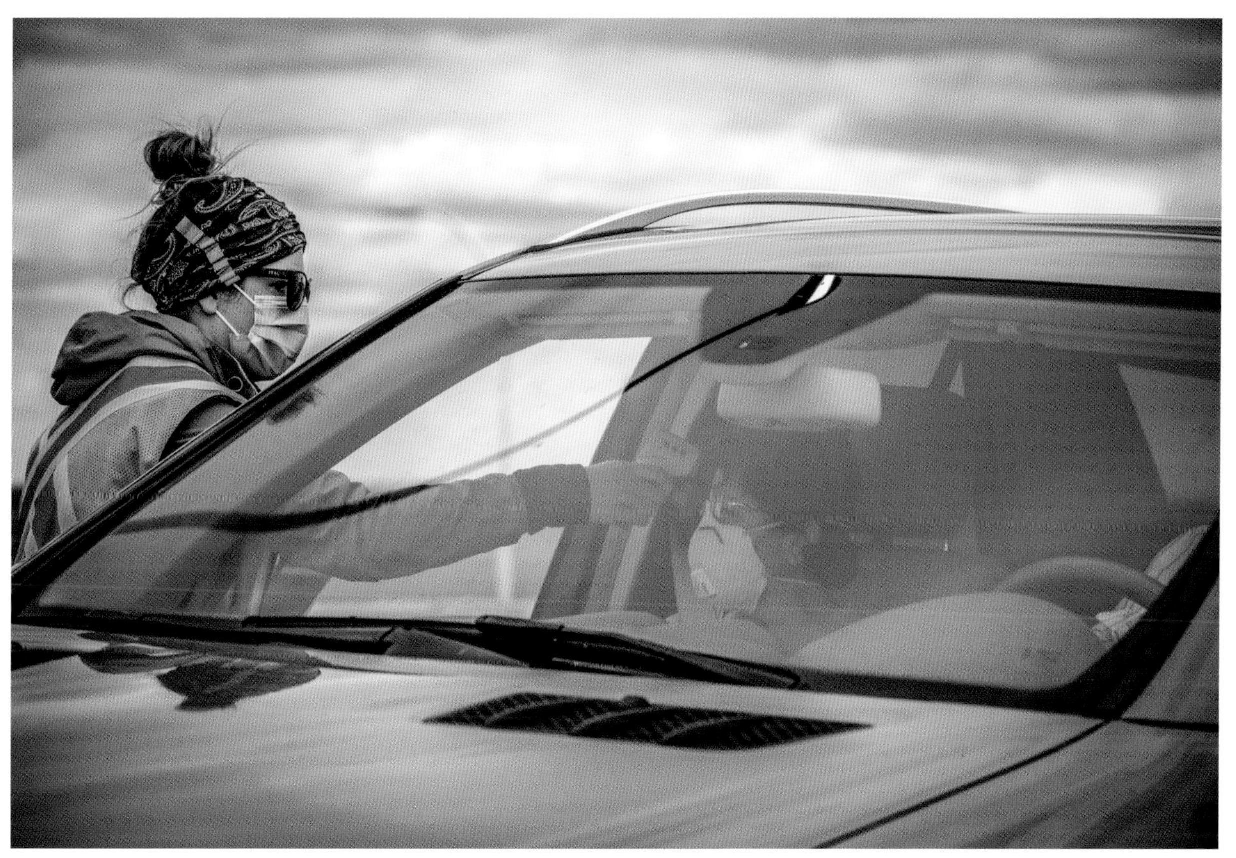

As part of the Alberta COVID-19 Border Testing
Pilot Program, licensed practical nurse Judy Wiebe
checks the temperatures of people coming into
Canada from the United States on June 4, 2020.

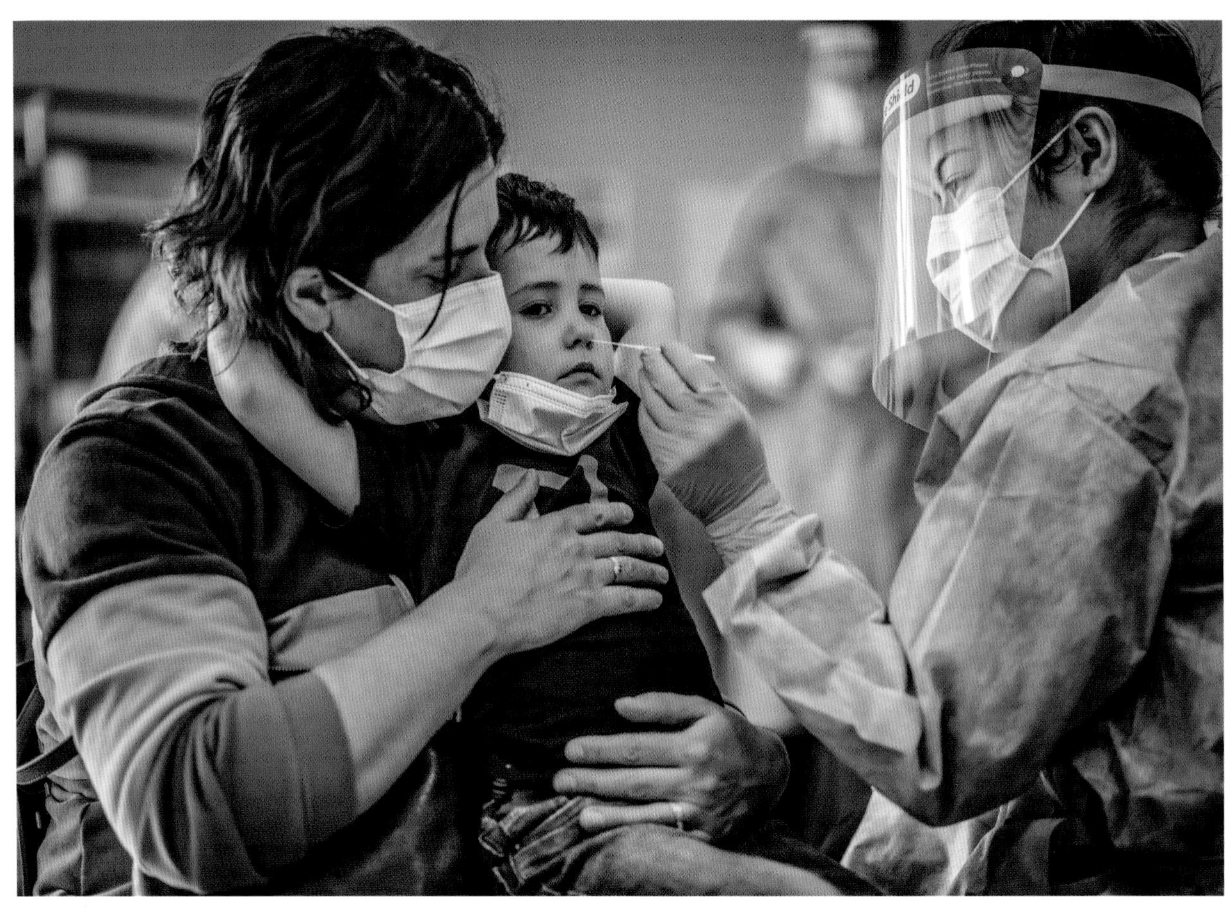

Adrienne Plaza holds her son Oscar, 3,
as he gets a COVID-19 swab from Miyeko
McInnes at the rapid-testing site in
Okotoks, Alberta, on April 15, 2021.

Hundreds of cars line up at the fast track
assessment centre in Calgary, Alberta,
on July 8, 2020.

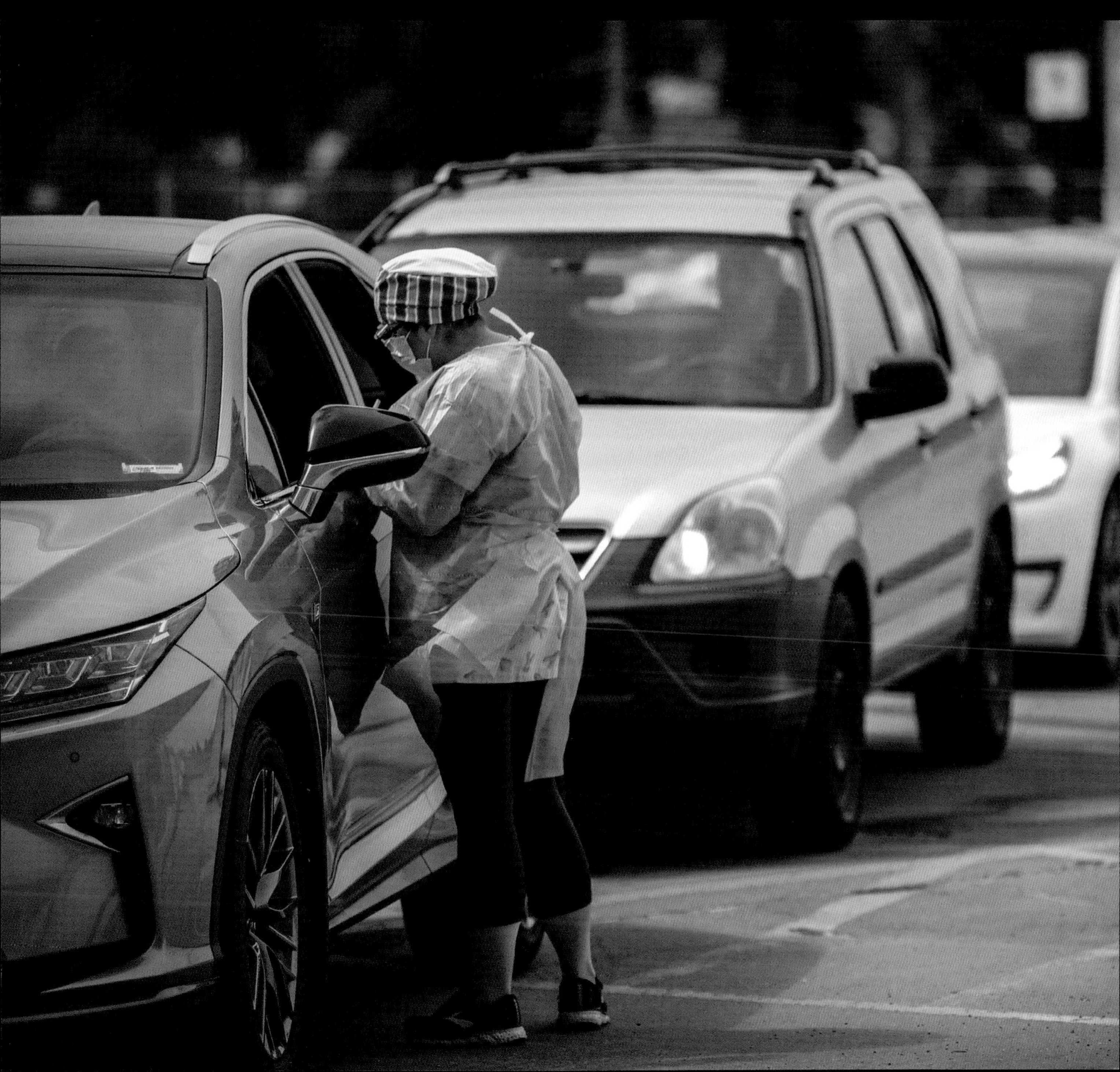

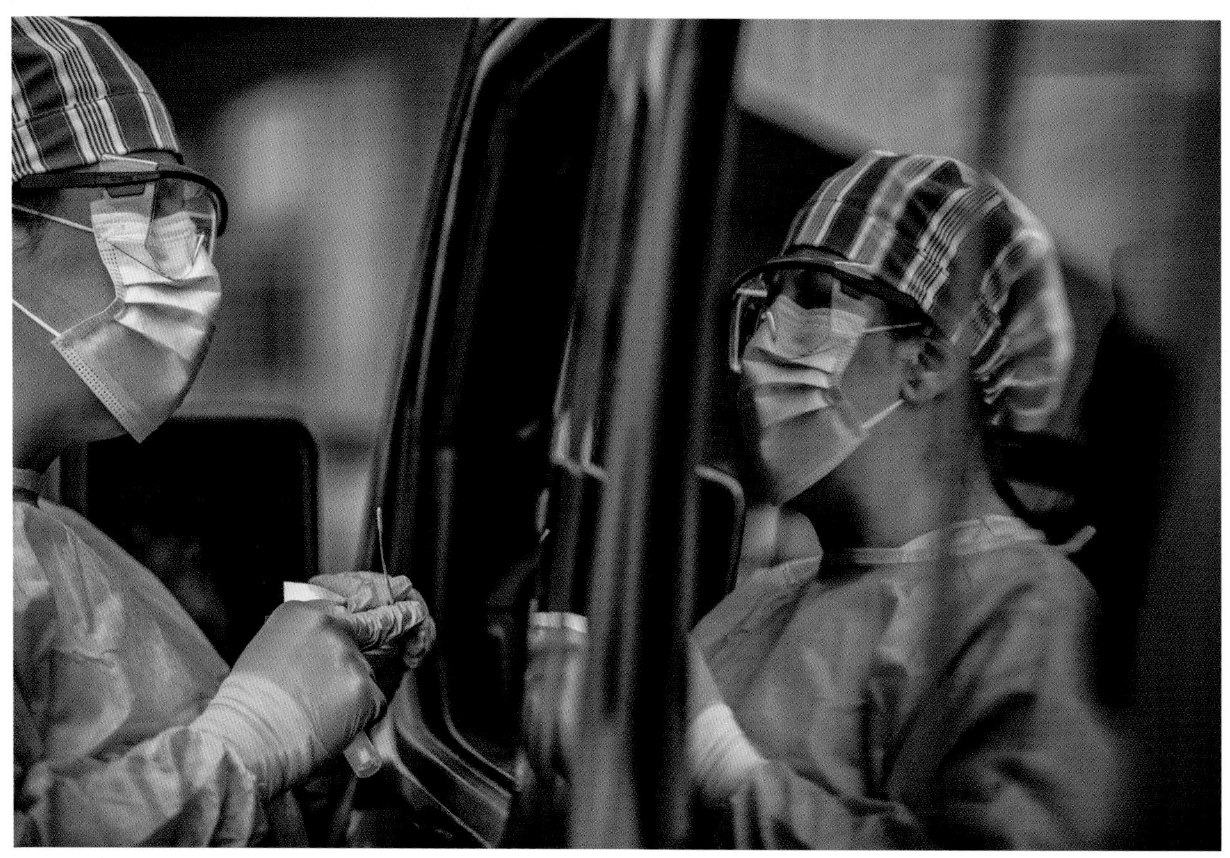

Jennifer Nakaska, speech language pathologist, gets a swab ready at the fast track assessment centre in Calgary, Alberta, on July 8, 2020.

Dr. Stephen Freedman, a pediatric emergency medicine physician, gives a COVID-19 swab to a five-day-old baby boy at Alberta Children's Hospital in Calgary. August 2020.

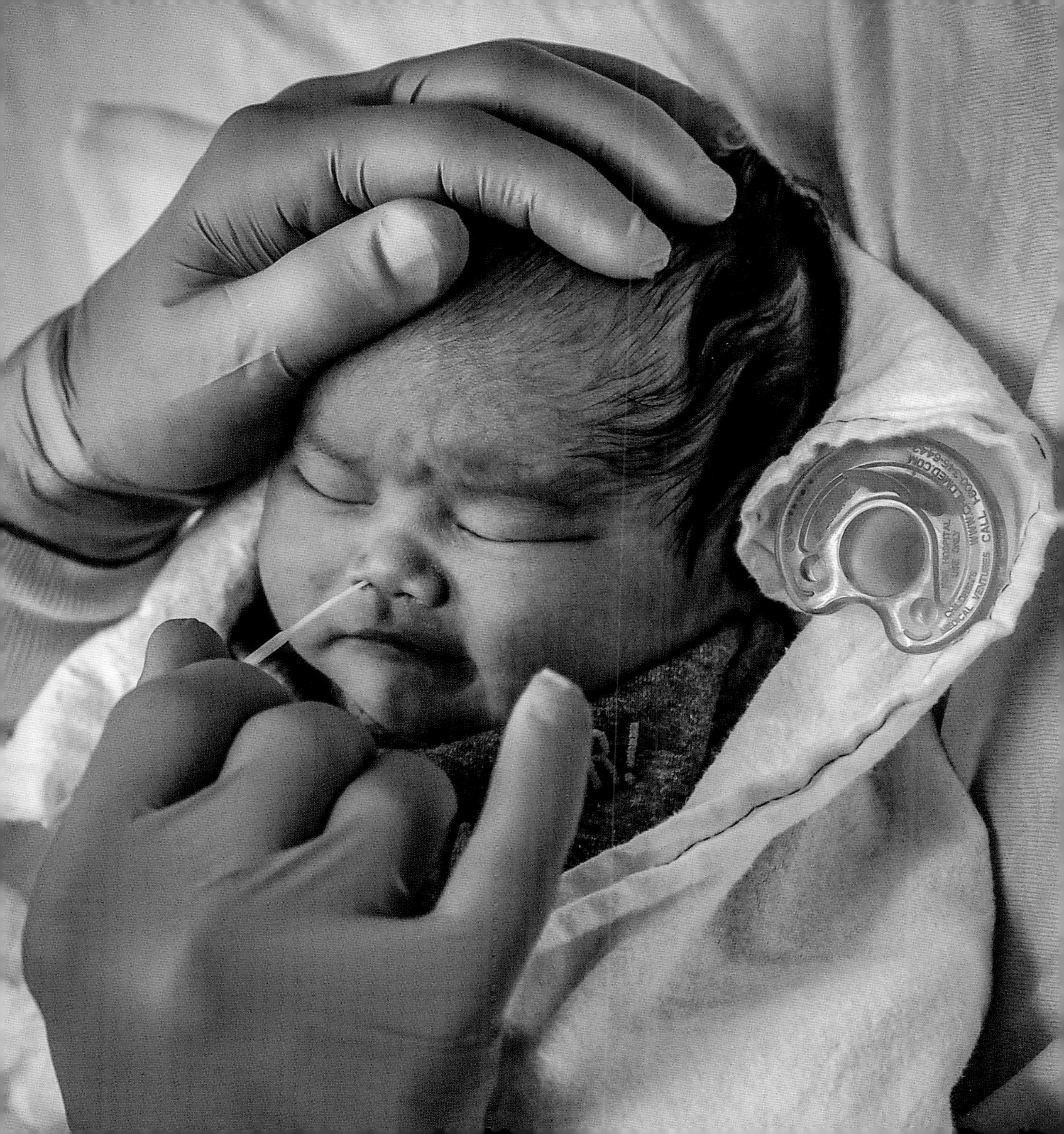

FOR HOSPITAL
USE ONLY
CHILDREN'S
WWW.CHILDMED.COM
MEDICAL VENTURES CALL 1-800-345-6443

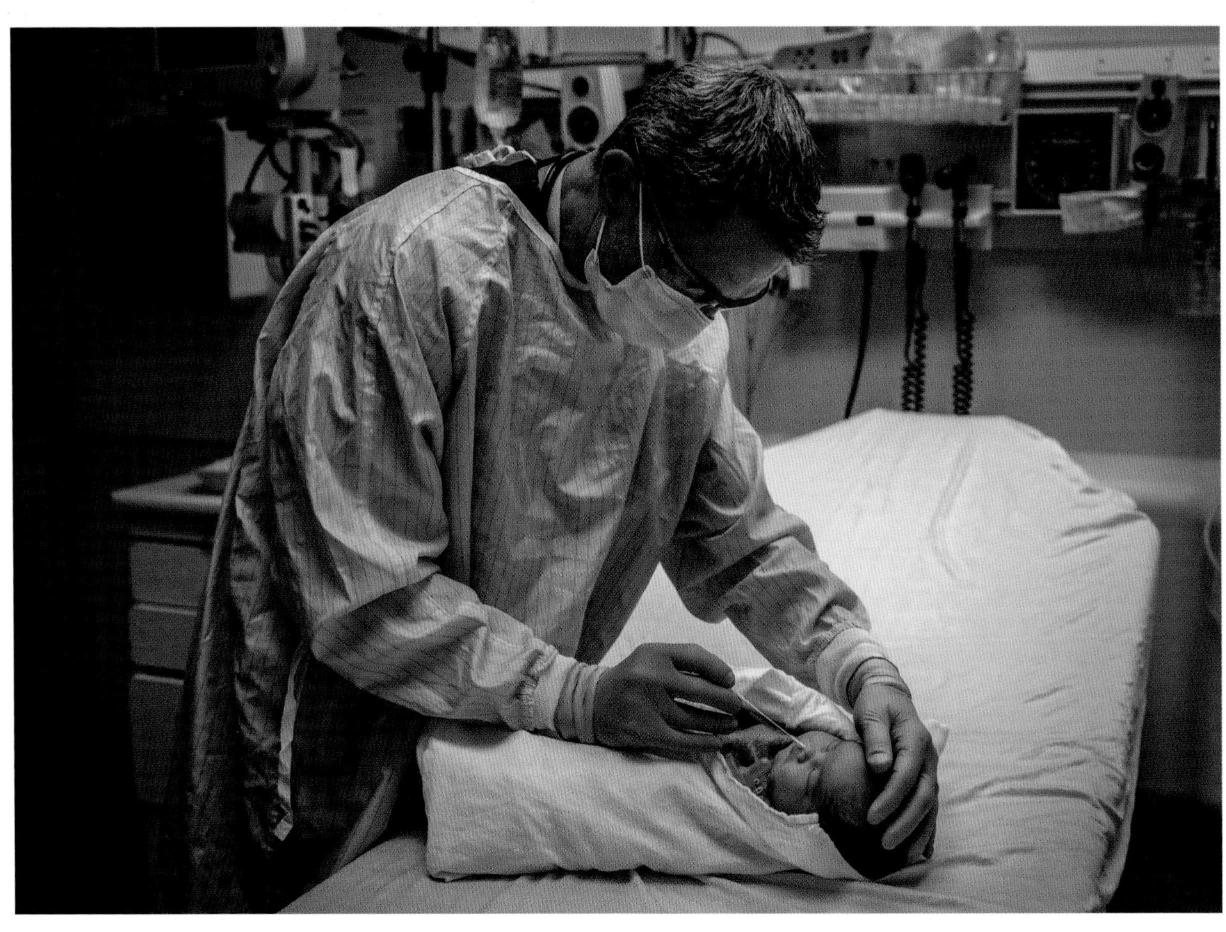

Pediatric emergency medicine physician Dr. Stephen Freedman administers a COVID-19 swab to a new baby at Alberta Children's Hospital in Calgary. Dr. Freedman is the lead investigator on an international study exploring the impact of COVID-19 on kids. August 2020.

Stephen Avenue in downtown Calgary, Alberta, is deserted in March 2020.

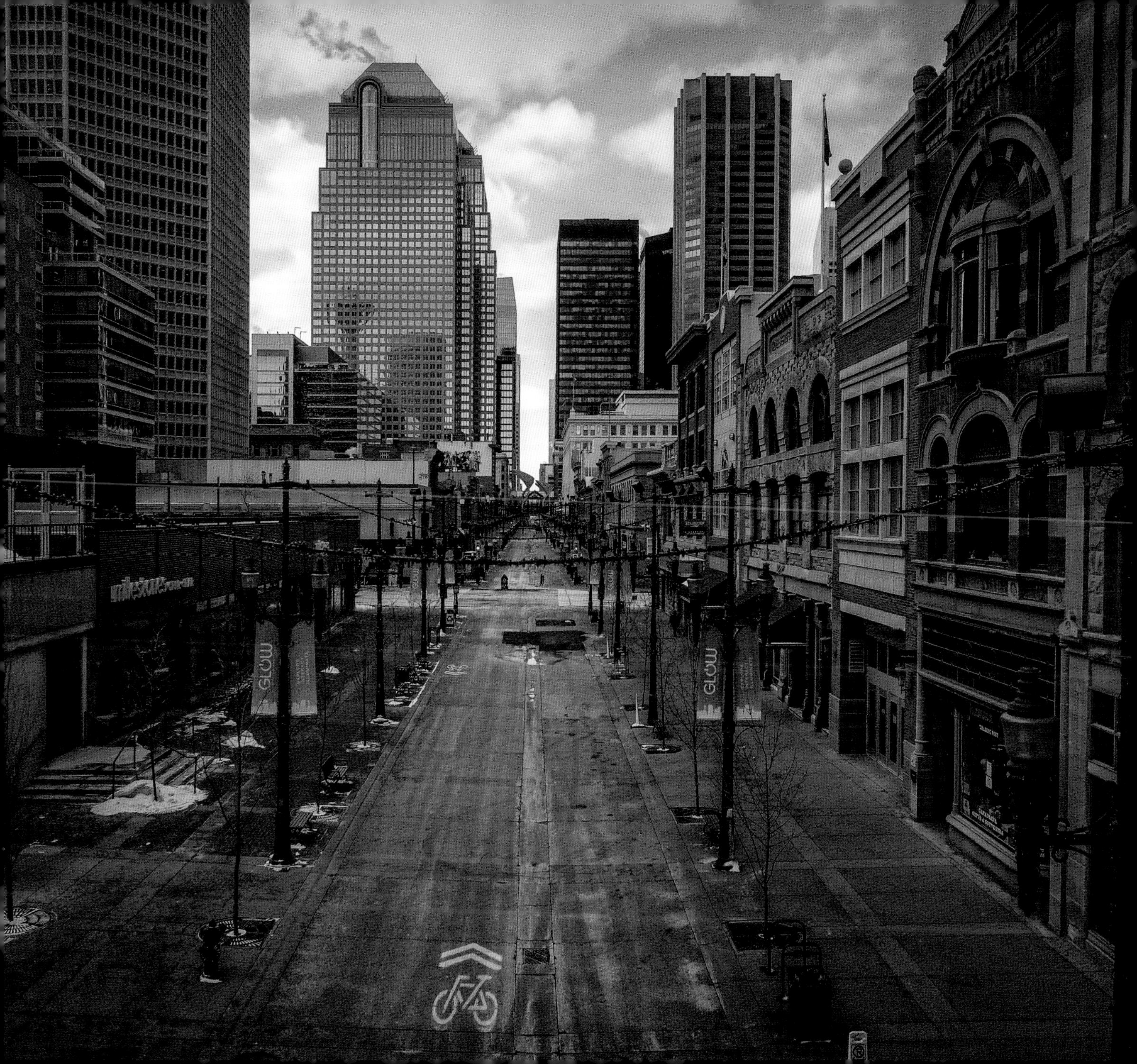

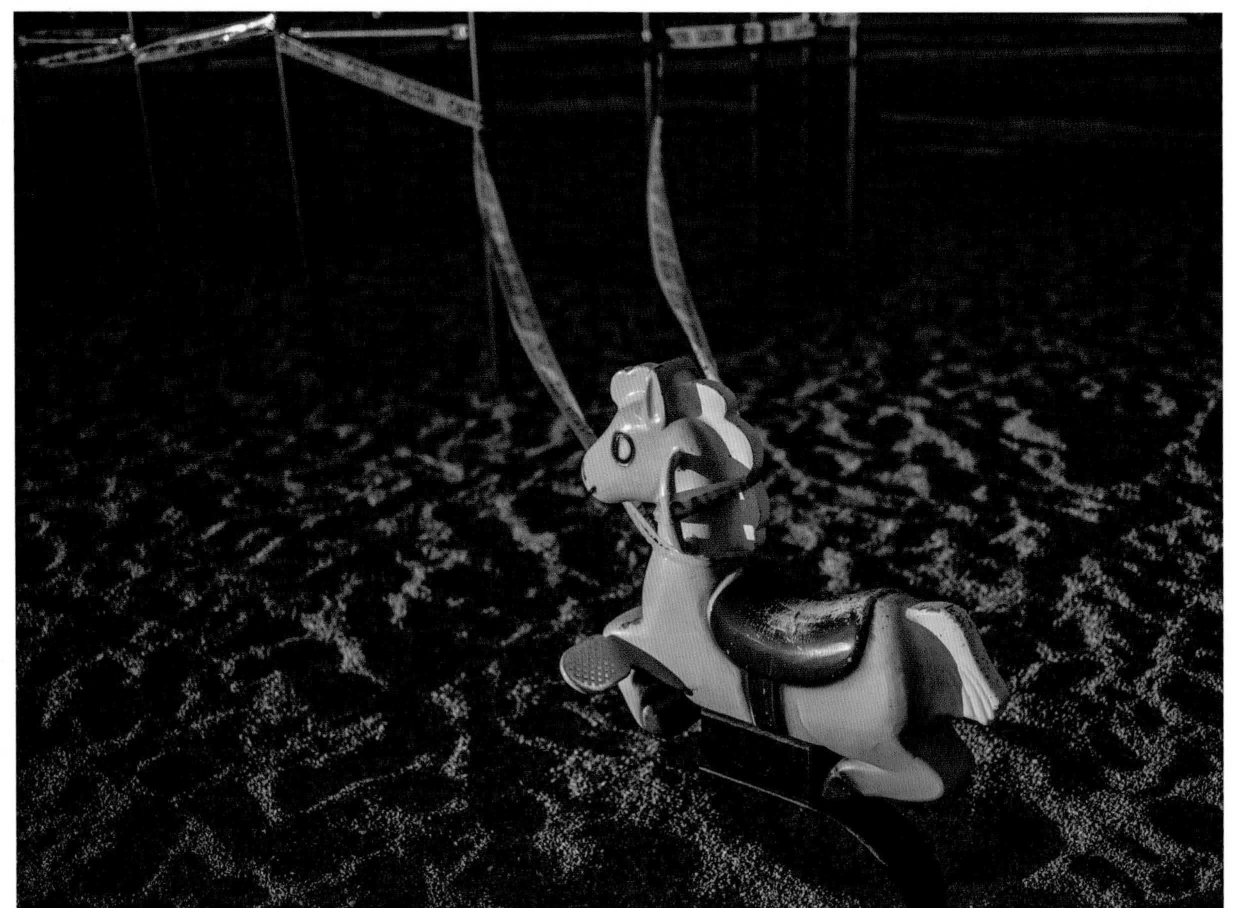

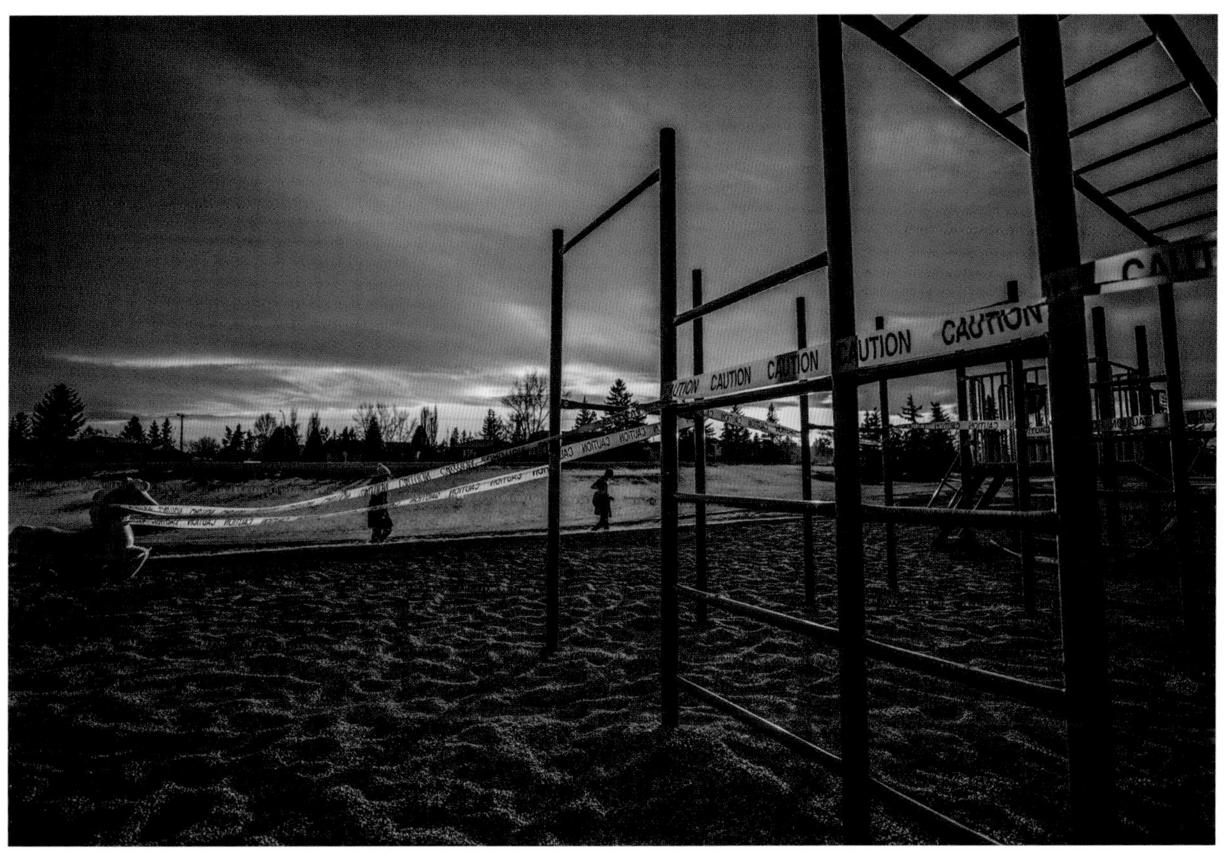

Yellow caution tape around a neighbourhood playground becomes the norm during the early days of the pandemic. March 2020.

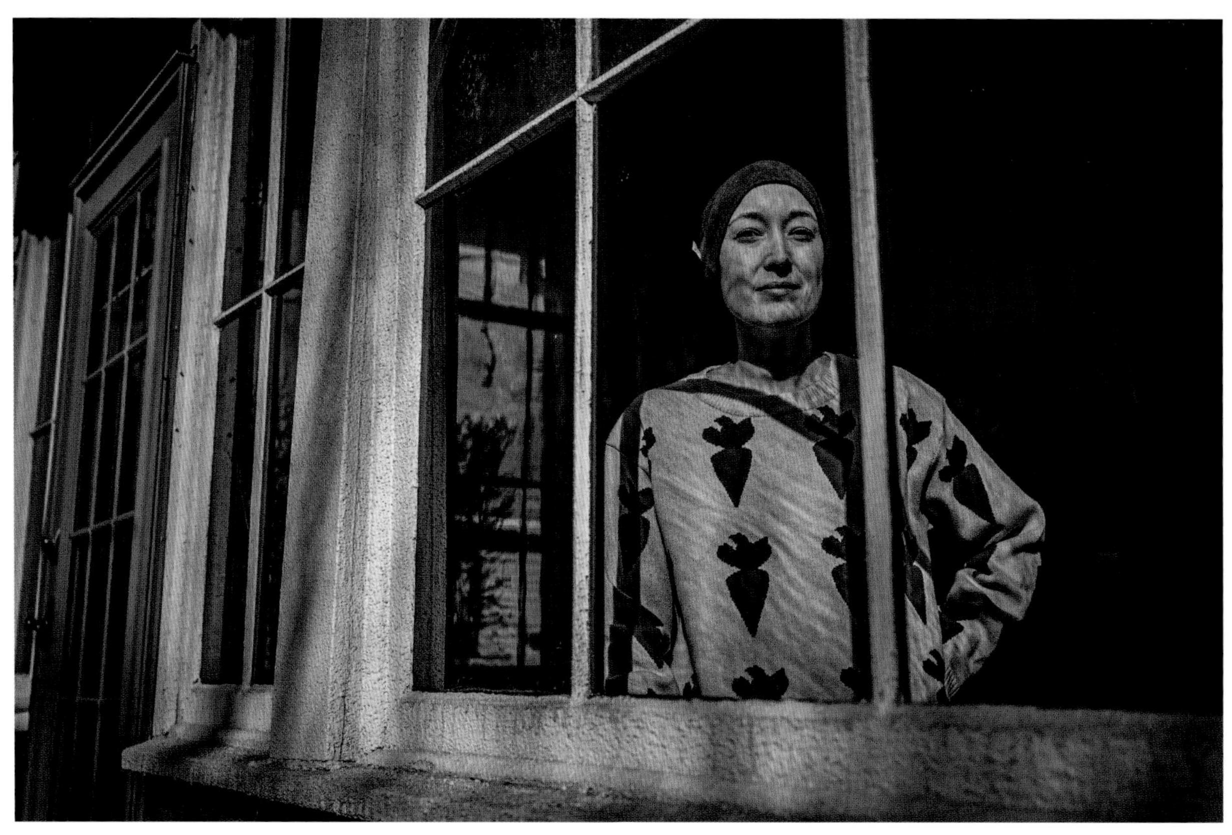

Kelly Cook was diagnosed with breast cancer in November 2019.
In late March, she shared some of her self-isolation positivity: "My
daughter is so incredibly happy and curious and hilarious. My husband has been my rock day-in and day-out. My family has shouldered
so much of the burden for me. As well as other things like my dog, my
friends, fresh air, and laughing at the absurdity of everything."

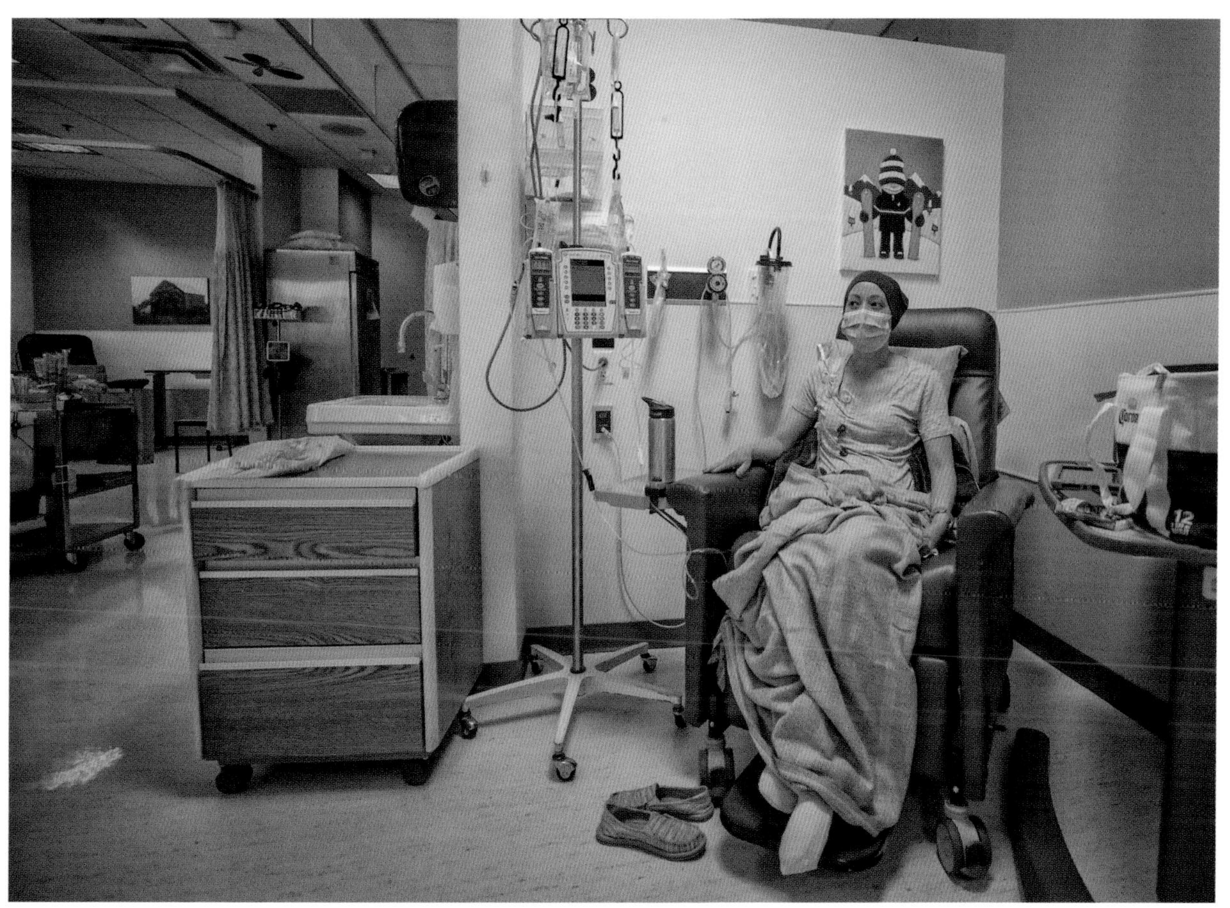

Kelly Cook goes through chemotherapy in isolation because of COVID-19 protocol in May 2020. Later that month, Cook rang the ceremonial bell after her last round of chemotherapy at the Tom Baker Cancer Centre.

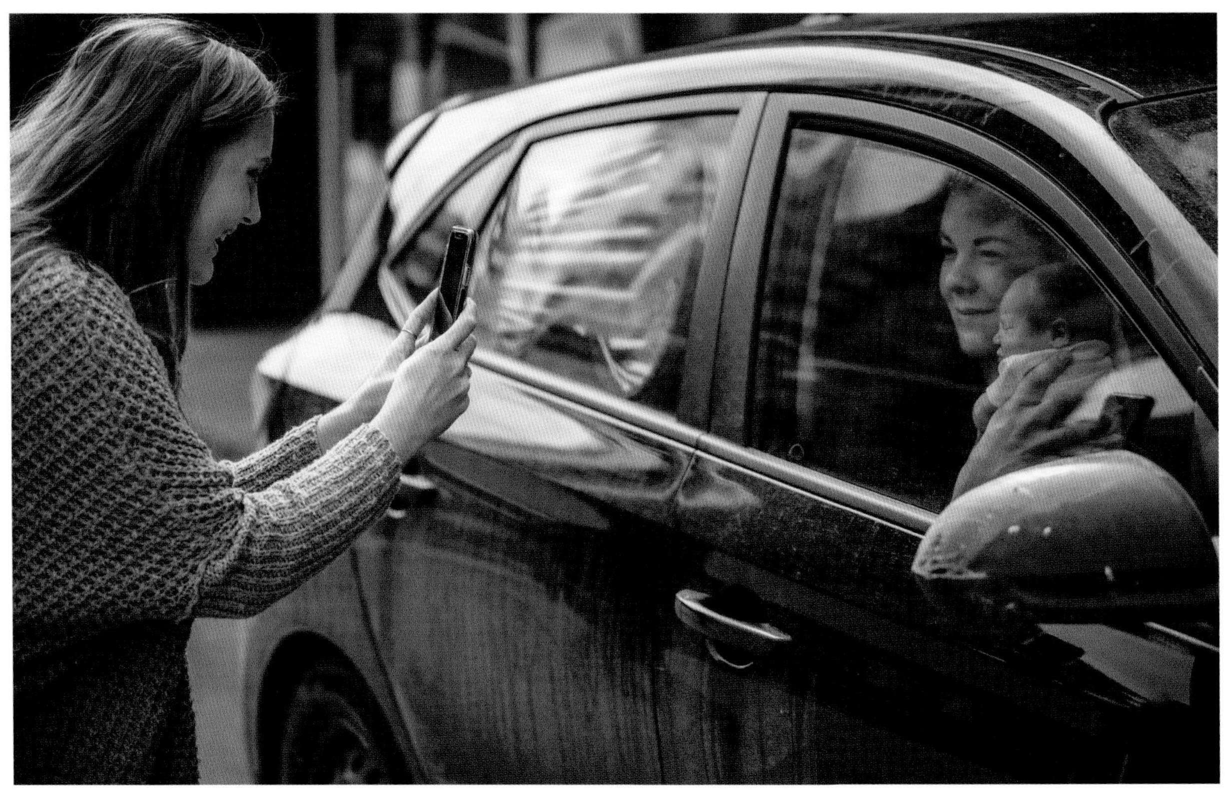

Evelyn Drake, showing off her newborn daughter Ivy May, keeps a safe distance from her friend in Calgary, Alberta, on April 13, 2020.

Josee Riehl, left, stays socially distanced from family members during a visit at Amica Aspen Woods in Calgary, Alberta, on May 7, 2020.

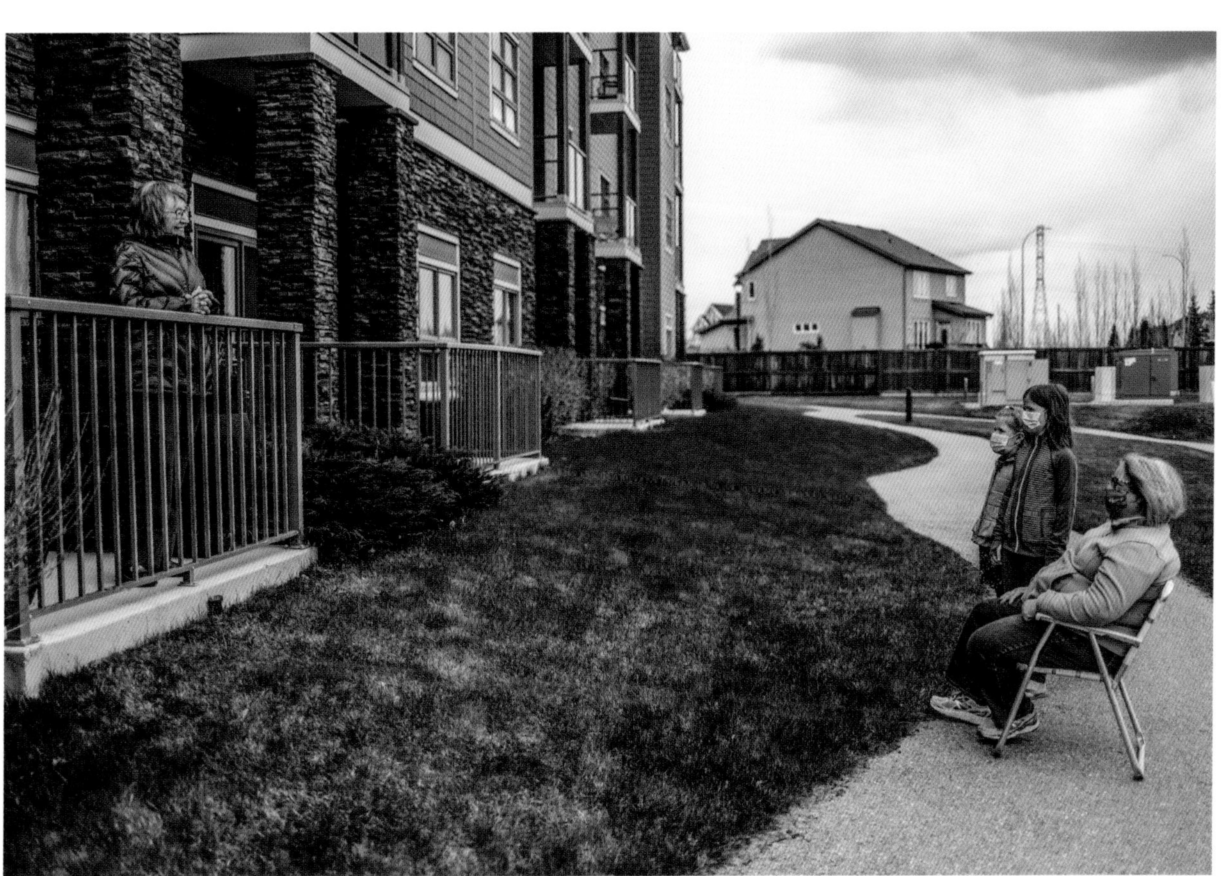

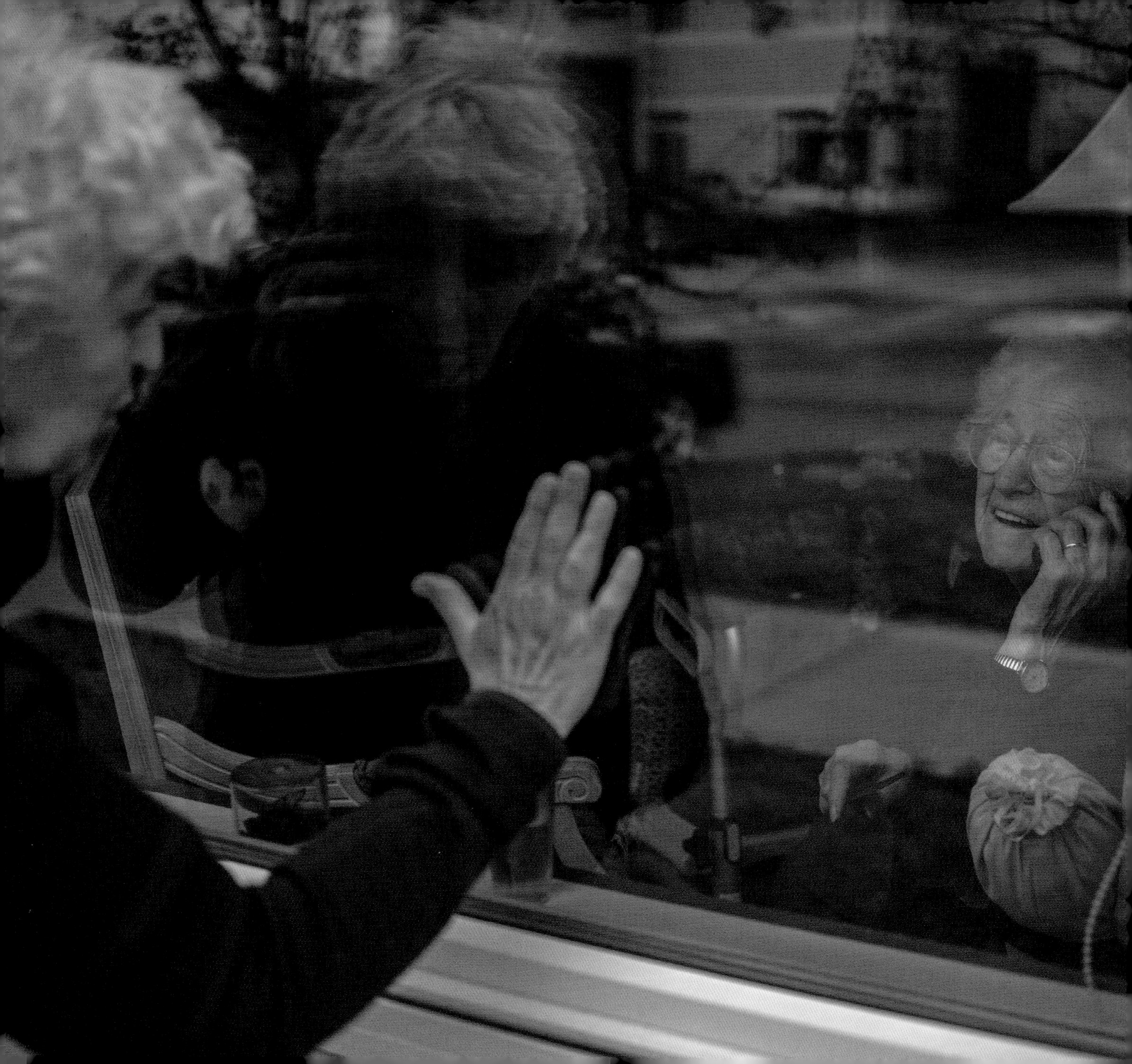

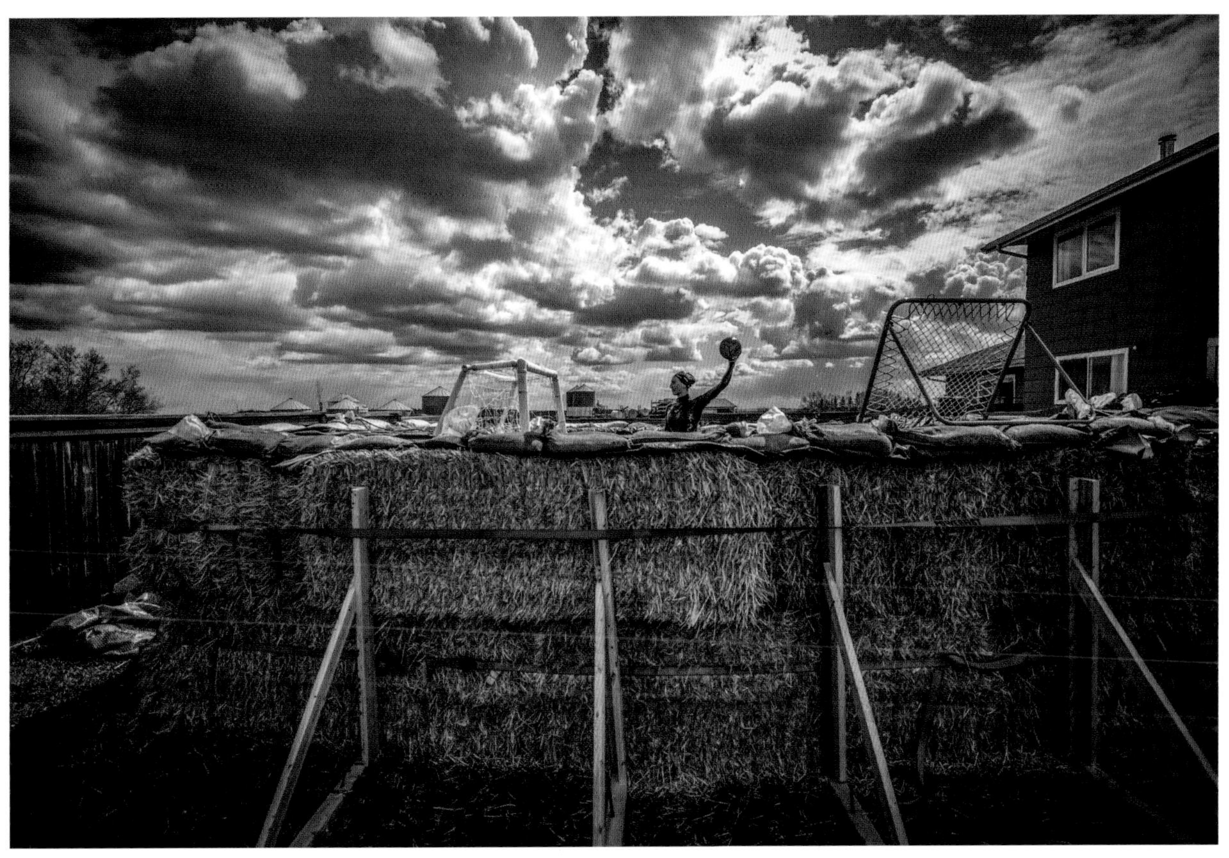

Linda Schmiegelt visits her mom, Emma, 92, in Calgary, Alberta, on June 6, 2020.

Kyra Christmas, a member of the Canadian women's water polo team, built a pool out of straw bales, with the help of her family, so she could train prior to the 2020 Tokyo Olympics that were postponed until July 2021.

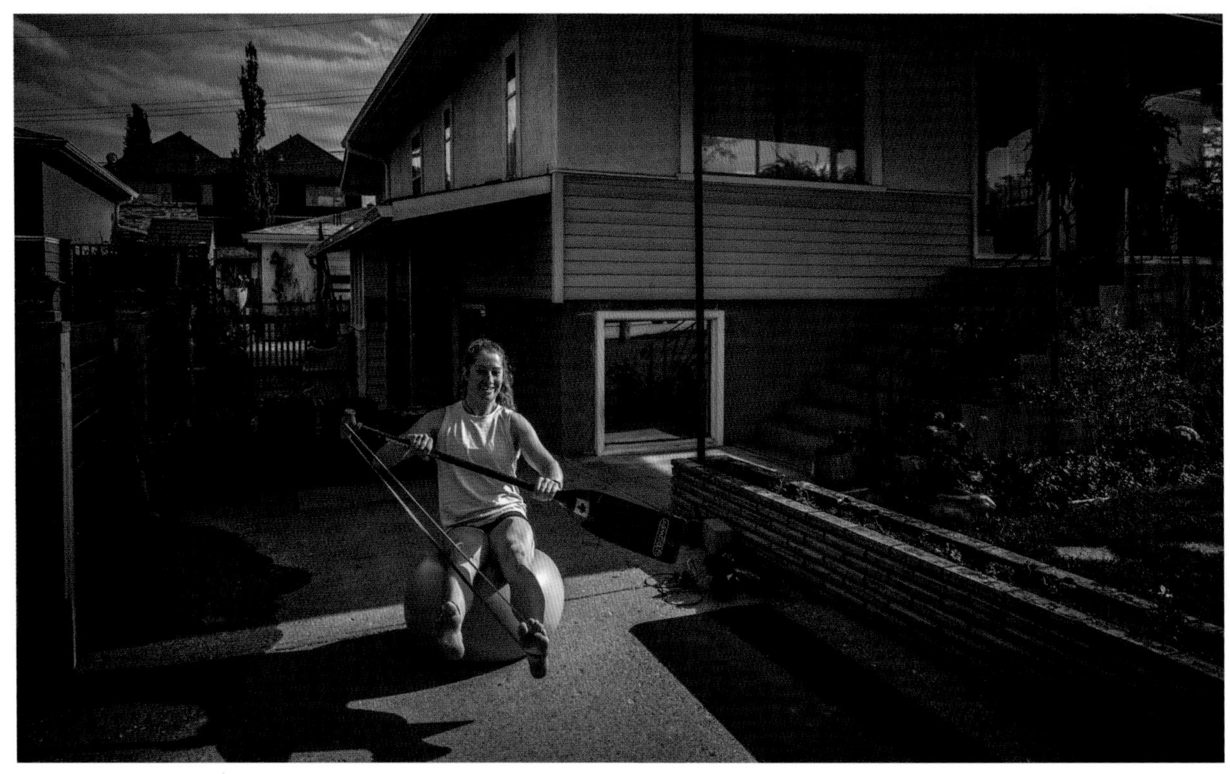

Because of closed gyms, Canadian slalom canoe-
ist Haley Daniels found ways to work out at home.
She competed at the Tokyo Olympics.

Rev. John Pentland, minister at the Hillhurst
United Church in Calgary, Alberta, stands in
front of pews adorned with photos of community
members. Because of the COVID-19 pandemic,
many churches switched to online services.
March 2020.

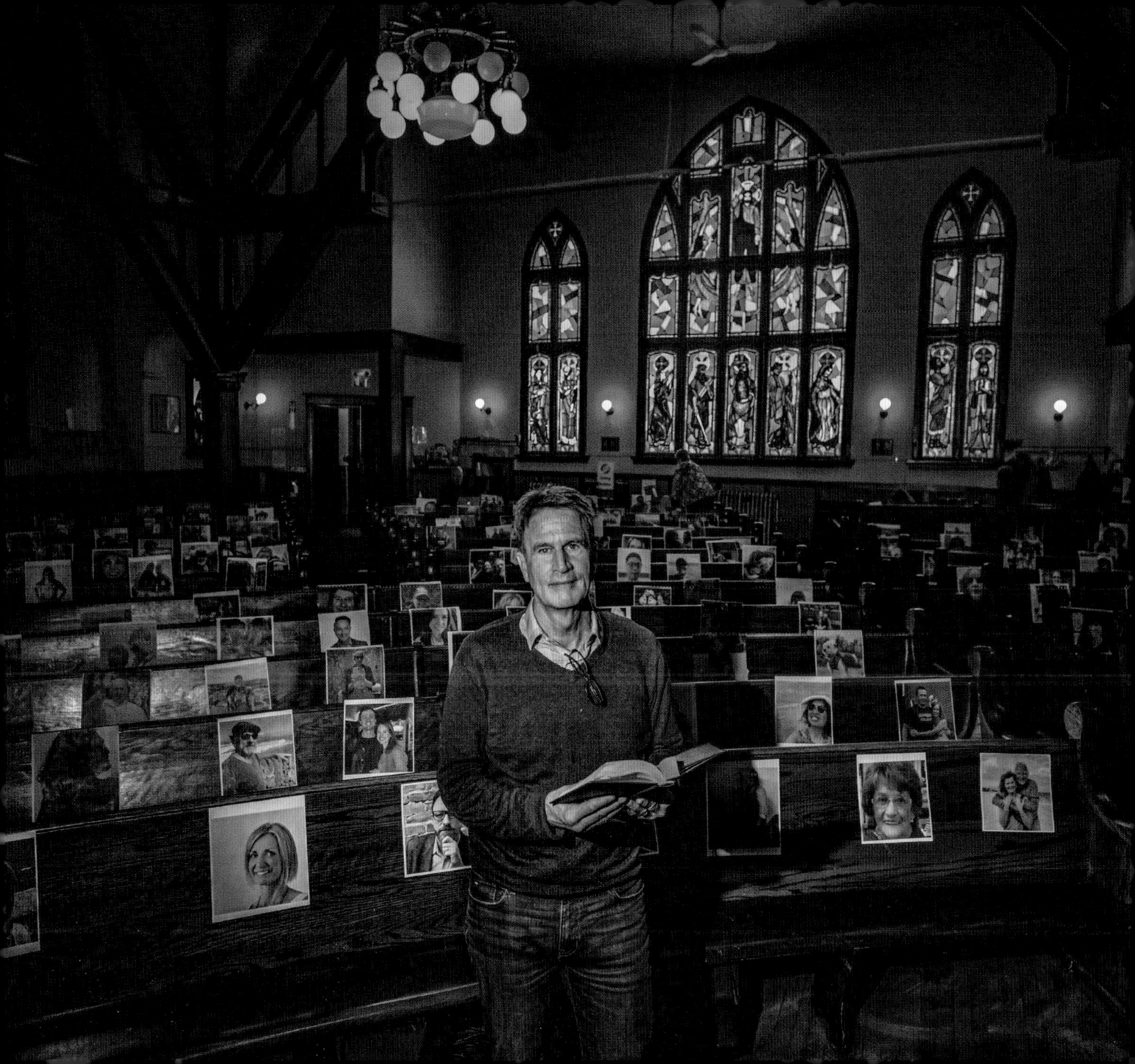

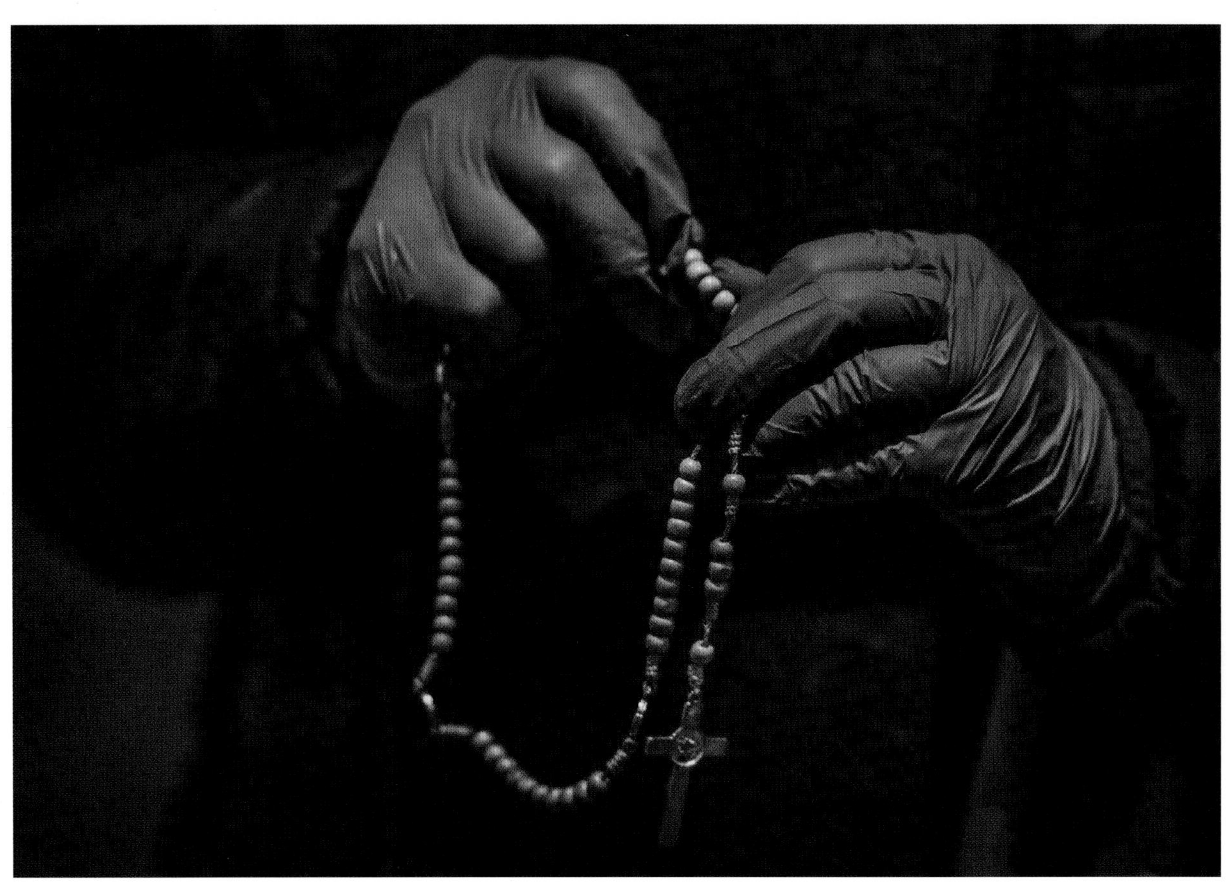

Maria Kacperska holds her rosary during
Palm Sunday, April 5, 2020, at Sacred
Heart Church in Calgary, Alberta.

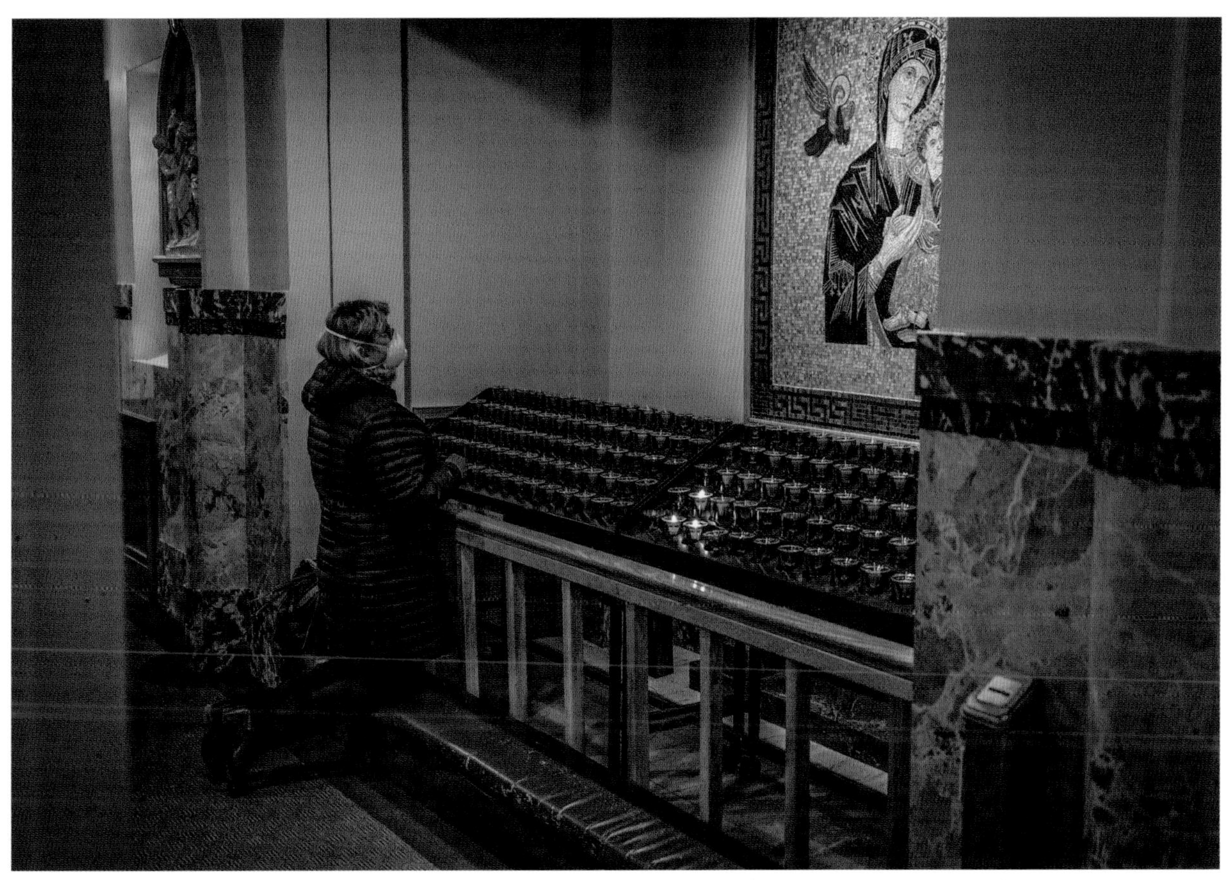

Maria Kacperska prays during Palm
Sunday, April 5, 2020, at Sacred Heart
Church in Calgary, Alberta.

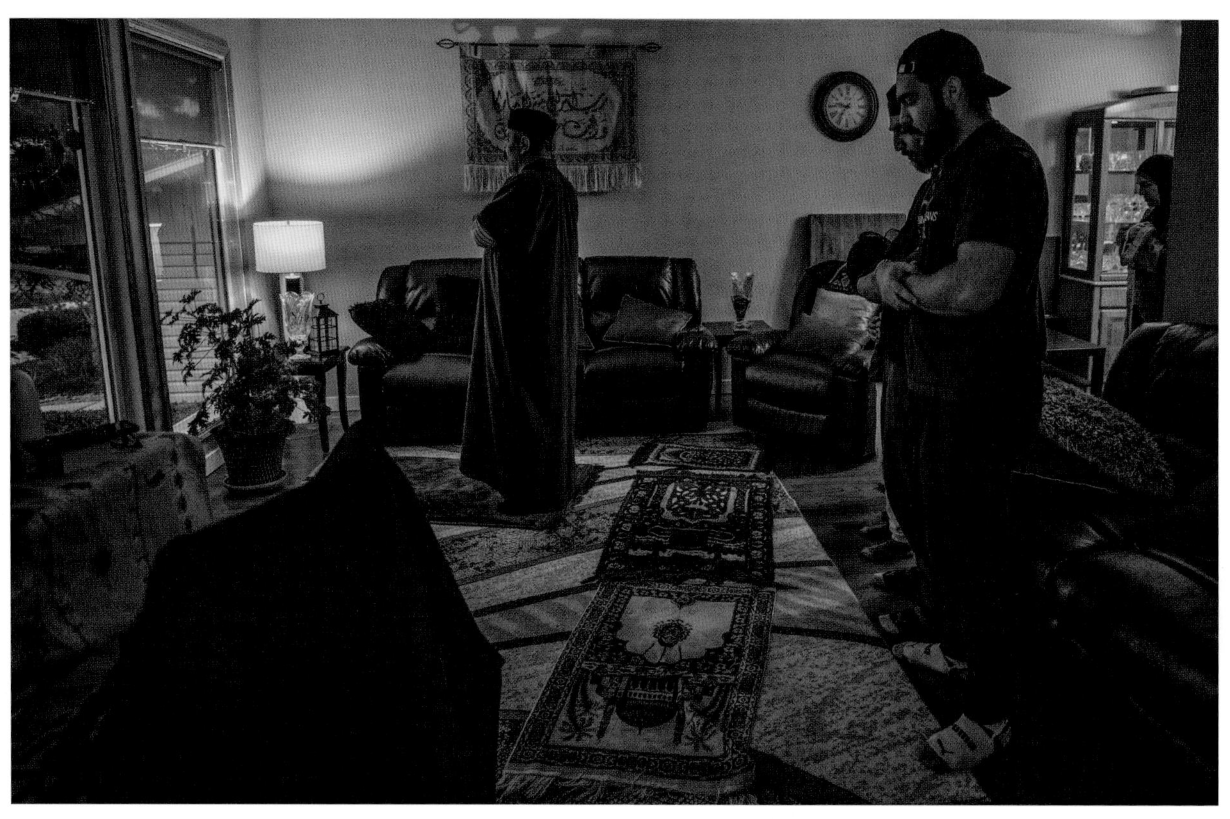

With the mosque closed because of COVID-19, Souheil Merhi, left, and his family pray at their home in Calgary, Alberta, on May 23, 2020, the last night of the year's holy month of Ramadan.

Rana Omar hands out bags filled with treats to children during the drive-by Eid celebration at Al-Salam Centre in Calgary, Alberta, on May 24, 2020.

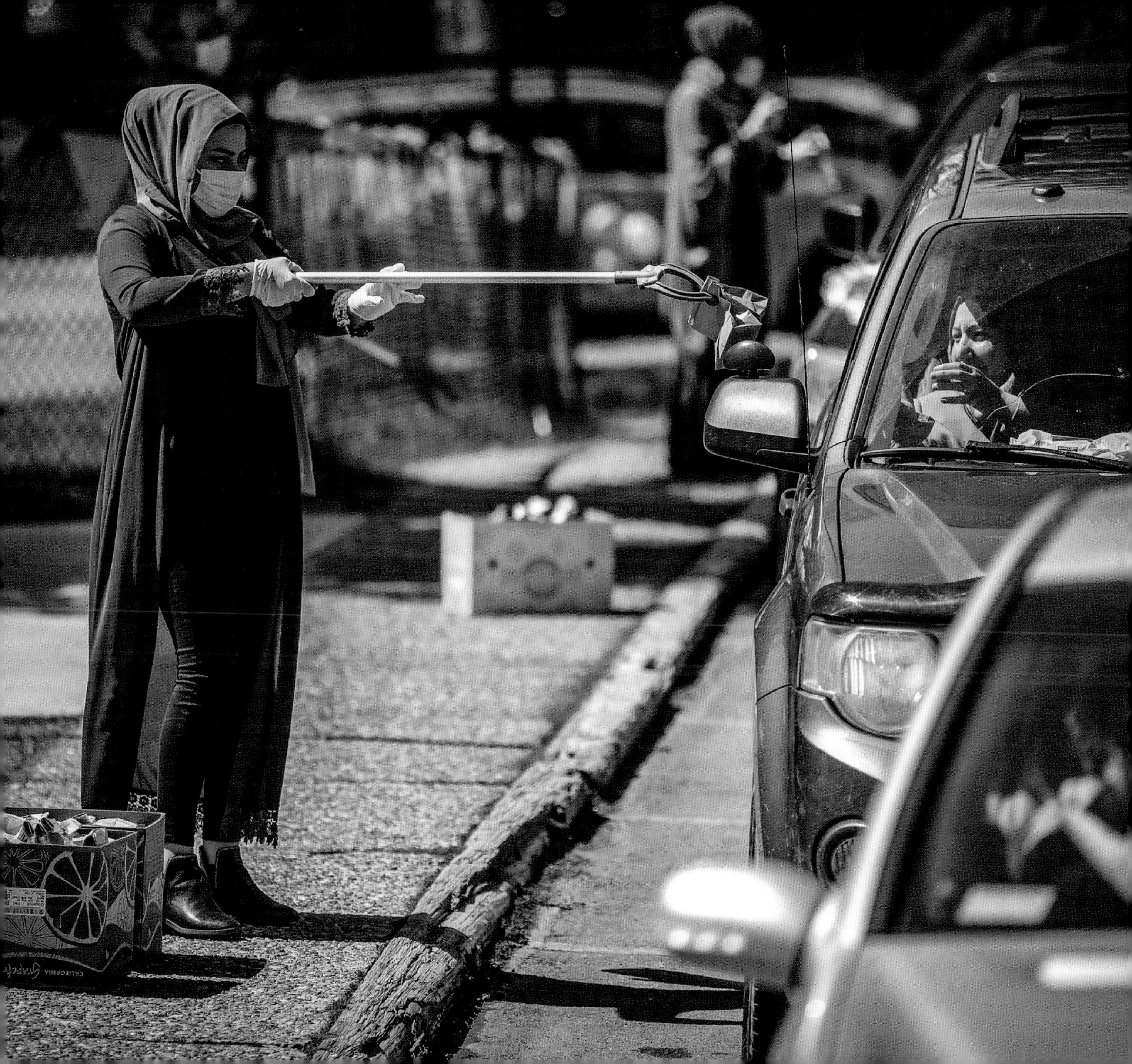

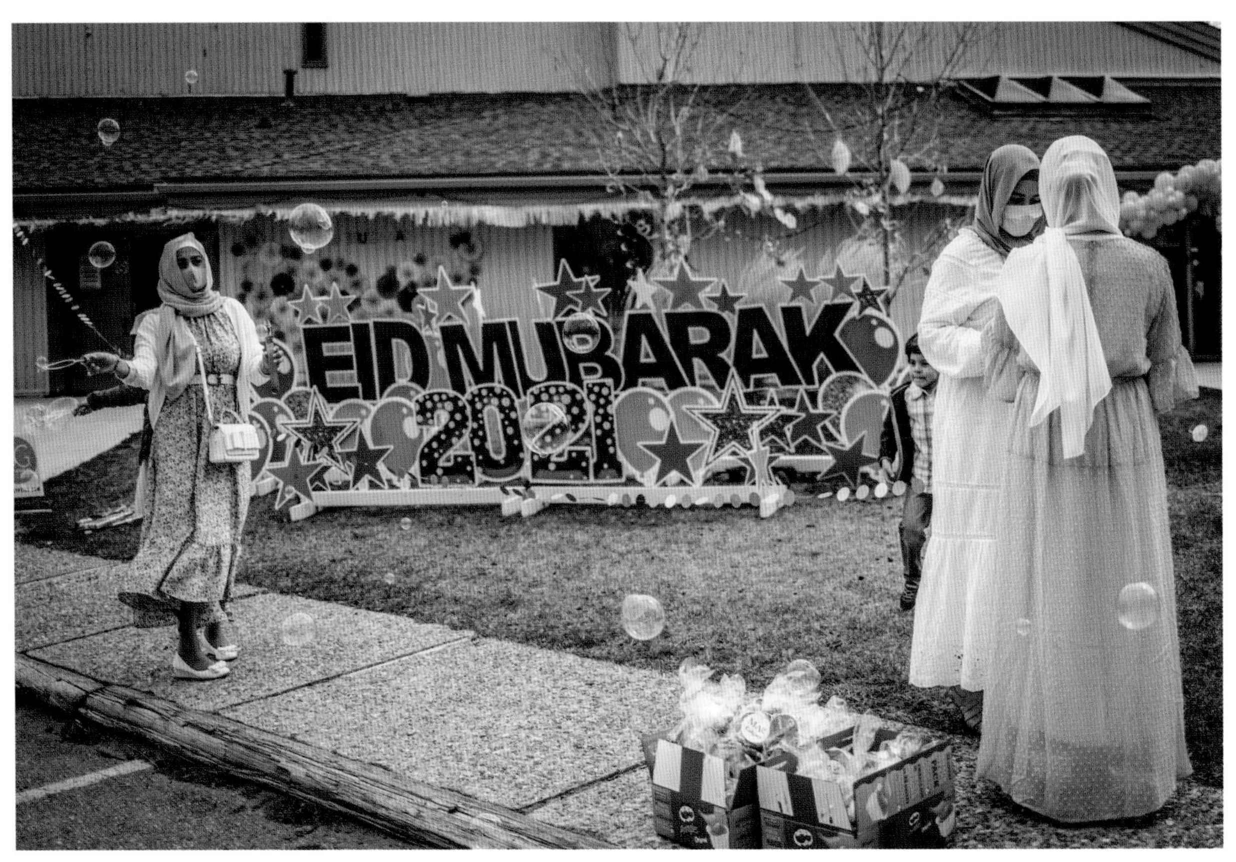

For the second straight year, drive-by Eid
celebrations are held at Al-Salam Centre
in Calgary, Alberta, on May 12, 2021.

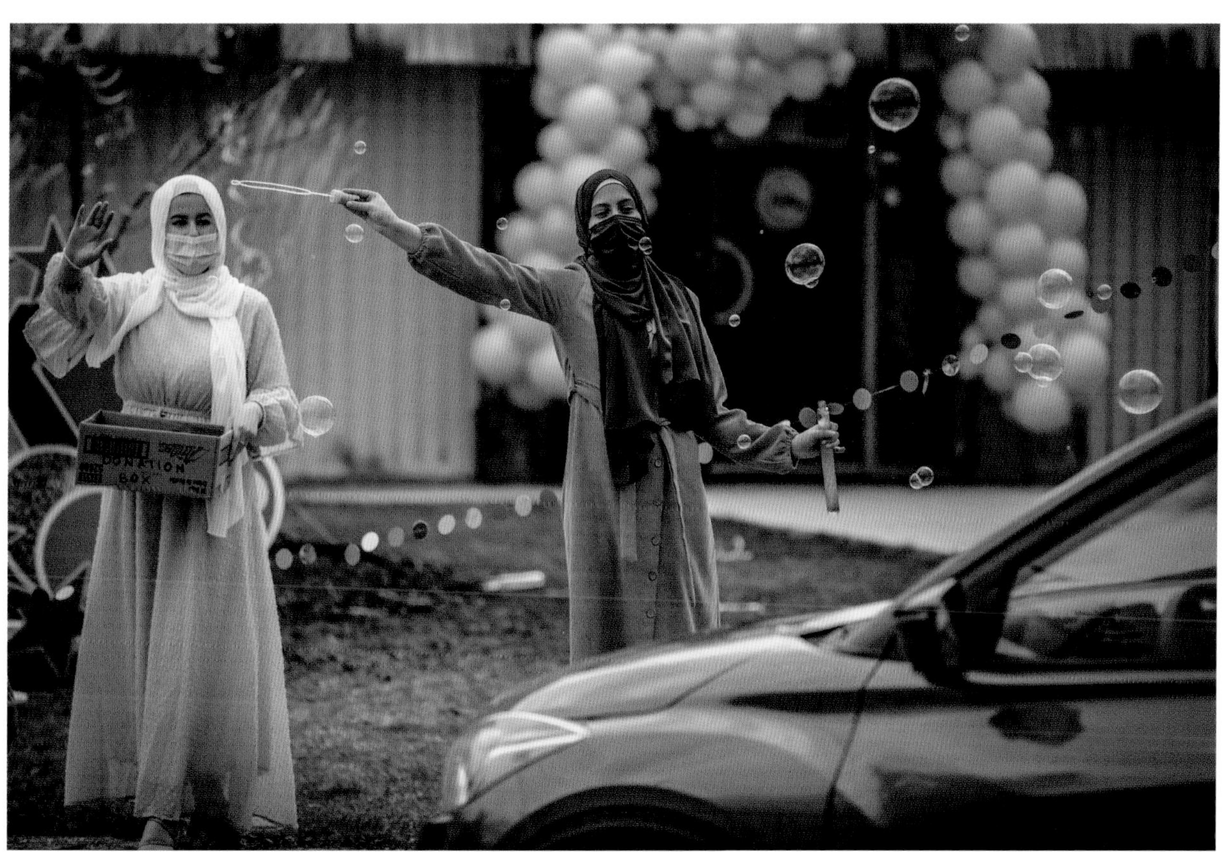

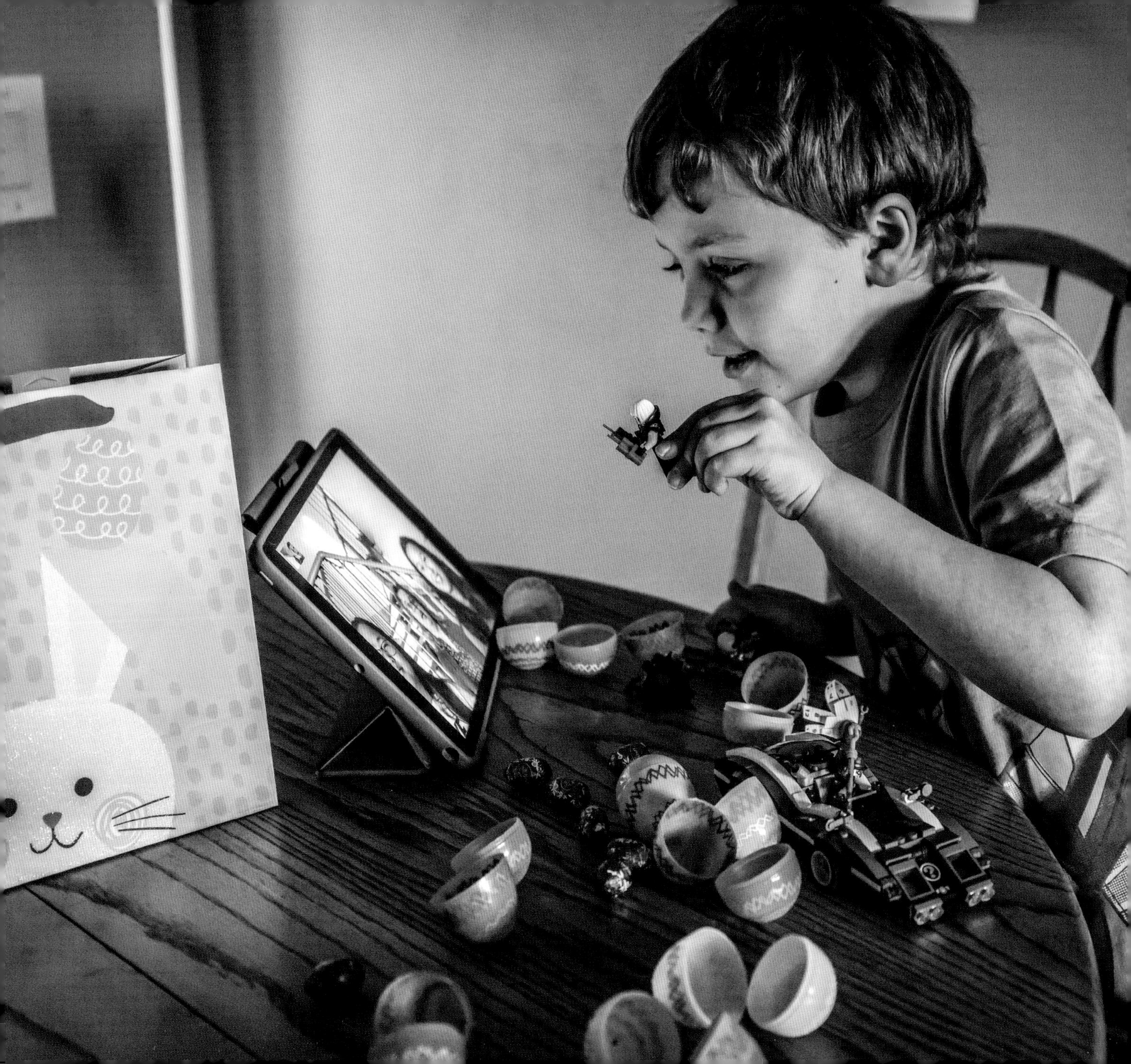

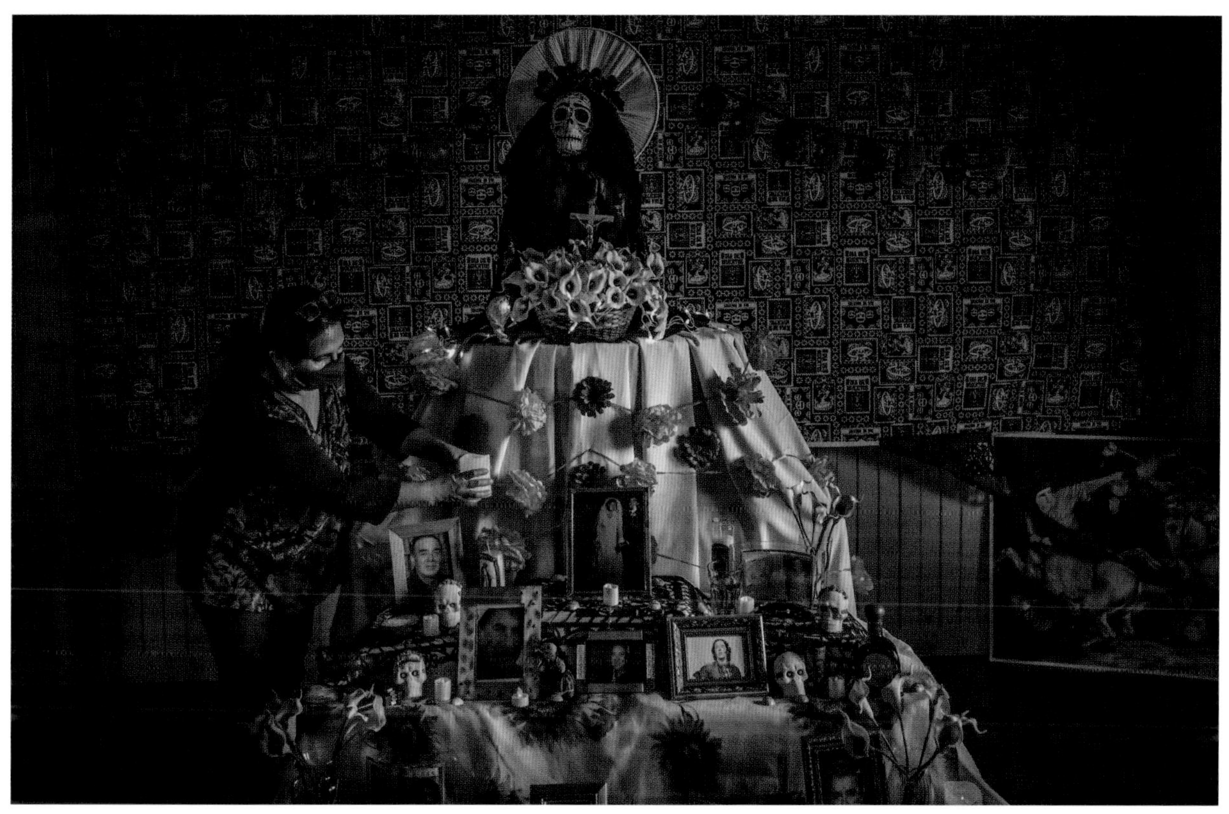

A.J. Hall uses FaceTime to visit with out-of-town family members during a socially distanced Easter 2021.

Liz Vigueras finishes the altar at the Highwood Museum in High River, Alberta, for Day of the Dead celebrations in 2020. This year the altar includes those who have died from COVID-19.

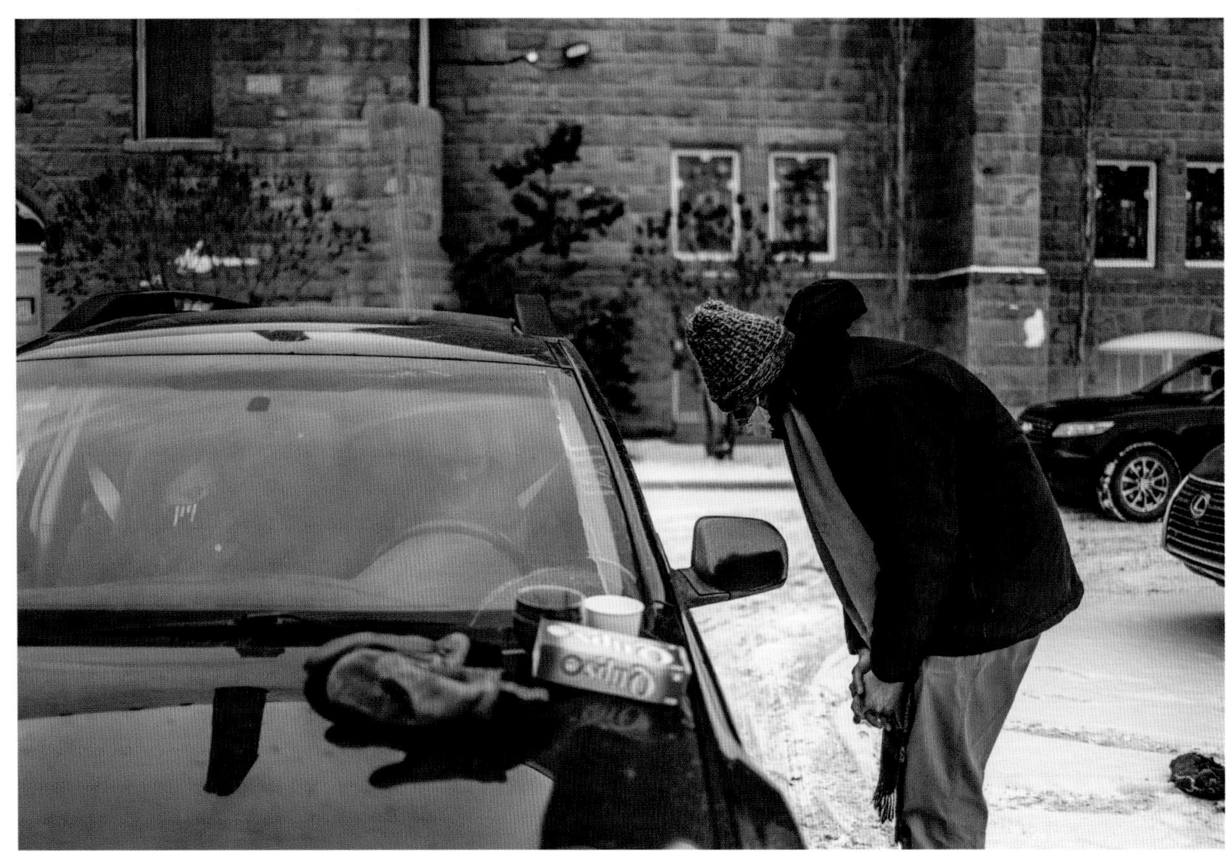

Rev. Jake Van Pernis takes part in the drive-through
Ashes on Ash Wednesday at Grace Presbyterian Church
on February 17, 2021. Although ashes are normally
placed on the foreheads of the parishioners, this year,
because of the COVID-19 pandemic, the ashes are put
on parishioners' hands with clean cotton swabs.

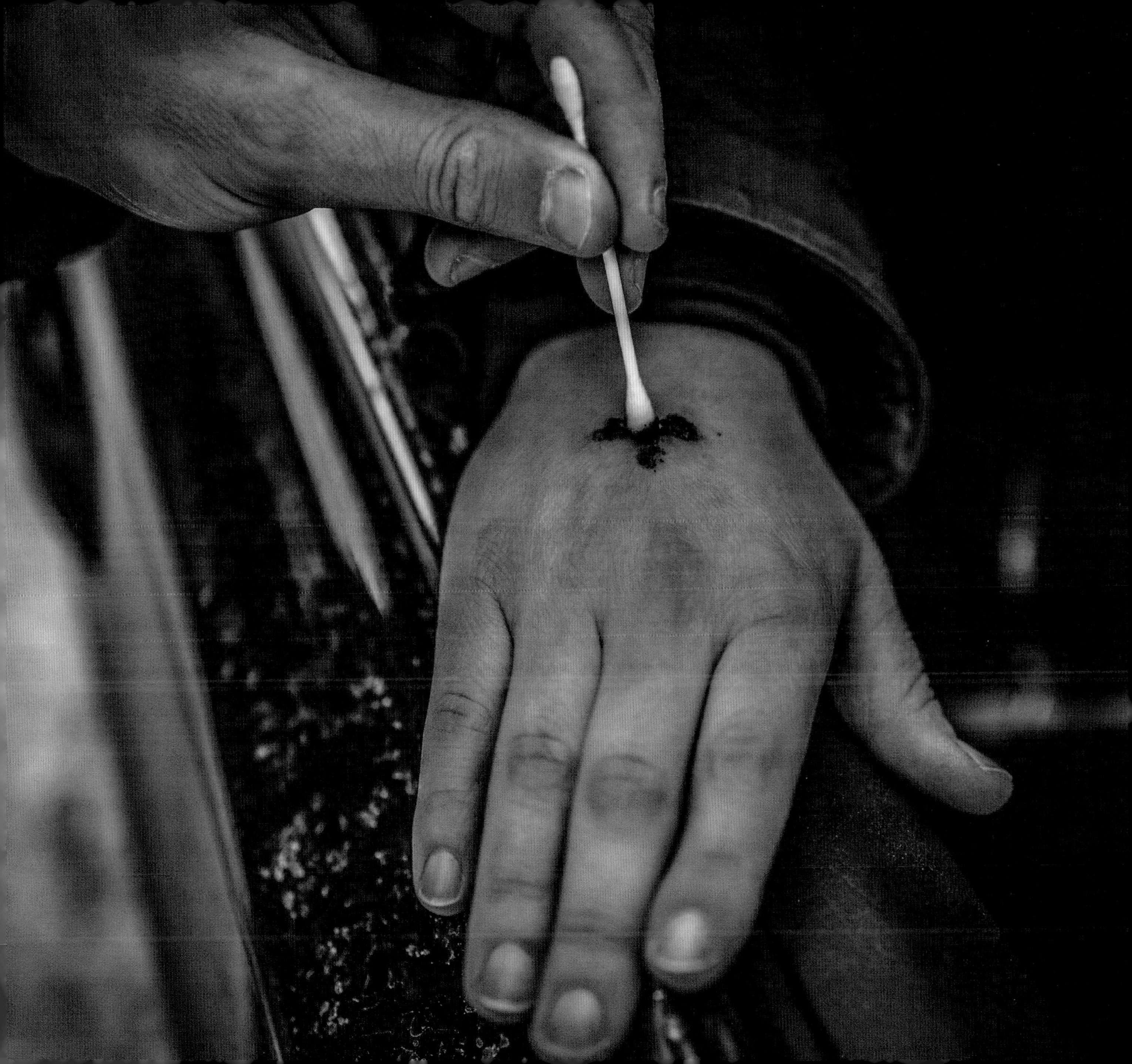

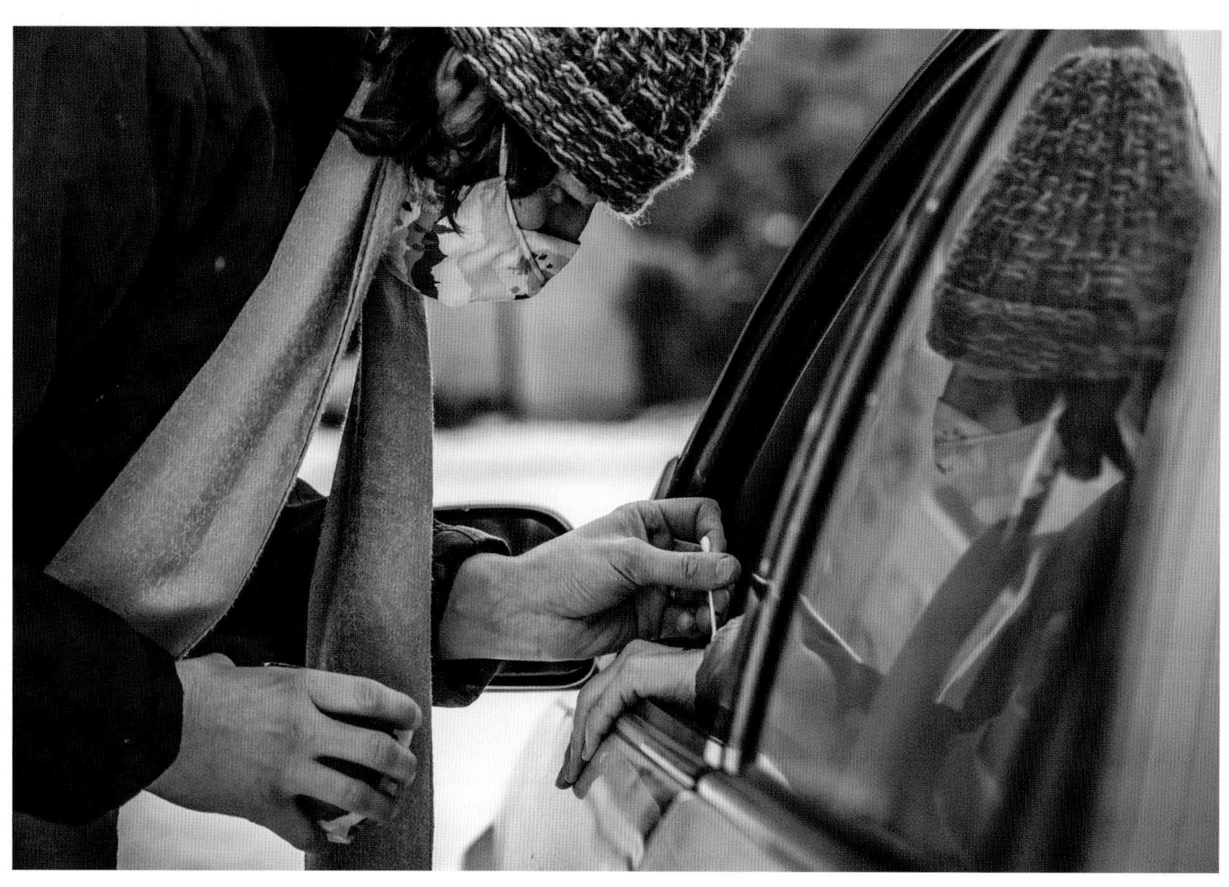

Rev. Jake Van Pernis applies ashes at the drive-through Ashes on Ash Wednesday at Grace Presbyterian Church on February 17, 2021.

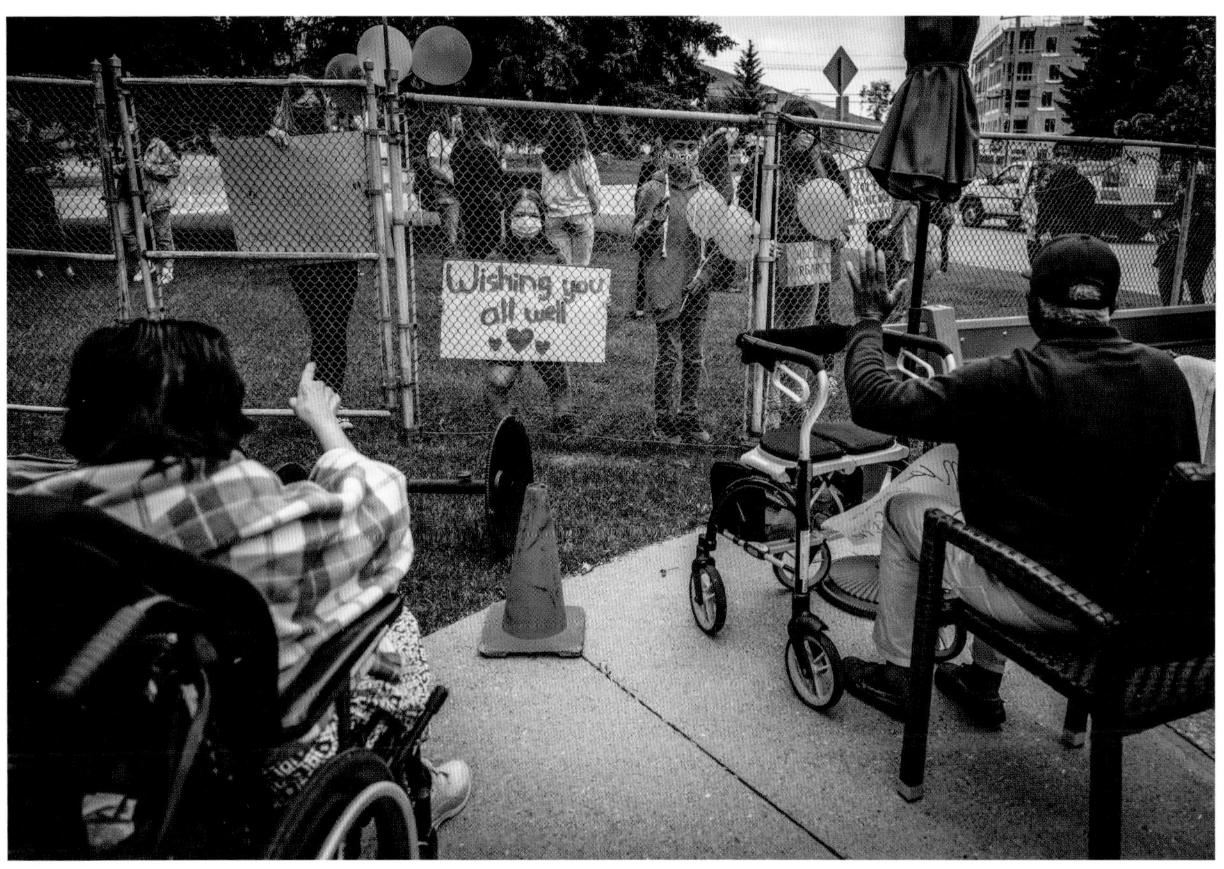

Calgary junior high LINKages students wave to
their senior friends at Carewest George Boyack
on June 18, 2020.

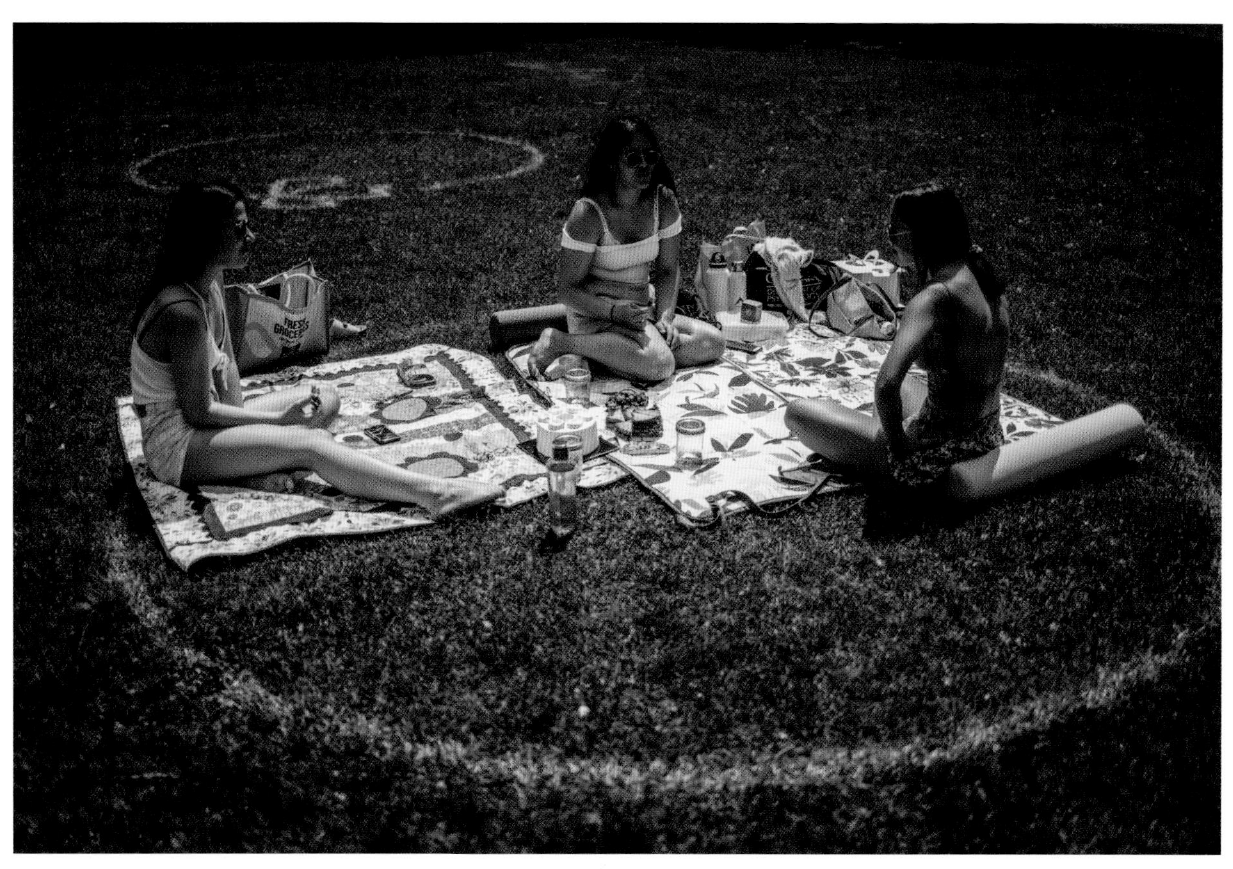

Keyana Paice, left, Katerina Shahim, centre, and Christine Novitsky enjoy a picnic in a circle that was spray-painted at Prince's Island Park to encourage social distancing. June 2020.

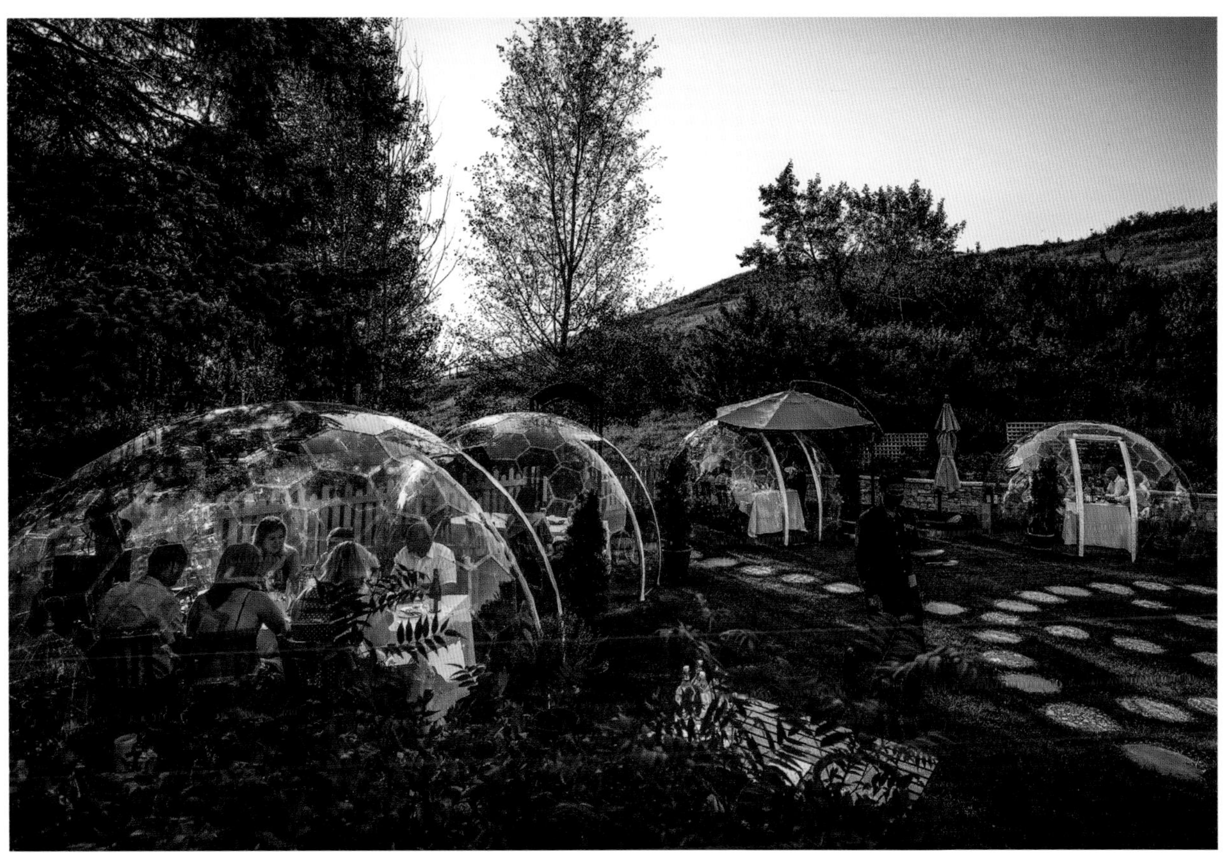

Patrons enjoy the pop-up garden globes at
Bow Valley Ranche Restaurant in Calgary,
Alberta, during the pandemic. July 2020.

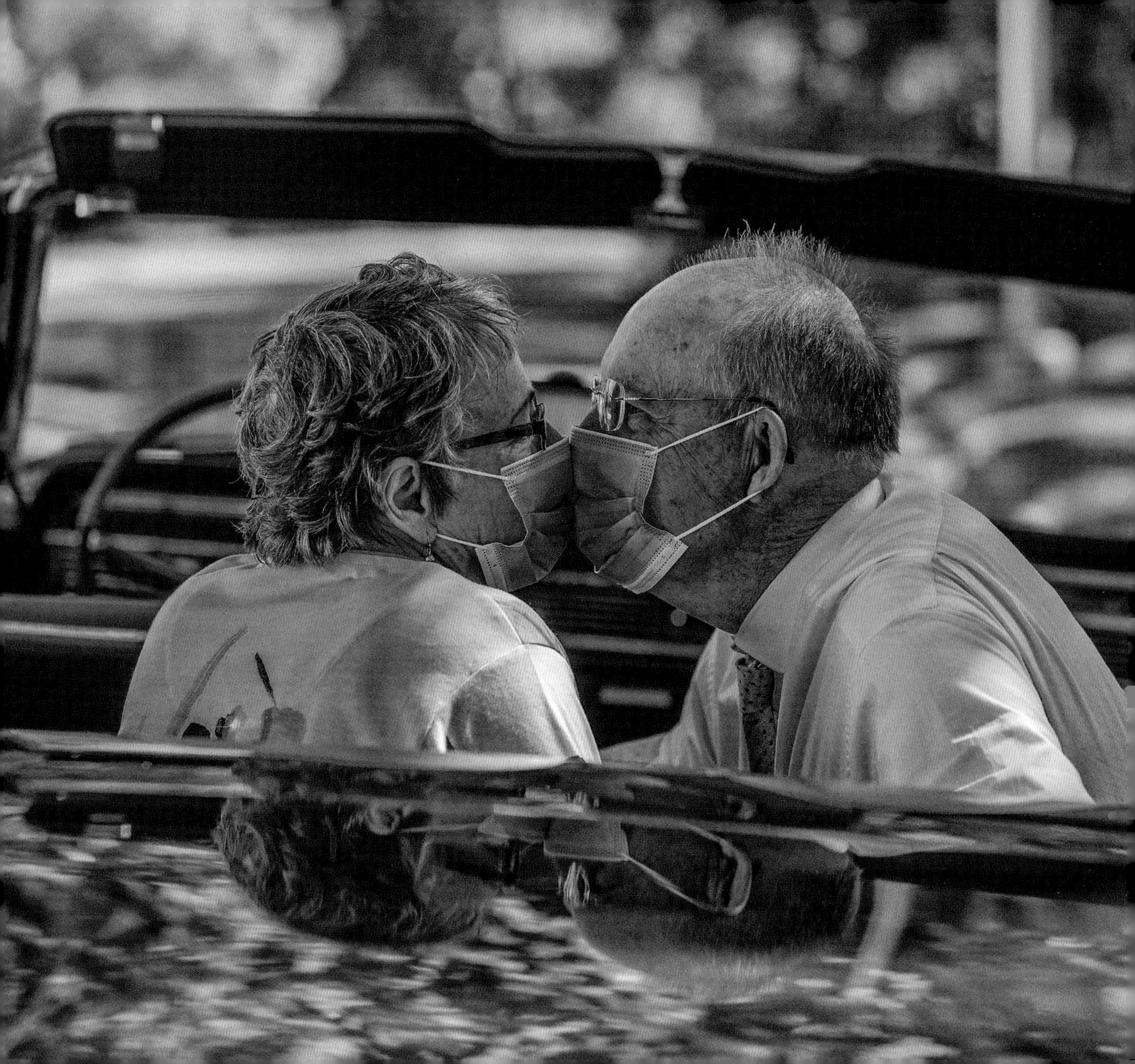

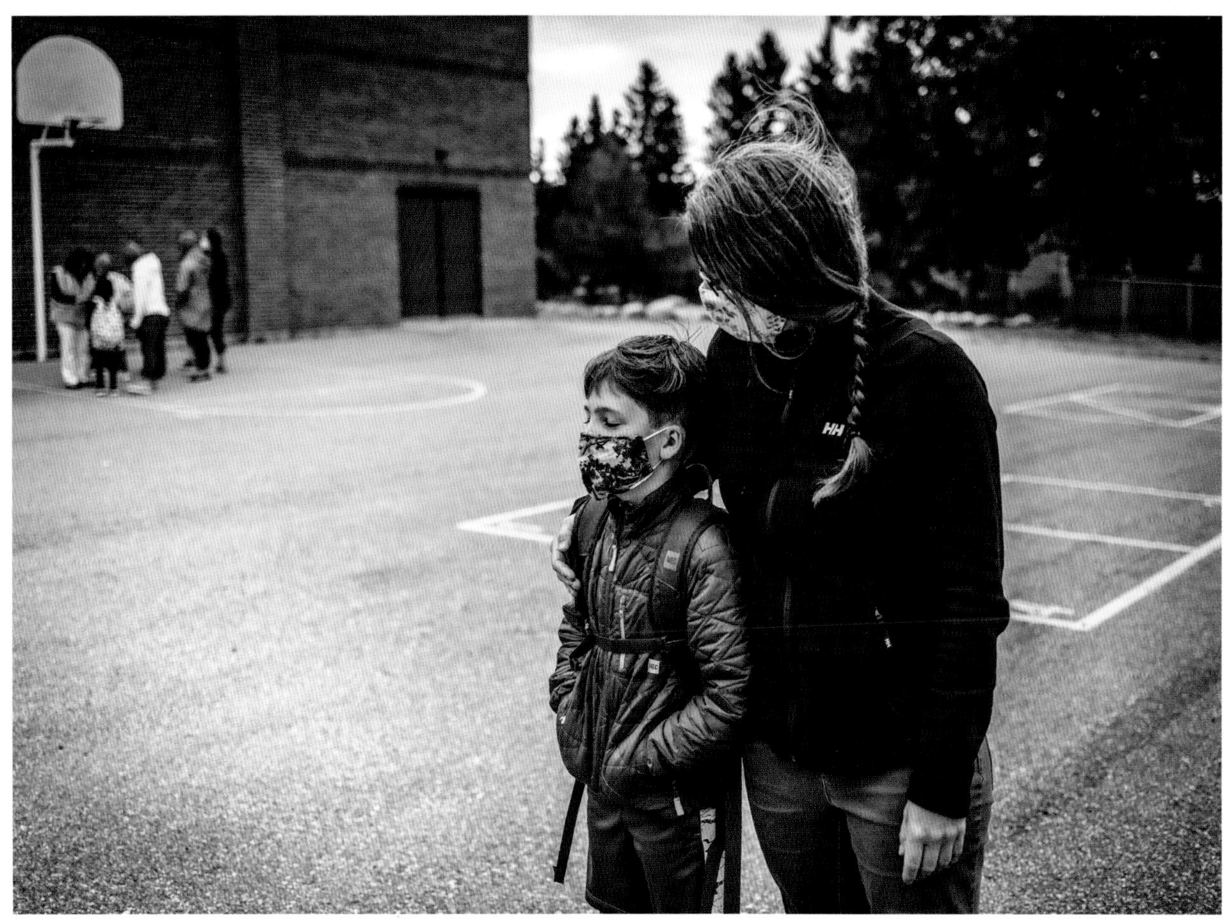

Marg and Dwight Gilliland celebrate their 50th wedding anniversary in a 1965 Lincoln in Calgary, Alberta, during the pandemic. August 2020.

Karilynn Simpson waits in the schoolyard with her son William on his first day of Grade 4 in Calgary, Alberta, on September 2, 2020.

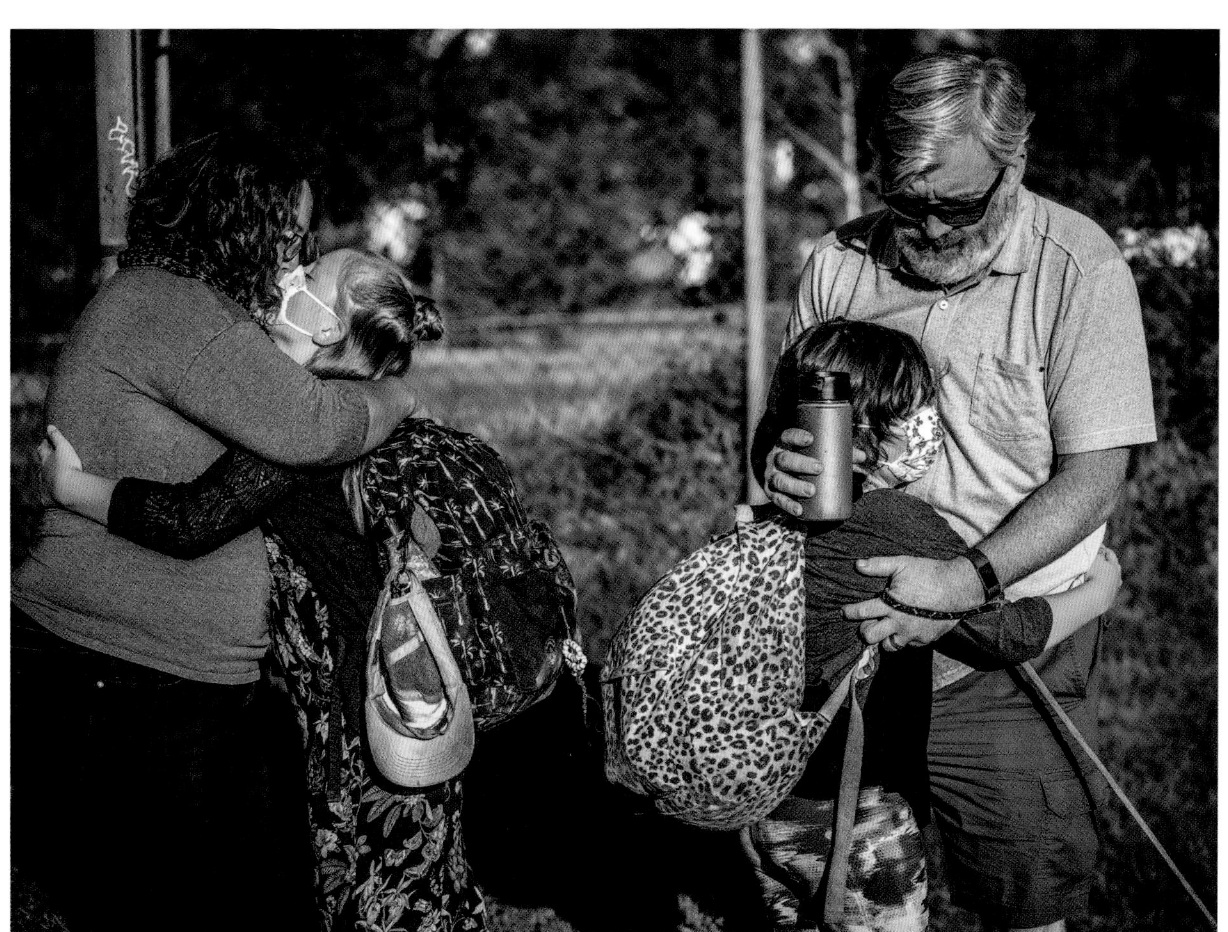

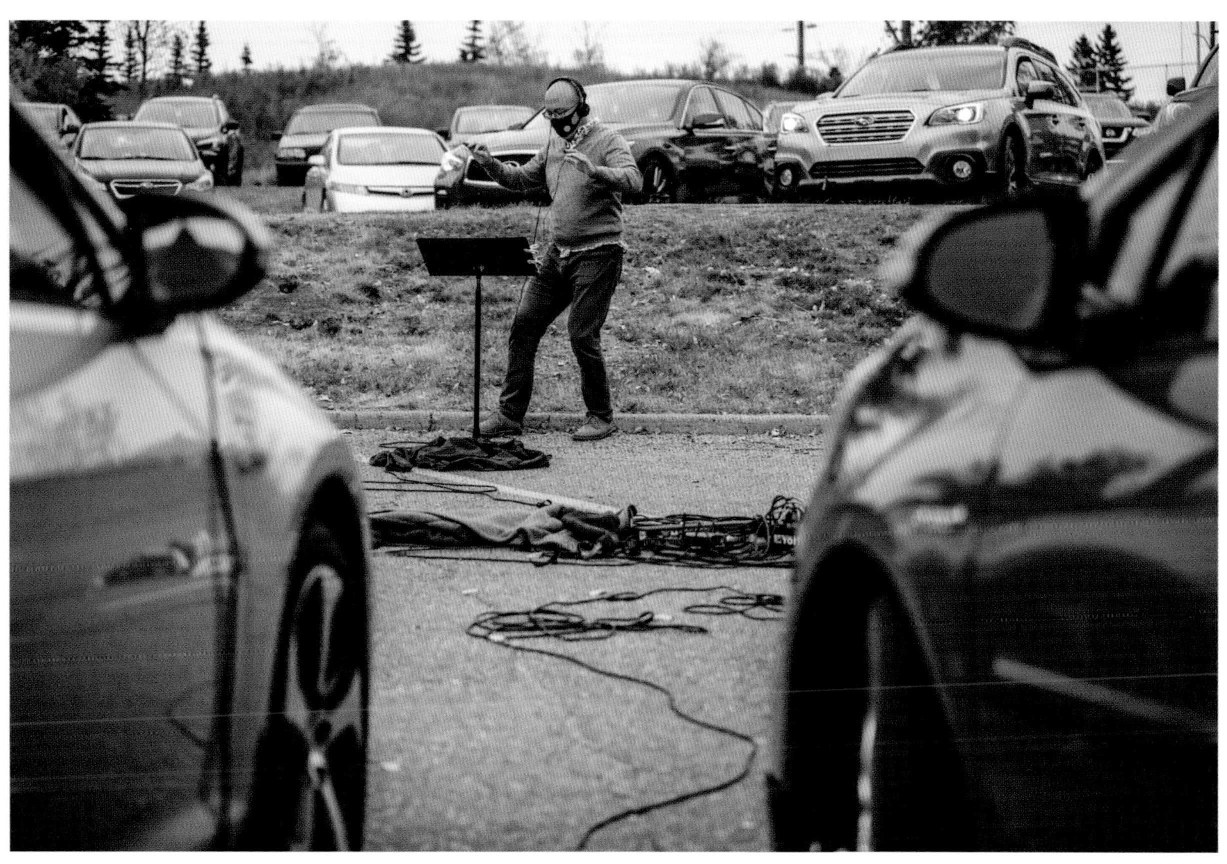

Parents Tara O'Donovan and Sean Myers say goodbye to their twin girls Abby, left, and Maggie on the first day of Grade 4 in September 2020.

Tim Shantz, artistic director and founder of Luminous Voices, performs during the LV Car Choir in the parking lot of Max Bell Arena in Calgary, Alberta. October 2020.

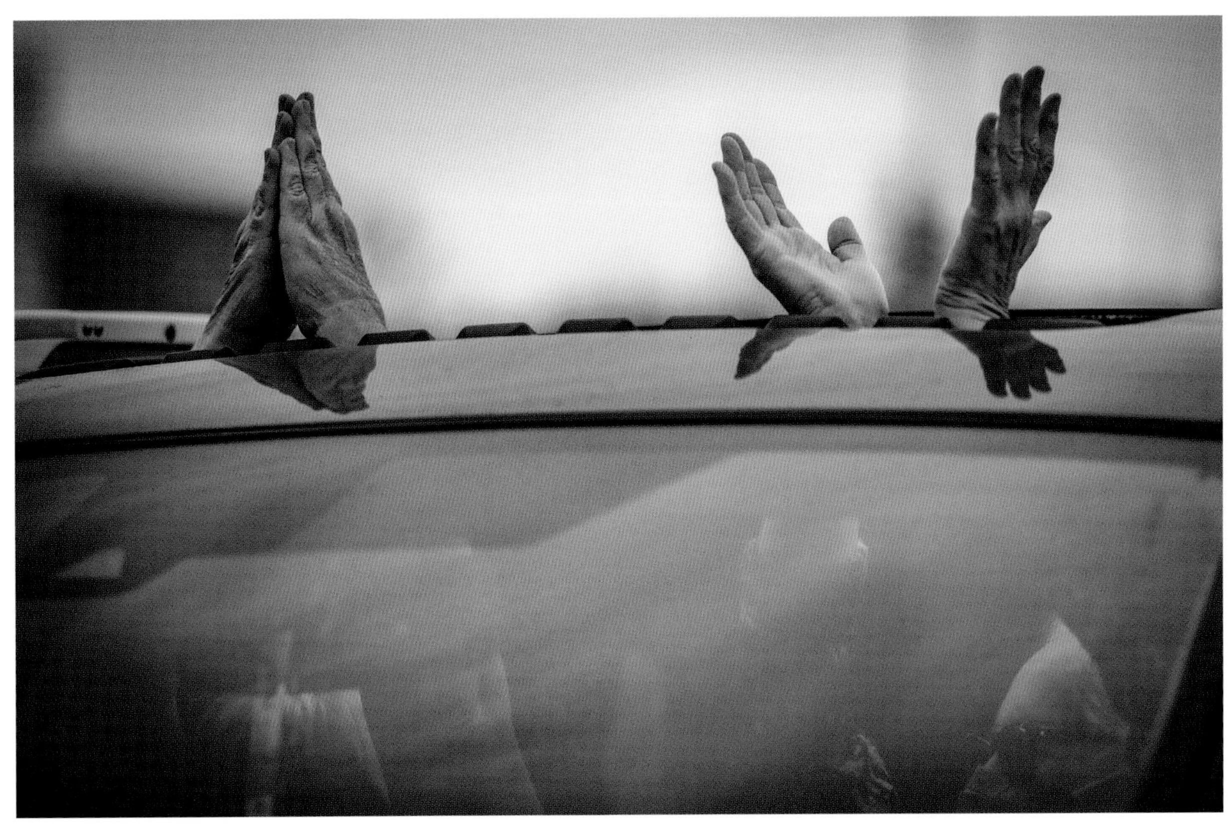

People listen in their vehicles to members
of Luminous Voices choir perform during
the LV Car Choir in the parking lot of Max
Bell Arena in Calgary, Alberta, 2020.

A member of Luminous Voices performs
during the LV Car Choir in the parking
lot of Max Bell Arena in Calgary, Alberta.
October 2020.

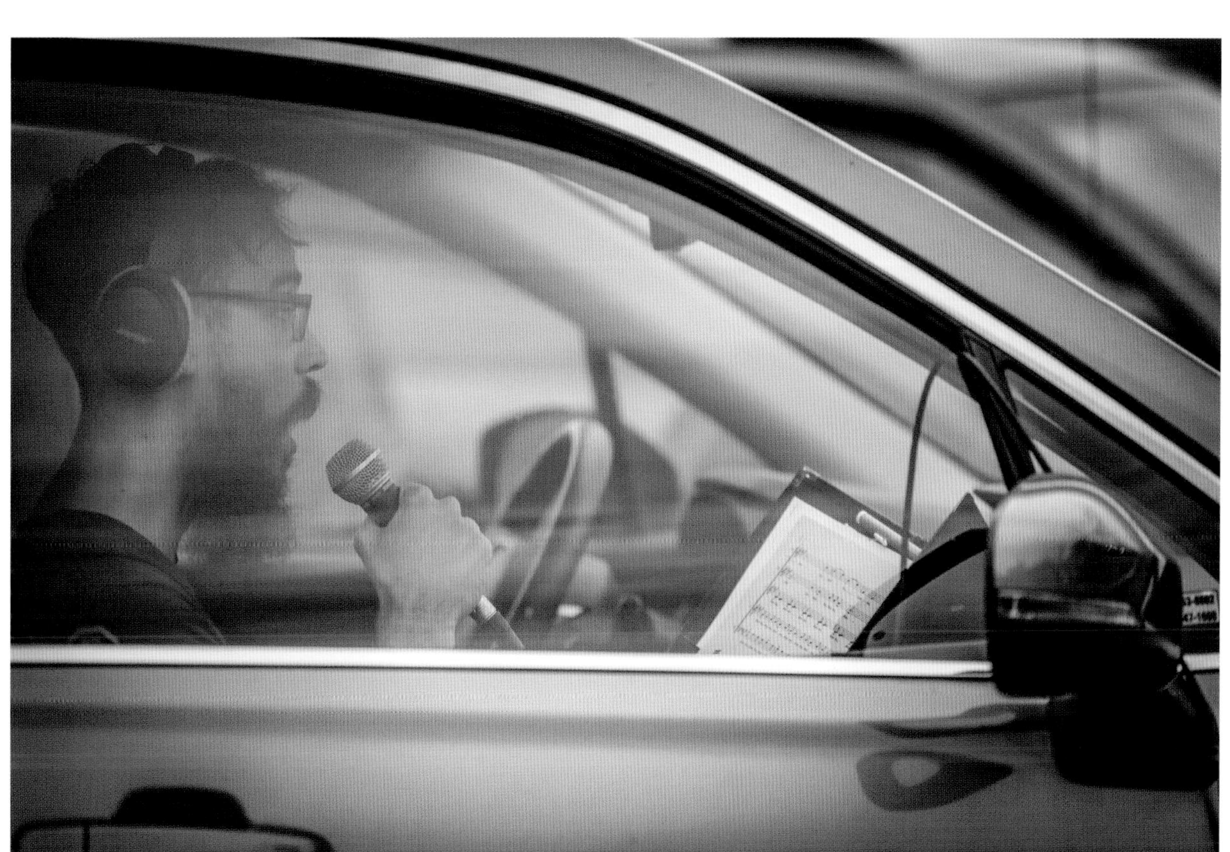

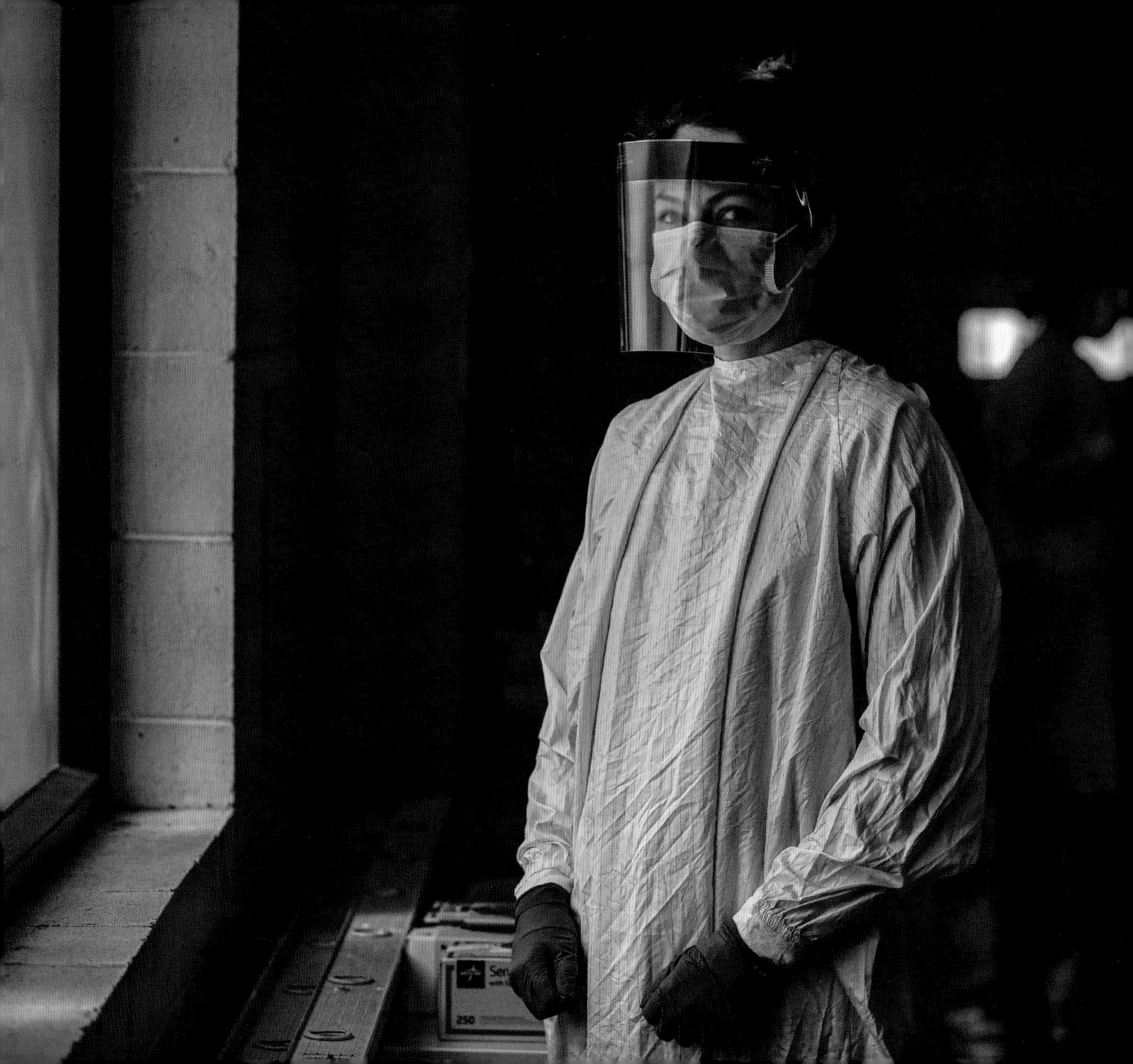

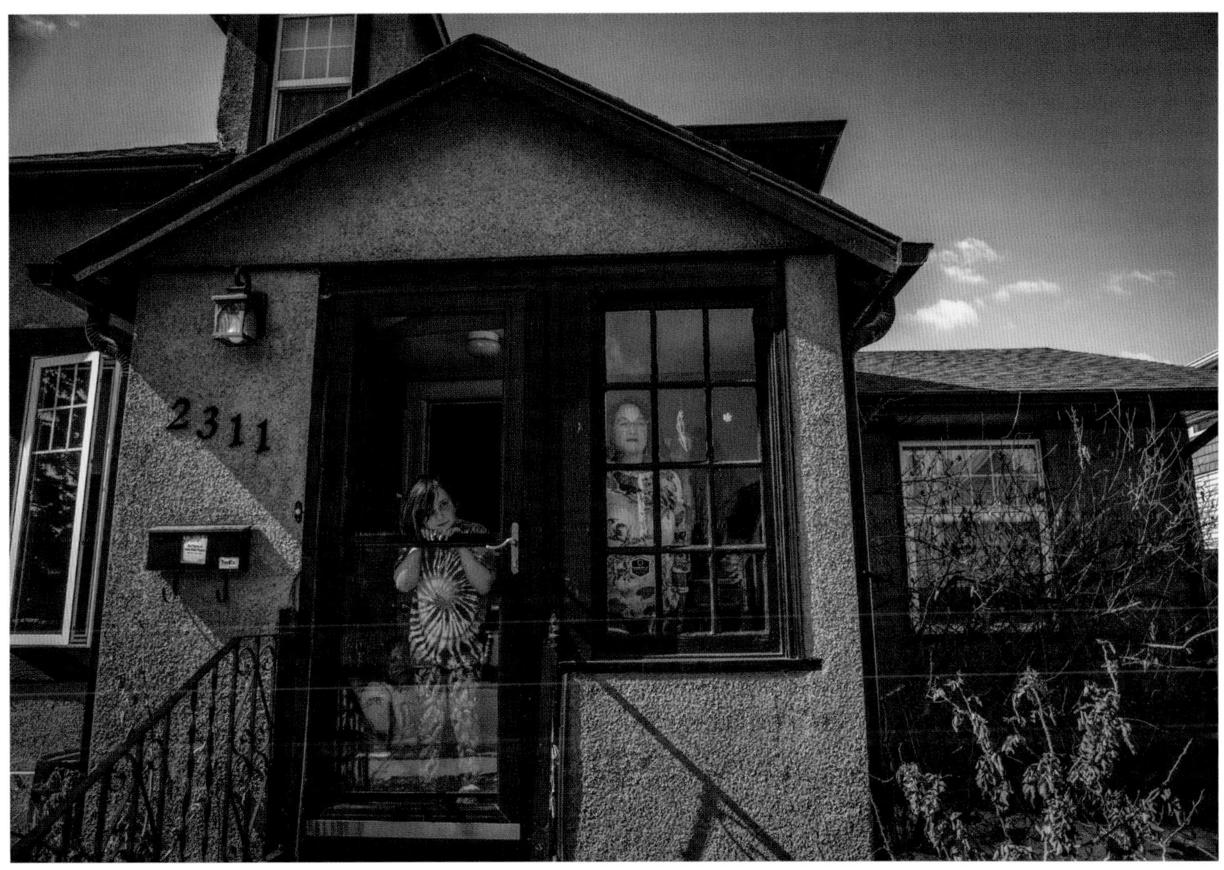

Registered nurse Julie Stanton works at the
Richmond Road COVID-19 assessment site in
Calgary, Alberta.

Tara O'Donovan, who tested positive for COVID-19,
isolates with her daughter Maggie at their home
in Calgary, Alberta, on March 30, 2021.

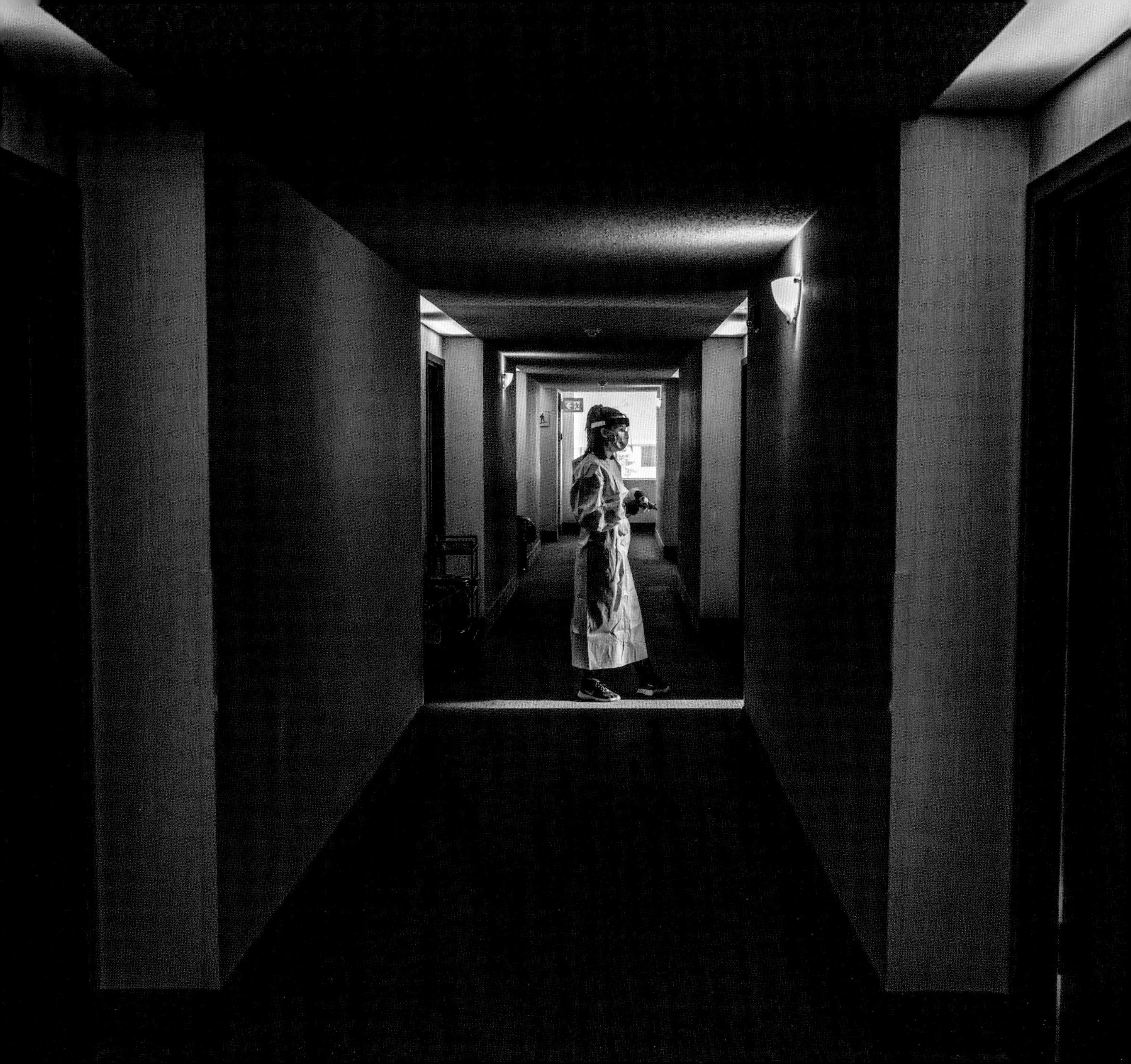

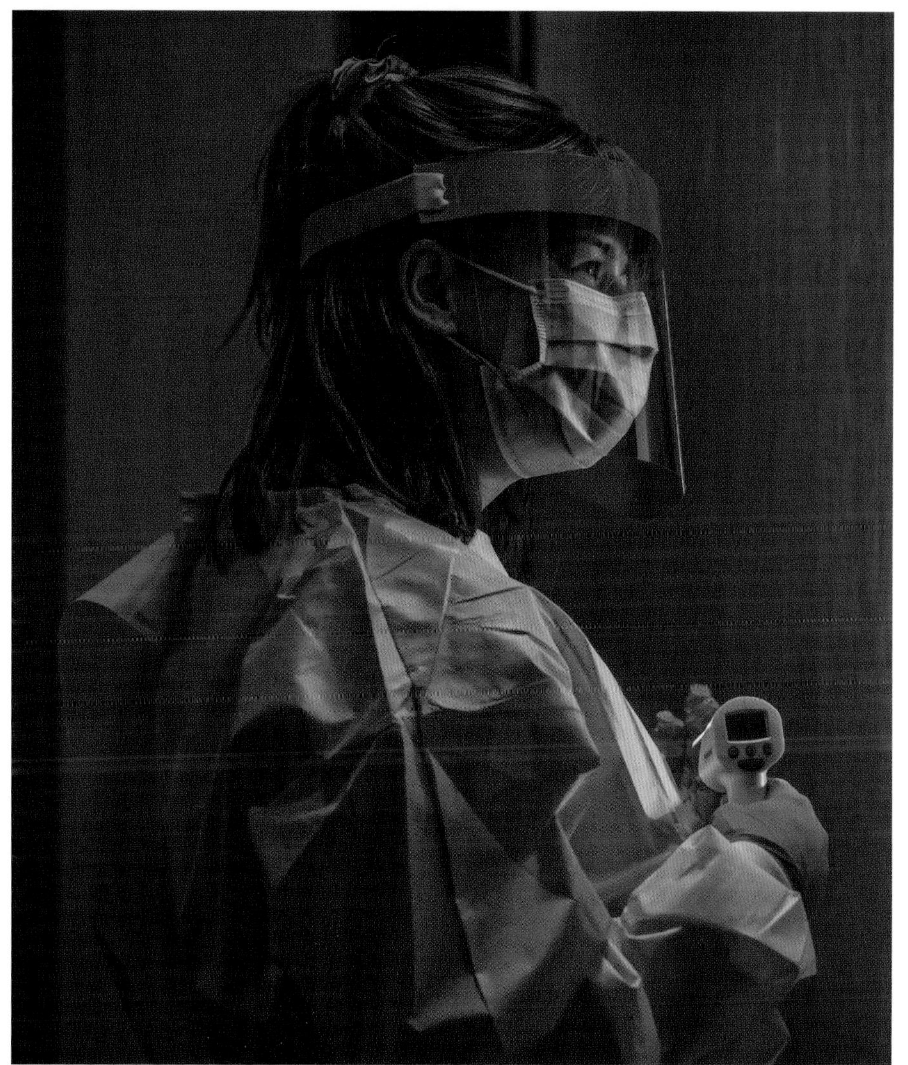

Licensed practical nurse Kassidy Czerniak is pictured inside the Assisted Self-Isolation Site (ASIS) in Calgary. The ASIS uses available hotel space to provide isolation venues for people experiencing homelessness who have symptoms or have been diagnosed with COVID-19. The Alex, Alberta Health Services and CUPS Calgary provide medical support for the site.

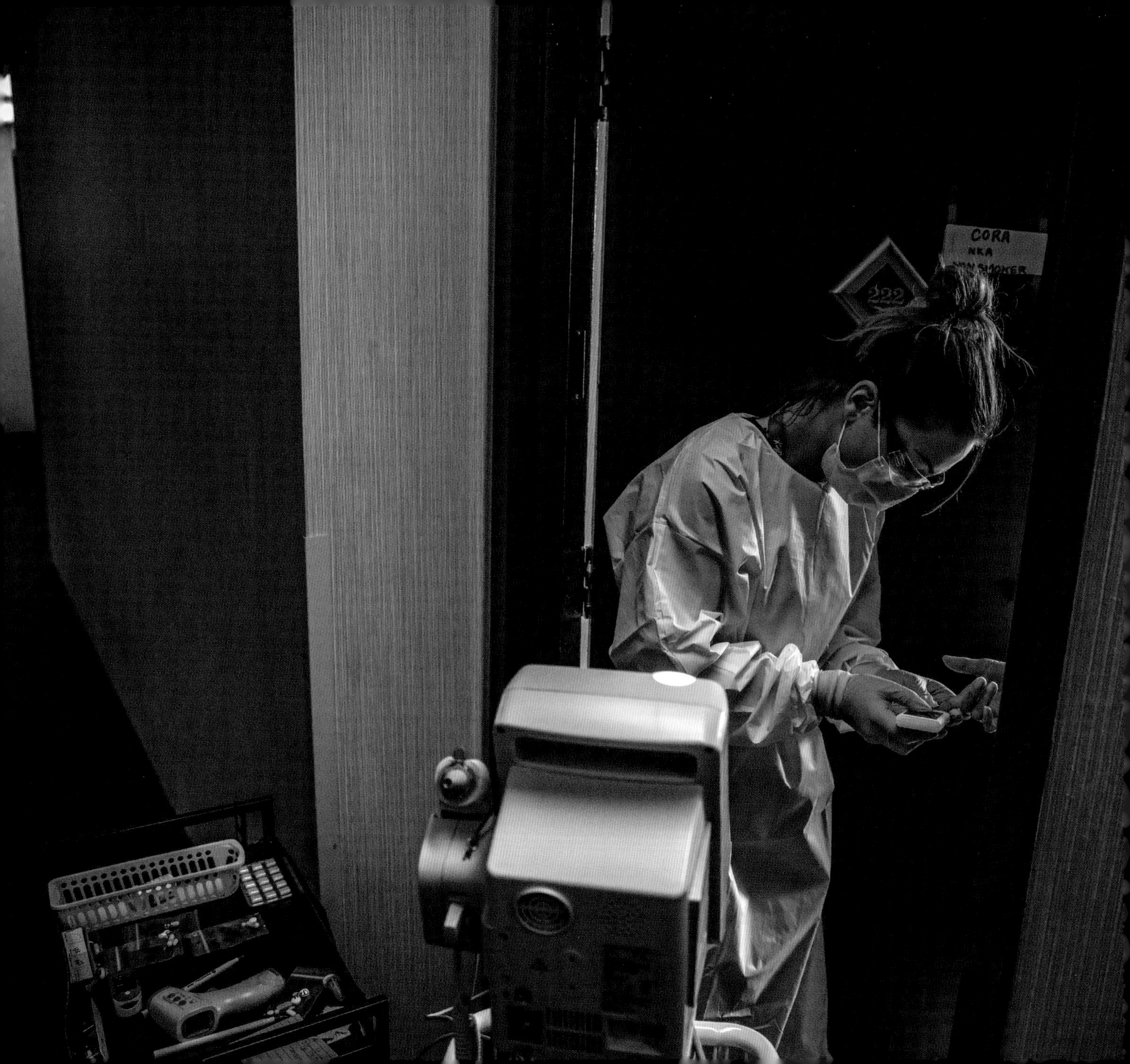
CORA
NKA
NON SMOKER
222

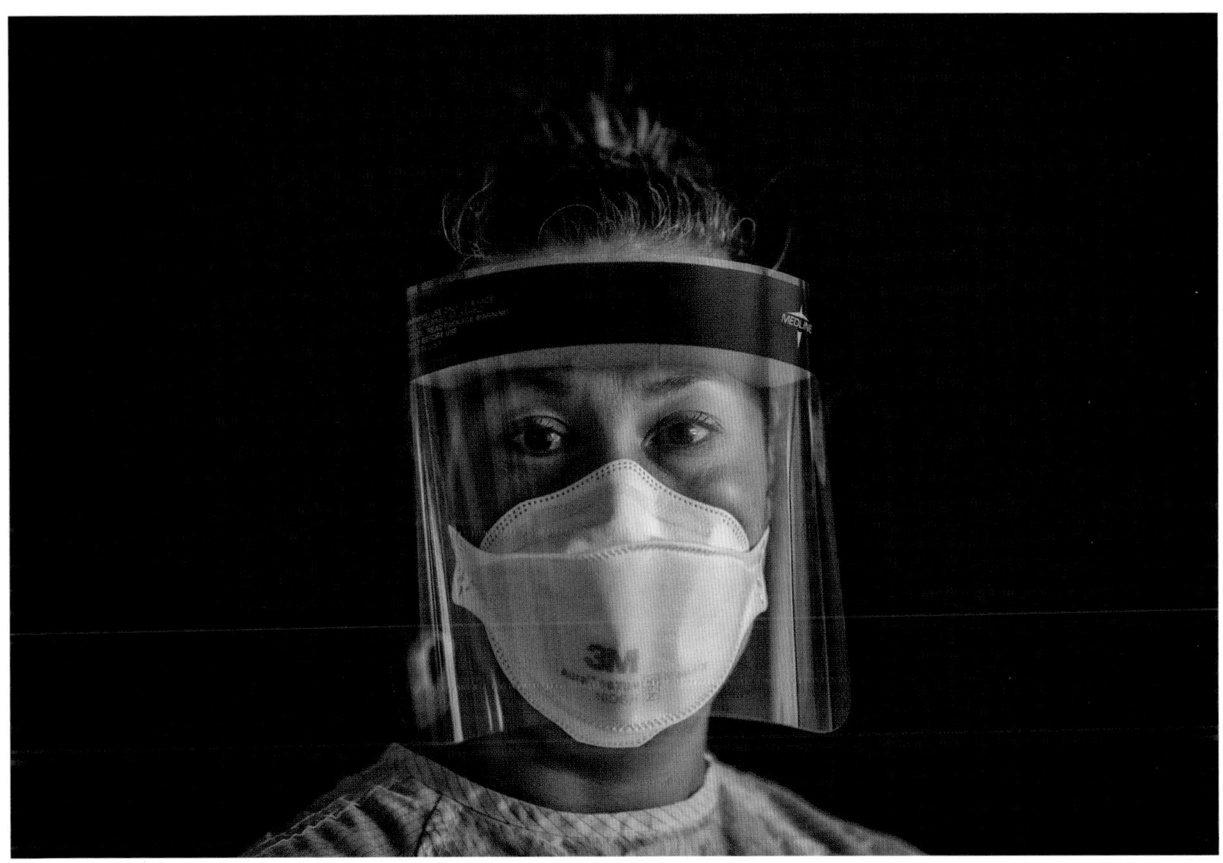

Anastazia Cline is pictured inside the Assisted Self-Isolation Site (ASIS) in Calgary. The ASIS uses available hotel space to provide isolation venues for people experiencing homelessness who have symptoms or have been diagnosed with COVID-19. The Alex, Alberta Health Services and CUPS Calgary provide medical support for the site.

A registered nurse wears full personal protective equipment at Alberta Children's Hospital in Calgary.

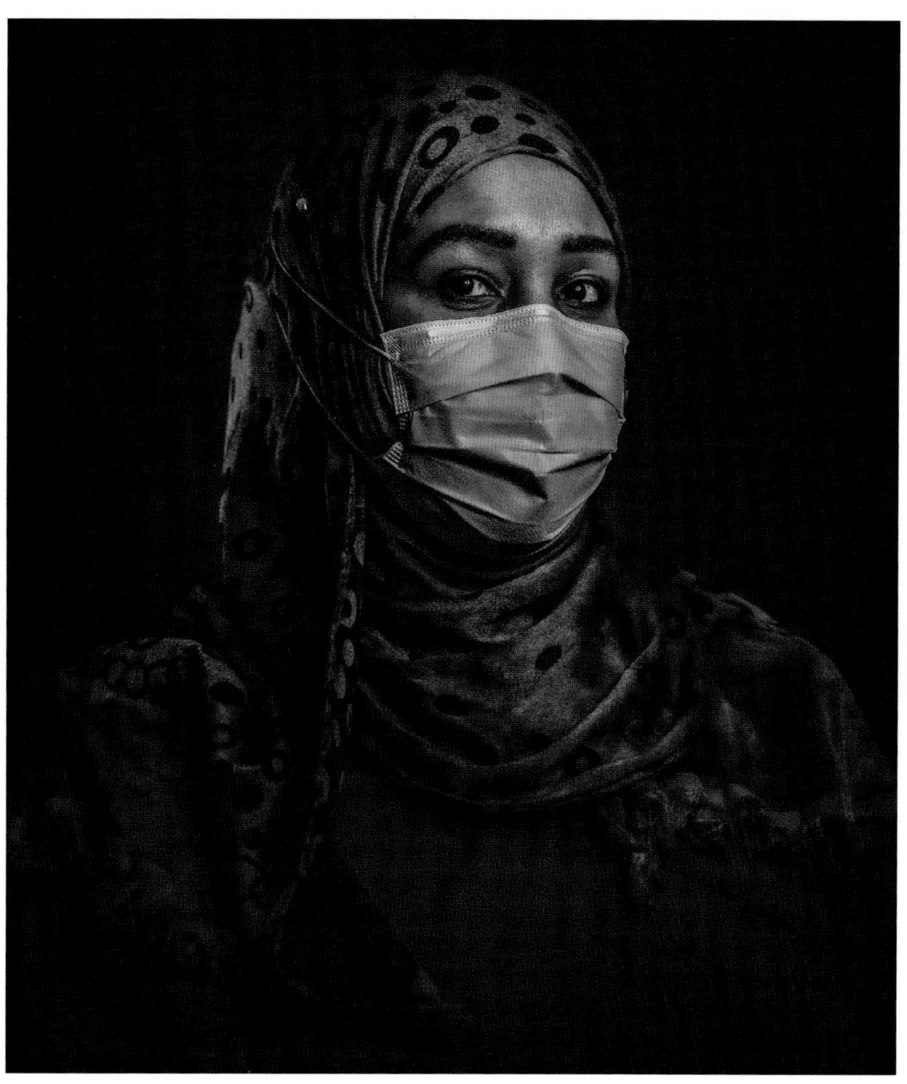

Hana Ibsa is a porter at
Peter Lougheed Centre in
Calgary, Alberta. April 2020.

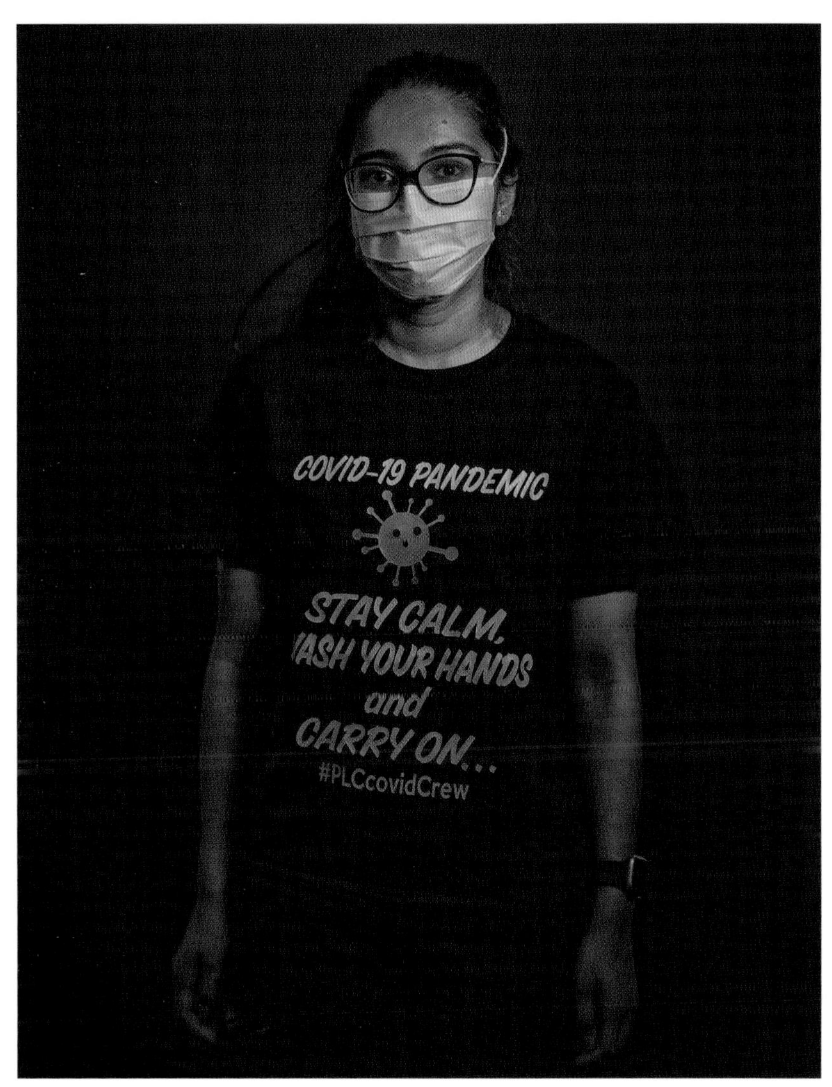

Sukhjit Parmar is a registered nurse at Peter Lougheed Centre in Calgary, Alberta. April 2020.

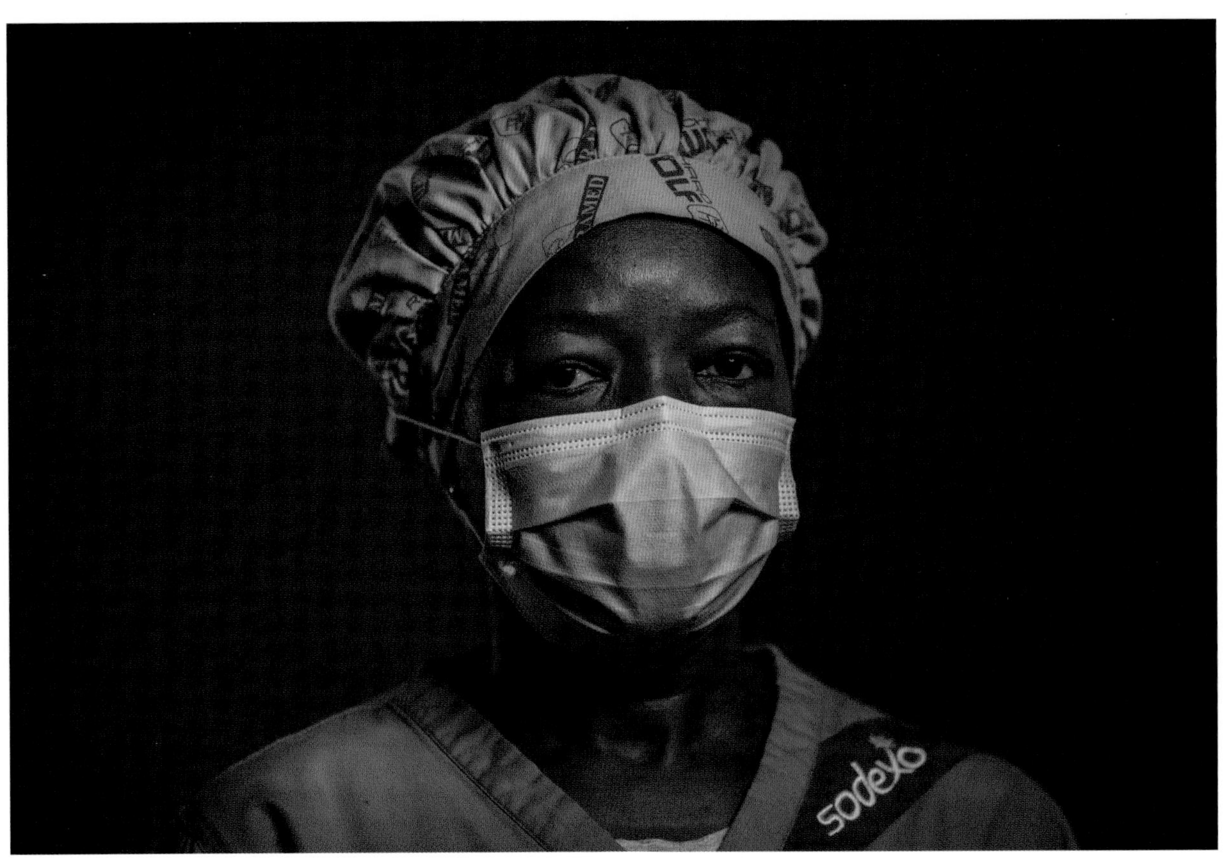

Joy Kamari, housekeeping, at Peter Lougheed
Centre in Calgary, Alberta. April 2020.

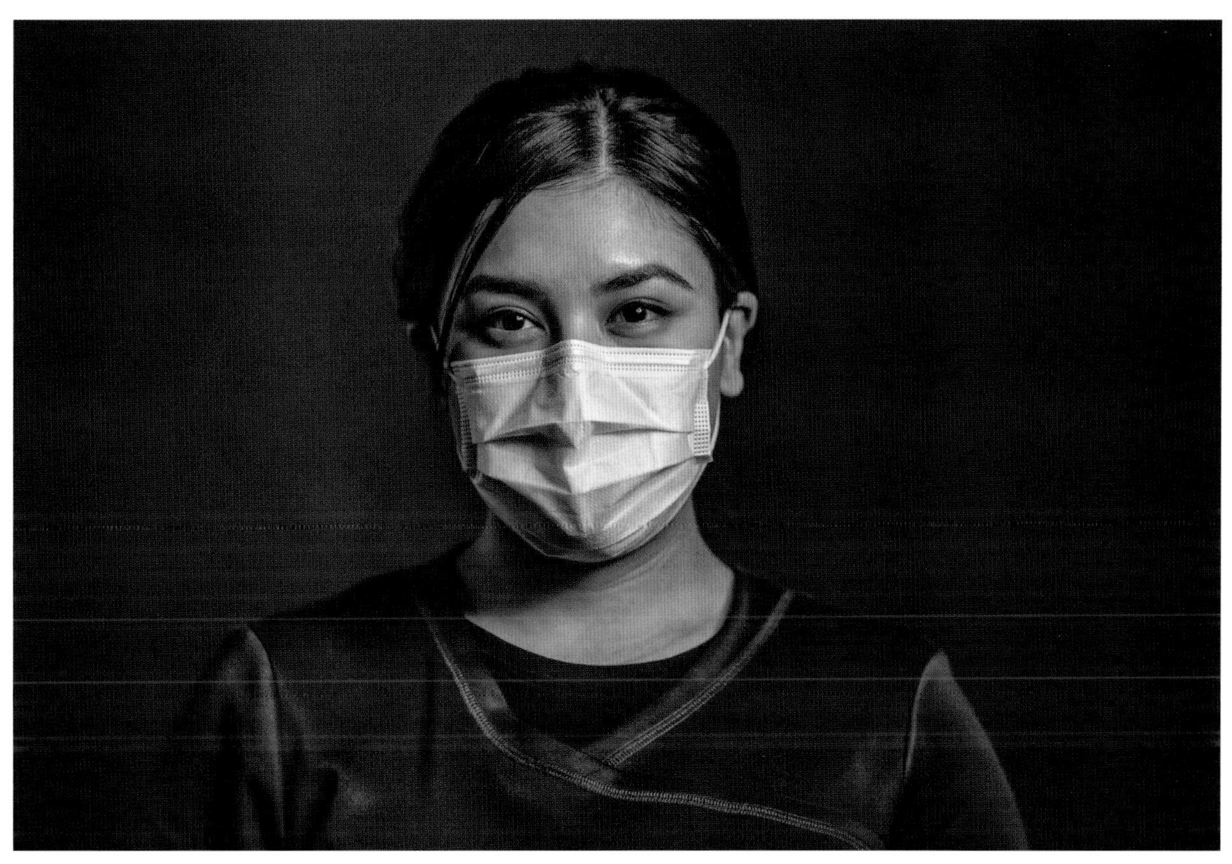

Herpreet Sandhu is a registered nurse at Peter
Lougheed Centre in Calgary, Alberta. April 2020.

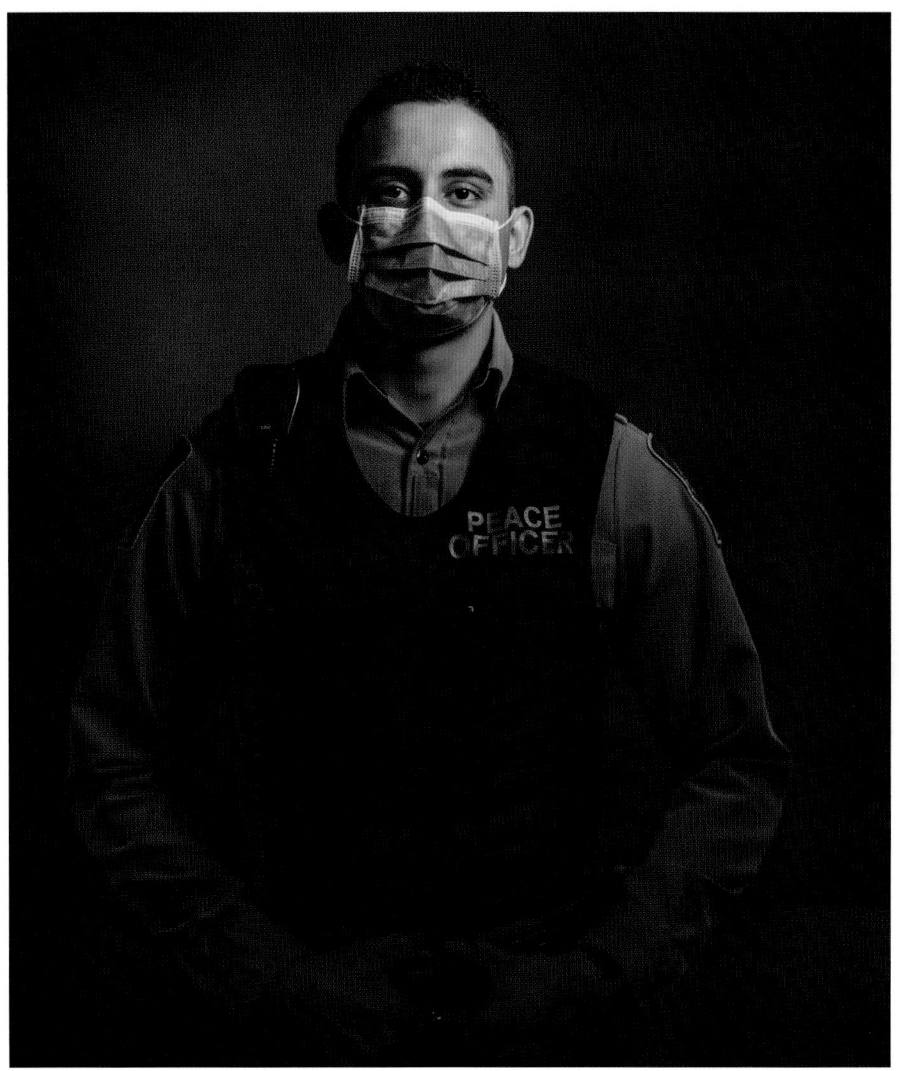

Vishal Mittu, peace officer at Peter Lougheed Centre in Calgary, Alberta. April 2020.

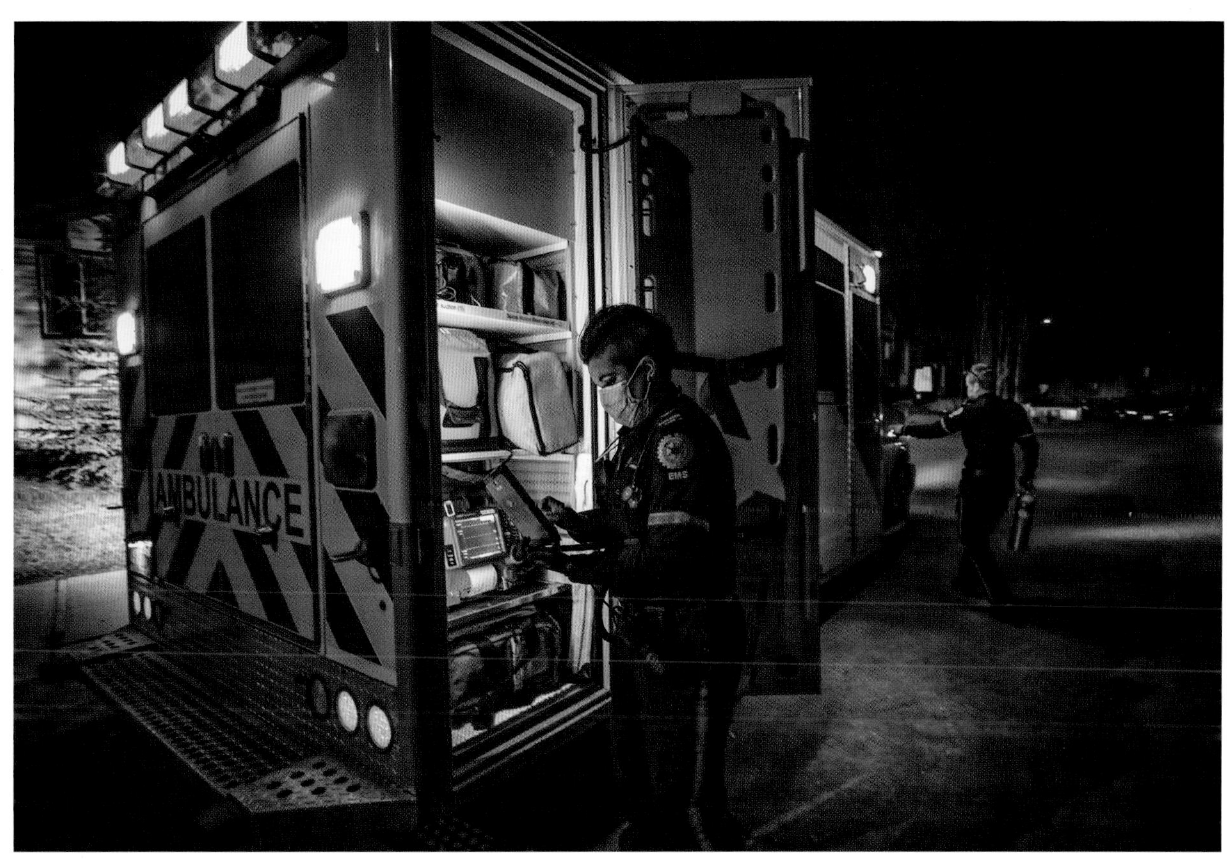

Paramedics Erin Corbett, left, and Liz
Leeder work a night shift in Calgary,
Alberta, during the pandemic.

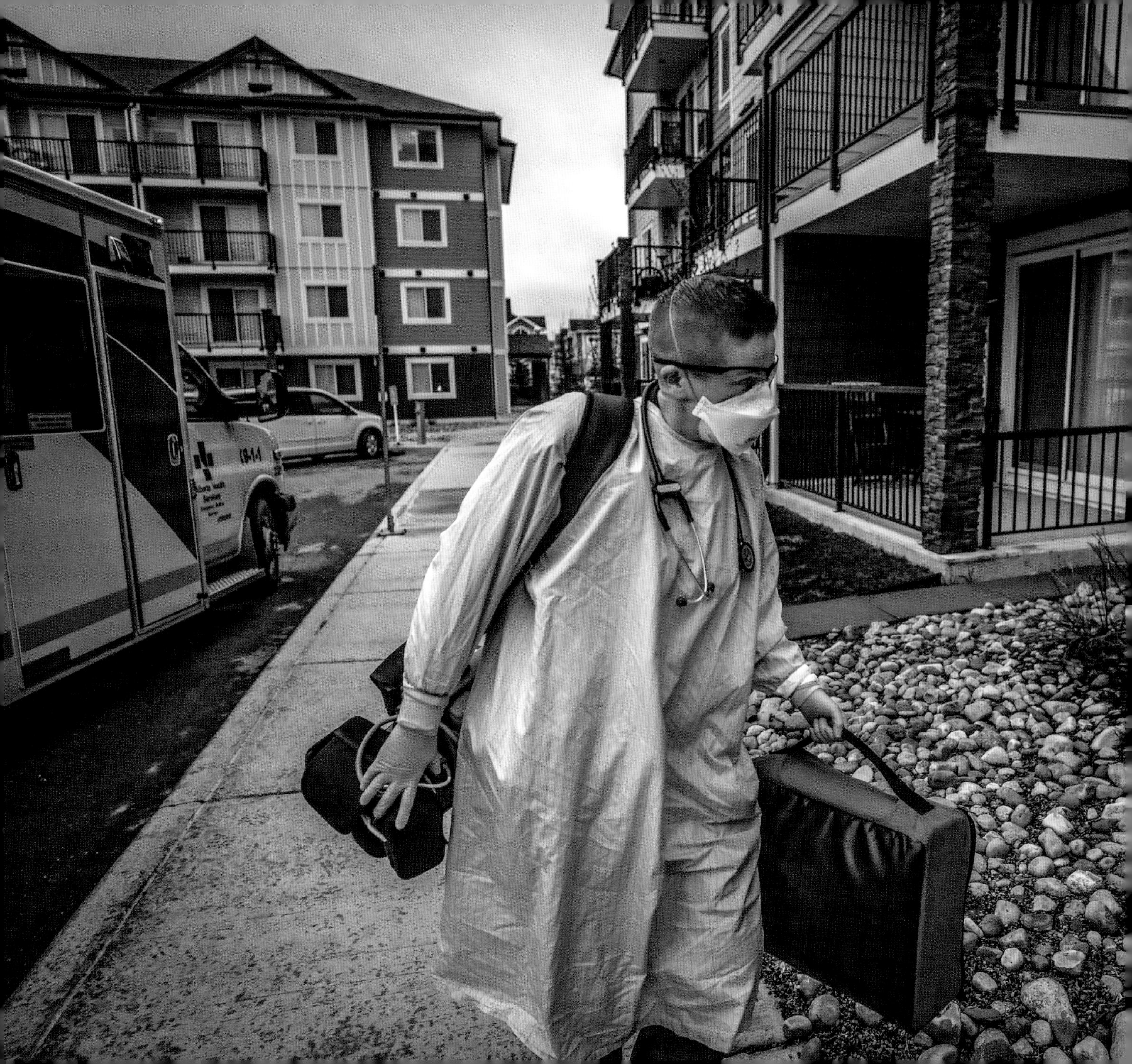

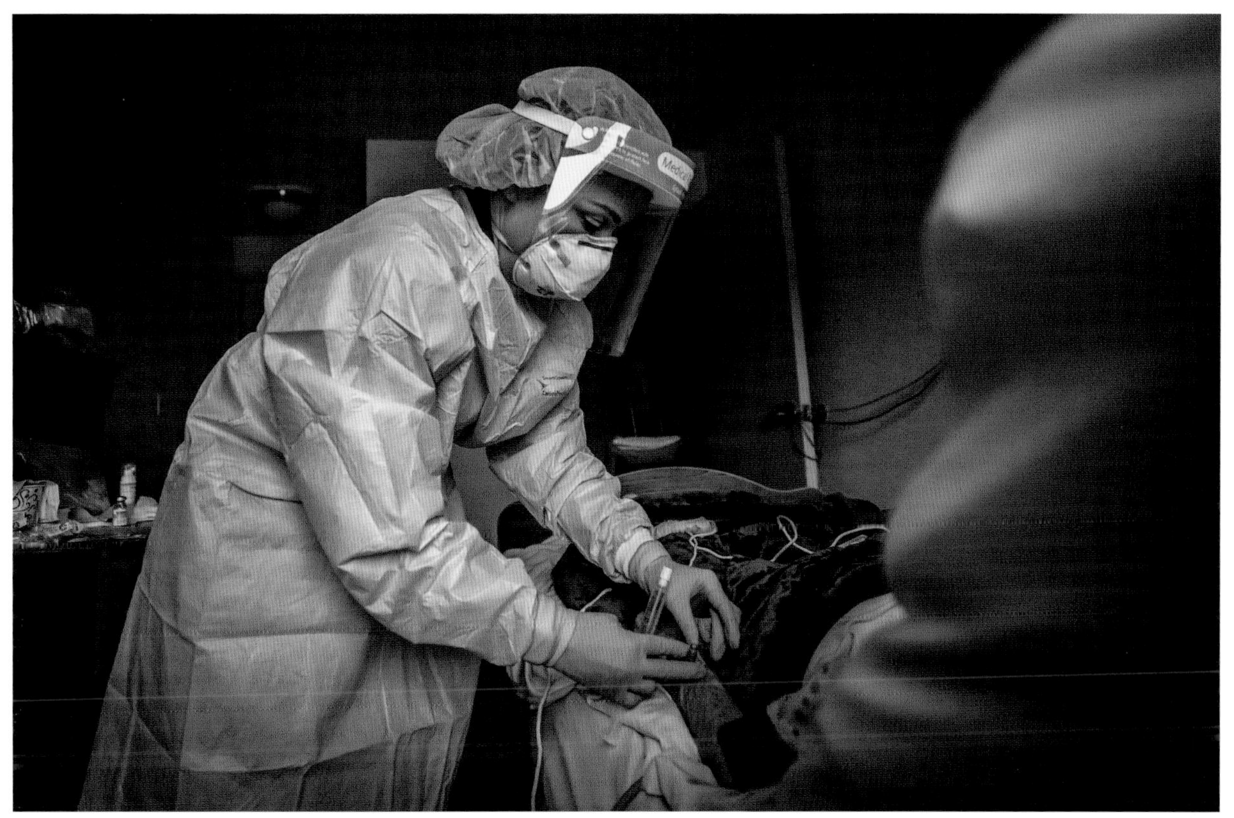

Paramedic Liz Leeder, in personal protective gear, enters the home of a potential COVID-19 patient in Calgary, Alberta.

Community paramedic Natalie Walker works on a patient at a seniors facility in Calgary, Alberta, in November 2020.

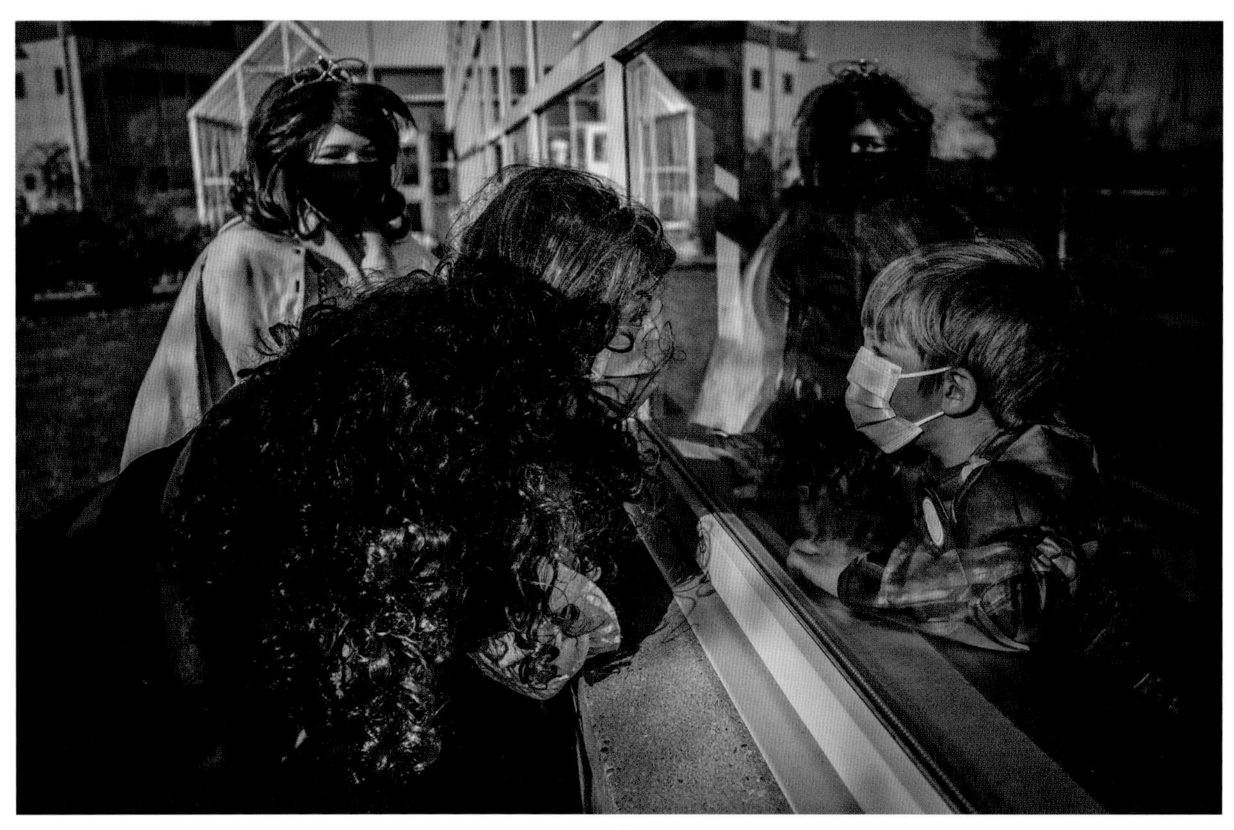

Owen Cotteril, 6, in his Iron Man
costume, waves to princesses during
Halloween celebrations at Alberta
Children's Hospital in 2020.

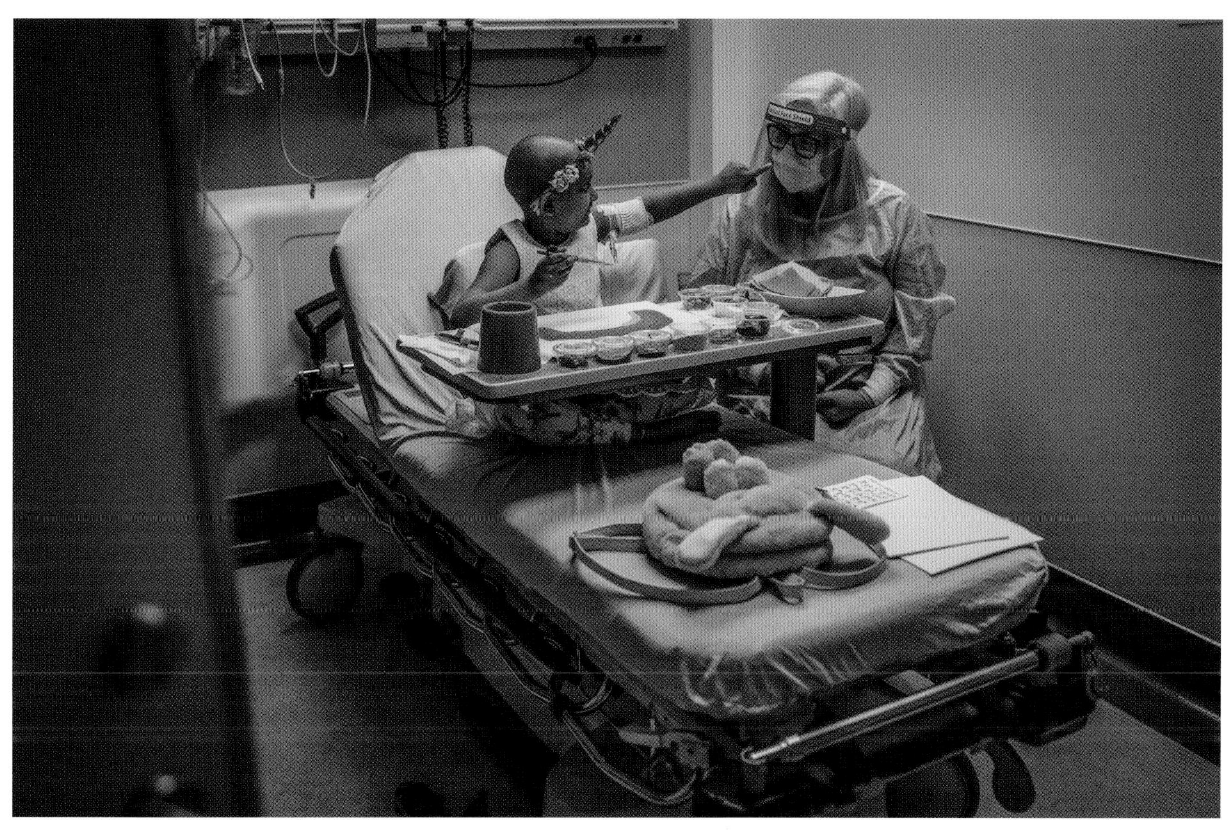

Child life and art specialist Deb Wozny
paints with Alizah Lewis, 8, at Alberta
Children's Hospital in November 2020.

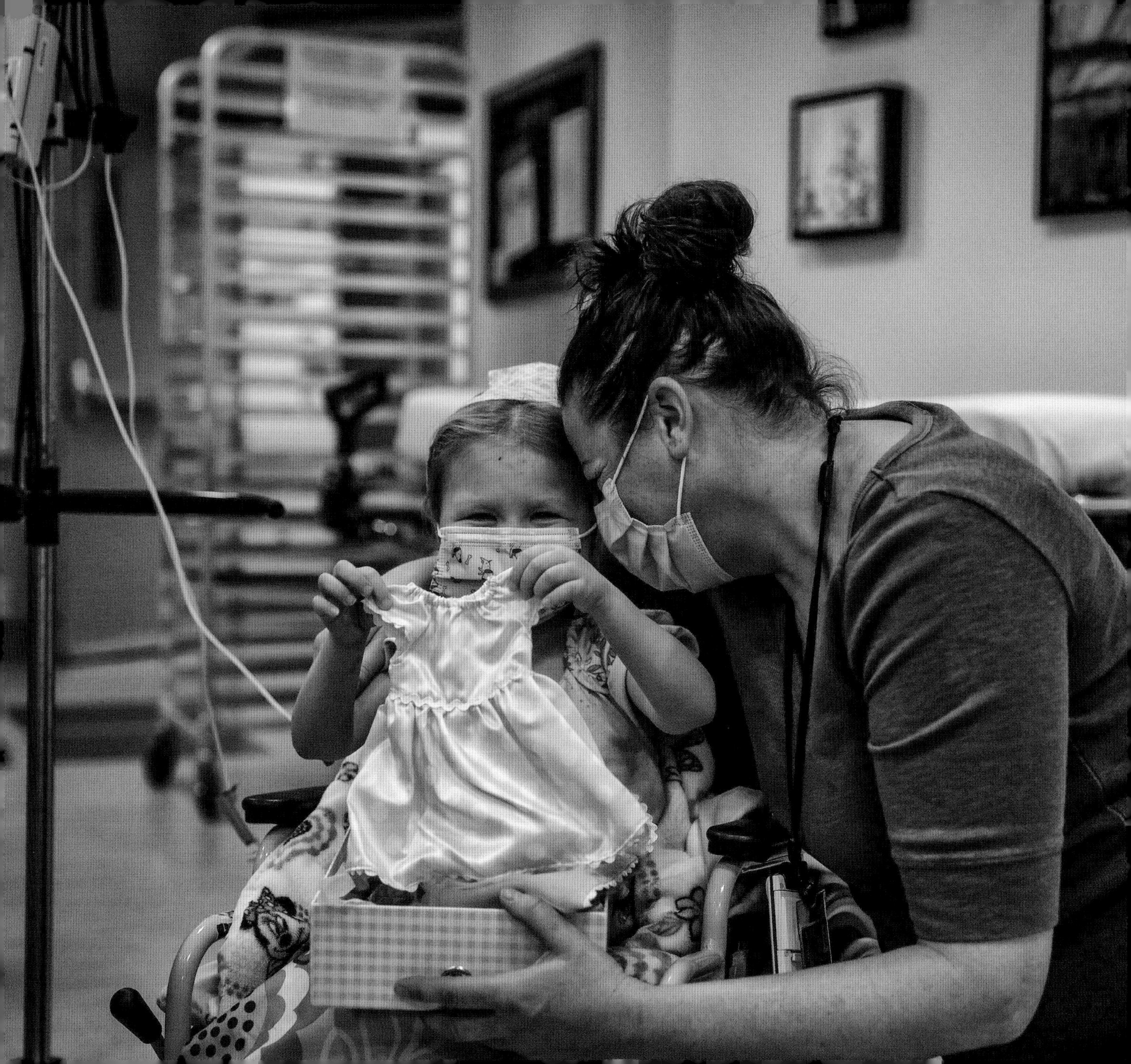

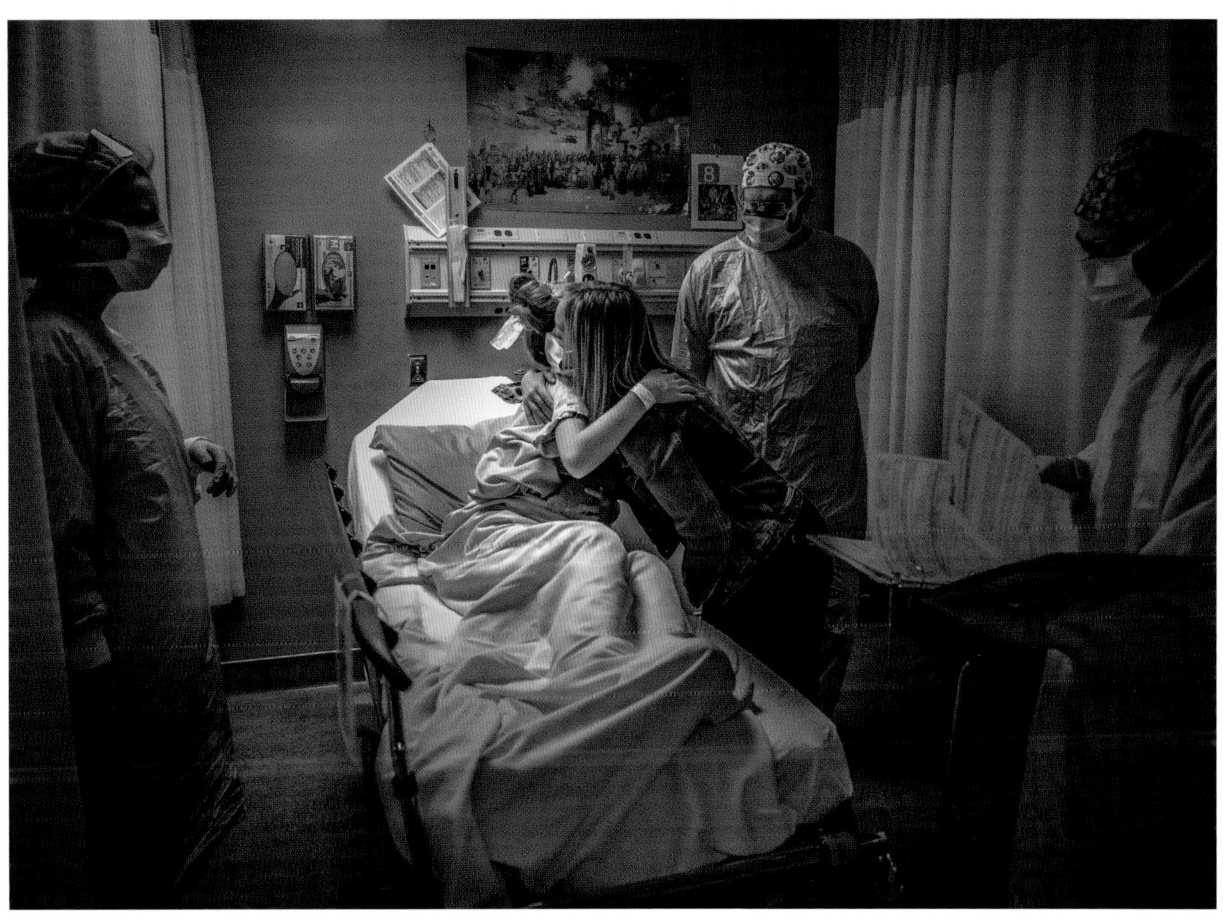

Chantal Newman, a child life specialist, hugs Shannon Mendel, 8, at Alberta Children's Hospital in November 2020.

Meagan McCance, right, embraces her daughter Hailey before the 13-year-old goes in for surgery at Alberta Children's Hospital in 2020.

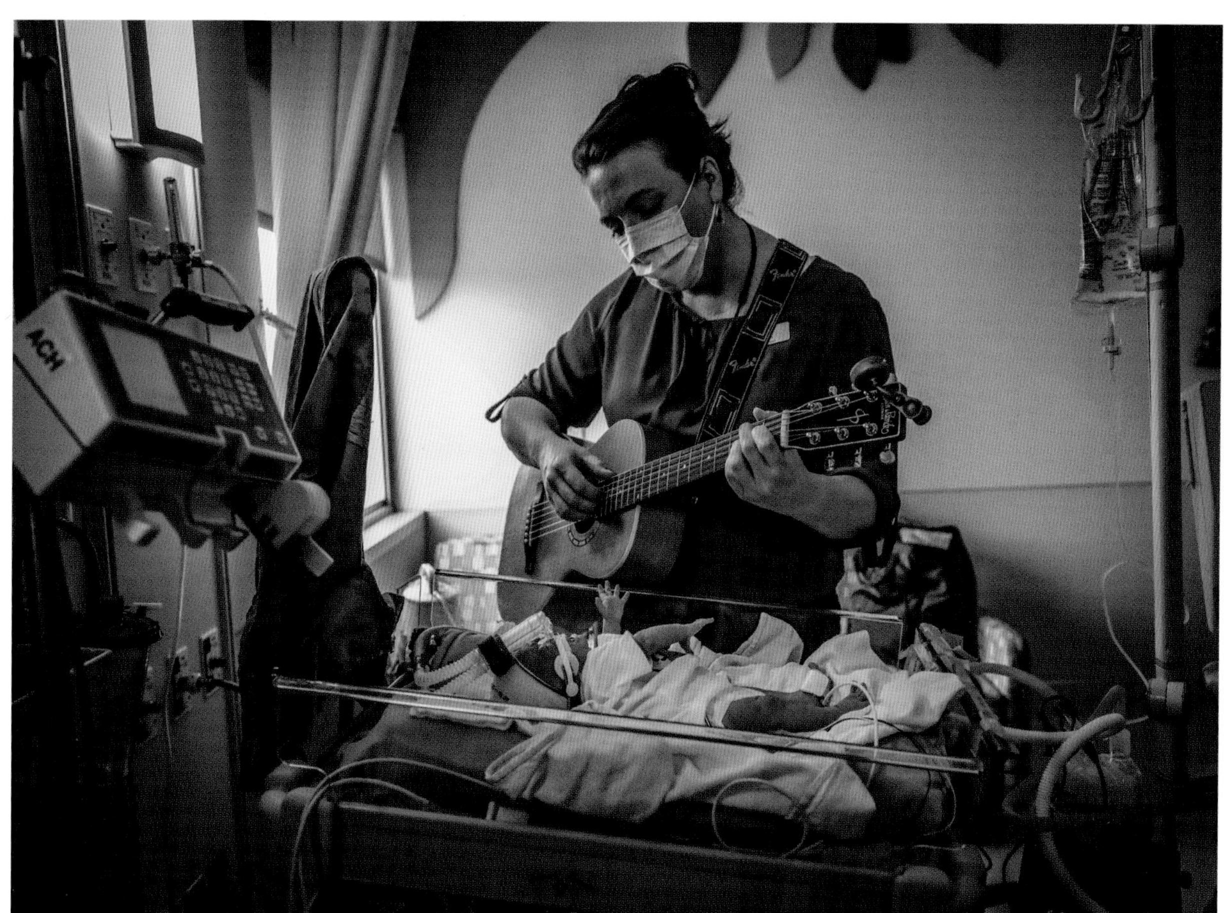

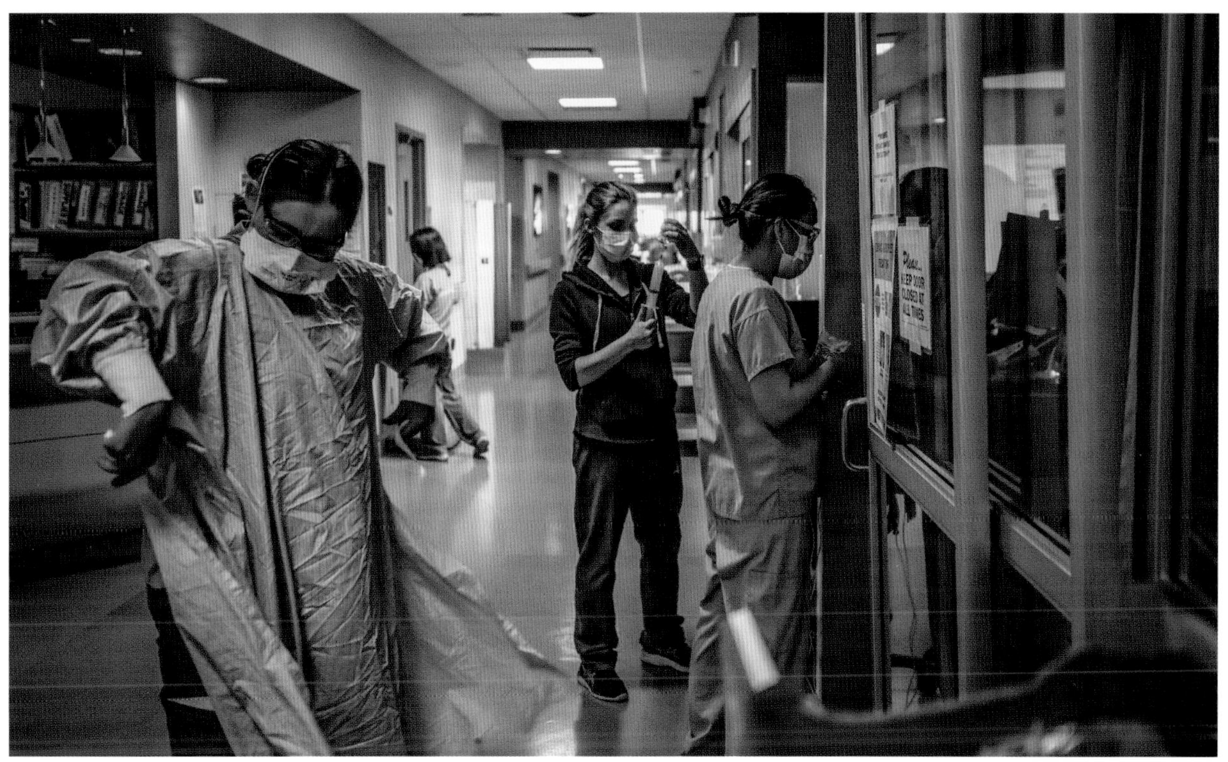

Music therapist Sarah Van Peteghen plays a song for an infant in the neo-natal intensive care unit at Alberta Children's Hospital in 2020.

Healthcare workers gather outside a COVID-19 patient's room in the intensive care unit at Peter Lougheed Centre in Calgary, Alberta. April 2020.

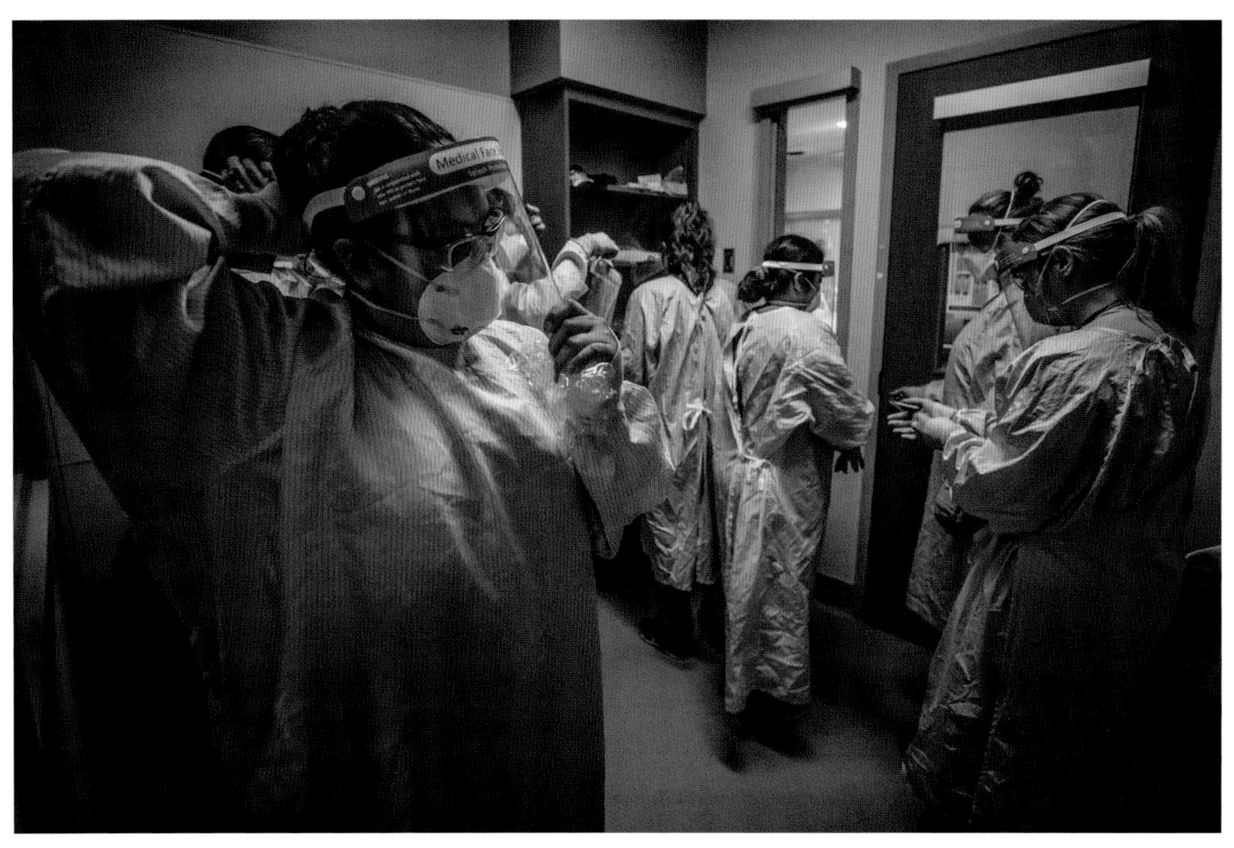

A healthcare team gets ready to
prone a COVID-19 patient in the
intensive care unit at Peter Lougheed
Centre in Calgary, Alberta, in
November 2020.

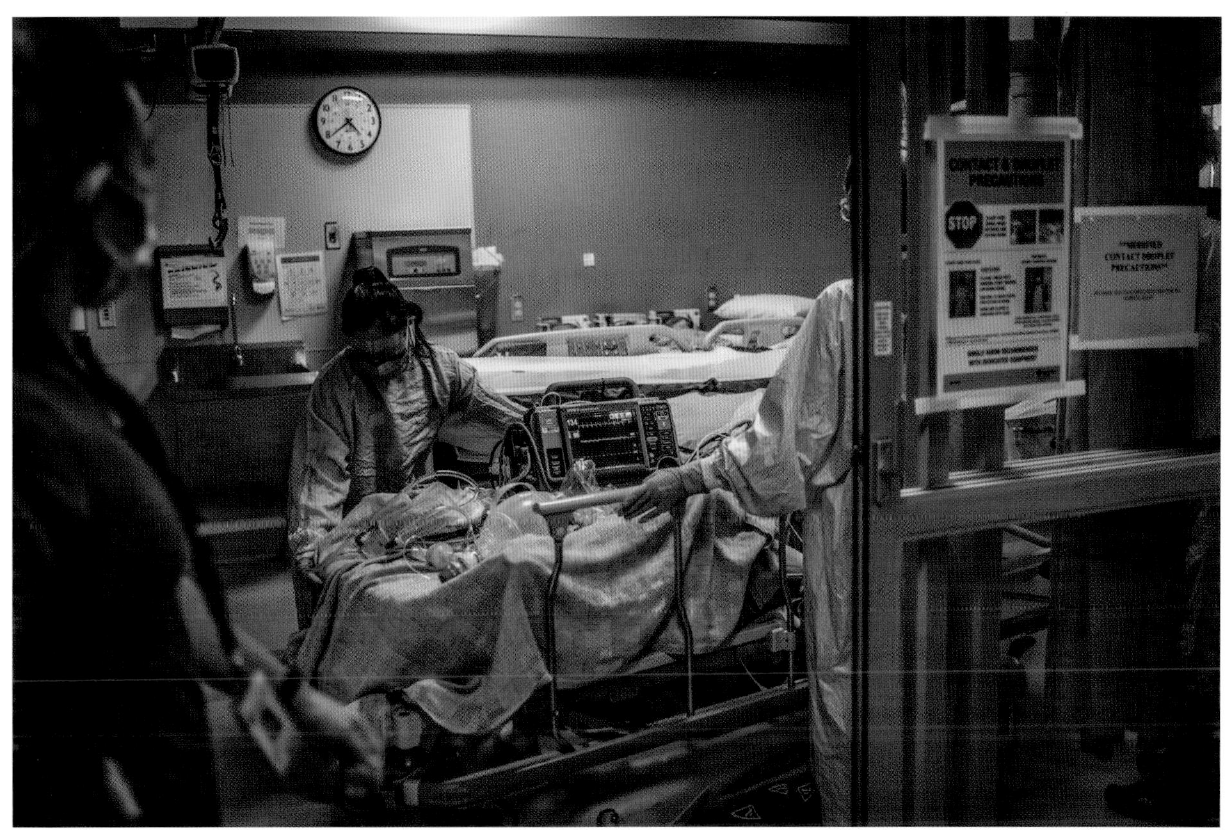

A healthcare team admits a COVID-19
patient to the intensive care unit at
Peter Lougheed Centre in Calgary,
Alberta, in November 2020.

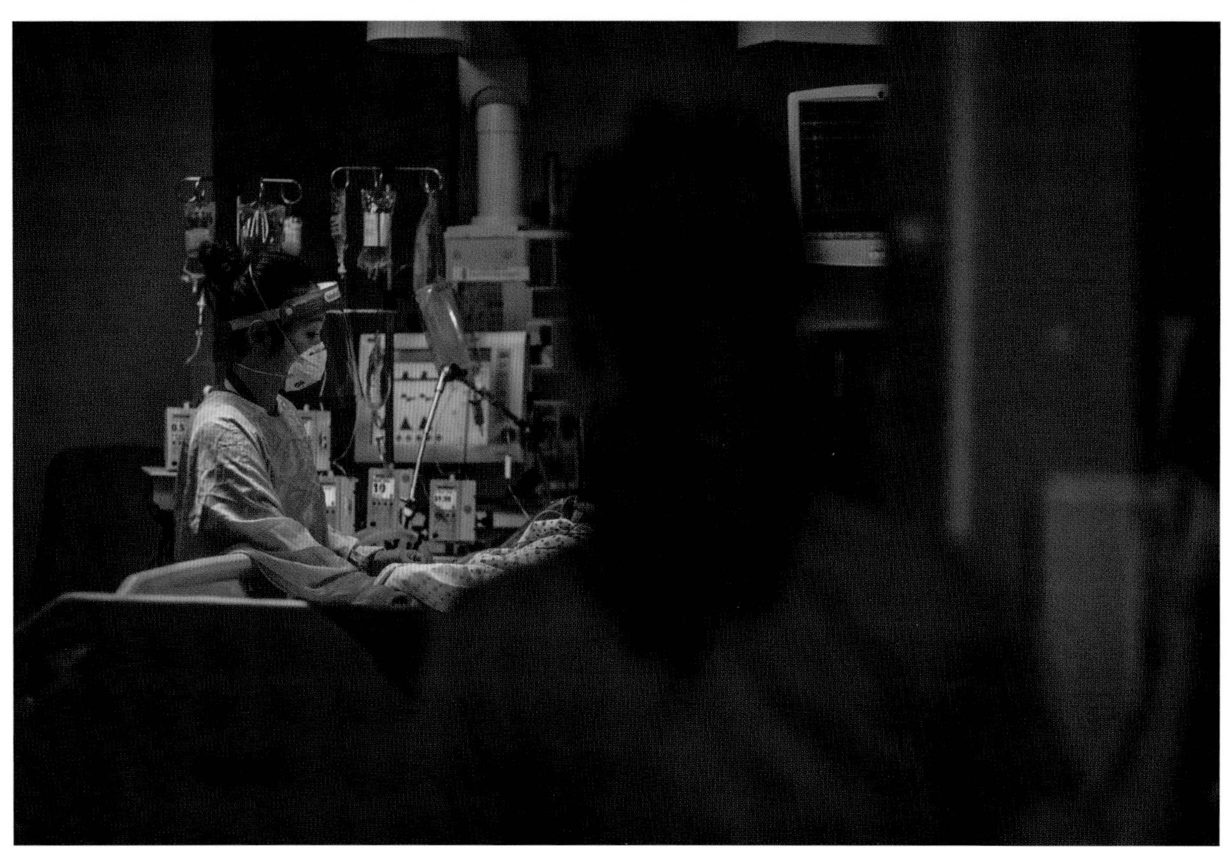

Healthcare staff attend to a COVID-19
patient in 2020.

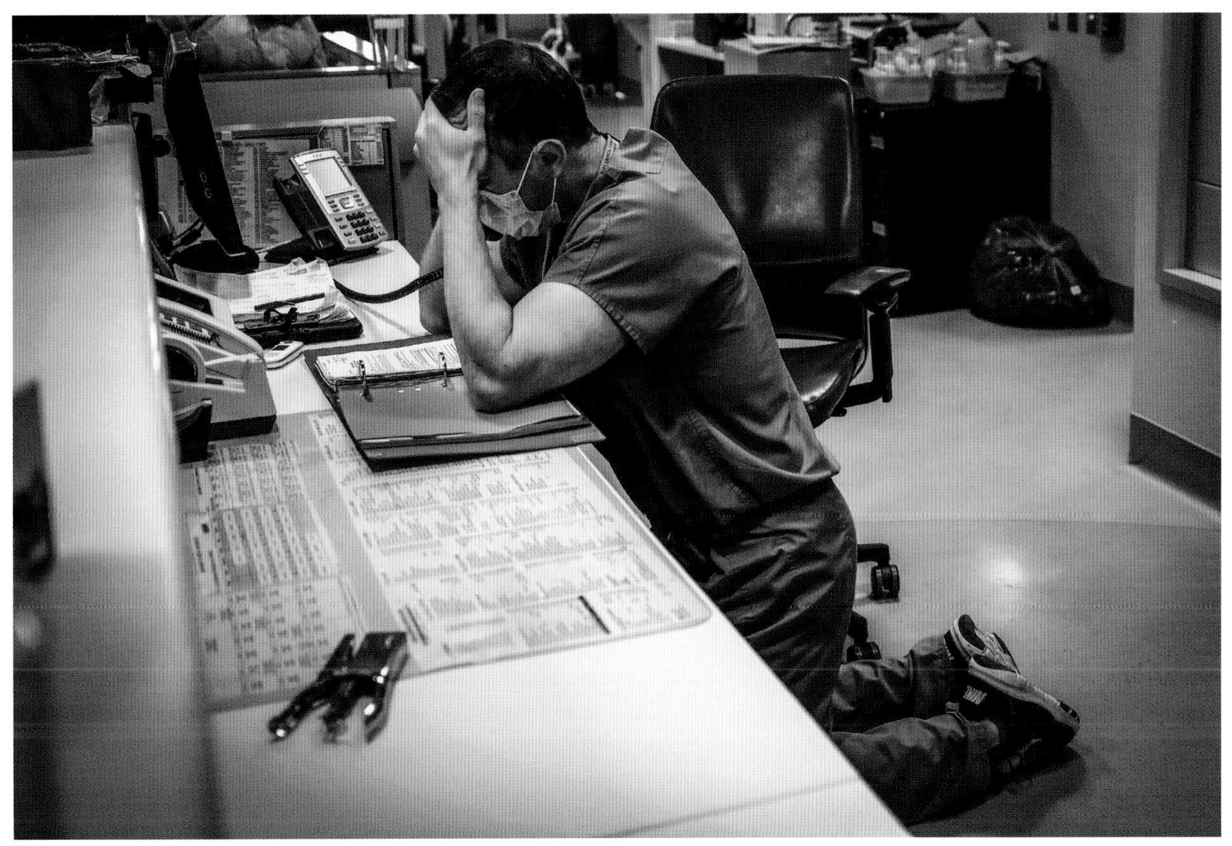

Dr. Simon Demers-Marcil, an intensive care physician in Calgary, Alberta, calls a family to tell them a loved one has died of COVID-19, in 2020.

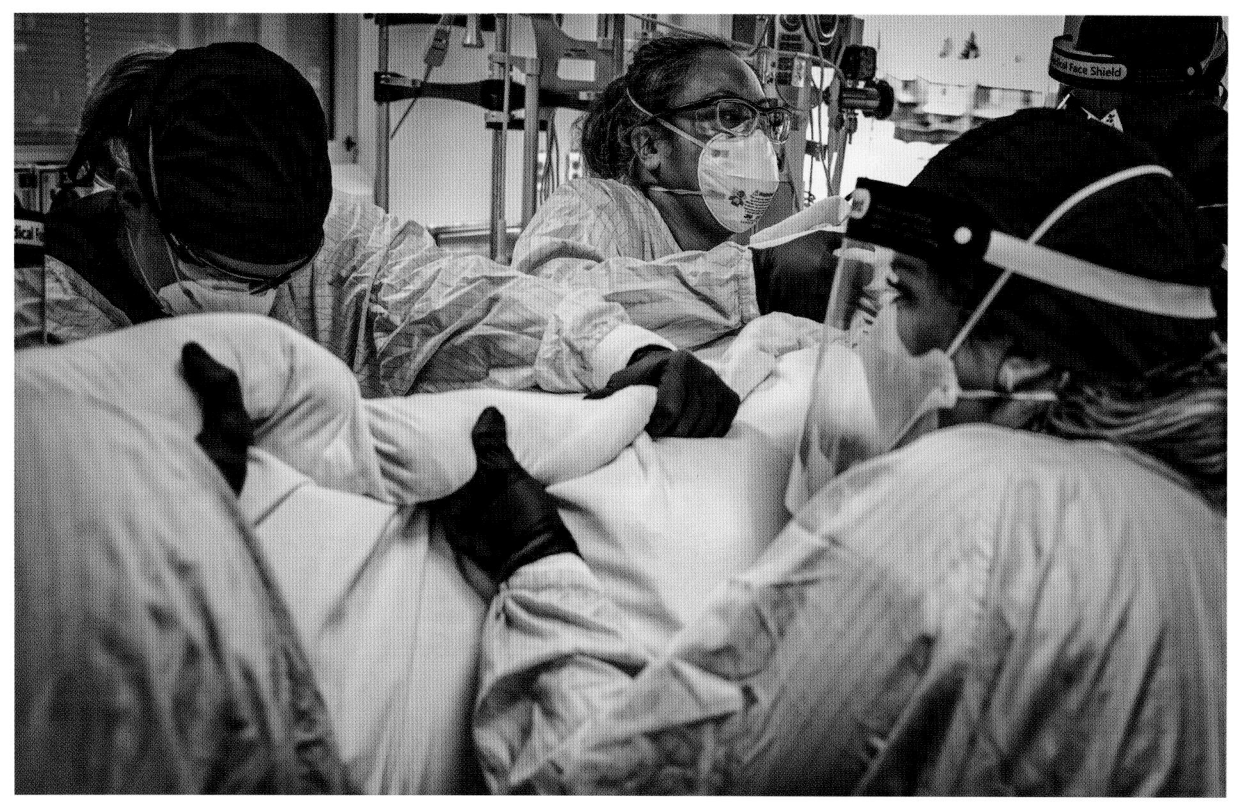

A healthcare team moves a patient with COVID-19 onto their stomach, which can help increase oxygen flow.

"Whatever happens, I got you," registered nurse Mia Torres, left, says to her colleague Joanna d'Abadie, a respiratory therapist. The pair works together in the intensive care unit at Peter Lougheed Centre.

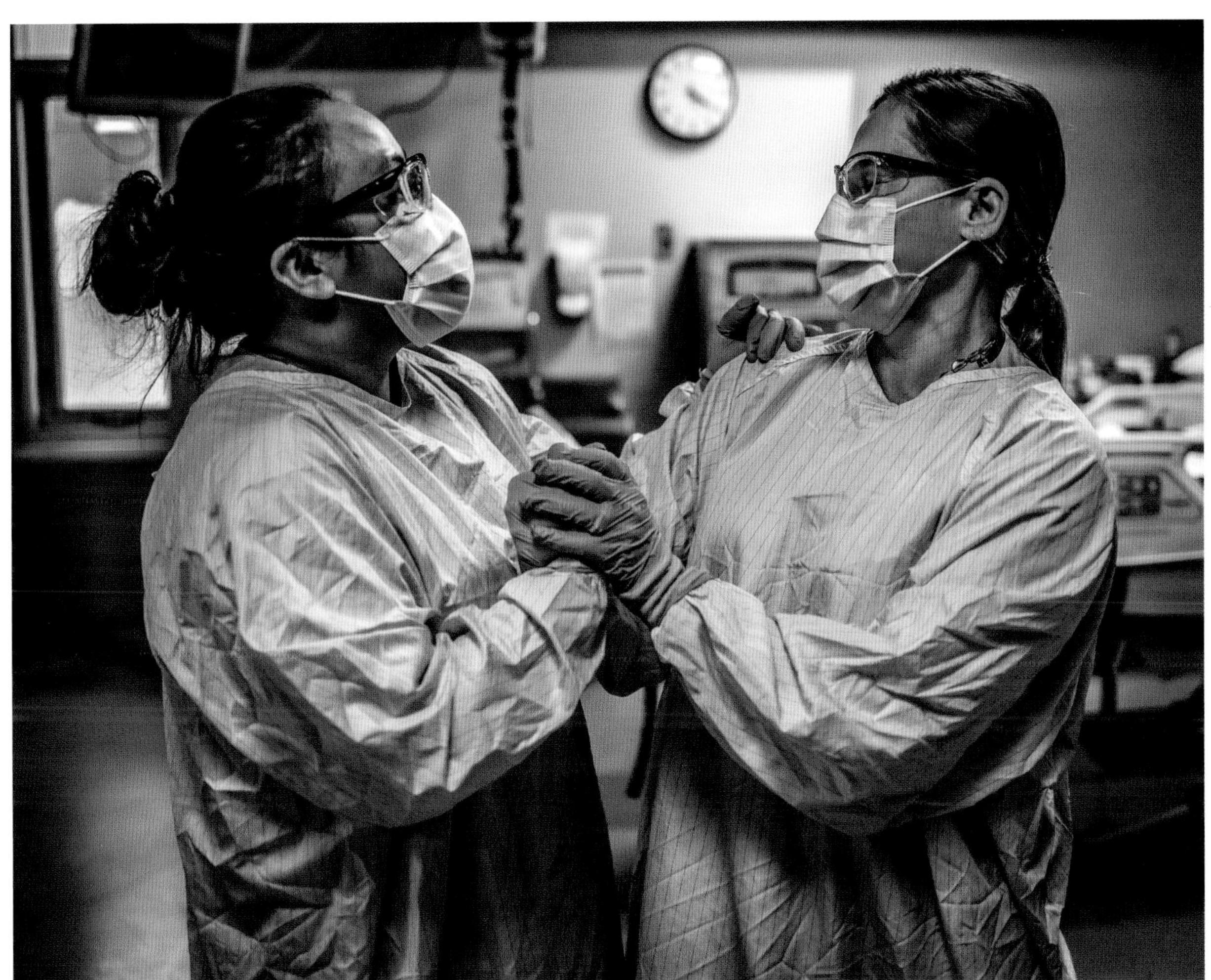

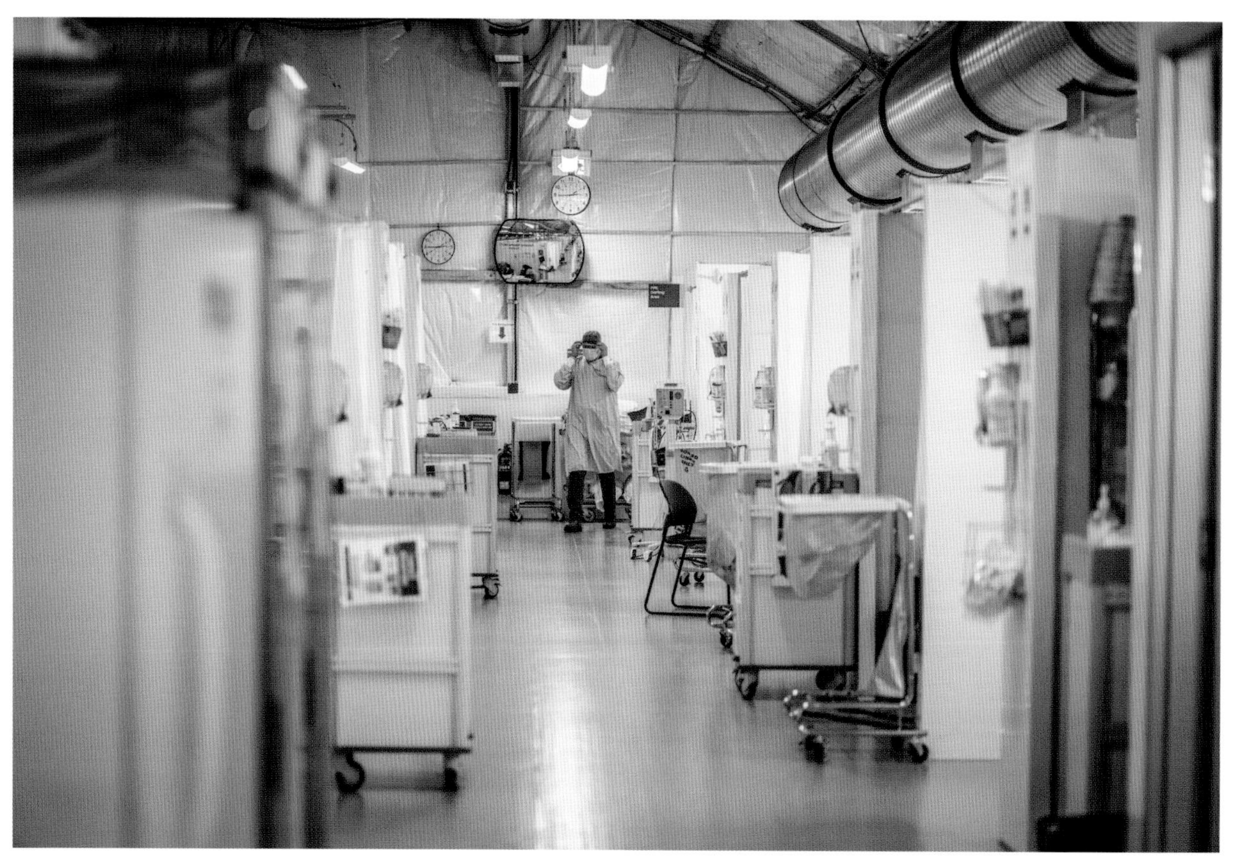

Healthcare staffer walks through
the temporary field hospital at Peter
Lougheed Centre in Calgary, Alberta.

Jenilee Mitzner, medical radiologic
technologist (left), helps a team
transfer a COVID-19 patient before a
chest X-ray at Peter Lougheed Centre.

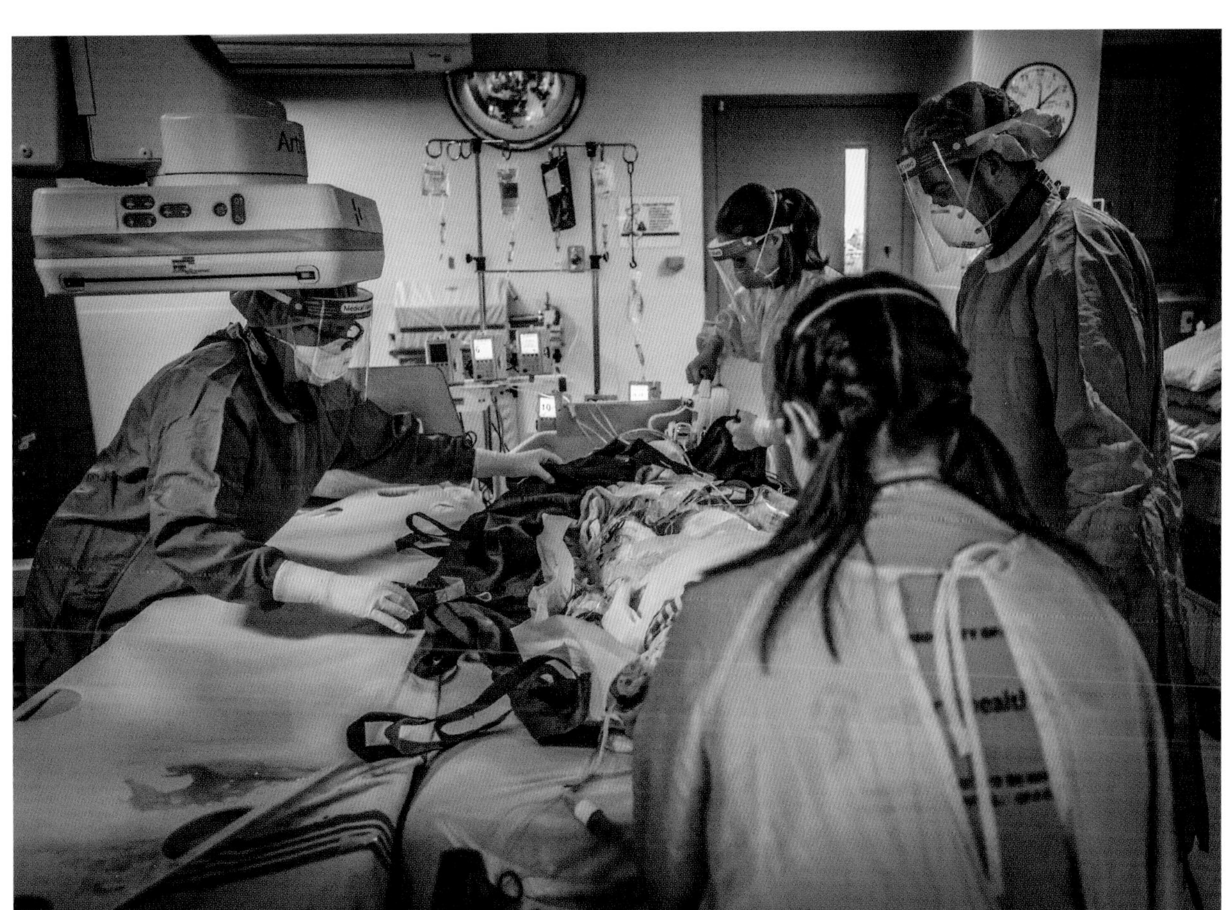

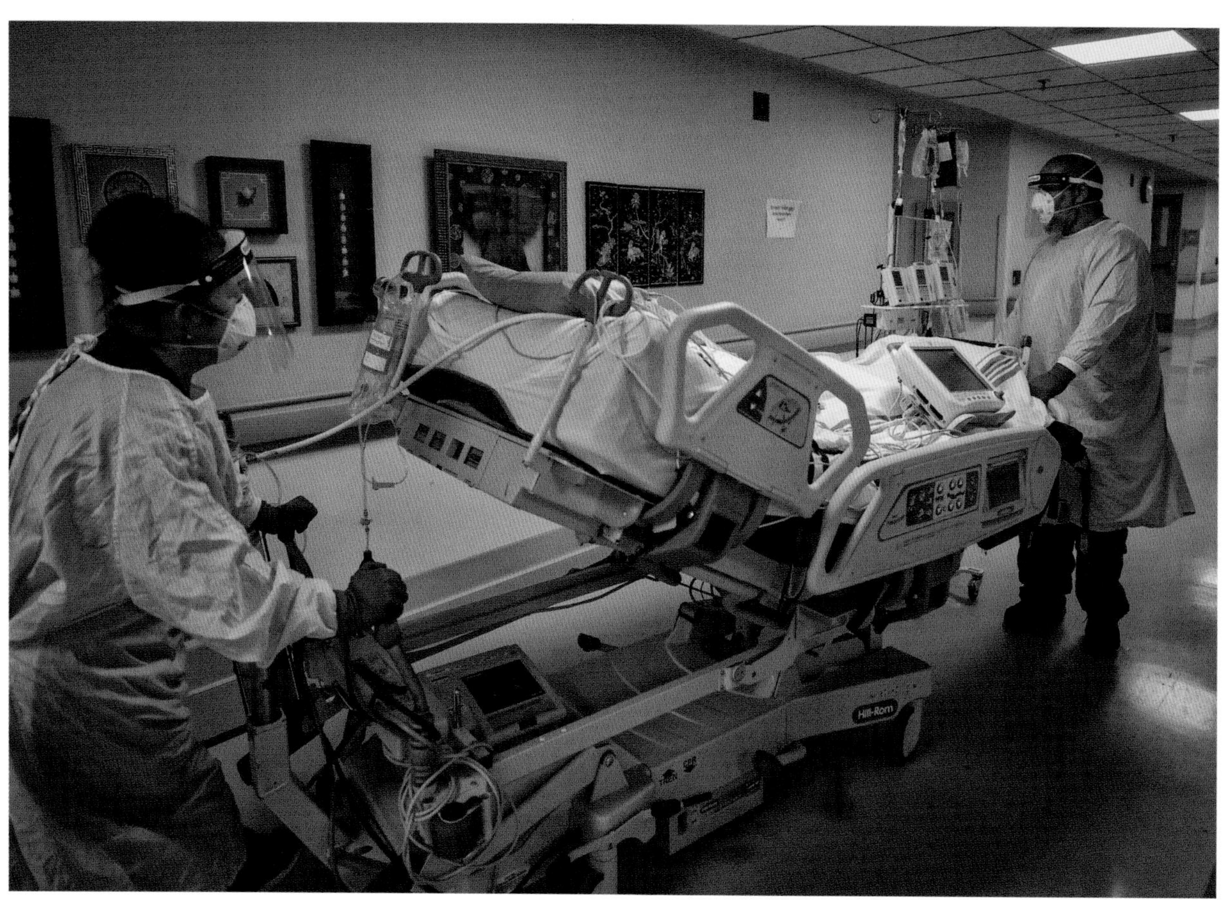

Sheila Shannon, left, and James Bond, porters, take a COVID-19 patient for a chest X-ray at Peter Lougheed Centre.

Registered nurse Anne Garcia comforts patient Chuck Dover, 76, in the COVID-19 unit at Peter Lougheed Centre in Calgary, Alberta, on January 20, 2021.

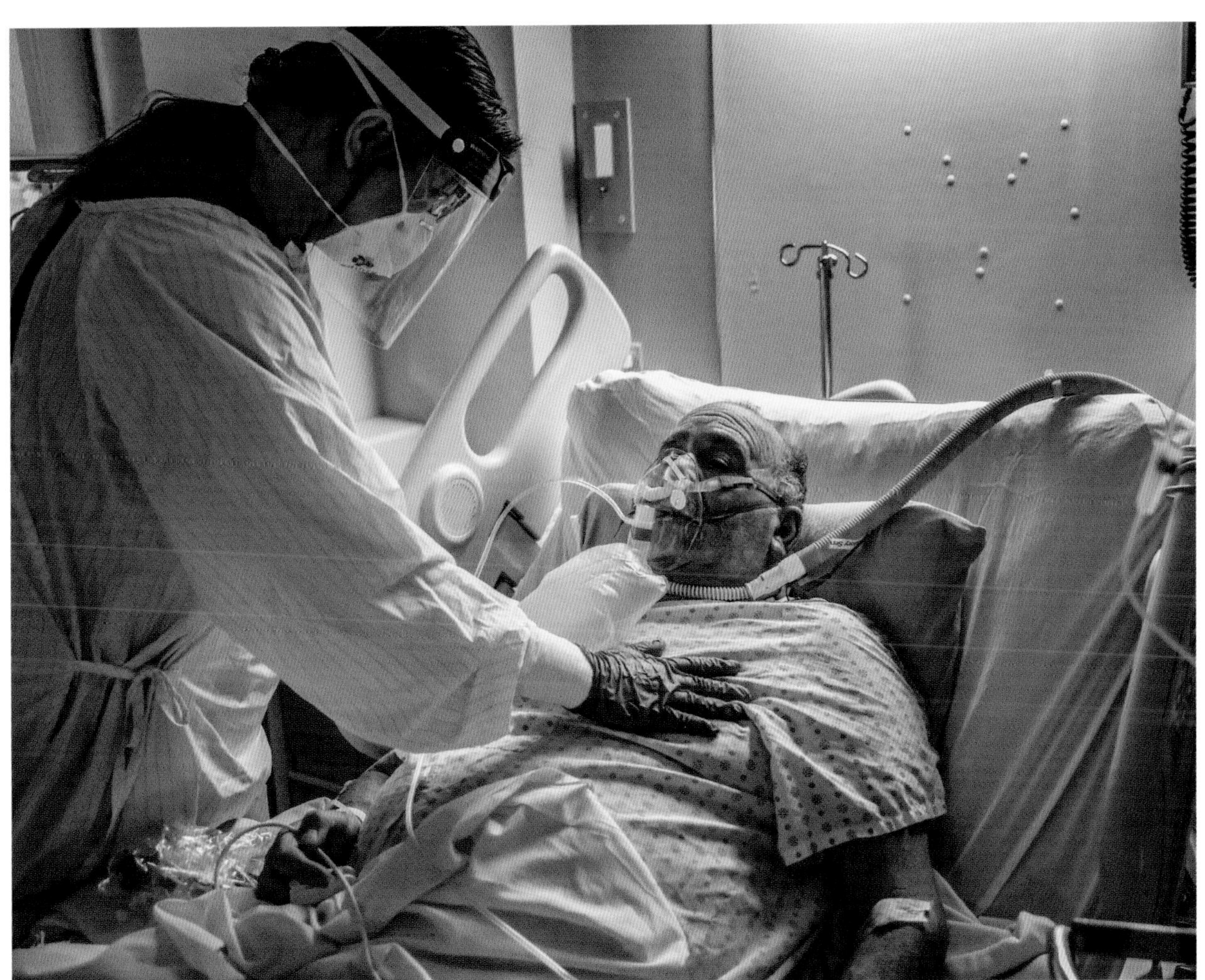

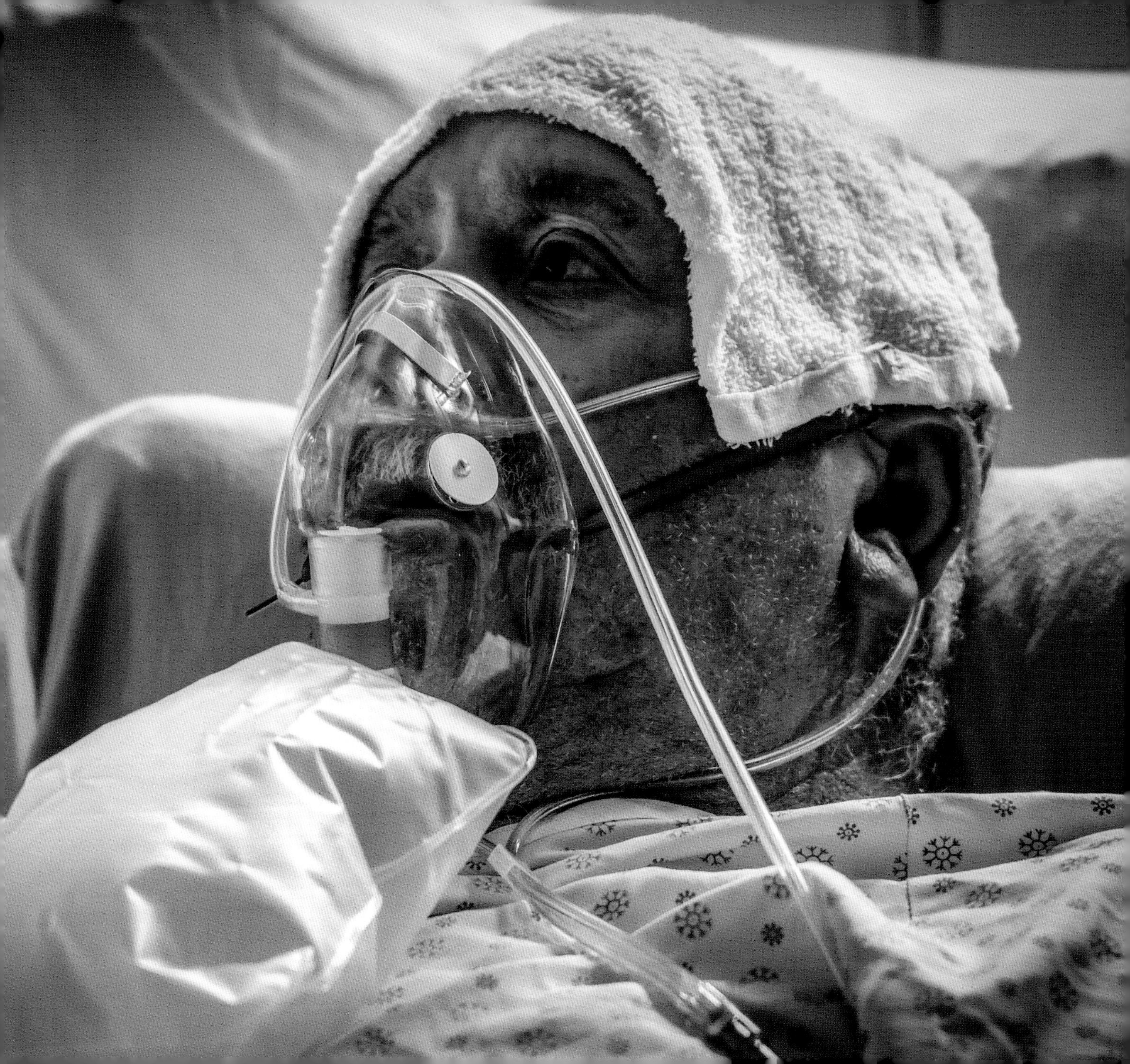

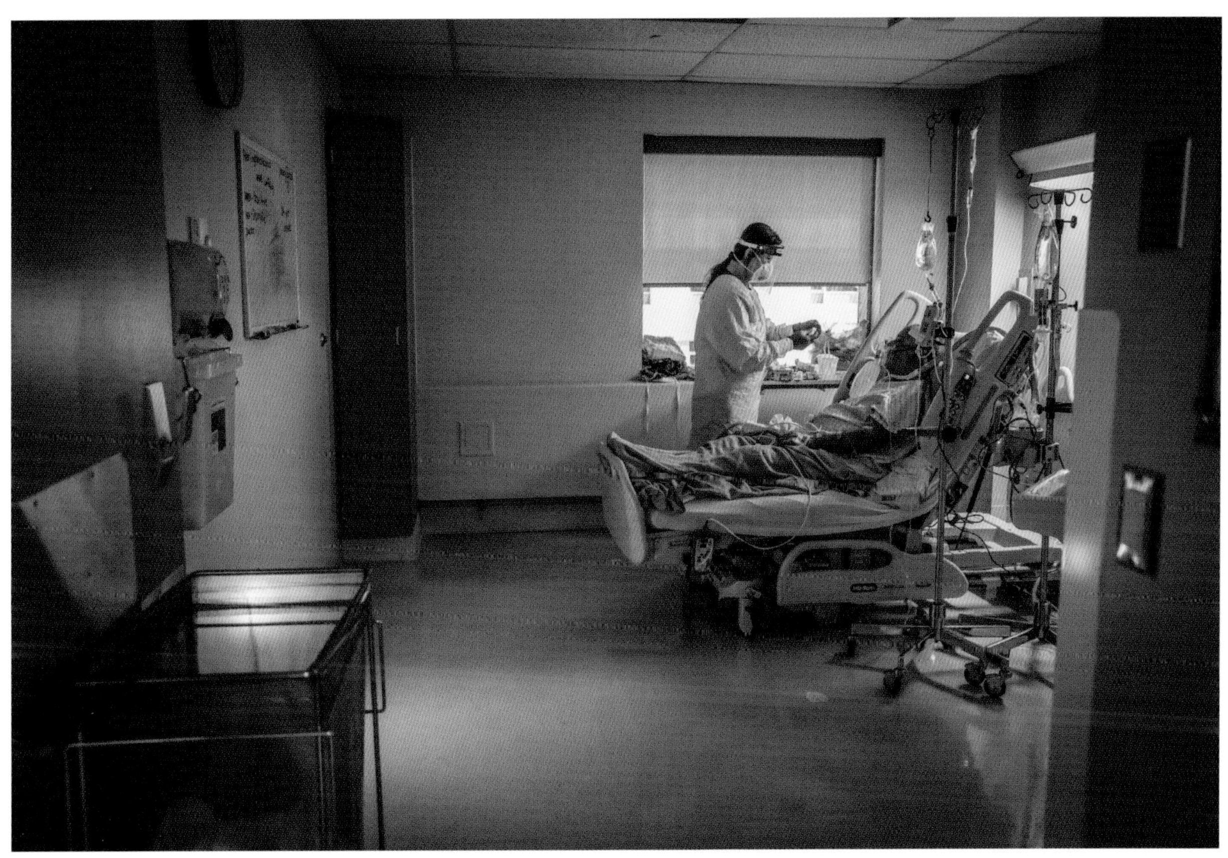

COVID-19 patient Chuck Dover, 76, is given
supplemental oxygen at Peter Lougheed Centre
in Calgary, Alberta, on January 20, 2021.

Registered nurse Anne Garcia comforts
COVID-19 patient Chuck Dover, 76, at Peter
Lougheed Centre in Calgary on January 20, 2021.

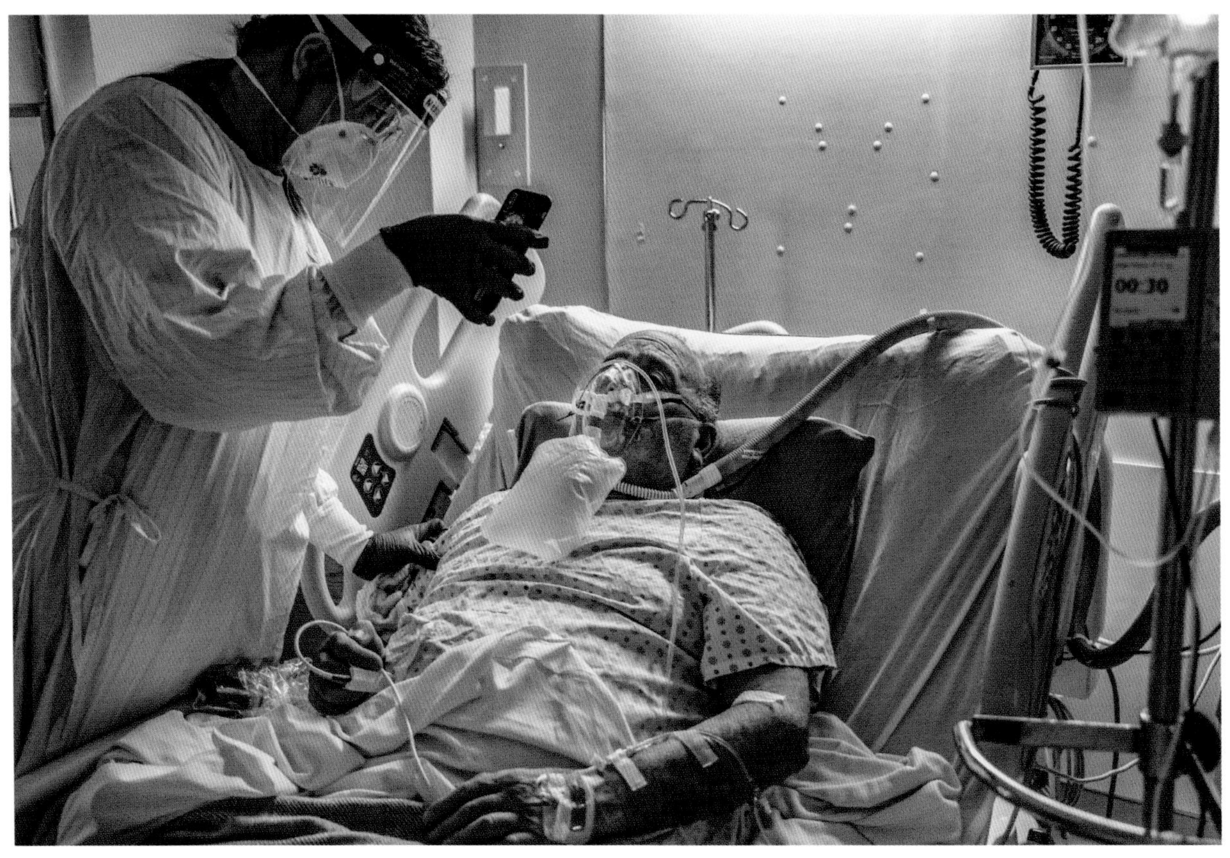

Registered nurse Anne Garcia holds the phone so COVID-19 patient Chuck Dover, 76, can FaceTime his wife Dixie at Peter Lougheed Centre in Calgary, Alberta, on January 20, 2021.

Dixie Dover puts on personal protective equipment before visiting her husband Chuck, who was intubated at Peter Lougheed Centre in January 2021.

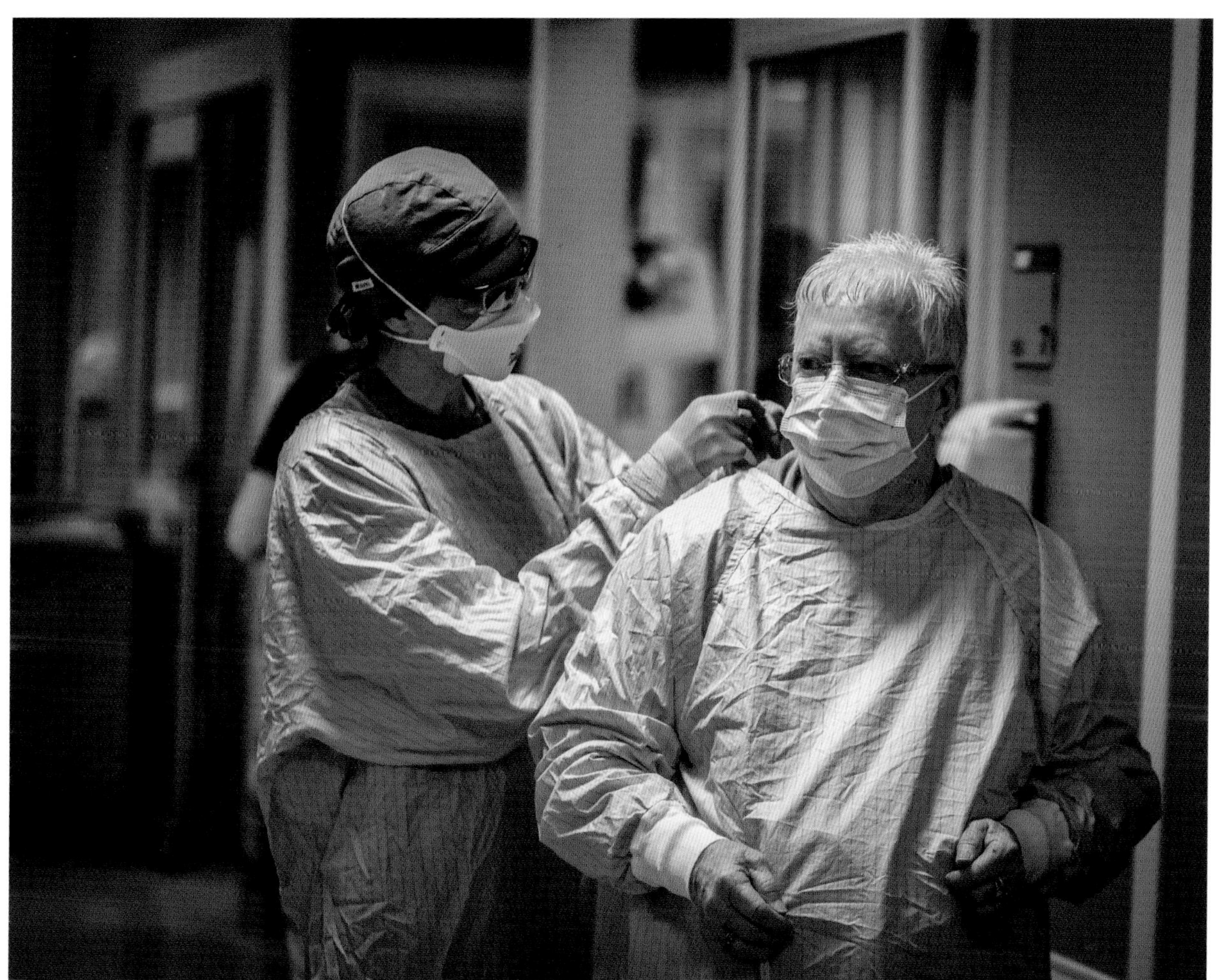

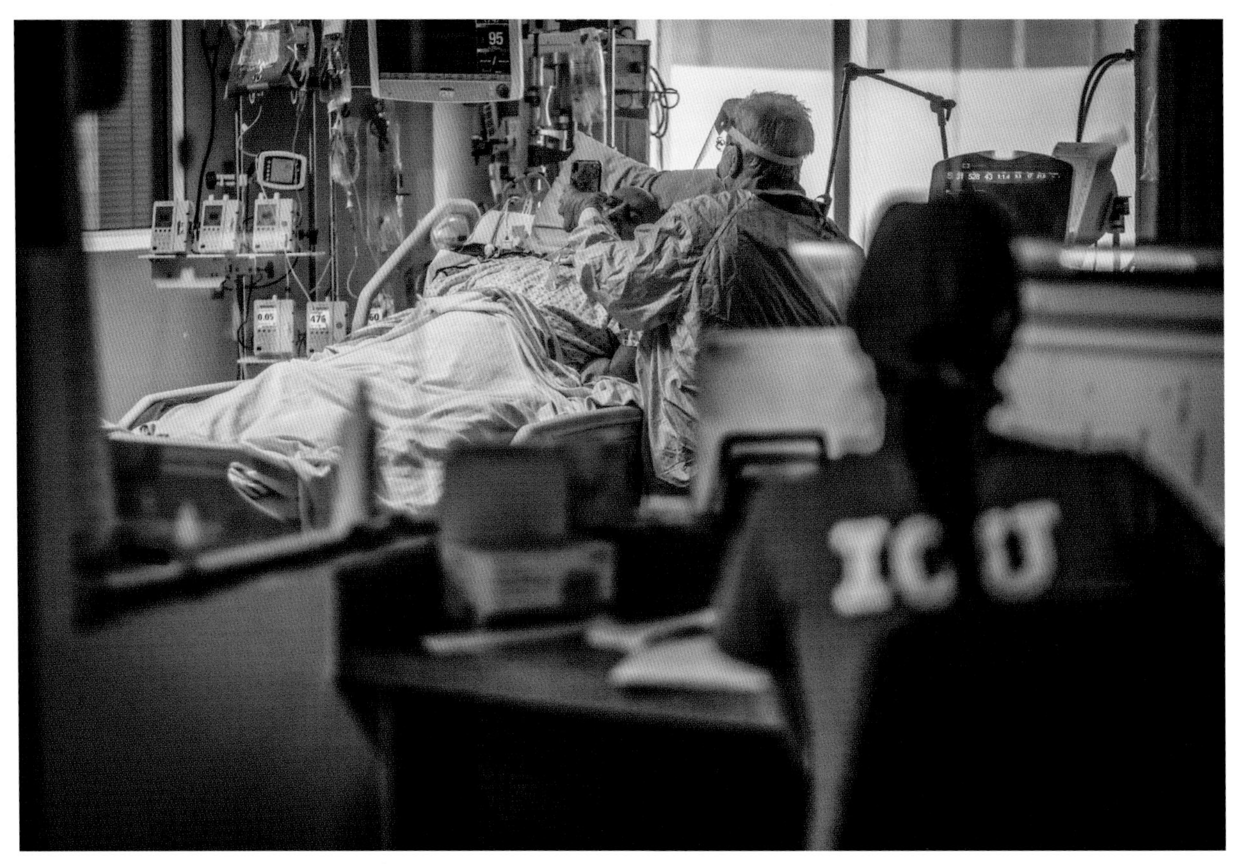

Dixie Dover visits her husband of almost
52 years in the intensive care unit at Peter
Lougheed Centre on February 5, 2021.

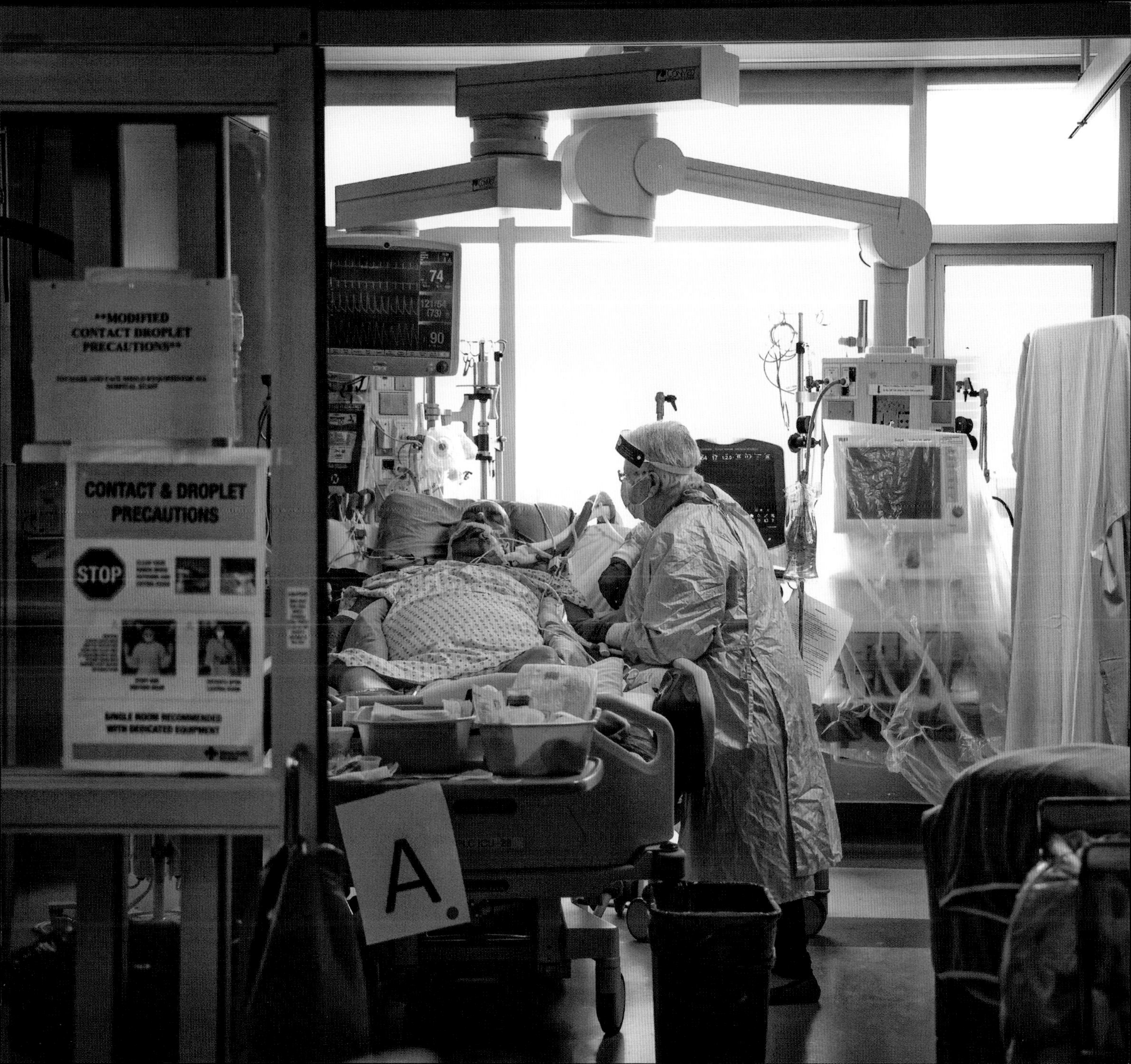
**MODIFIED
CONTACT DROPLET
PRECAUTIONS**

CONTACT & DROPLET
PRECAUTIONS

STOP

SINGLE ROOM RECOMMENDED
WITH DEDICATED EQUIPMENT

74
121/54
(73)
90

A

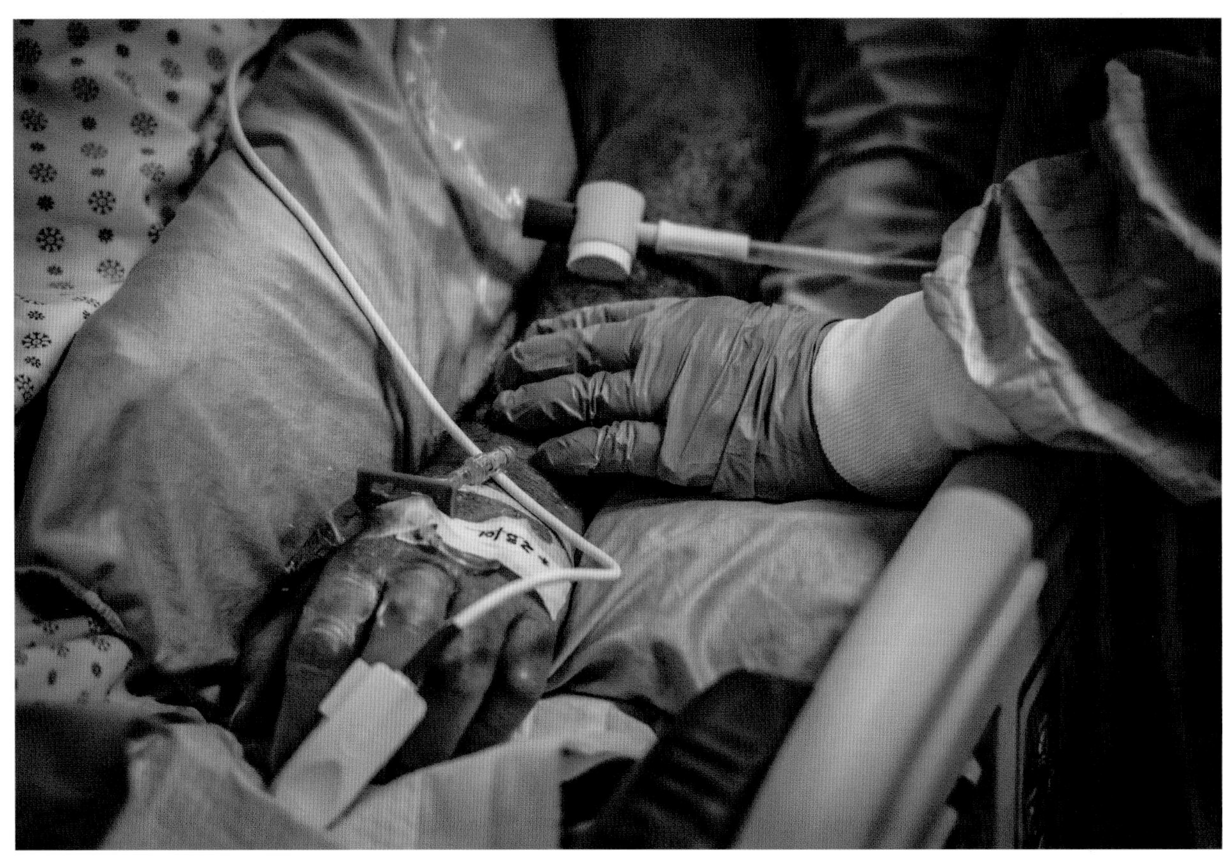

Dixie Dover holds the hand of her husband
Chuck Dover, a COVID-19 patient.

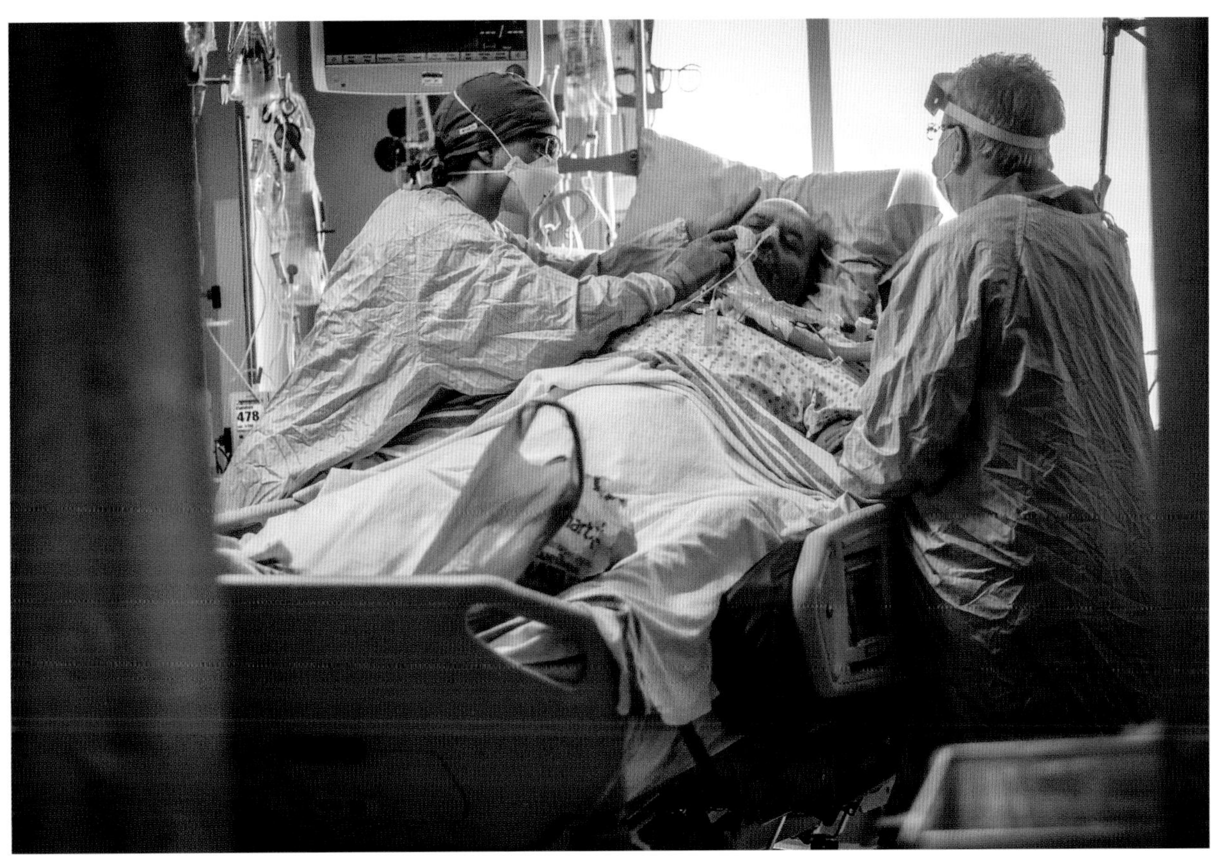

Dixie Dover, right, watches her husband
Chuck as intensive care unit nurse
Victoria cares for him.

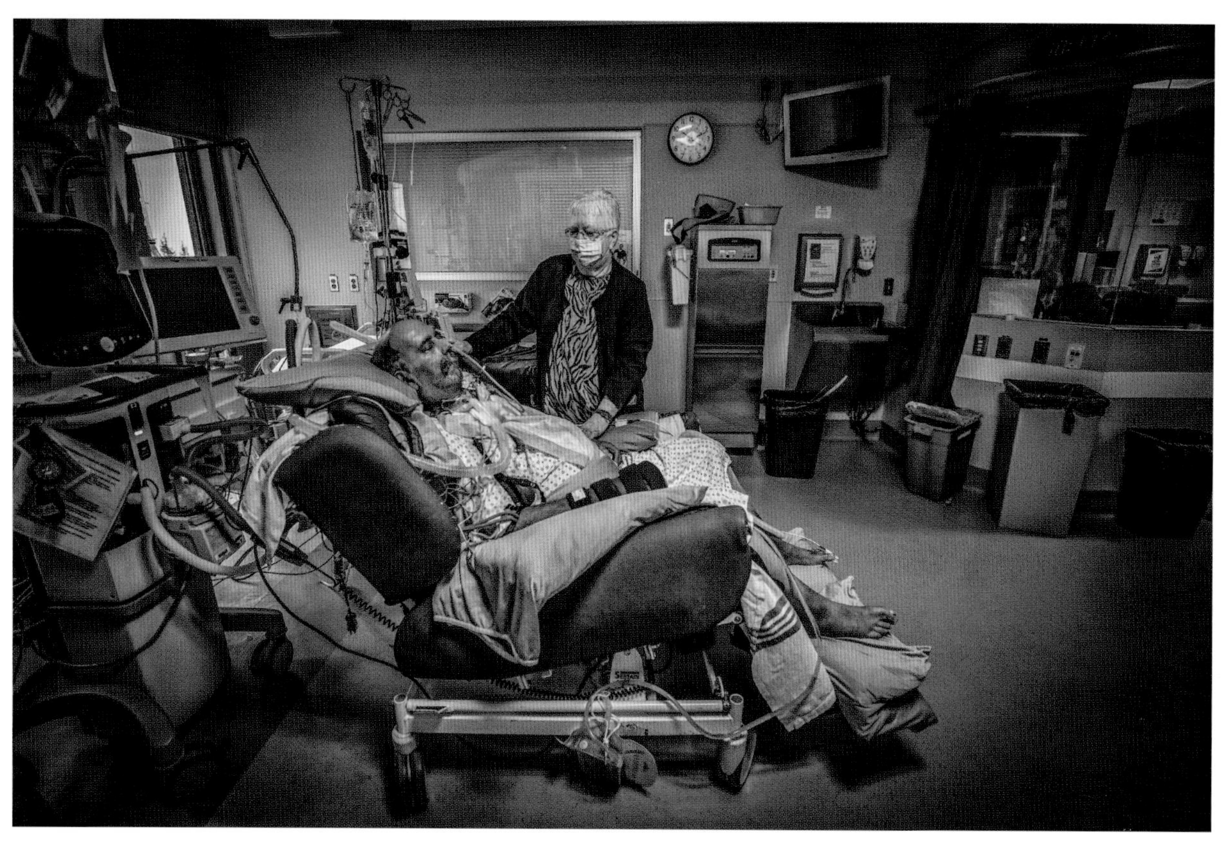

At the intensive care unit at Peter Lougheed
Centre, Dixie Dover visits her husband
Chuck, who is no longer infectious for
COVID-19, on February 26, 2021.

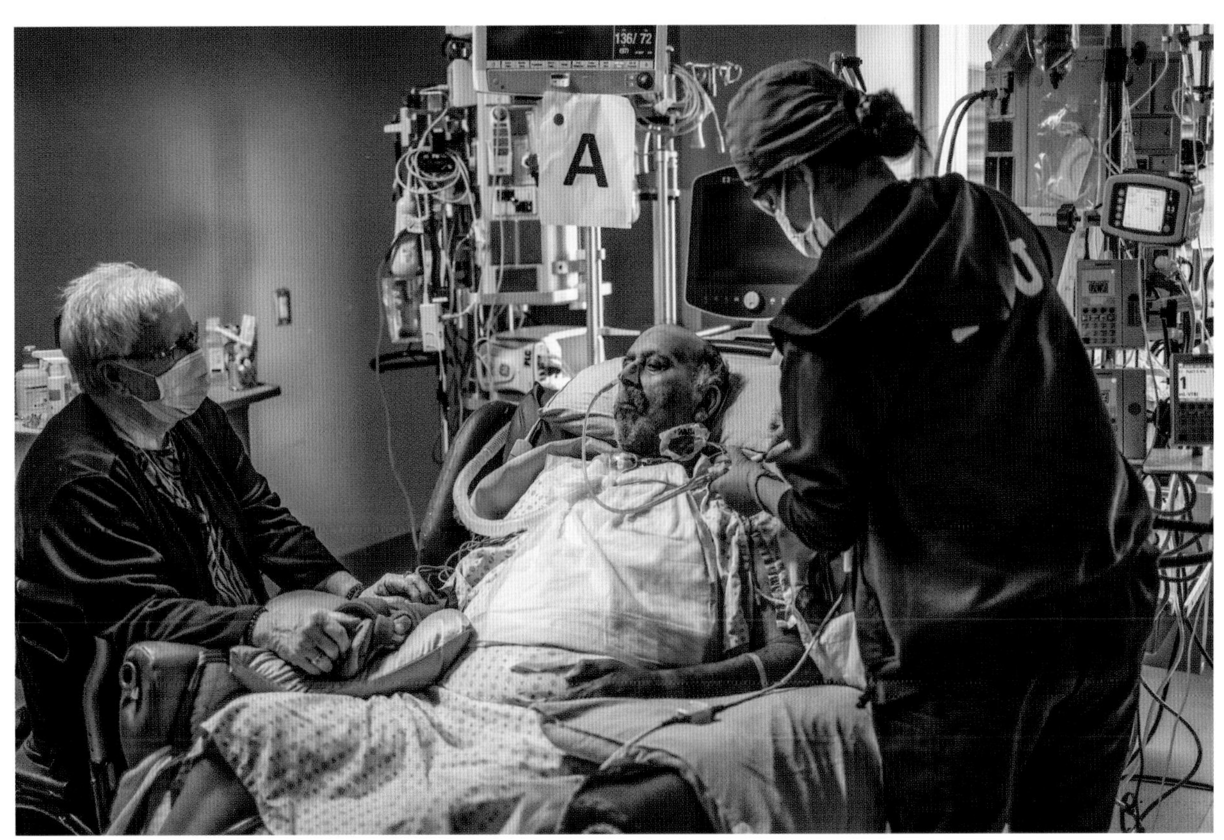
136/ 72
A

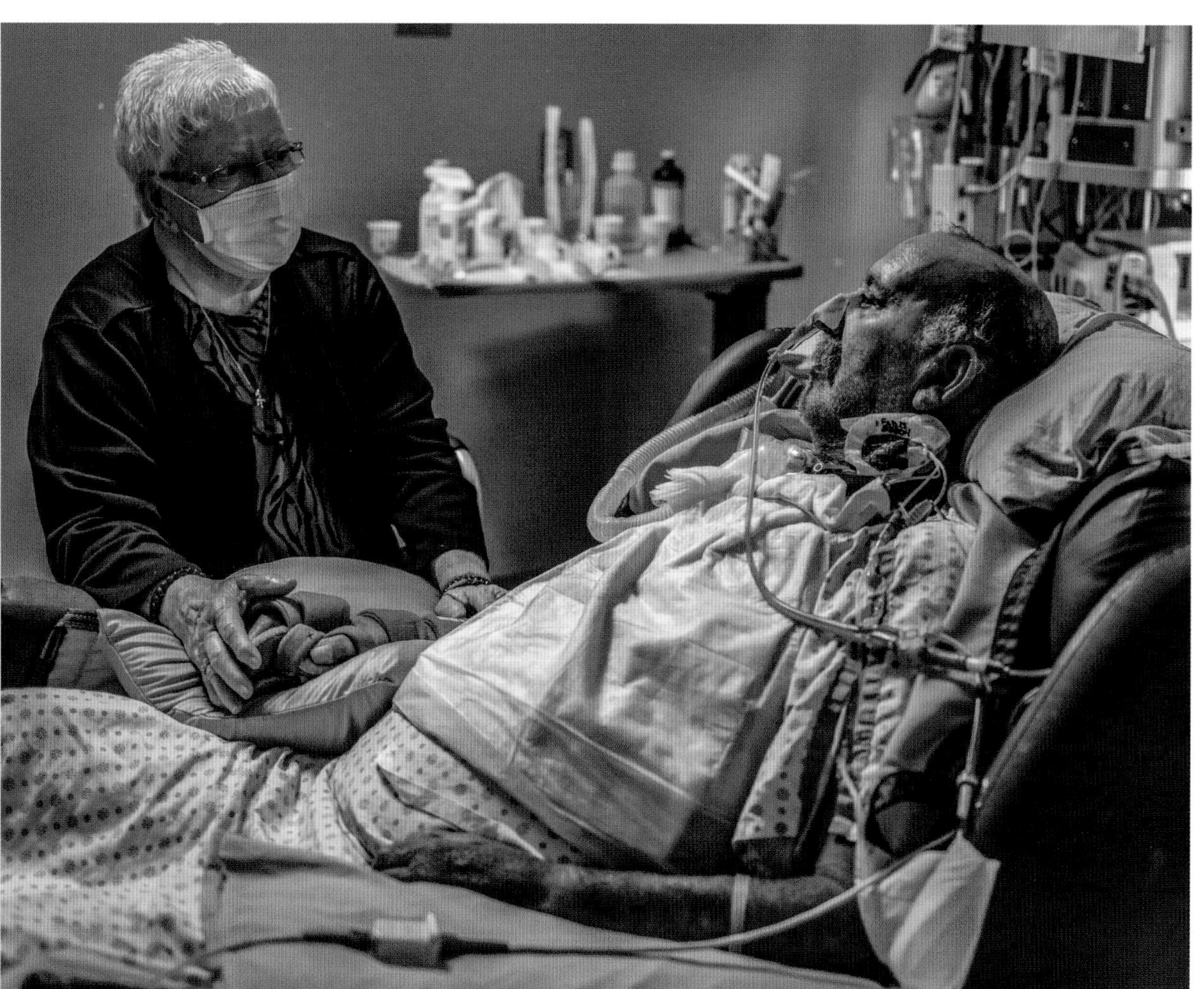

"There were four or five infections. Finally the doctor said the last one was a very aggressive one that was attacking his lungs. He said there's no coming back from this one. He would be hooked up to machines and ventilators for the rest of his life in care. Chuck and I have talked about this often, that if it was to ever come to that, I don't want to be alive just for the sake of being alive and neither did he. So I made the decision that we would take him off life support," says Dixie Dover. "Everybody got to go in and say their goodbyes."

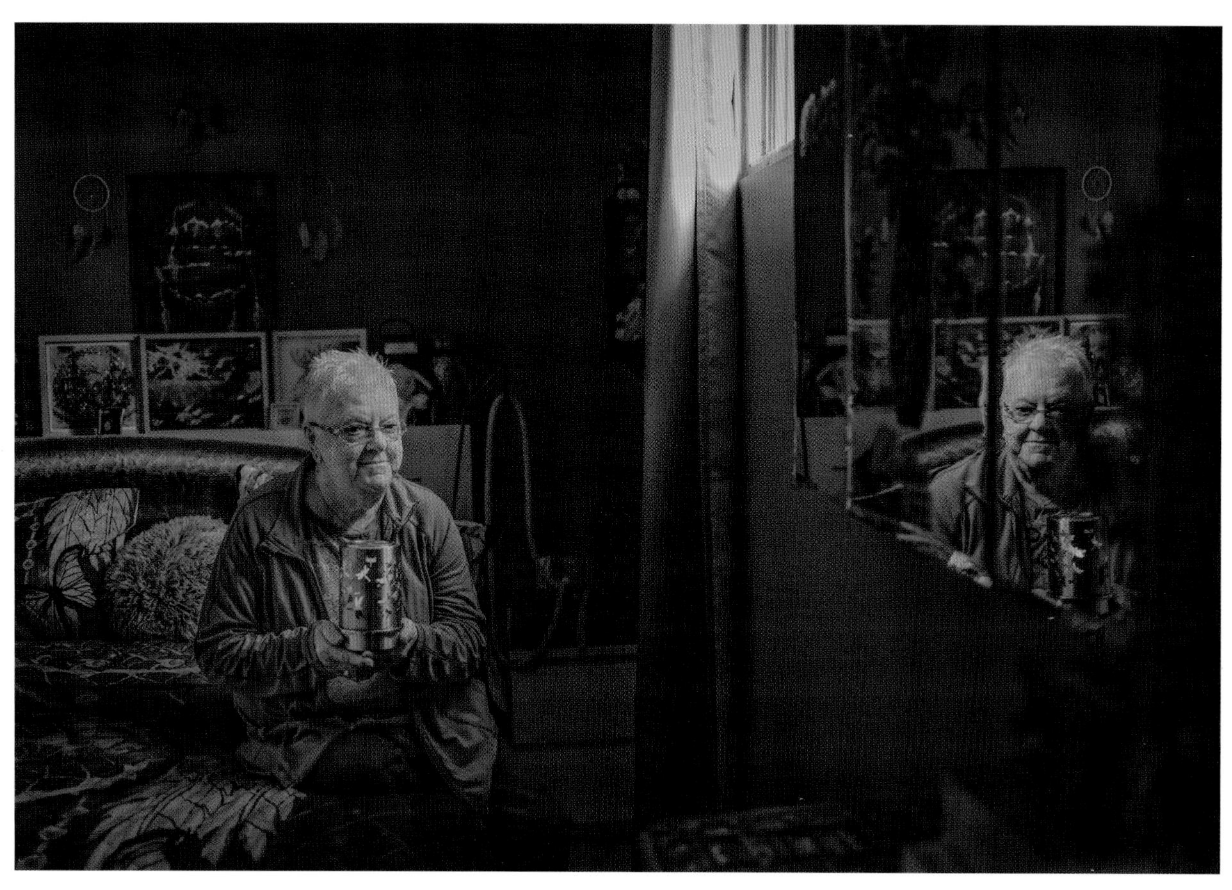

Dixie Dover holds an urn with her husband
Chuck's remains in their home in Calgary,
Alberta. Chuck died March 4, 2021. "Evenings
are the worst. I reach over and he's not there.
It's hard. It's very hard," says Dixie Dover.

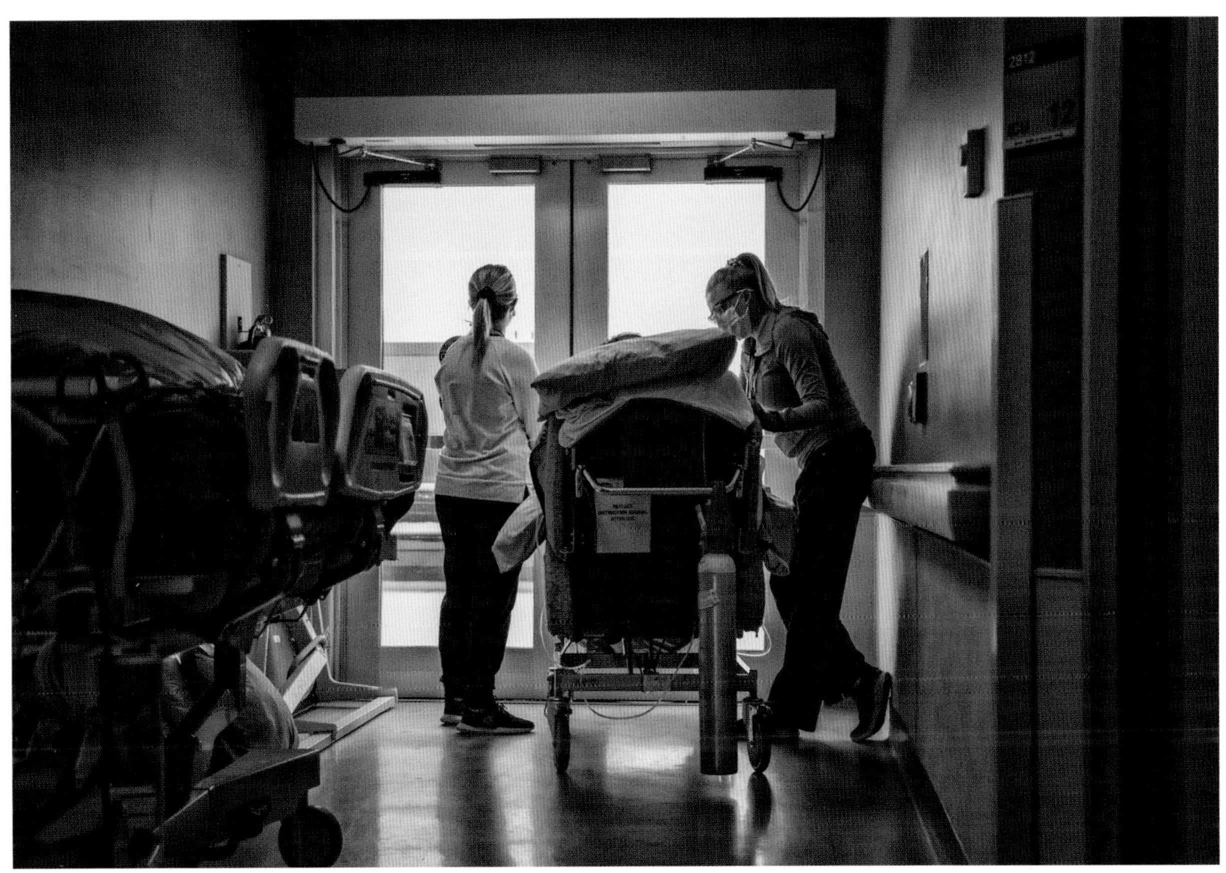

Therapy assistant Dianne Losey, left, and physiotherapist Paige Dorn take a COVID- 19 patient, who is off isolation, out of his intensive care unit room at Peter Lougheed Centre for a look out of a different window in January 2021.

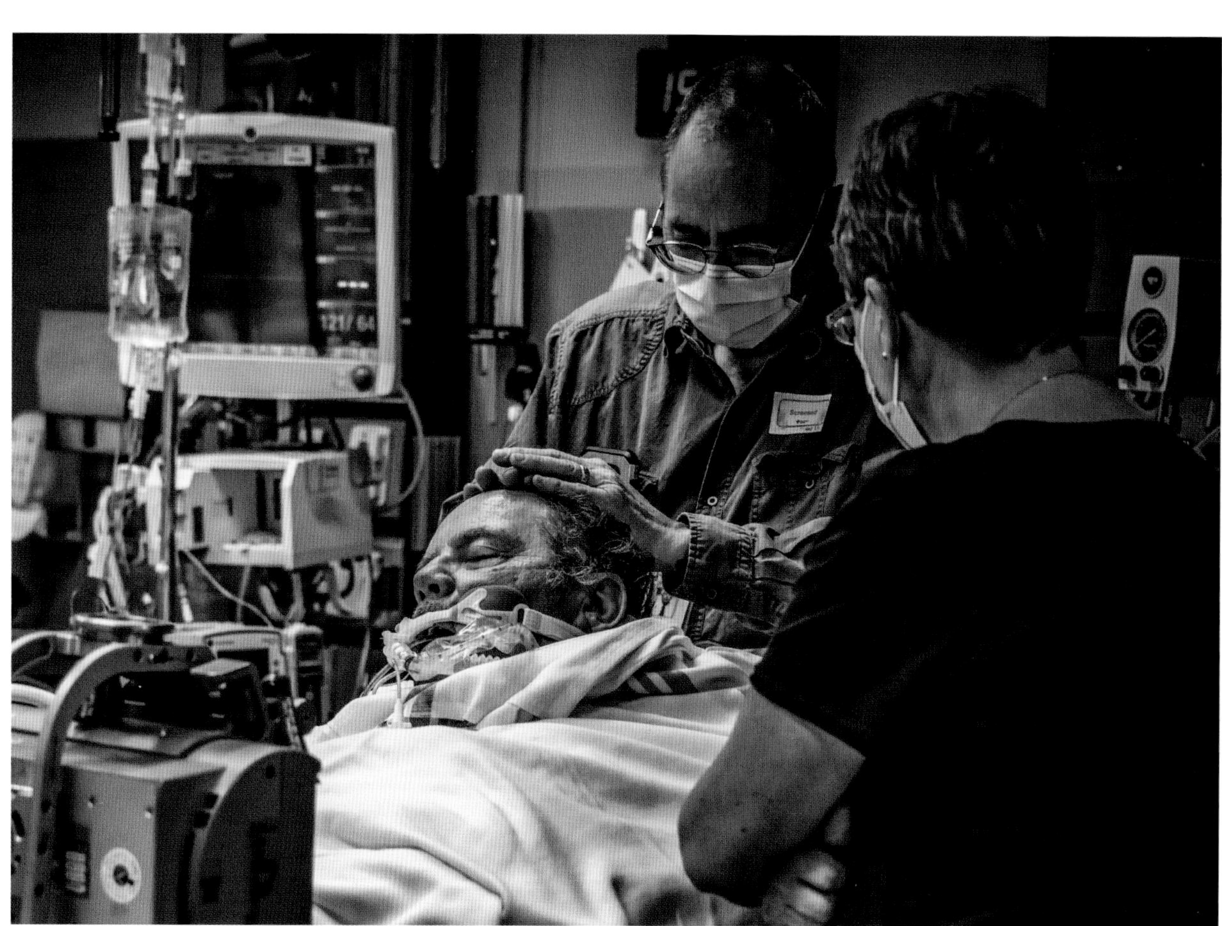

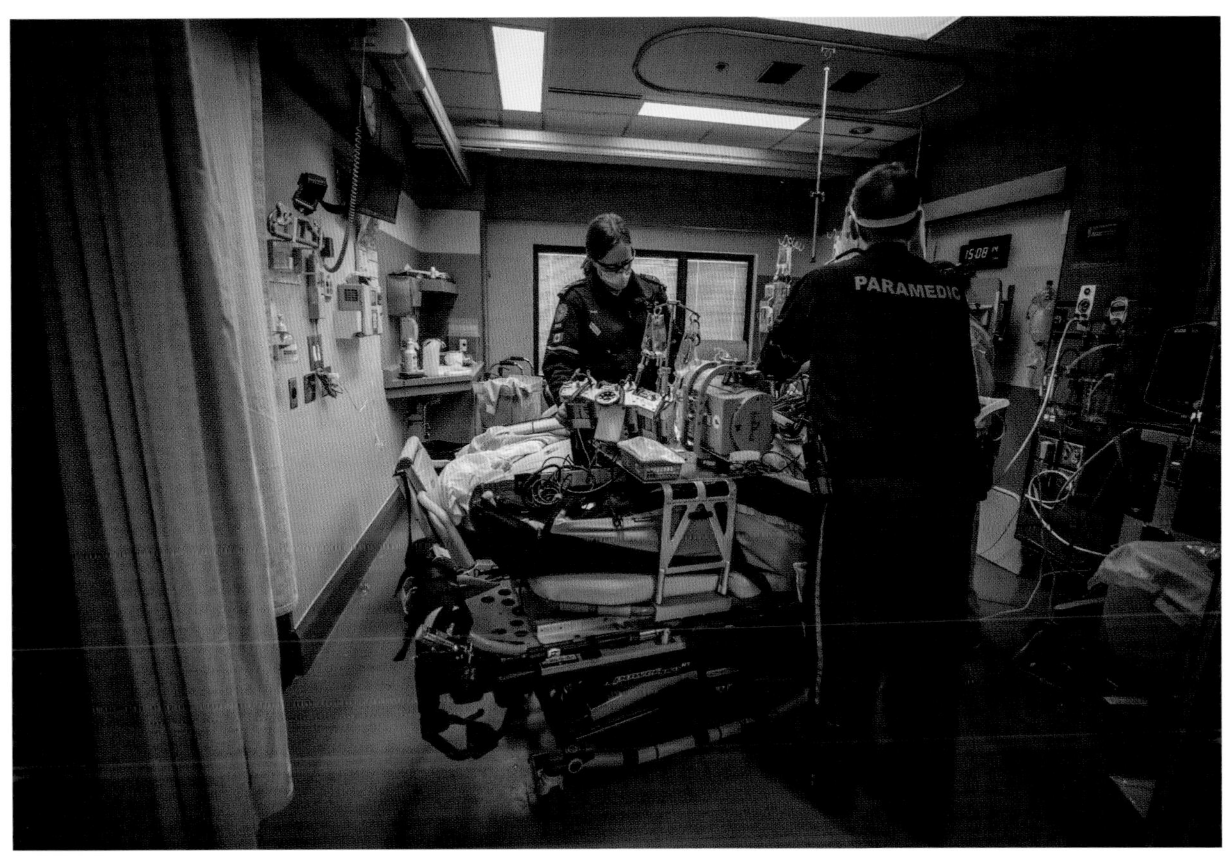

Marguerite Hagen is at her husband Roger's bed-side in Medicine Hat, Alberta, as their bishop, Dale Anderson, does a blessing before flight paramedics take Roger to a Calgary hospital on March 17, 2021.

Flight paramedics transport non-COVID-19 patient Roger Hagen from Medicine Hat to Calgary on March 17, 2021.

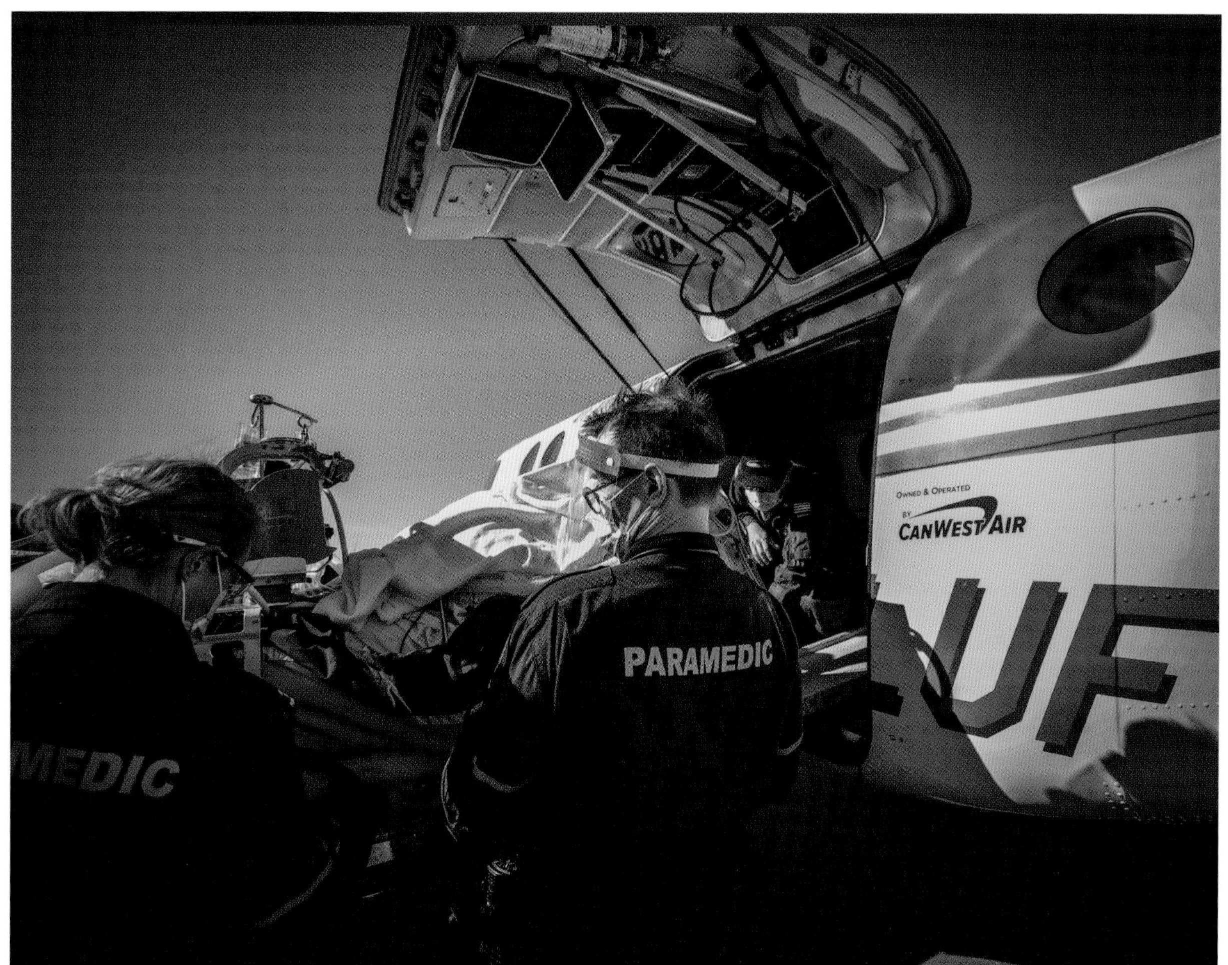
PARAMEDIC
MEDIC
OWNED & OPERATED
BY
CanWest Air
UF

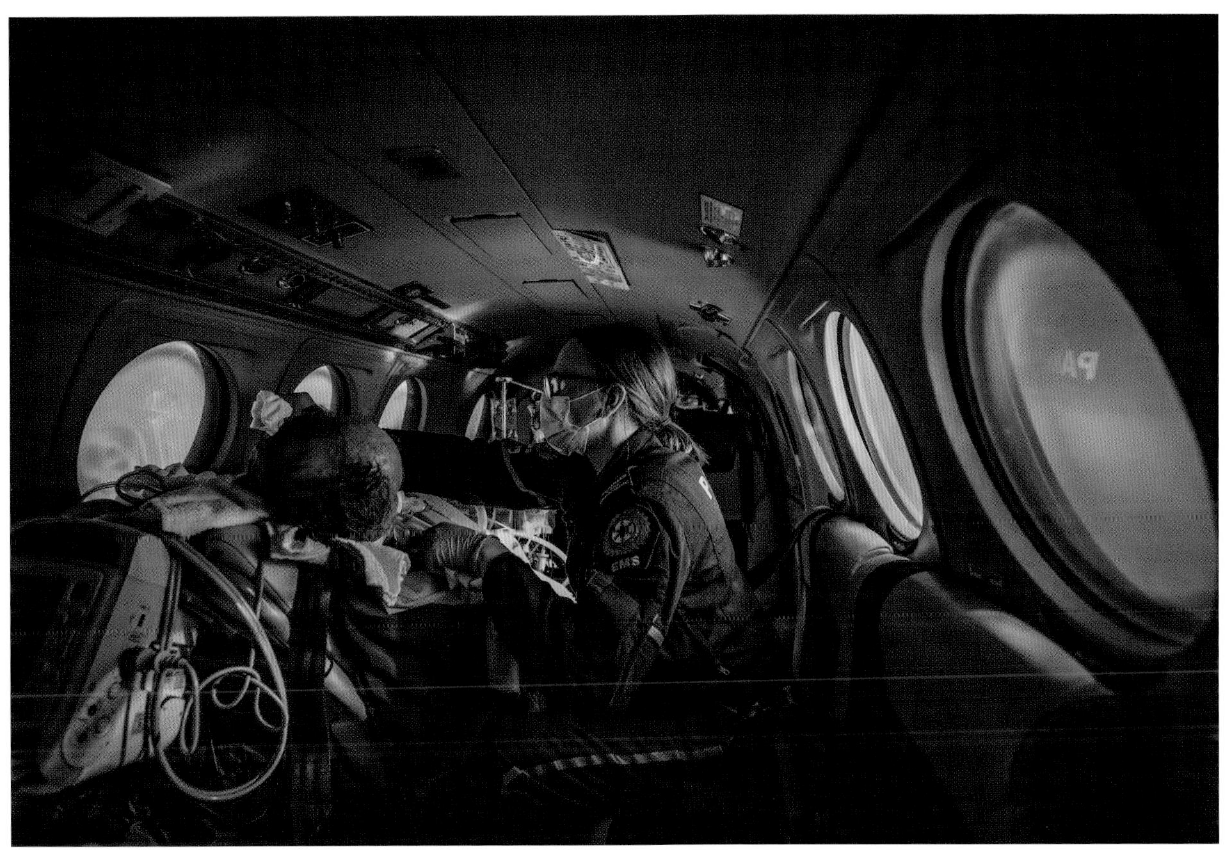

Flight paramedics transport non-COVID-19 patient Roger Hagen from Medicine Hat to Calgary on March 17, 2021.

Flight paramedic Denise Vanderkooi accompanies a patient to Calgary from Medicine Hat. Each plane in the air ambulance program is equipped with a cardiac monitor, IV pumps and trauma gear, to provide 24-hour air ambulance services throughout the province.

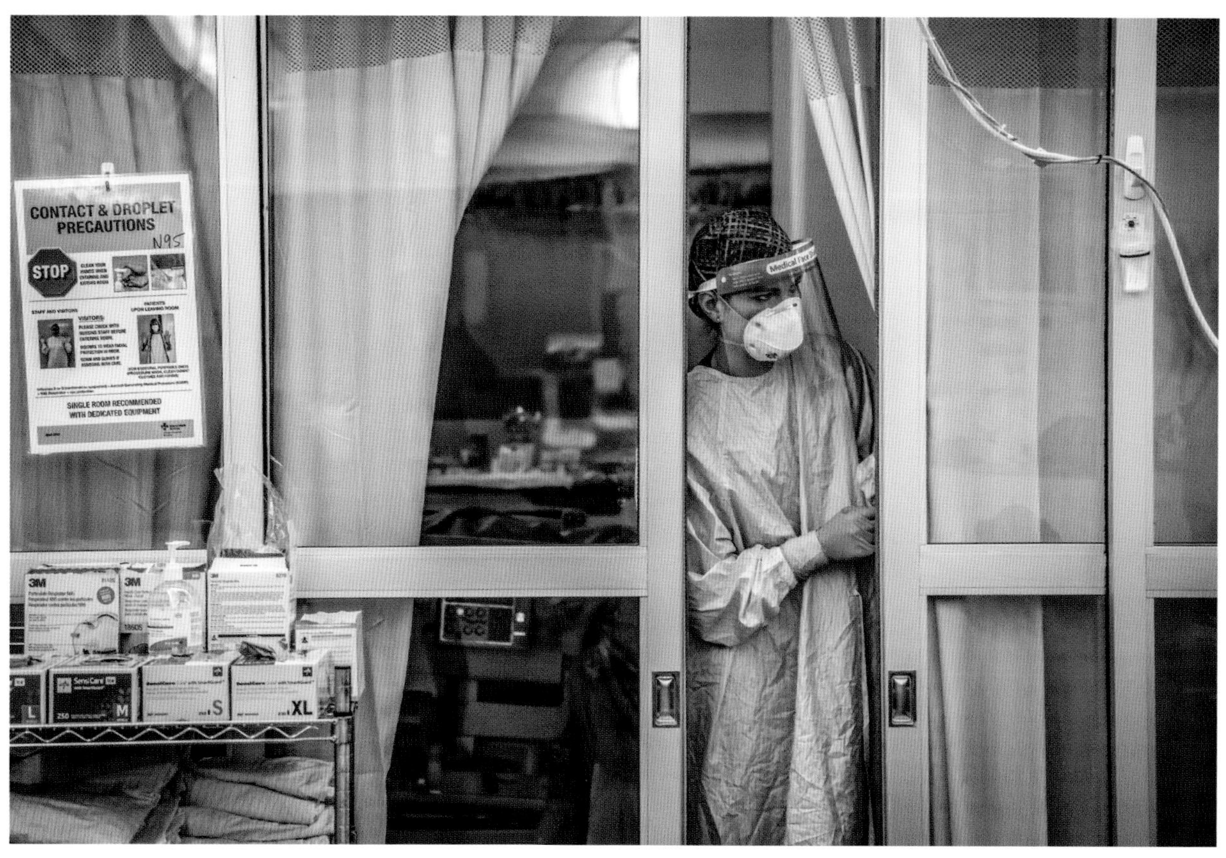

Jillian Harlock, registered nurse in the intensive care unit, at Rockyview General Hospital in Calgary, Alberta, in January 2021.

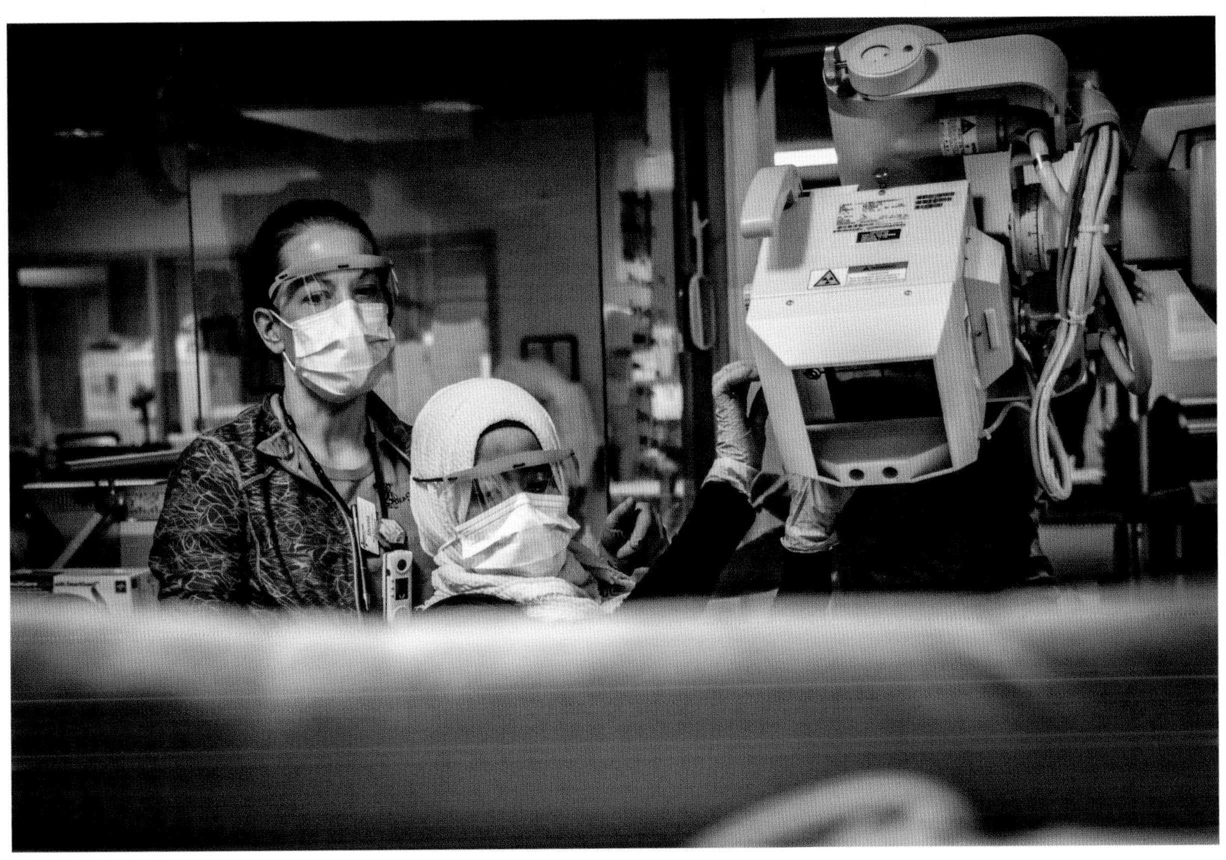

Shonna Sale, left, helps SAIT student Marufa
Chowdhury take a chest X-ray of a non-
COVID-19 patient in the intensive care unit at
Peter Lougheed Centre on January 28, 2021.

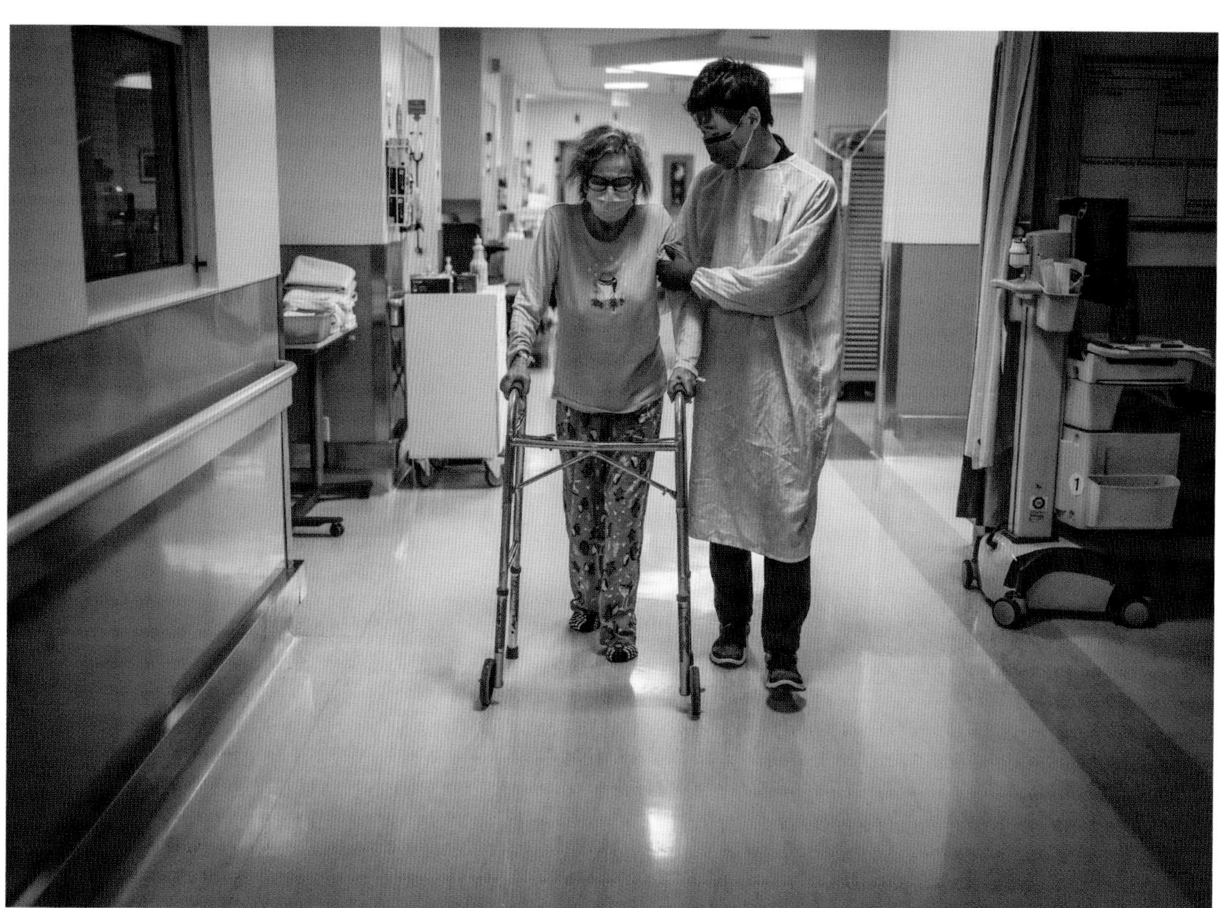

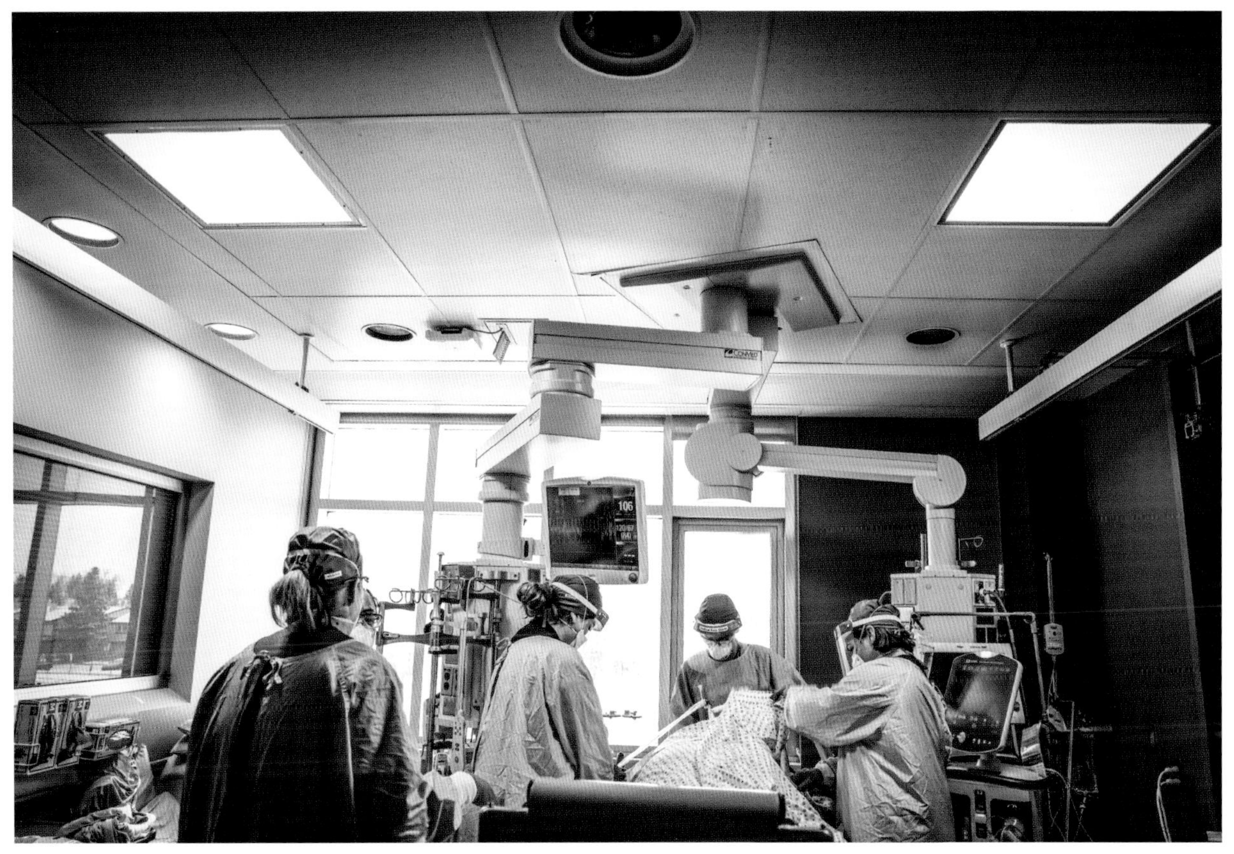

Nadia Enjeneski, recovering from COVID-19
and off isolation at Rockyview General
Hospital, goes for a walk with the assistance
of physiotherapist Kevin Shin.

A healthcare team prones a COVID-19 patient
in January 2021.

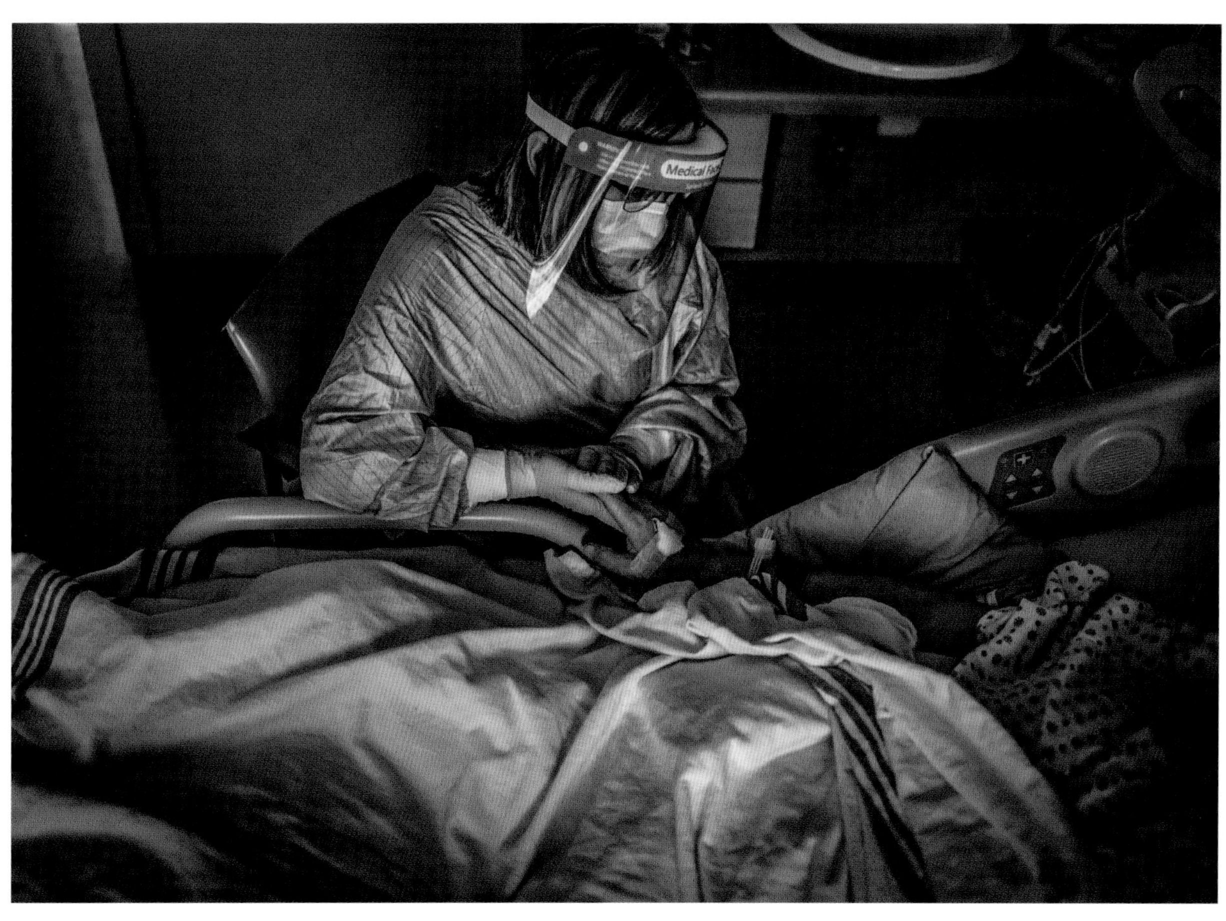

Jackie Long, a volunteer for No One Dies
Alone (NODA), sits with a patient at
Foothills Medical Centre in Calgary, Alberta.

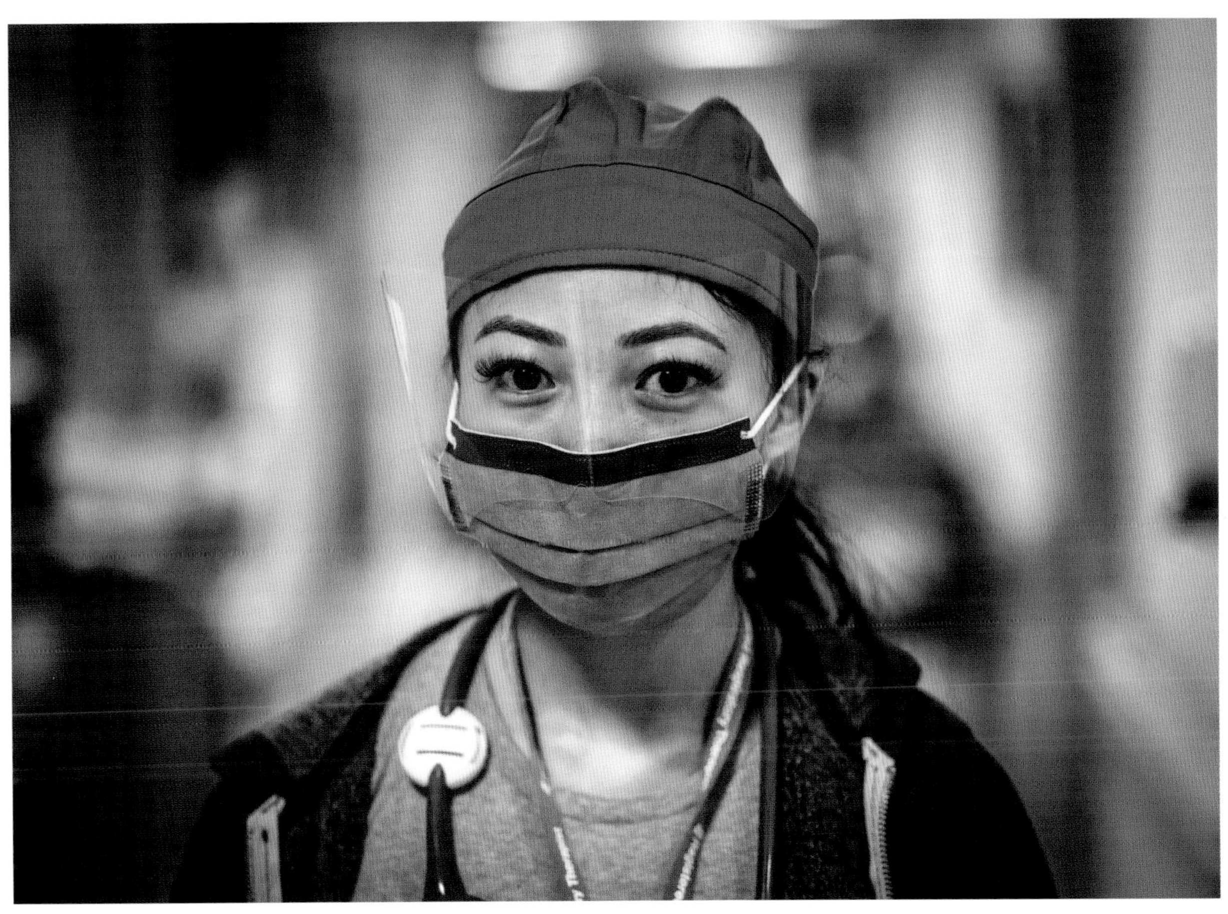

Connie Lo, a registered nurse in an intensive
care unit, in February 2021.

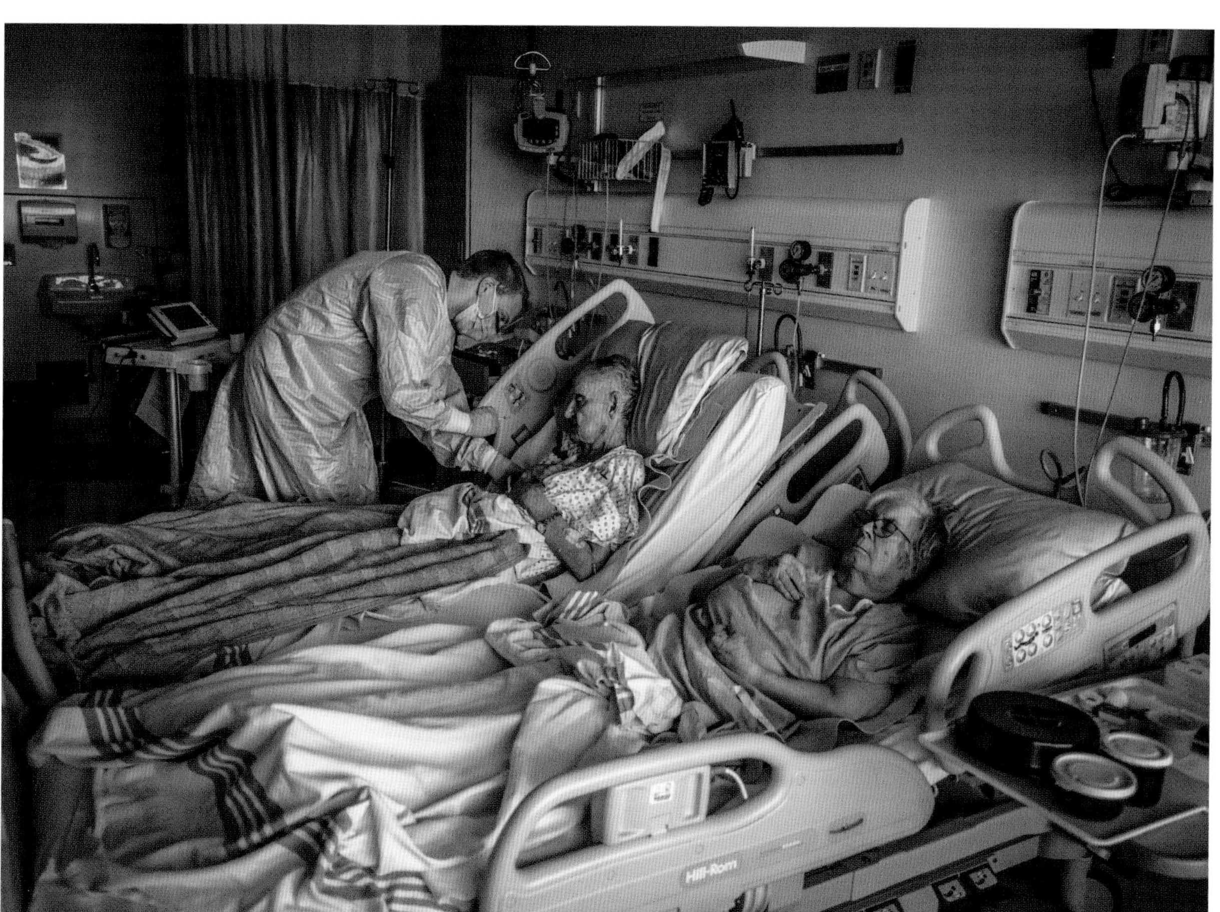

In the 1950s, Margaret Squire — then Margaret Murray — came to Canada from Scotland to work as a nurse and midwife for a year in Saskatoon. While she was there, she met George Squire, a Canadian geophysicist. The two fell in love and, on August 24, 1957, were married.

In January 2021, George, 94, and Margaret, 90, were both diagnosed with COVID-19. George was the first to end up in hospital, followed by Margaret a few days later.

The Rockyview General Hospital team on Unit 93 was able to keep the couple together, pushing their beds close to each other and setting up virtual visits with family.

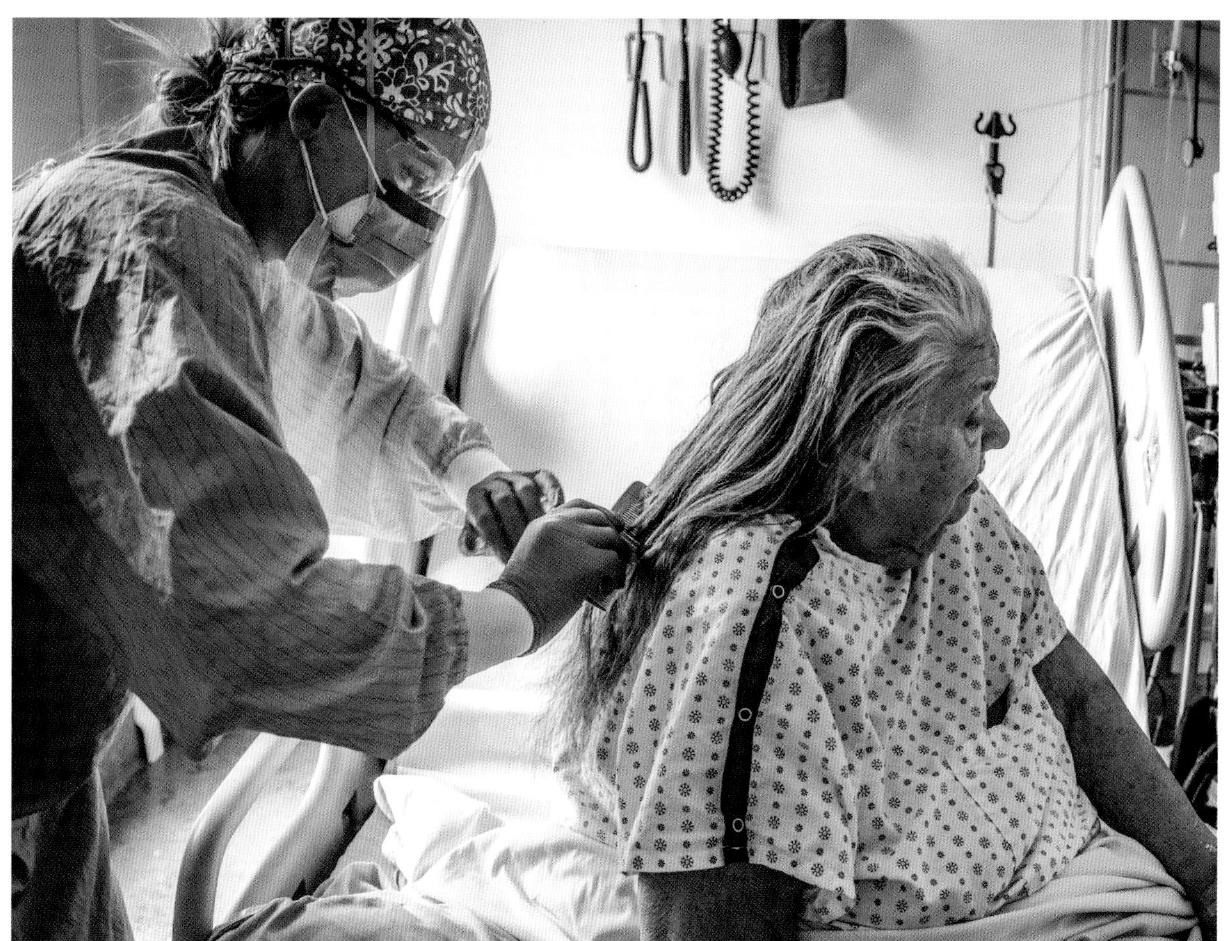

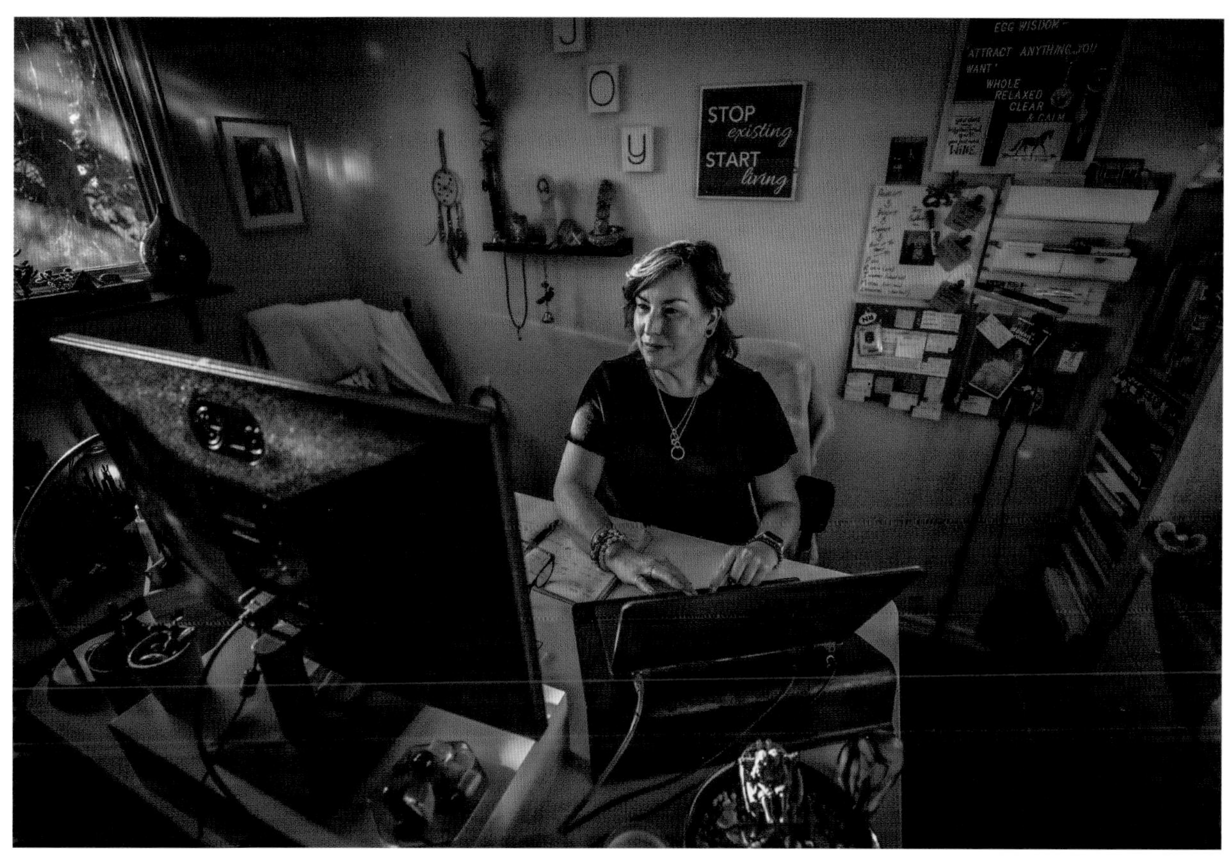

Frances Van Herk, 90, is cared for by registered nurse Kristina at Chinook Regional Hospital in Lethbridge.

Alberta Health Services contact tracer Samantha Tattersall in her home office in Calgary in February 2021.

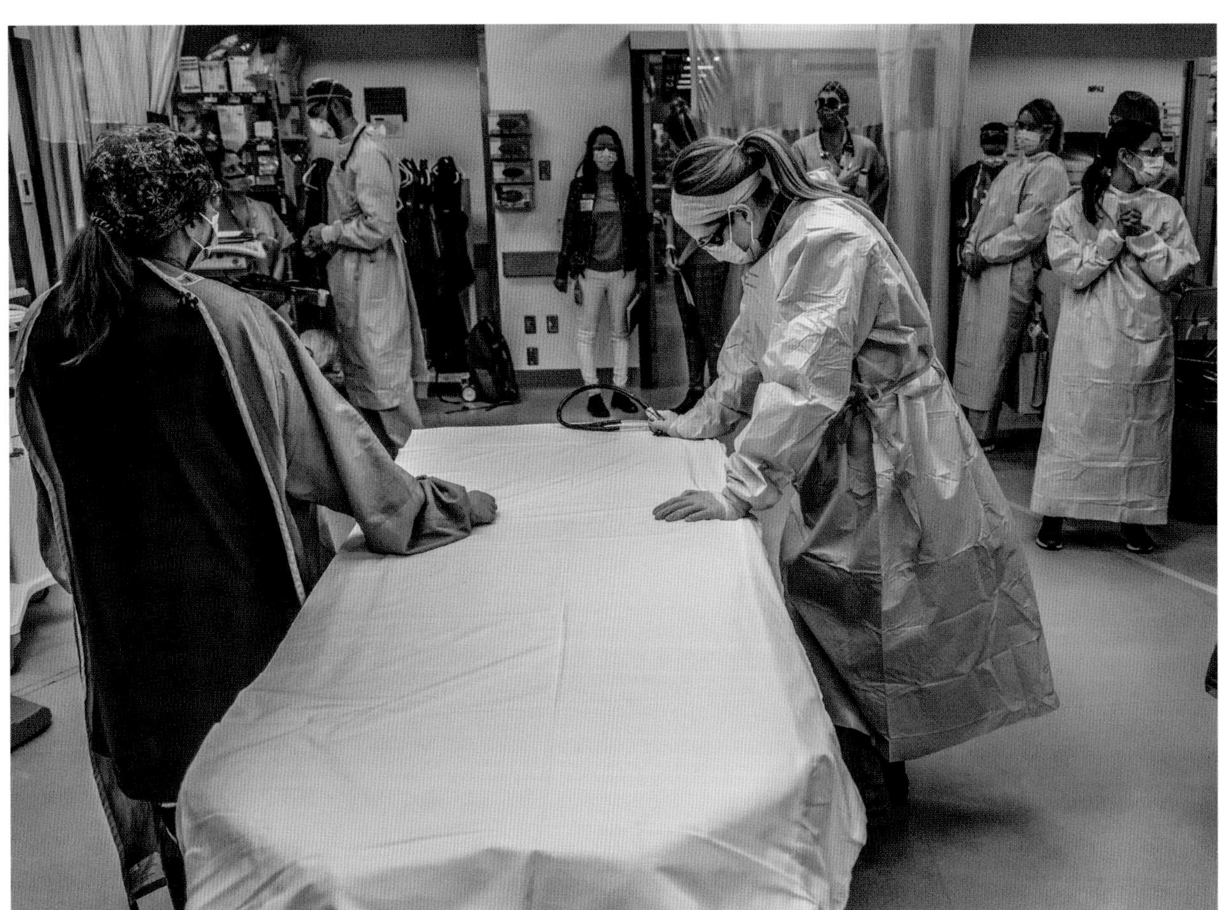

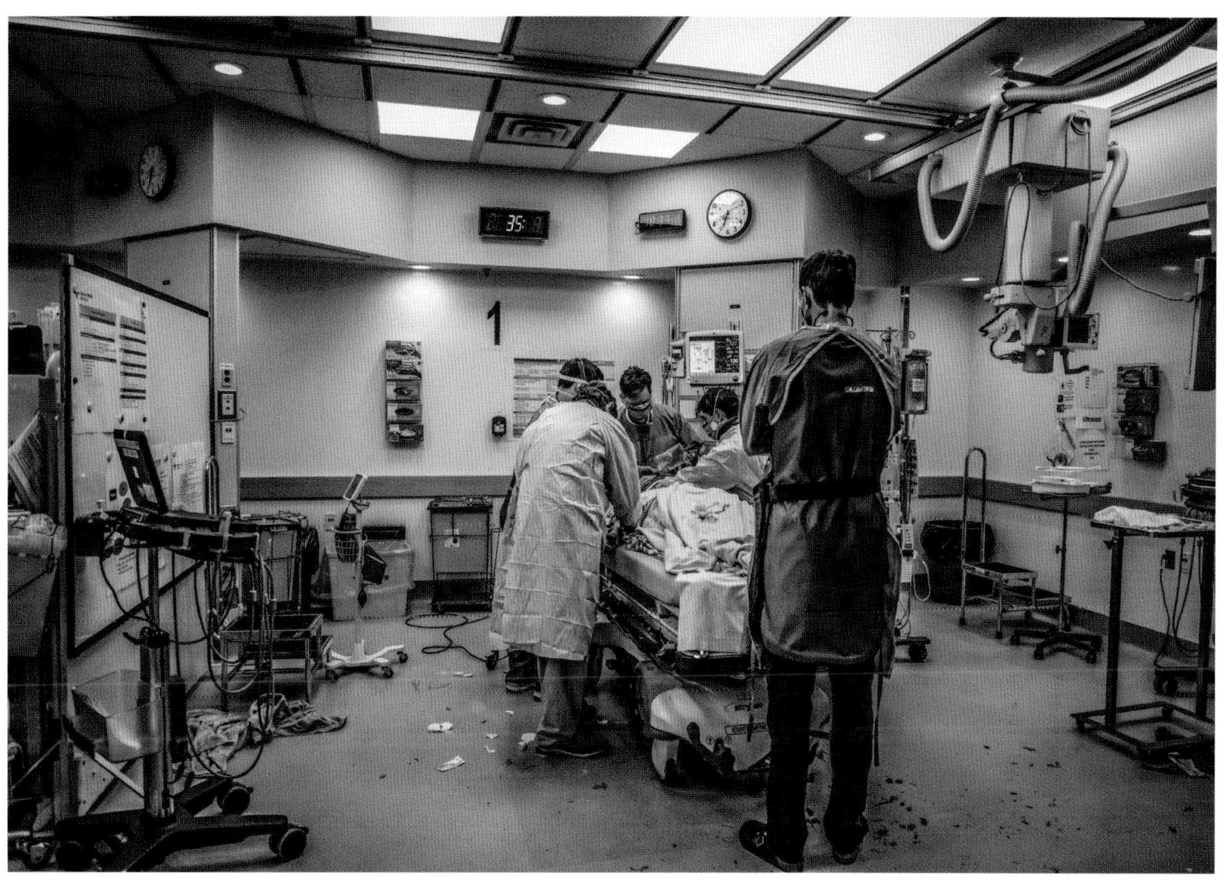

There is calm before a patient arrives in the trauma bay in emergency at Foothills Medical Centre.

A healthcare team works to save a patient in the trauma bay in emergency at Foothills Medical Centre in Calgary, Alberta.

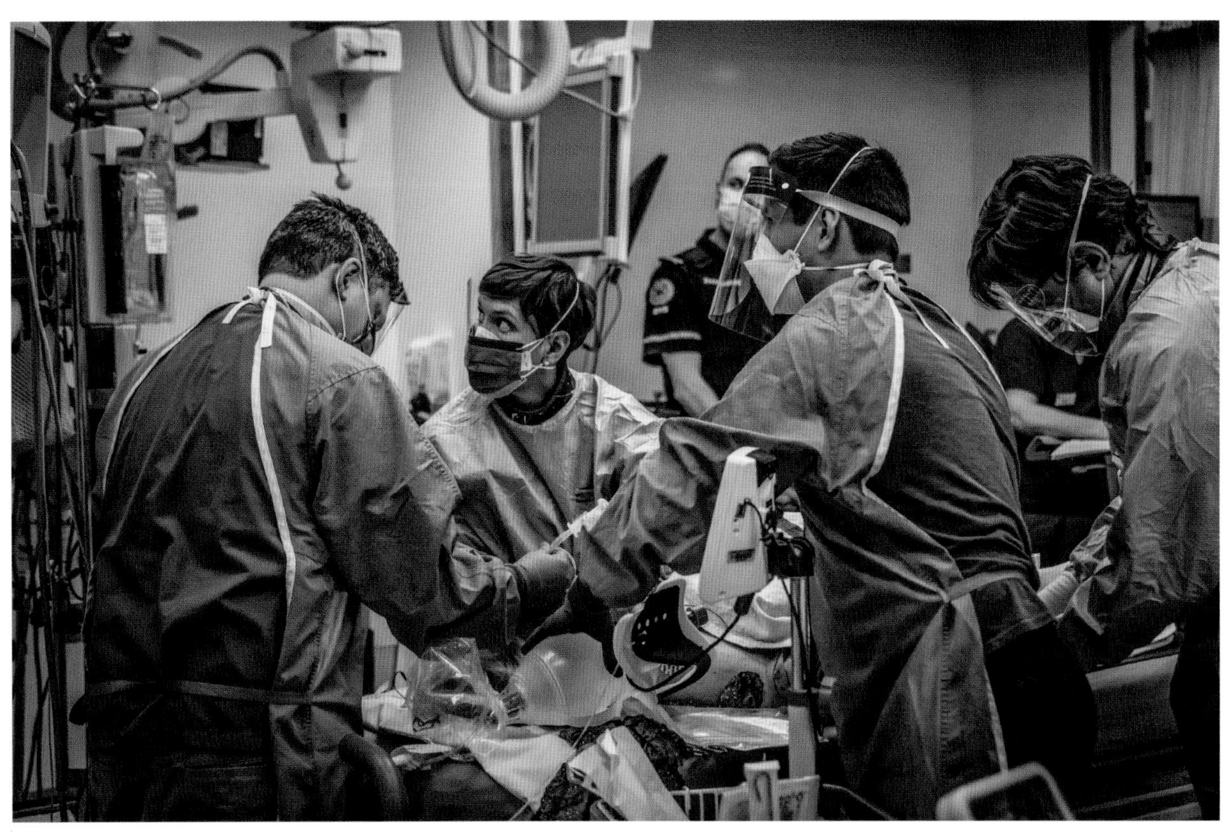

A healthcare team works to save a patient
in the trauma bay in emergency at Foothills
Medical Centre in Calgary, Alberta.

Registered nurse Nicole Ahmed visits her dad
Ron Barrett, a COVID-19 patient off isolation,
in the intensive care unit at Peter Lougheed
Centre in Calgary, Alberta, in June 2021.

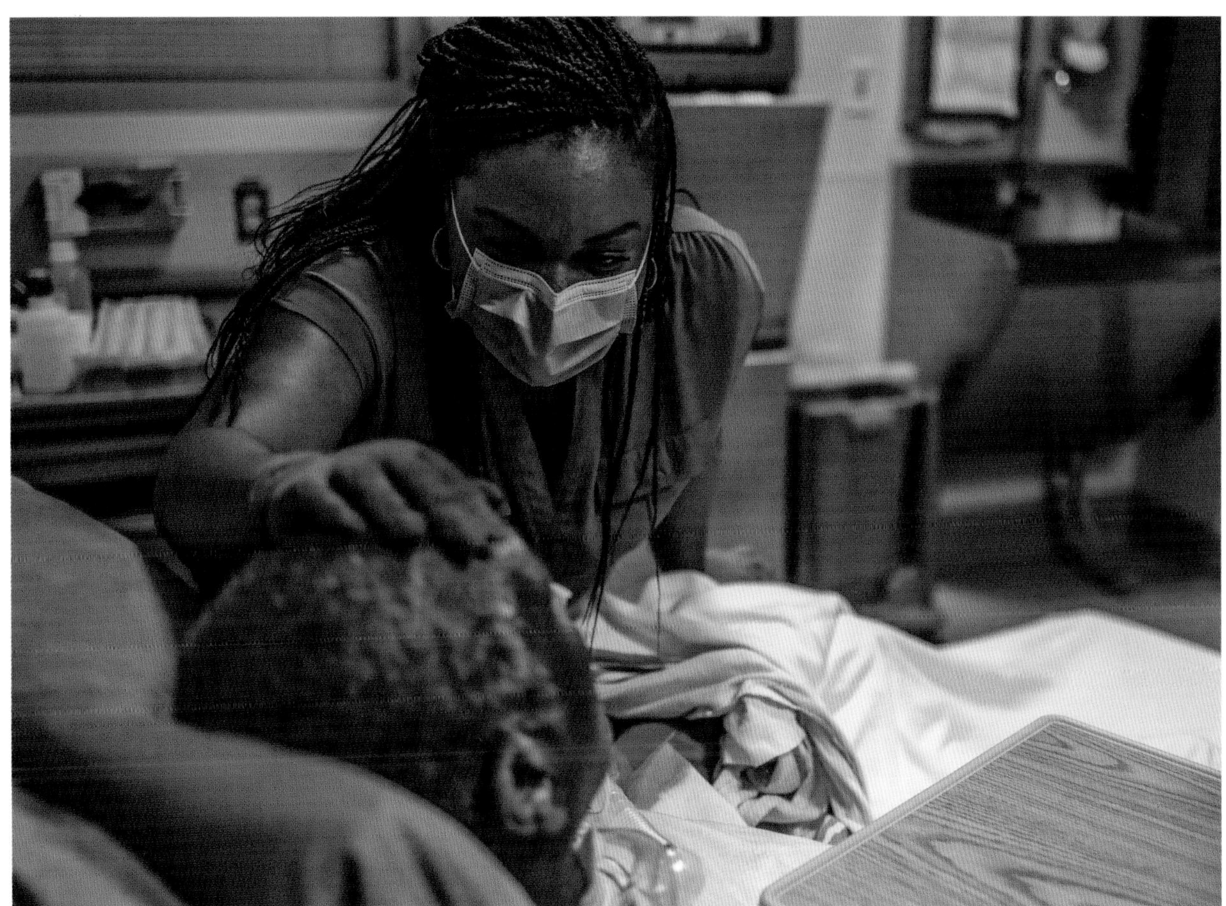

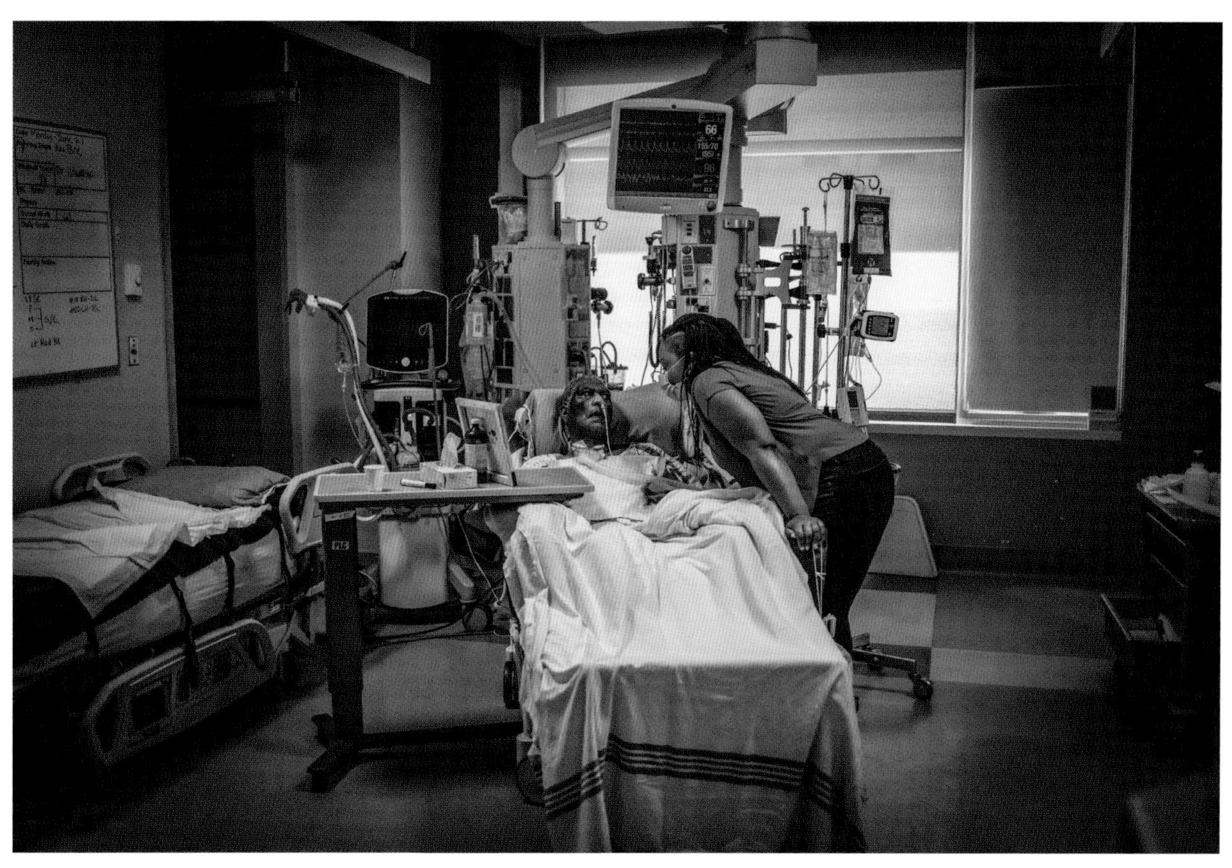

Registered nurse Nicole Ahmed visits her dad
Ron Barrett, a COVID-19 patient off isolation,
in the intensive care unit at Peter Lougheed
Centre in Calgary, Alberta, in June 2021.

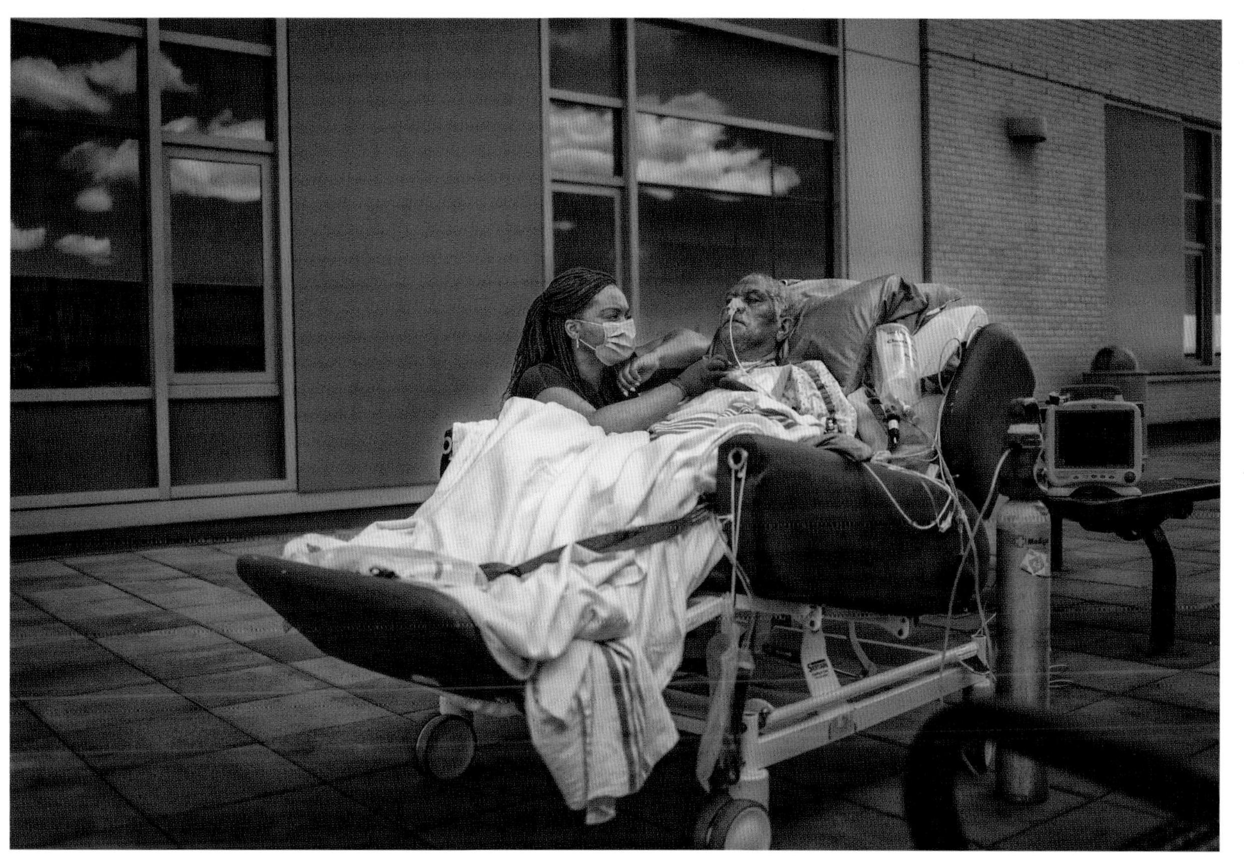

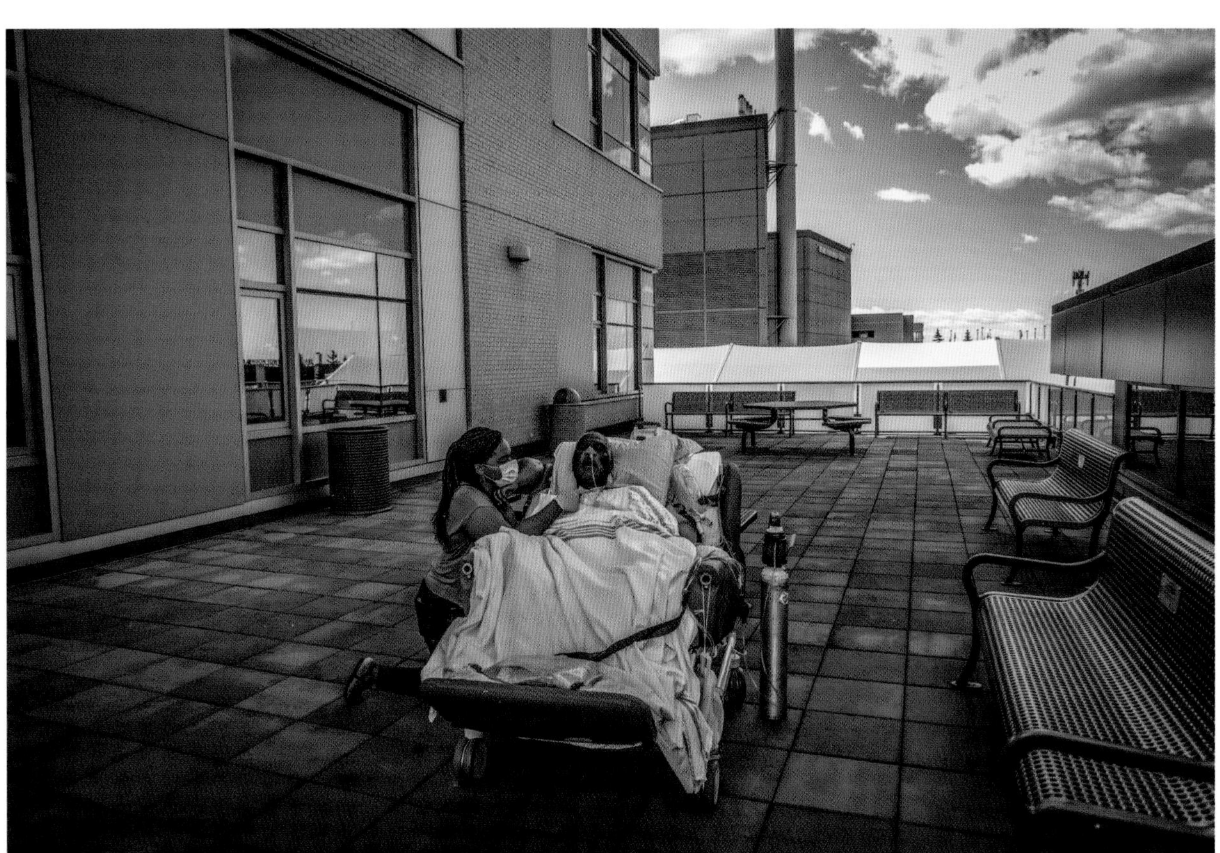

"COVID-19 is real. It came to my front door. As a healthcare worker, a daughter, a wife and mother, I see how real this is," says registered nurse Nicole Ahmed.

In May 2021, Ahmed's father Ron Barrett was admitted with COVID-19 to the intensive care unit at Peter Lougheed Centre. "Within 10 minutes of being admitted, he was intubated and on oxygen," Ahmed says.

"I was in shock. I was numb. It felt like it was a bad dream."

Her dad spent five weeks in a medically induced coma and nearly died twice. His partner also became sick with COVID-19 and had to be hospitalized.

When Barrett, 72, finally turned a corner and started to get better, his first words were "Amazing. The staff is amazing."

"We all had tears in our eyes," Ahmed recalls.

"He has a lot of gratitude for the staff: the doctors, nurses, respiratory therapists, housekeepers, you name it. My whole family does."

Barrett was released from hospital in late August. He continues to recover from COVID-19 at home.

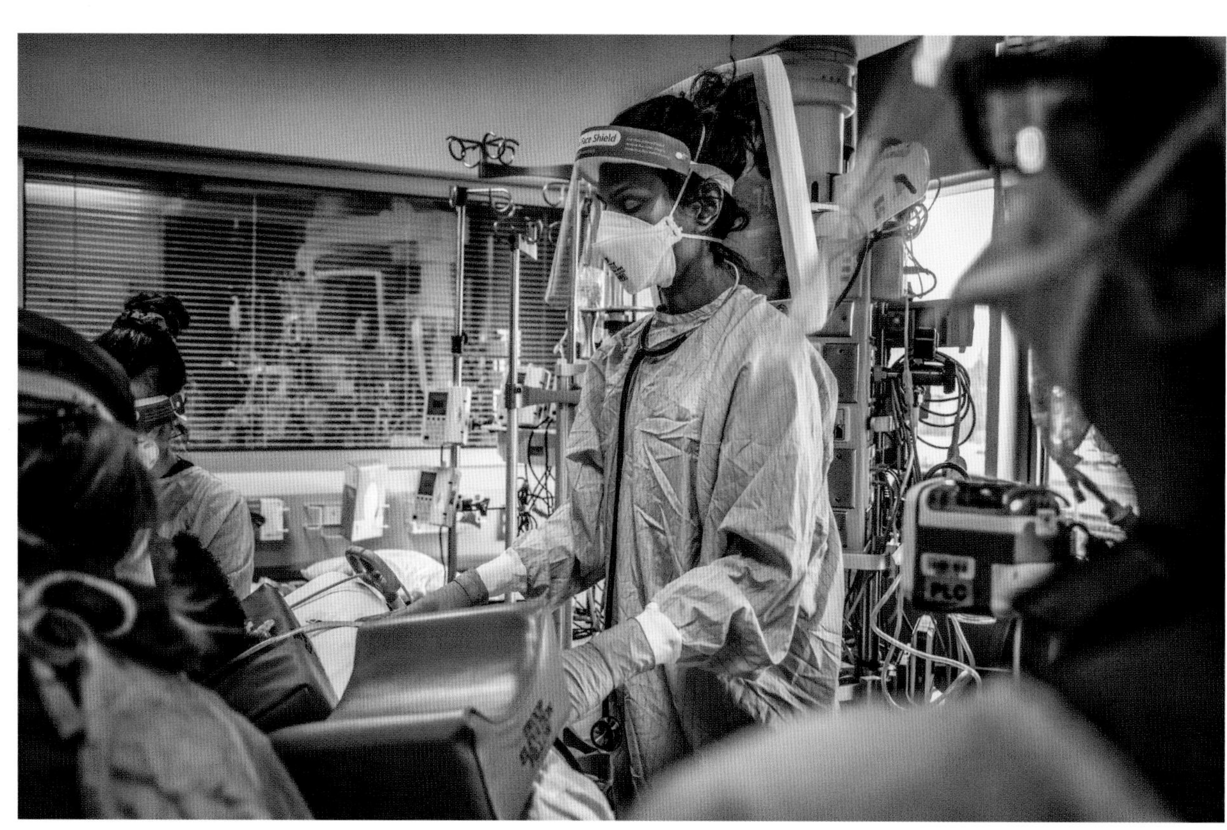

Dr. Ayesha Khory is pictured in the moments before intubating a COVID-19 patient in the intensive care unit.

"COVID-19 is a virus. Its goal is to reproduce and spread in any way possible. It's like any other virus: Anyone can get it. It's not selective about who it infects," says Dr. Khory.

Dr. Khory worked as an engineer in the province's oil industry before going to medical school and has been in practice for eight years. An emergency physician in Calgary, she works primarily at Rockyview General Hospital. She also works with the Assisted Self-Isolation Site (ASIS), which provides healthcare and a safe place to isolate for some of the city's most vulnerable people.

Dr. Khory says she will never forget some of the people she has met this past year – including a healthcare worker with COVID-19 who worried about seeking medical help until it was too late. "She didn't want to burden a healthcare system that she felt was already overworked," Dr. Khory says.

"The hard days are when you have bad cases or someone you can't find a solution for or help in the way you wish you could. That's hard."

She knows what she's looking forward to most when the pandemic is done: "Hugs. I'm a big hugger," she says.

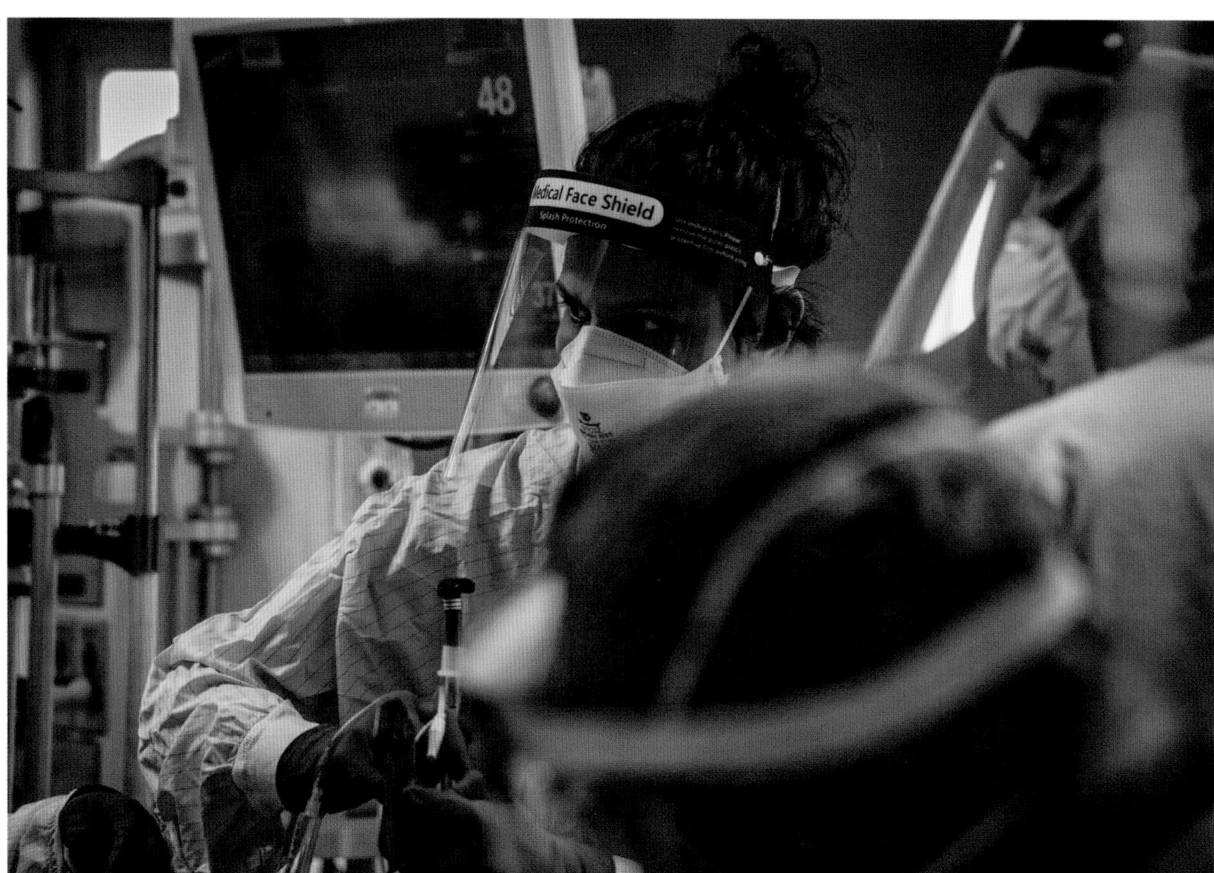
Medical Face Shield
Splash Protection

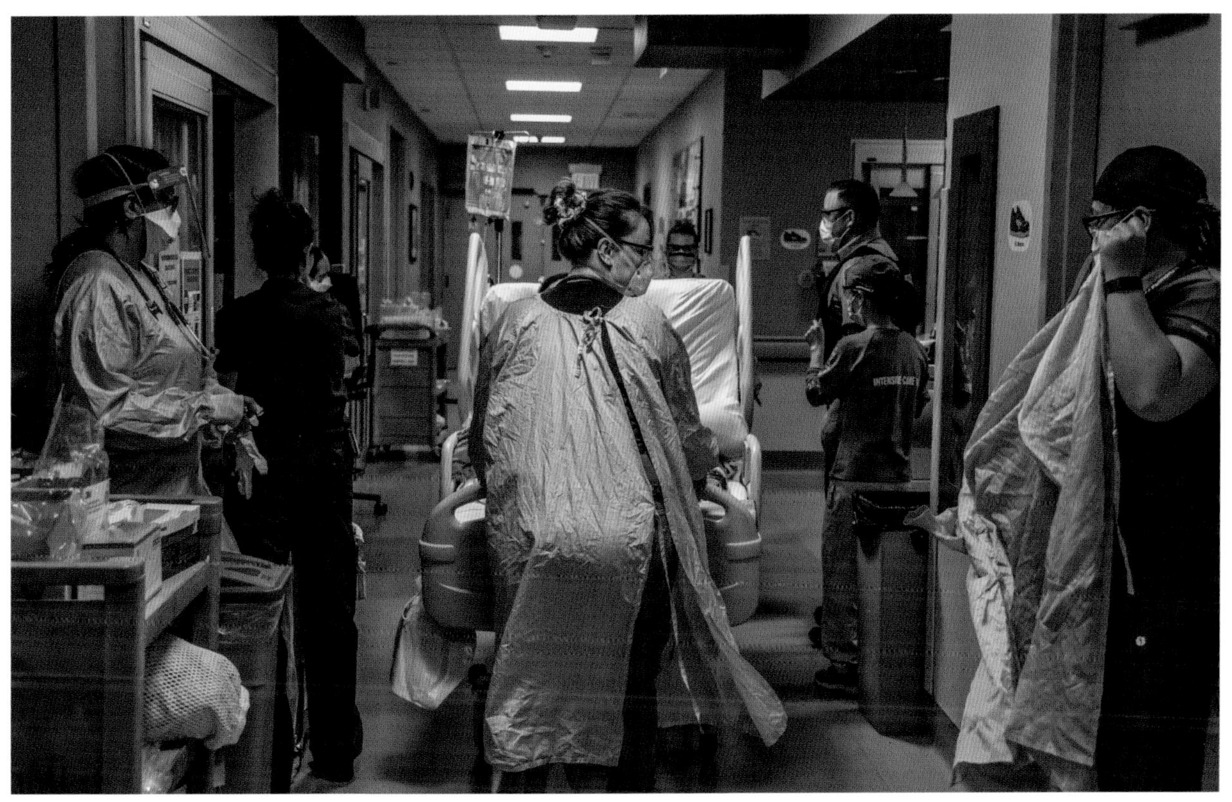

Dr. Ayesha Khory intubates a COVID-19 patient
in the intensive care unit at Peter Lougheed
Centre in Calgary, Alberta.

A healthcare team admits a COVID-19 patient
to the intensive care unit at Peter Lougheed
Centre in Calgary, Alberta.

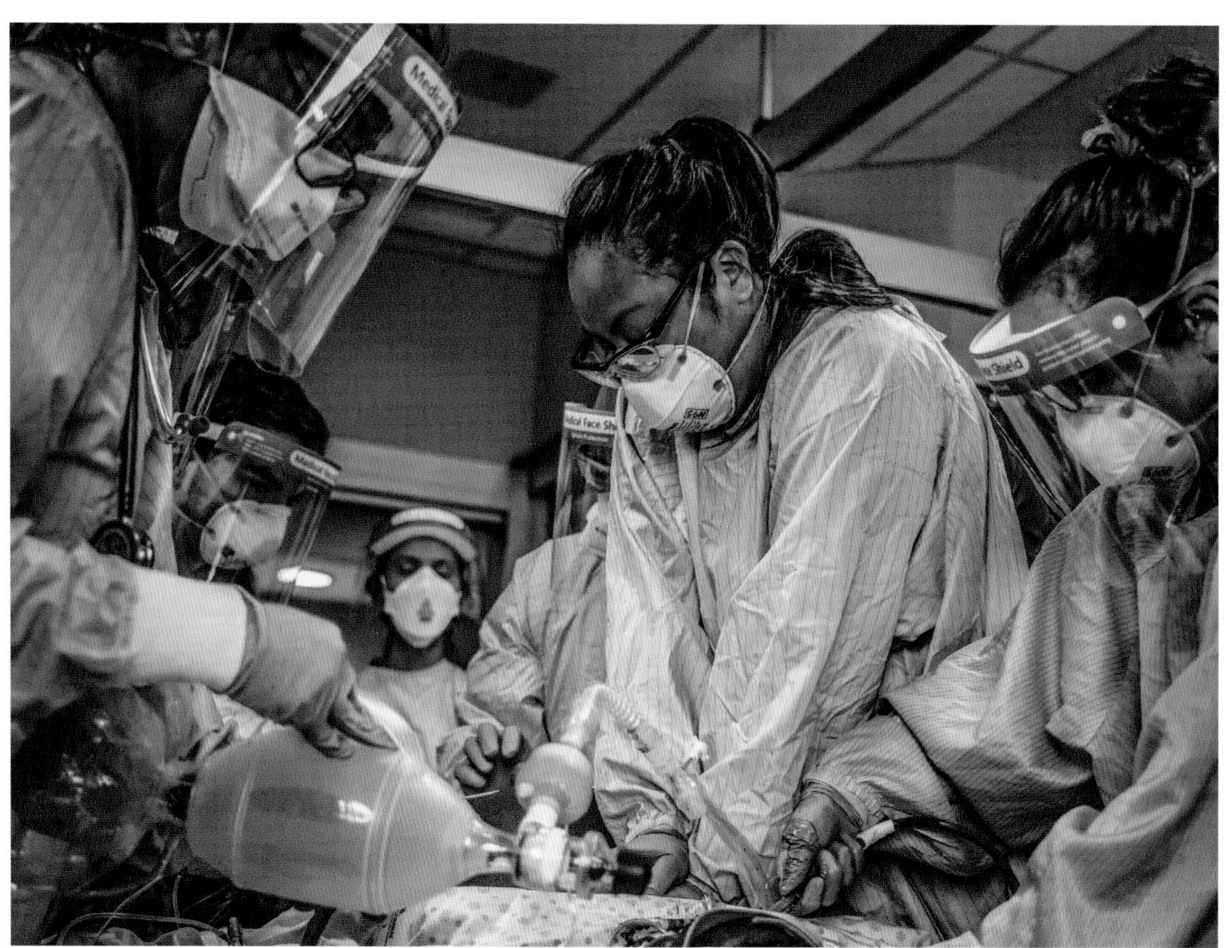

Medical
Medical face Shield
Medical face Shield
Face Shield

Registered nurse Mia Torres, centre, does chest compressions on a COVID-19 patient in the intensive care unit at Peter Lougheed Centre.

"My heart is broken for all the patients in our ICU who can only have their family members with them through a phone or an iPad calling in," says Torres.

"It isn't what I would want if I were in their shoes."

Torres is looking forward to many things once the pandemic has ended.

"Being able to hug my parents and grandmother again, to be able to have family dinners and get that lost quality time back. To be able to travel with my husband again and see the world. Being able to hang out with my co-workers and go for breakfast or a late dinner after a stretch of shifts."

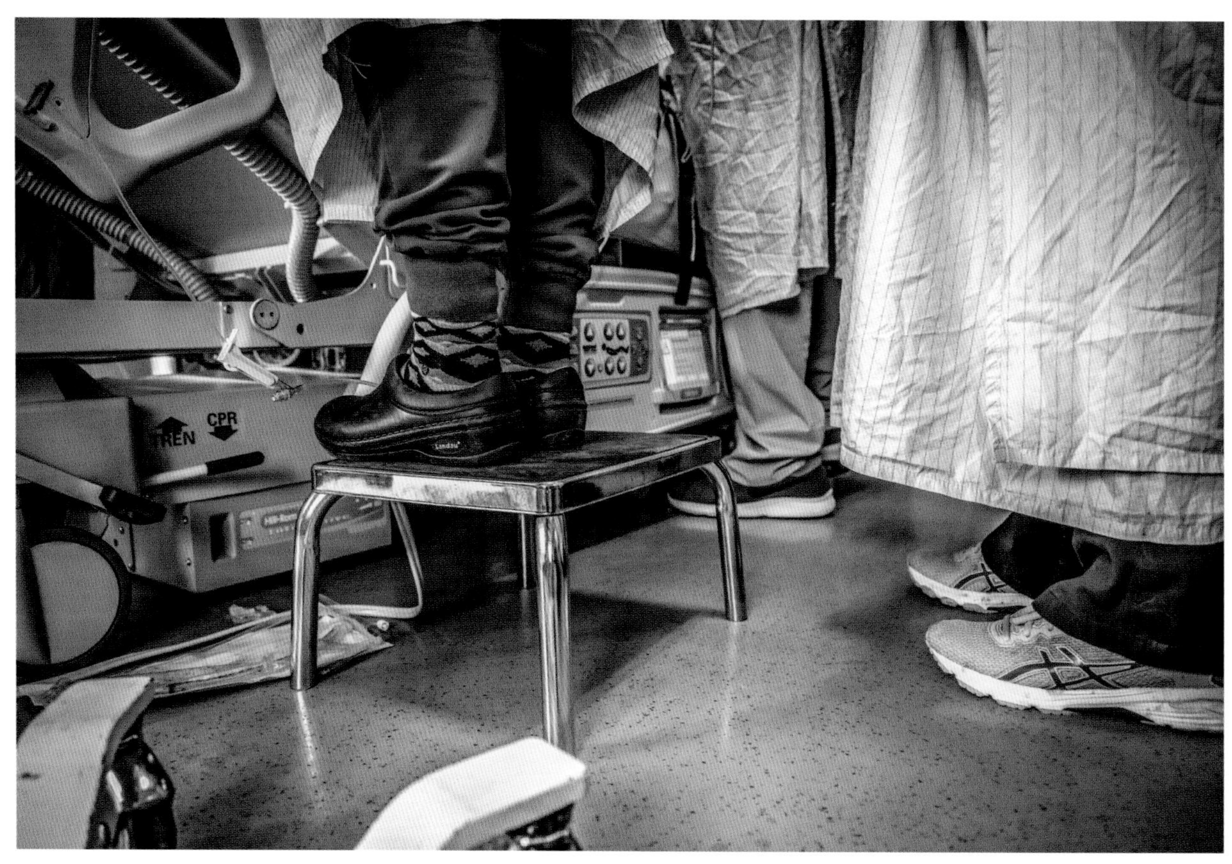

Healthcare team members use a stool to do chest compressions on a patient in an intensive care unit.

Family members, behind drawn curtains, say goodbye to a loved one dying of COVID-19 in the intensive care unit, while a registered nurse, left, and an AHS volunteer sit in the hallway

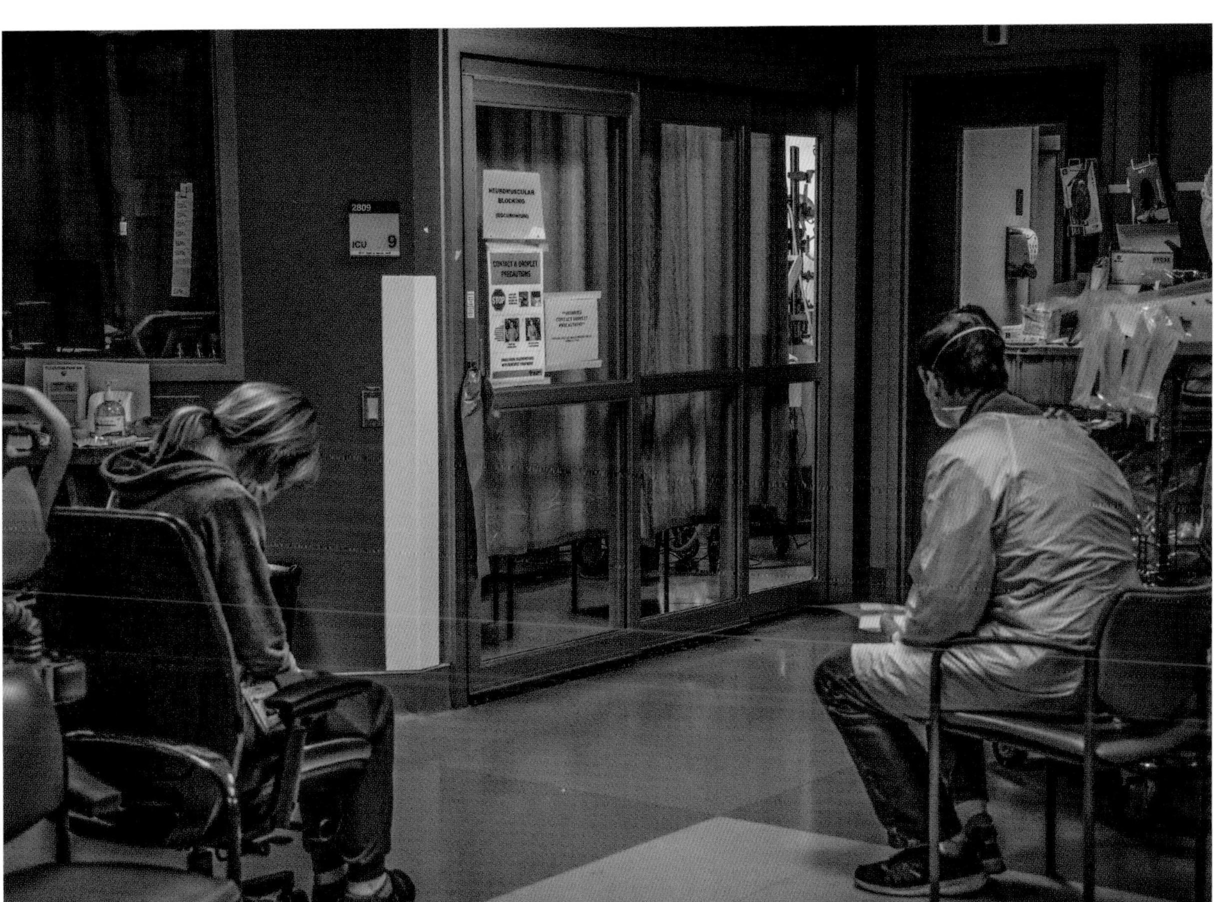

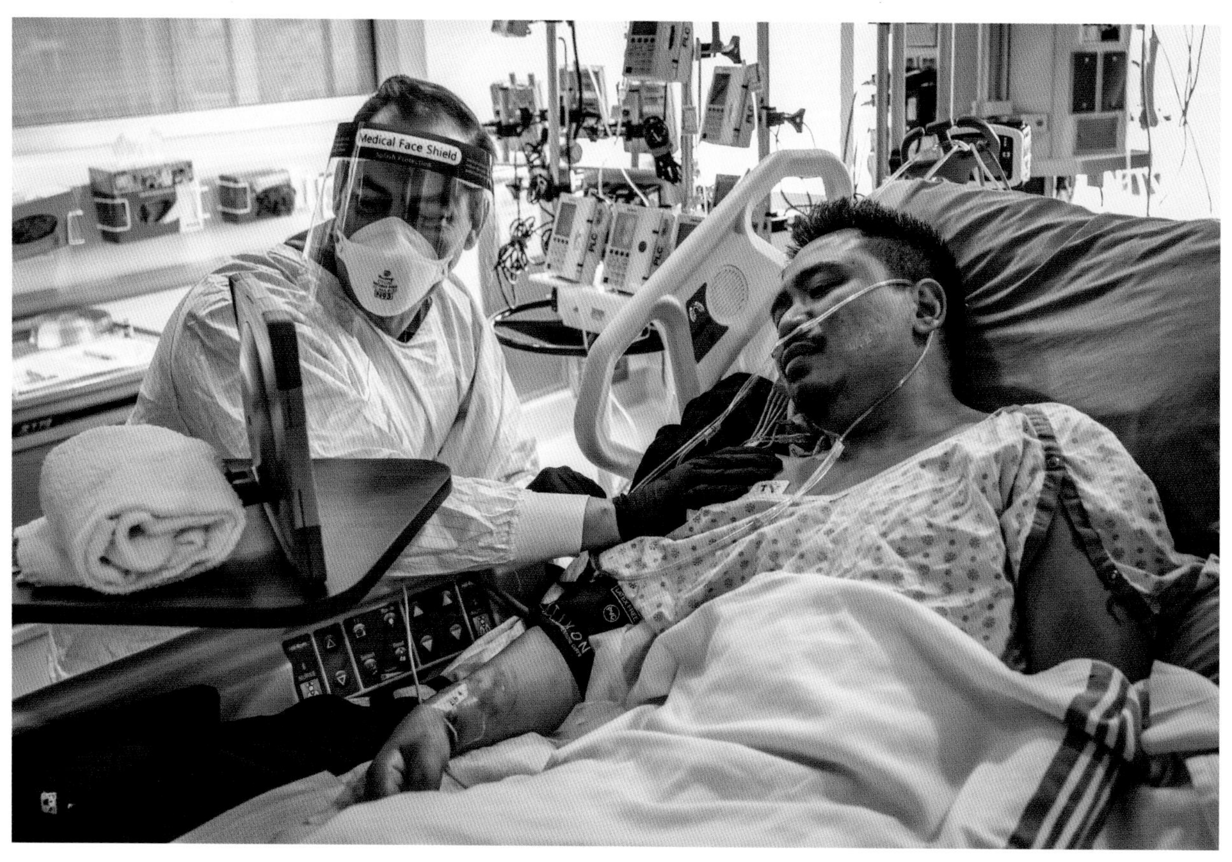

Volunteer Daniel Hughes sets up an iPad so COVID-19 patient Vincent Facullo can talk to his family from his room in the intensive care unit at Peter Lougheed Centre in April 2021.

The front of a respiratory therapist's shirt during a shift.

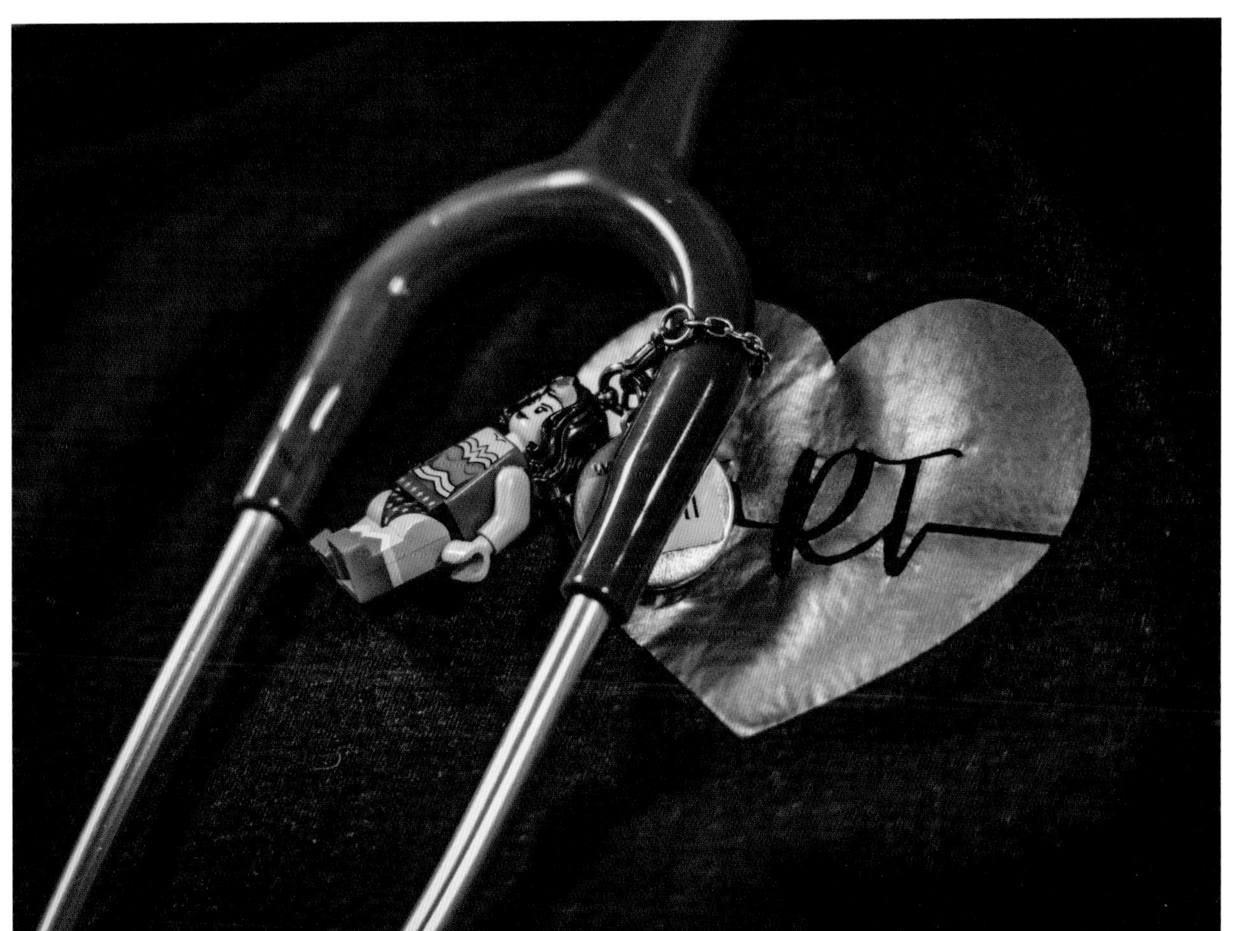

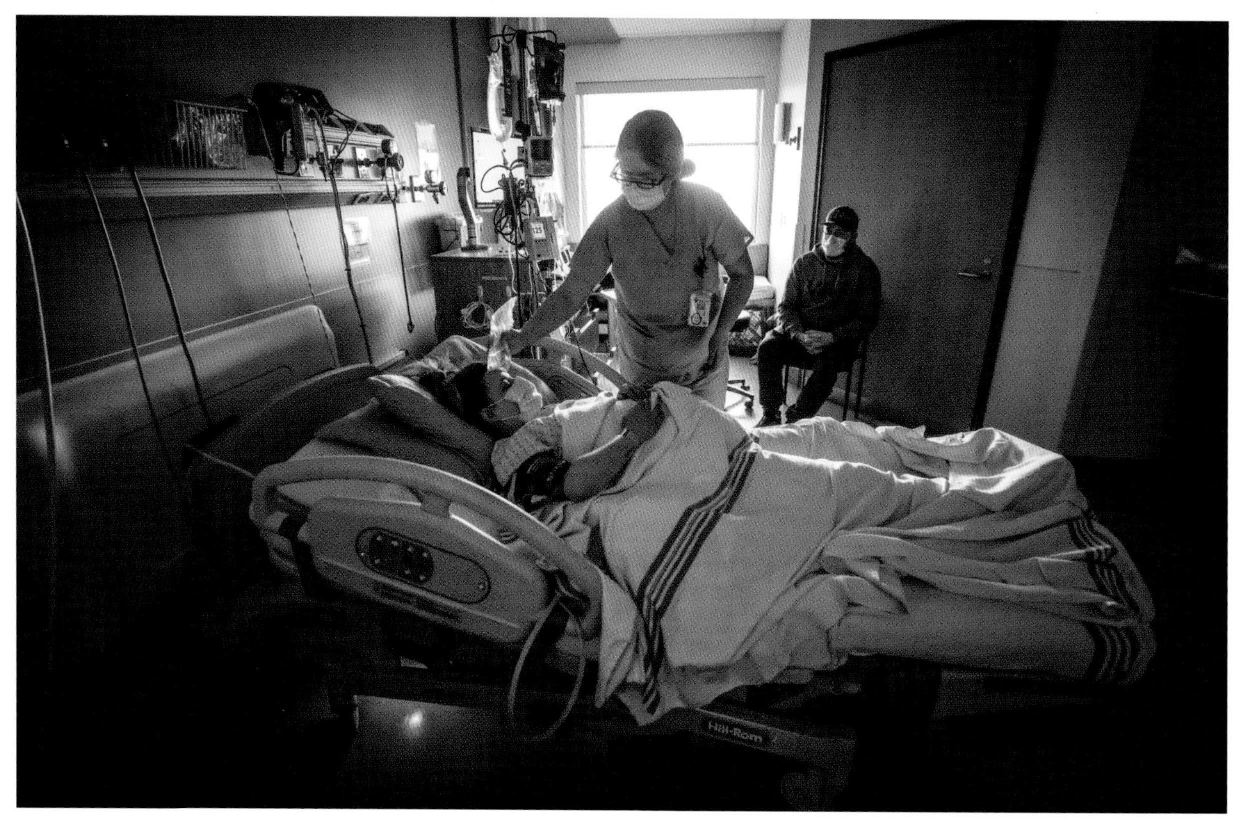

A healthcare worker puts an ice bag
on the forehead of Bea Matusko,
who's in labour.

Tolson Matusko cuts the cord after his
wife Bea delivers their first child.

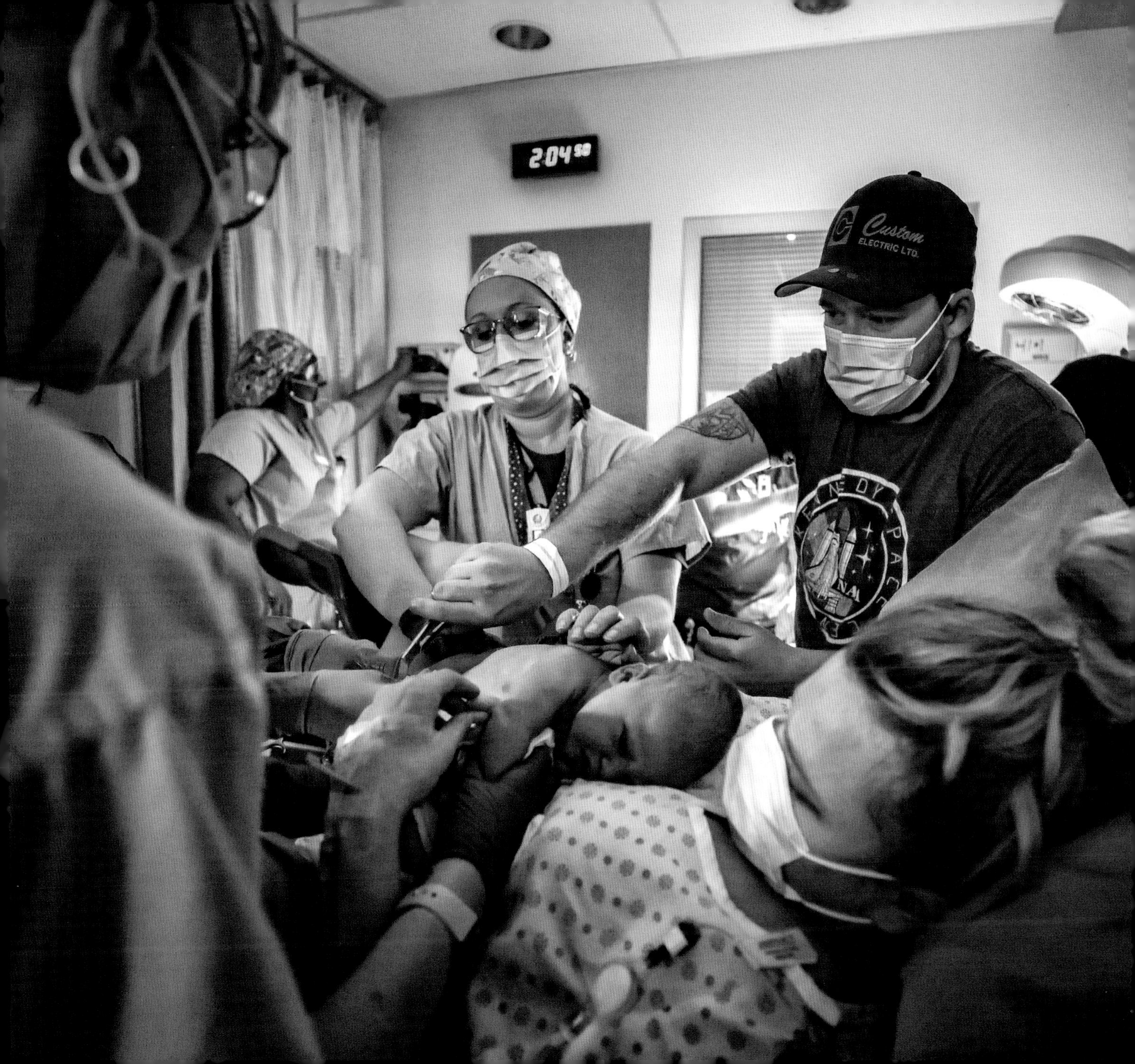

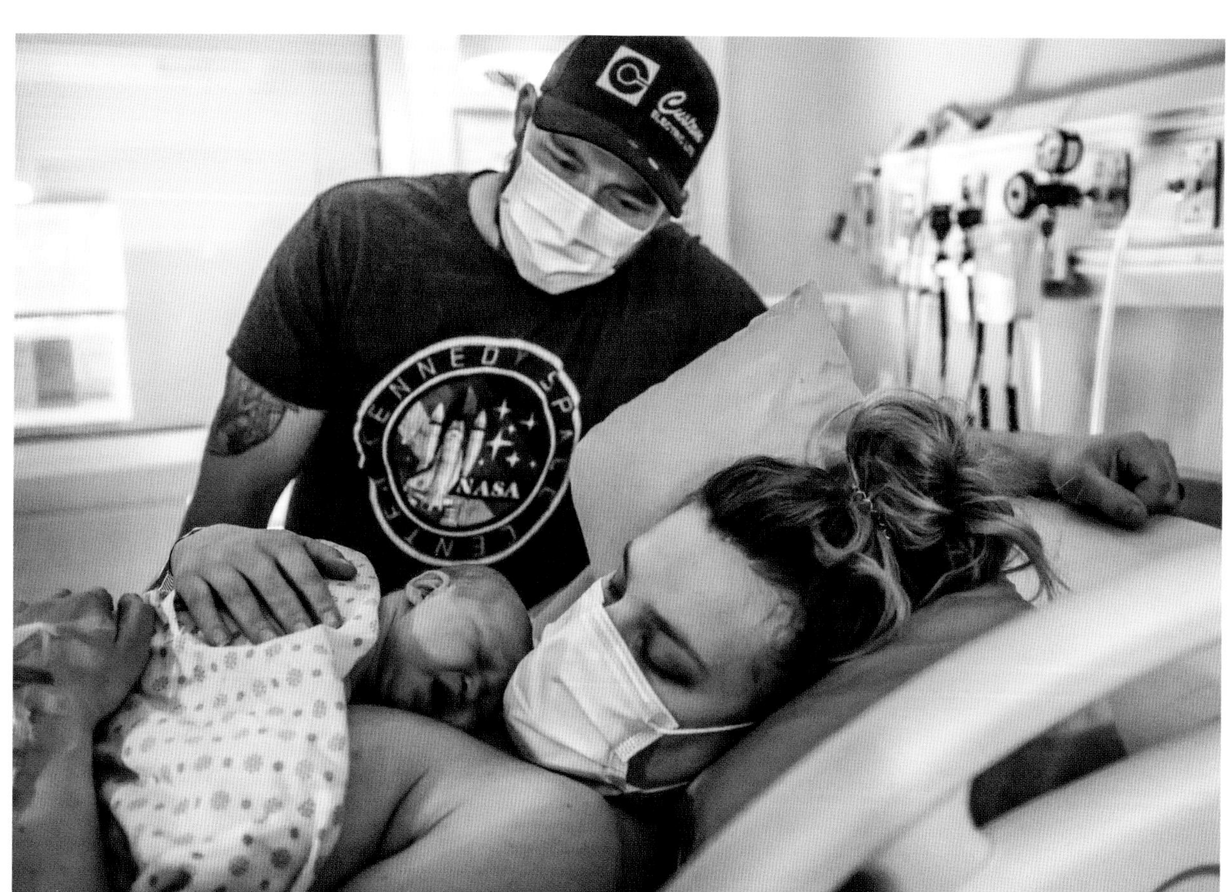

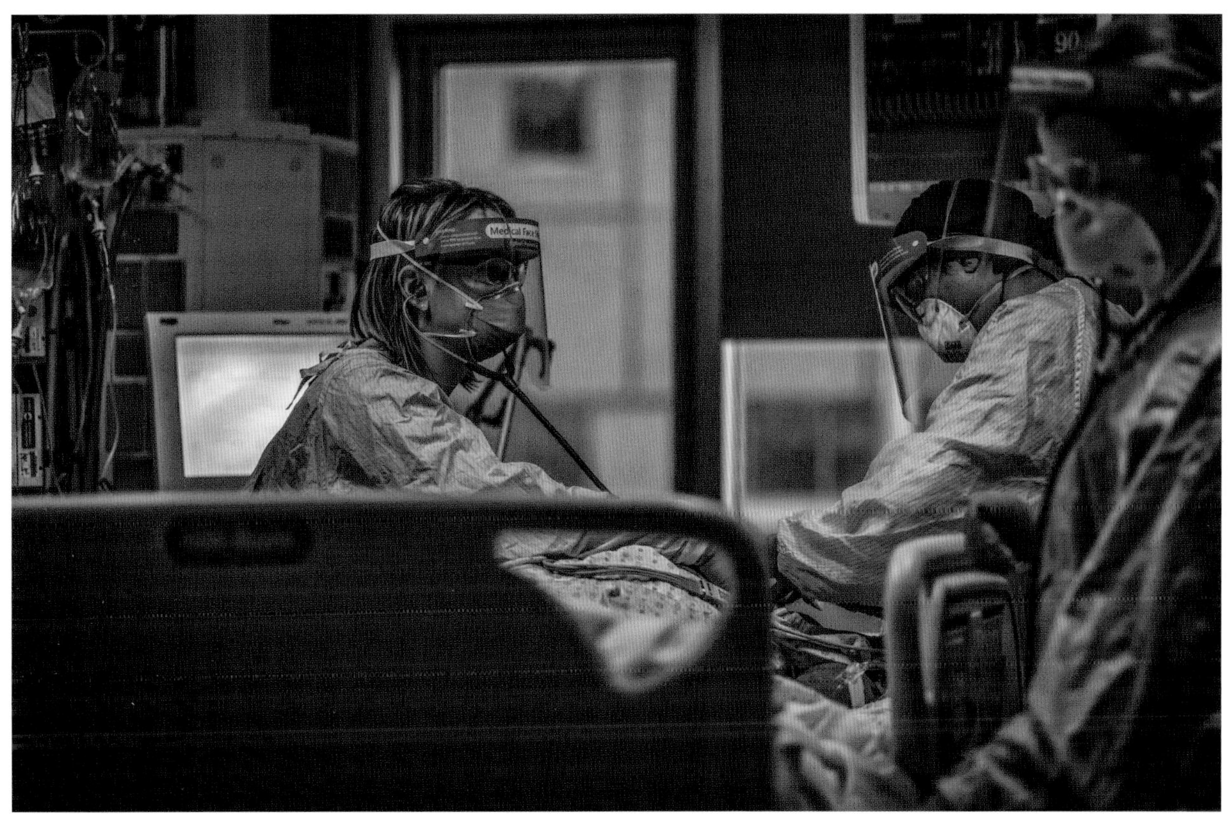

Parents in a pandemic, Tolson and Bea Matusko cuddle their newborn at South Health Campus in Calgary, Alberta, in 2021.

"Giving birth during a pandemic is surreal. Appointments are attended alone. You are isolated from friends and family due to risk of contracting COVID-19. And the fear that your partner will develop symptoms and not be able to be present for the birth is immense," says Bea Matusko.

Respiratory therapist Nancy Van Der Velden, left, and other staff members check the vital signs of a COVID-19 patient.

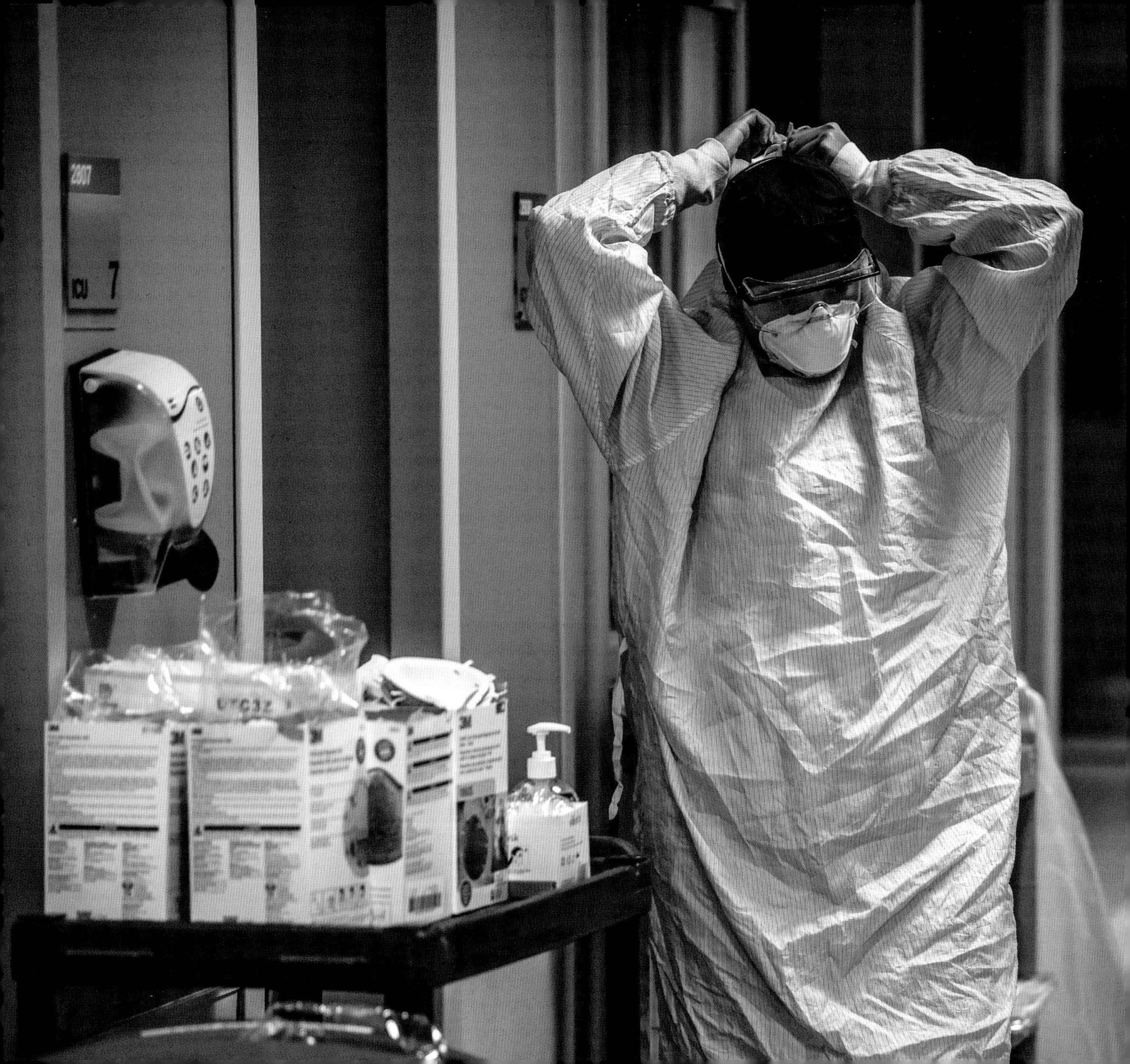

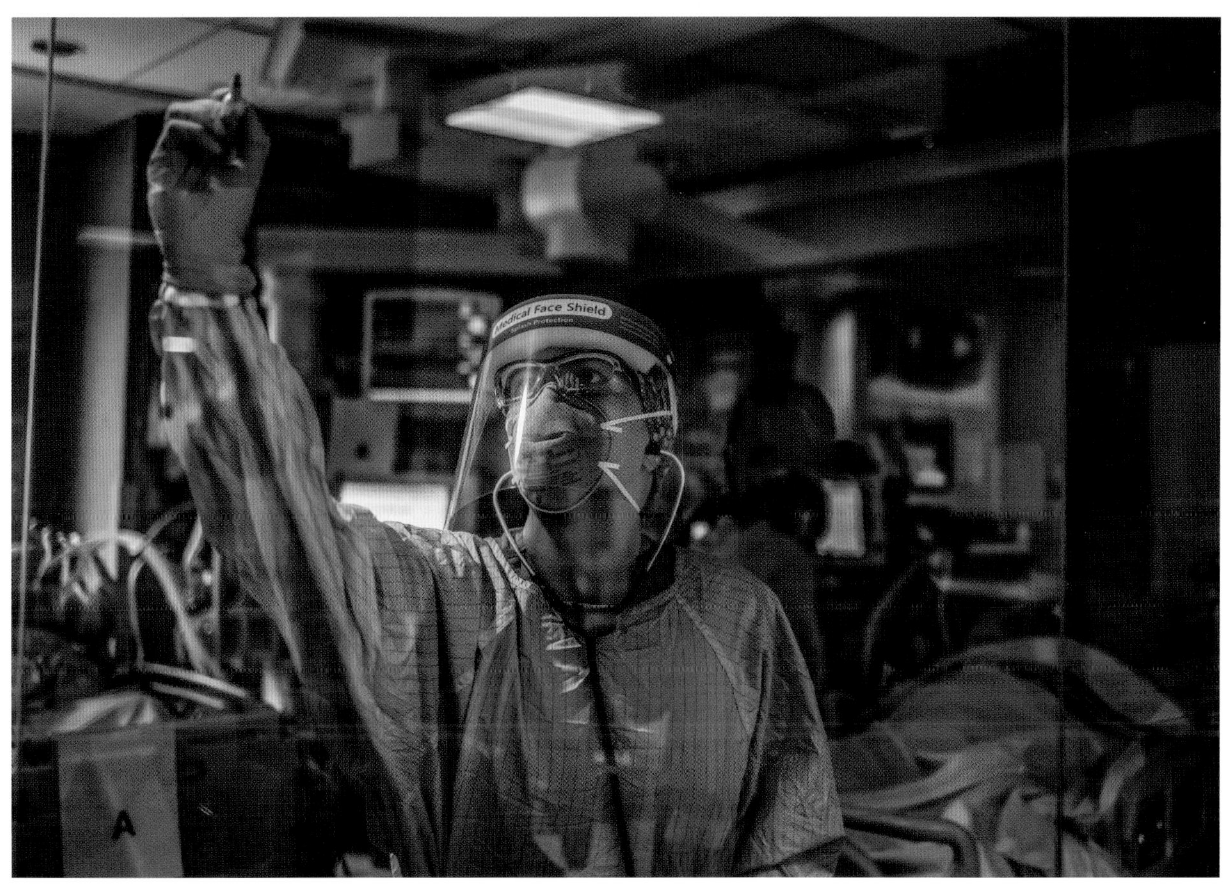

A healthcare professional dons personal protective equipment before entering the room of a COVID-19 patient.

A healthcare team member writes vital-sign information on the glass from inside the room of a COVID-19 patient in the intensive care unit at Peter Lougheed Centre.

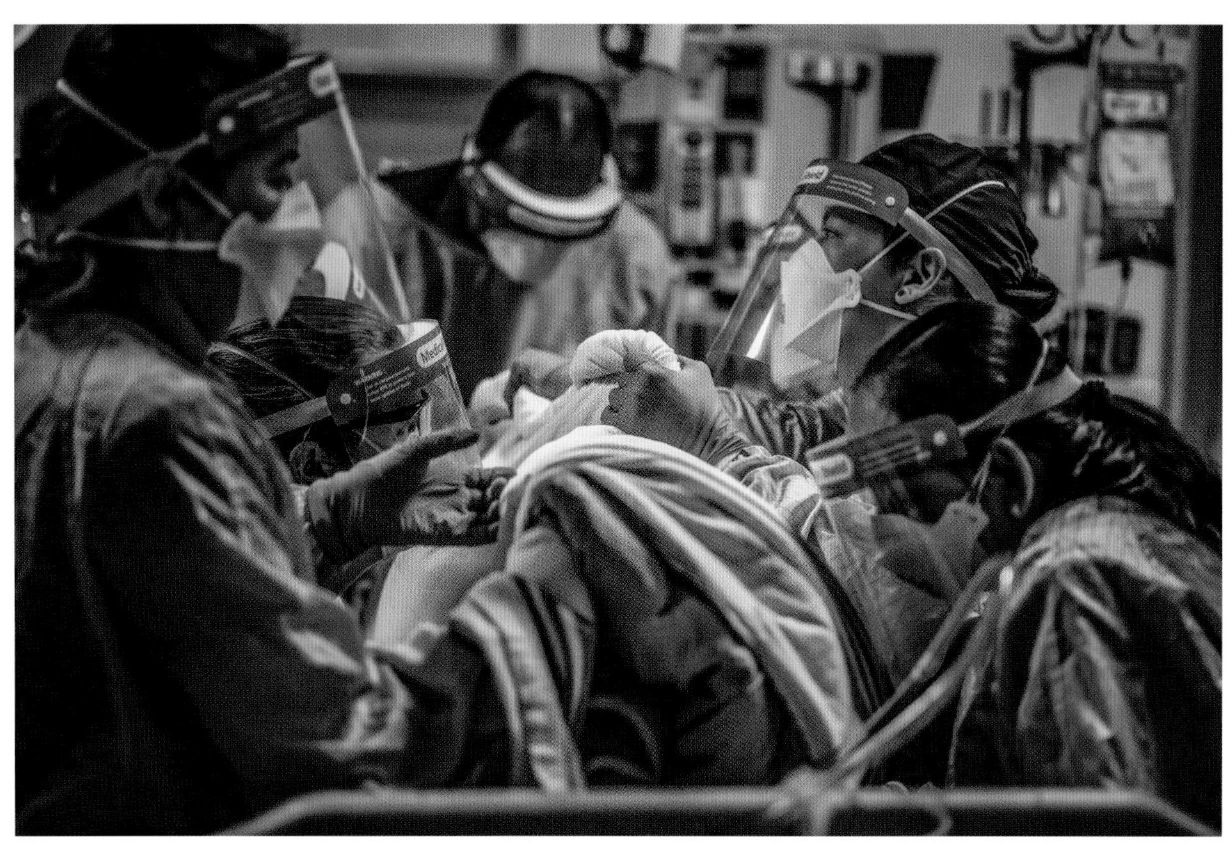

A healthcare team in the intensive care unit
at Peter Lougheed Hospital work together to
move a COVID-19 patient into "prone positioning." In prone positioning, patients lie on their
stomach rather than their back, which can help
increase oxygen flow to the patient's lungs.

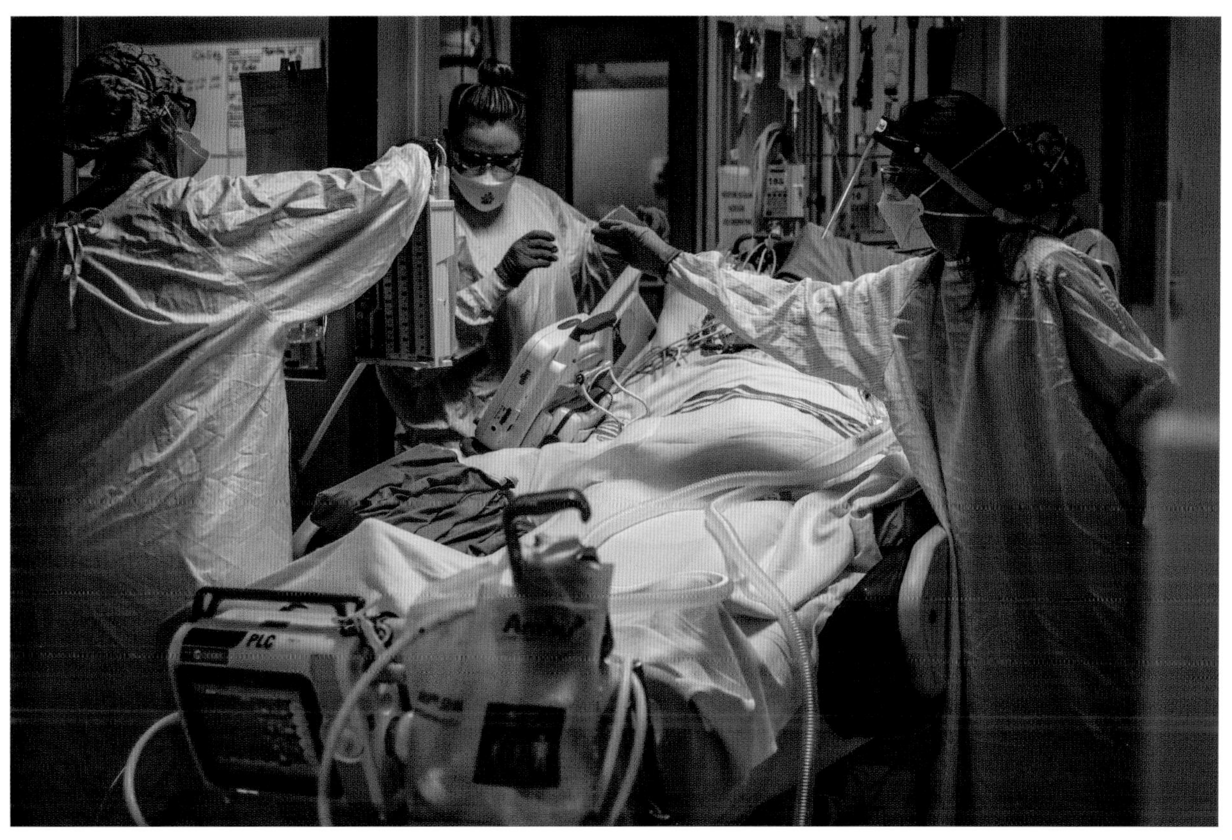

A COVID-19 patient is admitted to the intensive
care unit at Peter Lougheed Centre in Calgary,
Alberta.

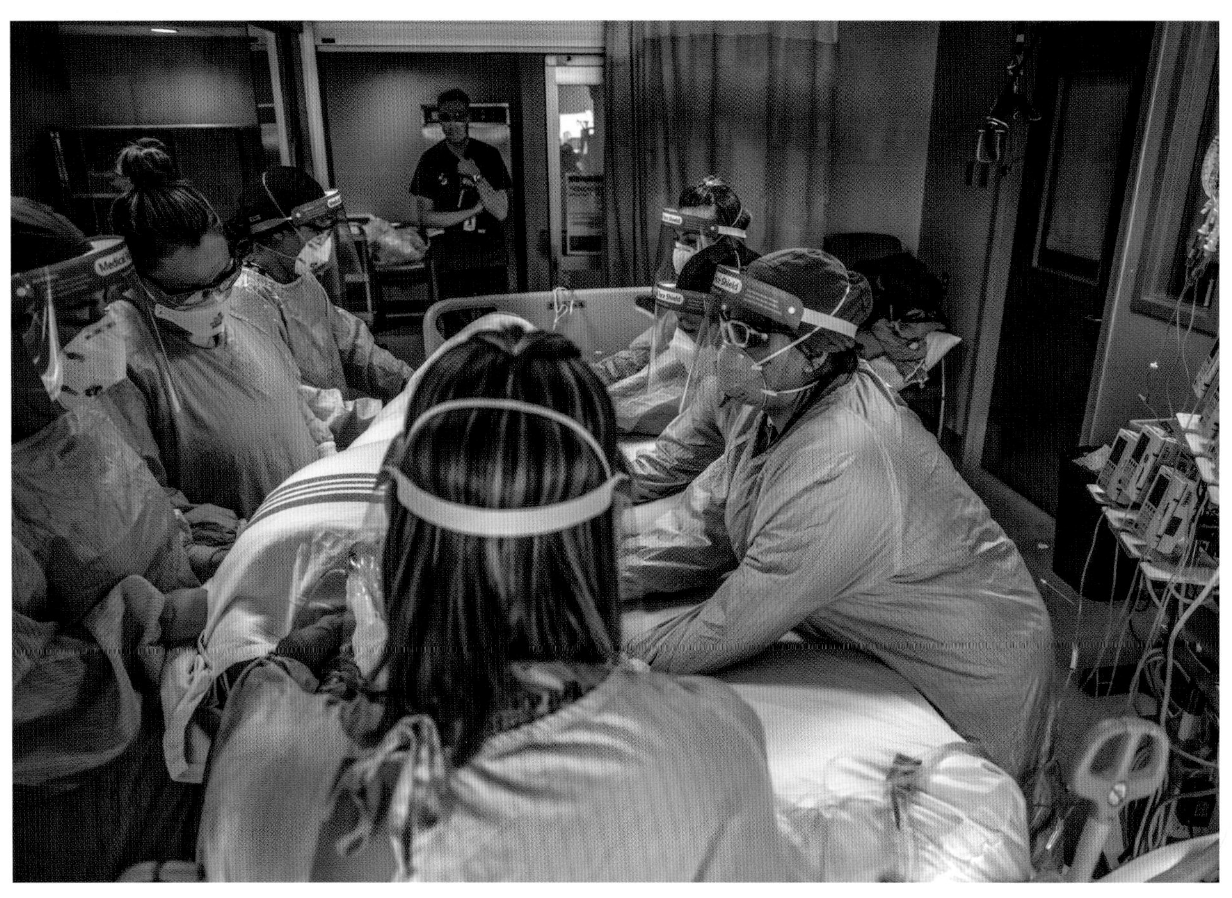

A healthcare team moves a COVID-19
patient.

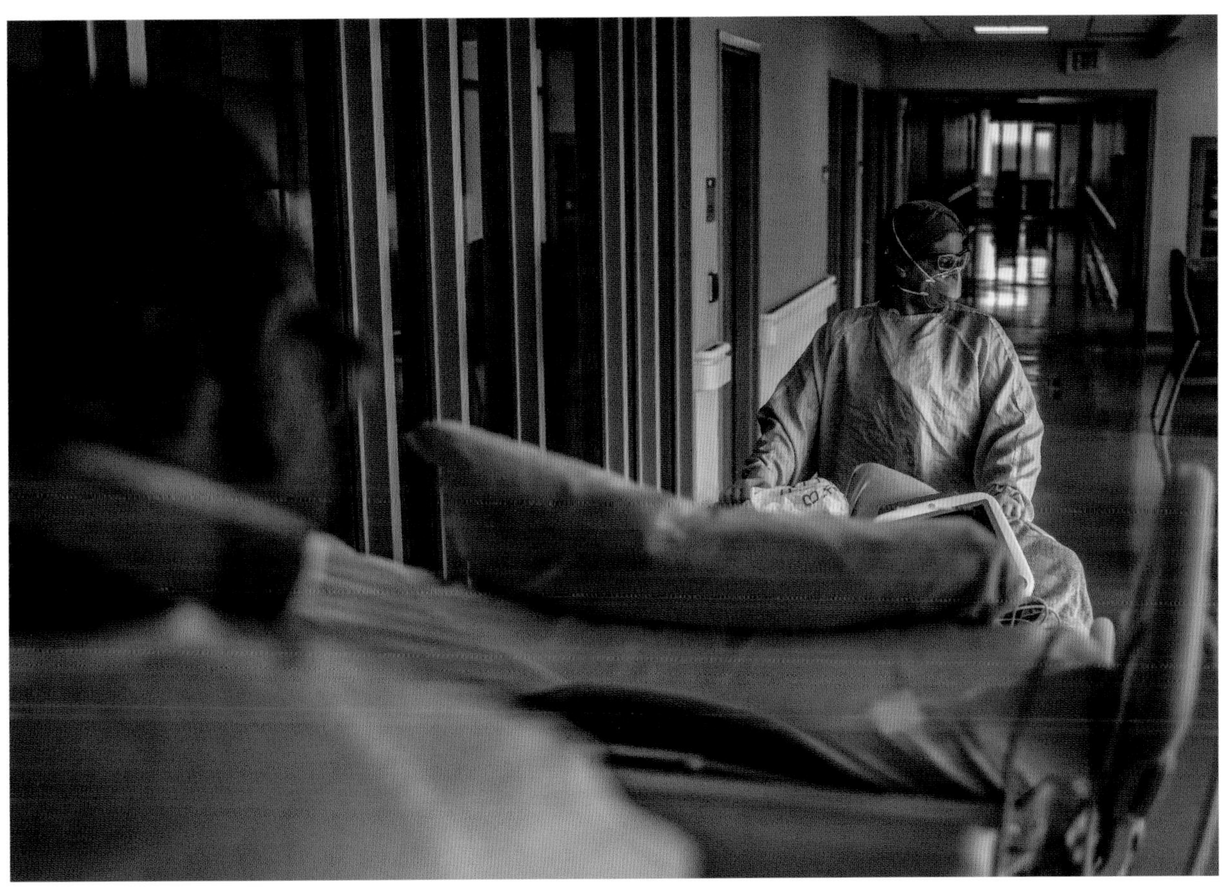

A healthcare team moves a patient
from the COVID-19 unit at Peter
Lougheed Centre to the intensive
care unit to be intubated.

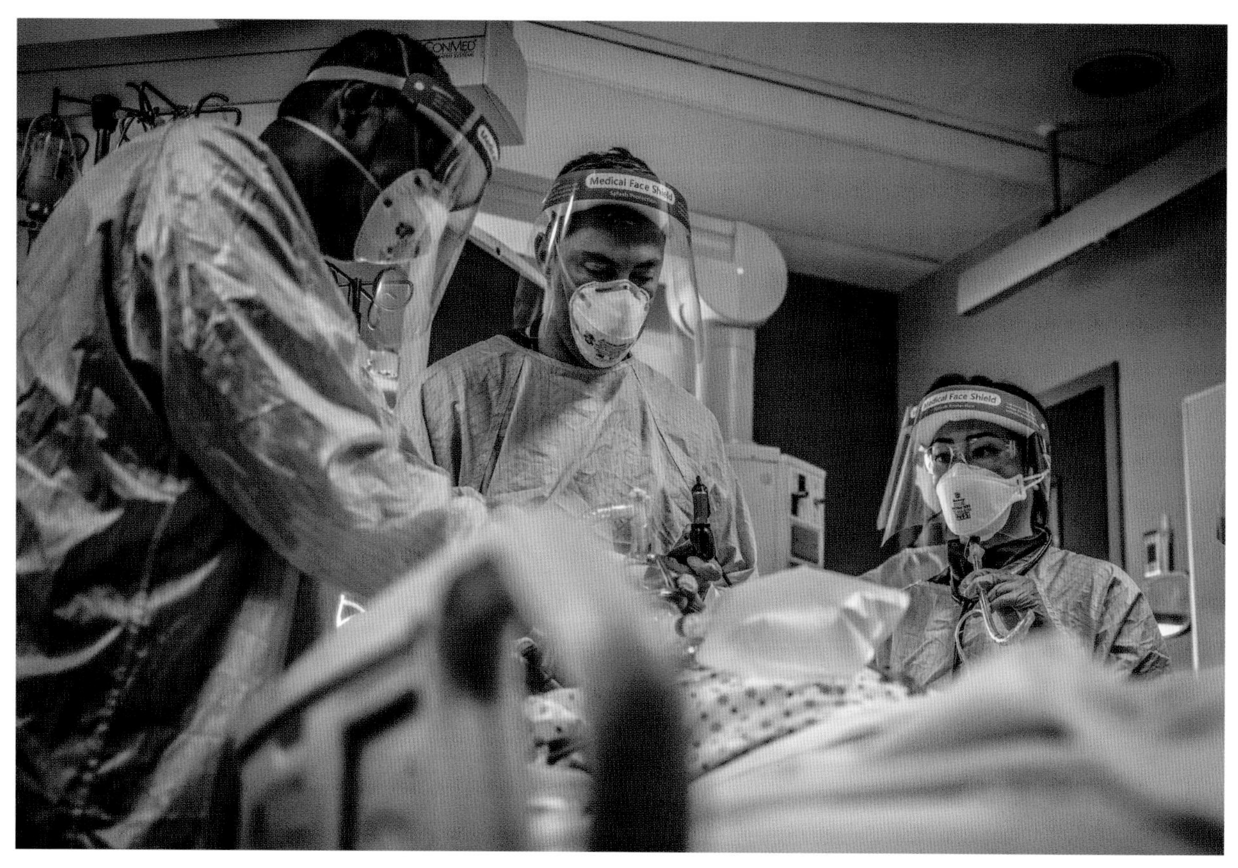

A healthcare team works together to
intubate a COVID-19 patient.

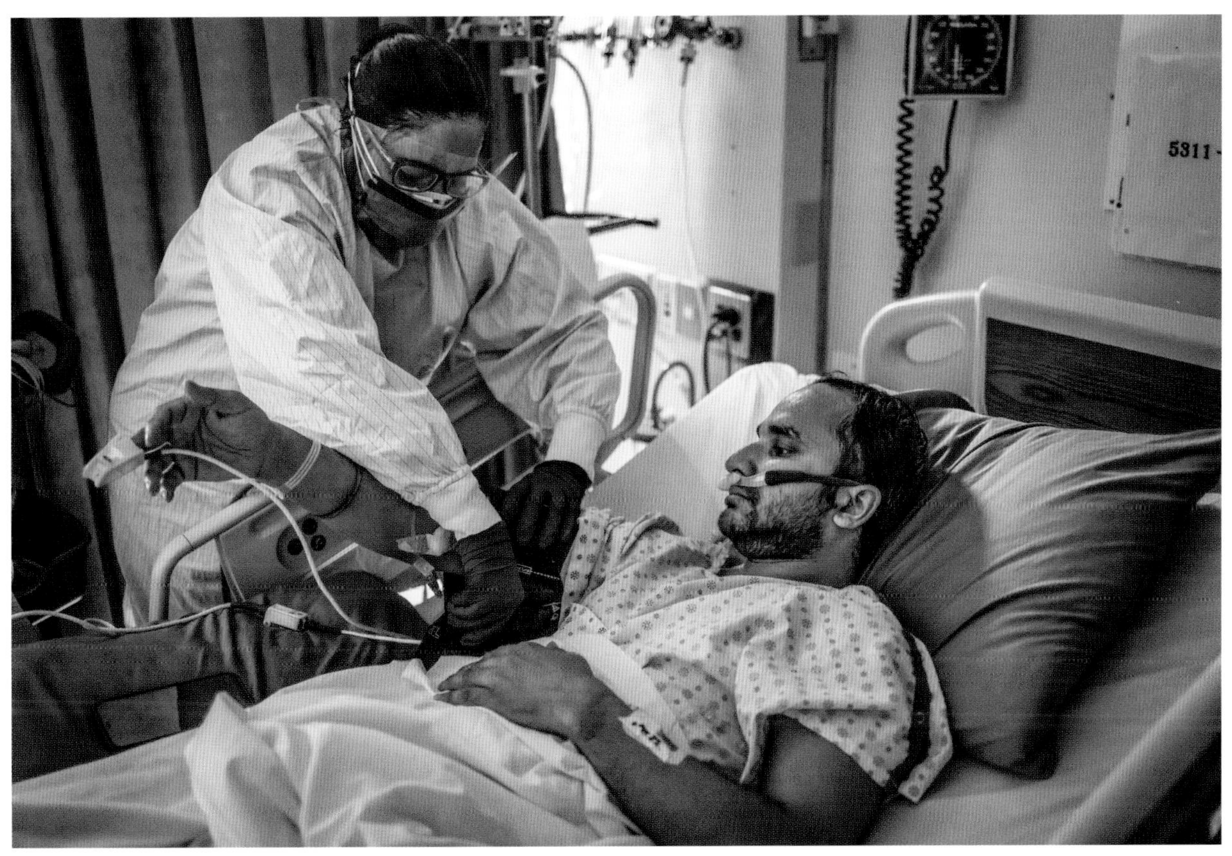

A registered nurse checks the vital signs
of Dalwinder Dub, 38, who required high-
flow oxygen in the COVID-19 unit at Peter
Lougheed Centre in Calgary, Alberta, in
April 2021.

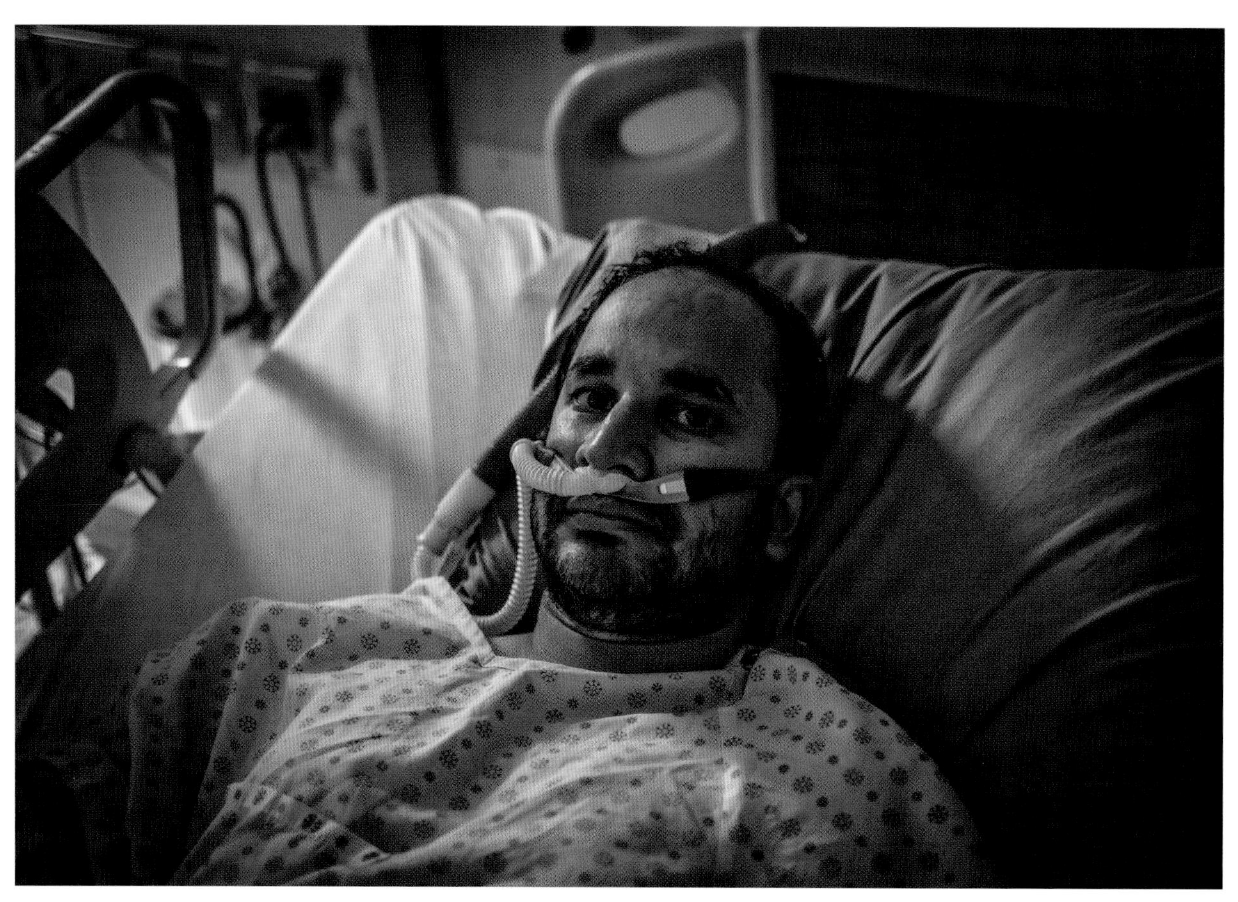

Dalwinder Dub, 38, required high-flow oxygen in the COVID-19 unit at Peter Lougheed Centre in Calgary, Alberta, in April 2021.

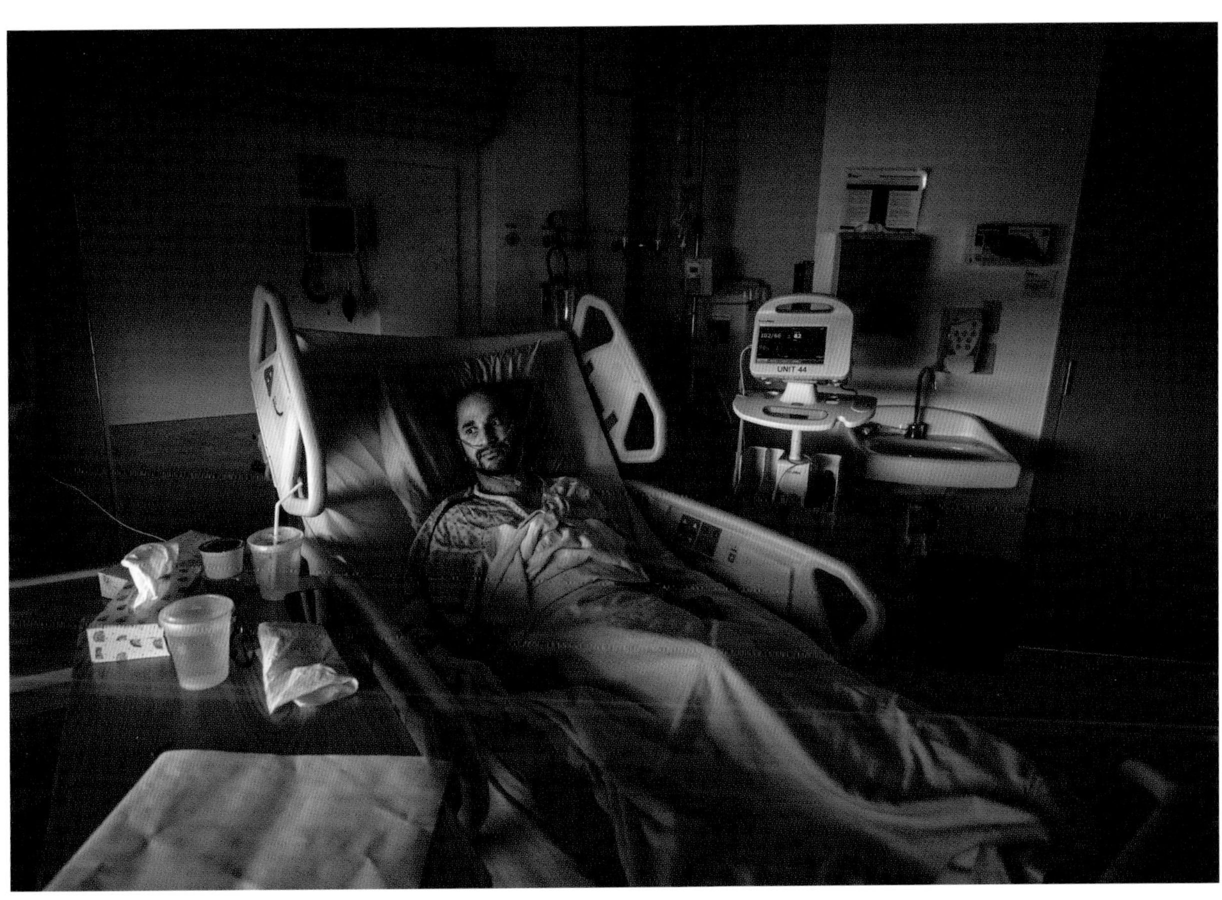

Dalwinder Dub rests a few days before
being discharged from the COVID-19 unit
at Peter Lougheed Centre.

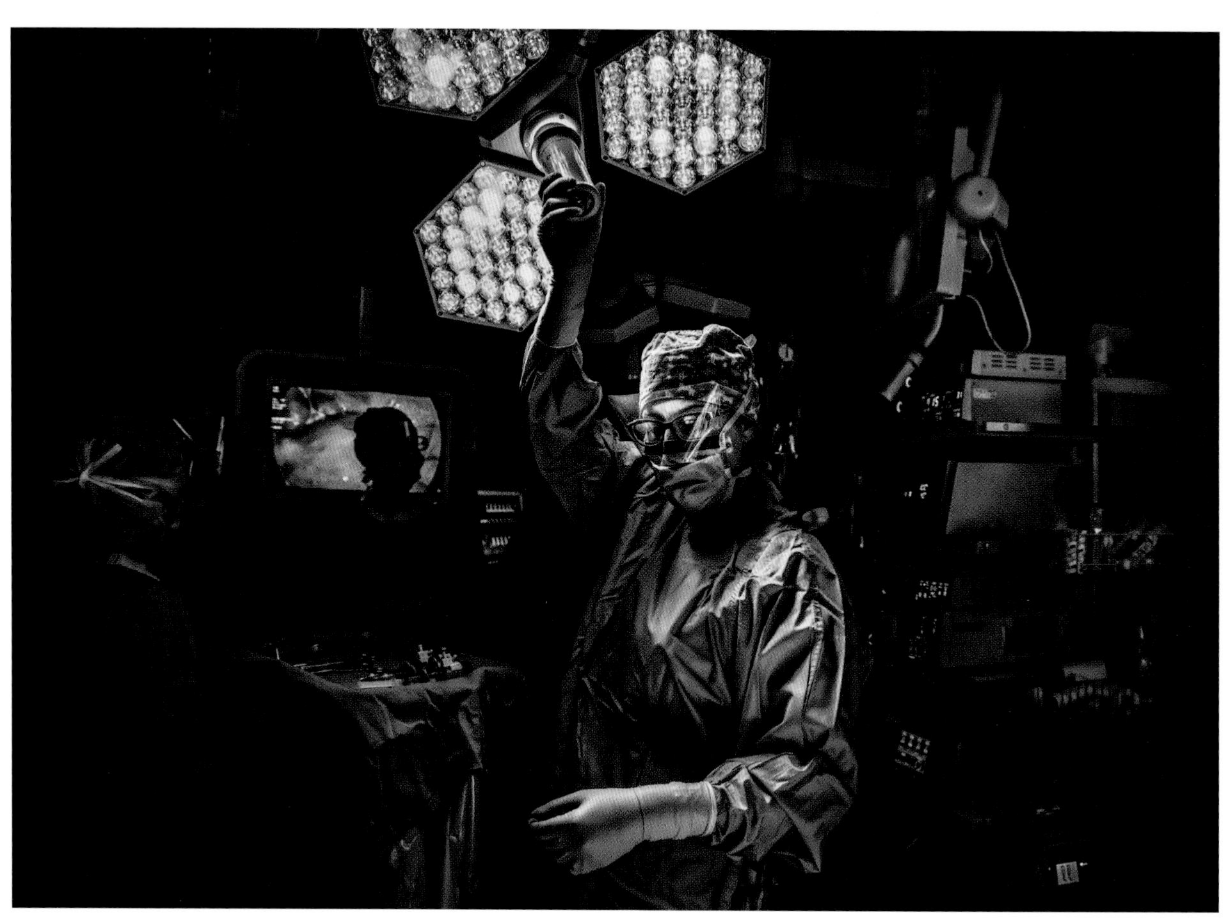

Amanda McBurney, a licensed practical nurse, works in an operating room at Peter Lougheed Centre in Calgary, Alberta.

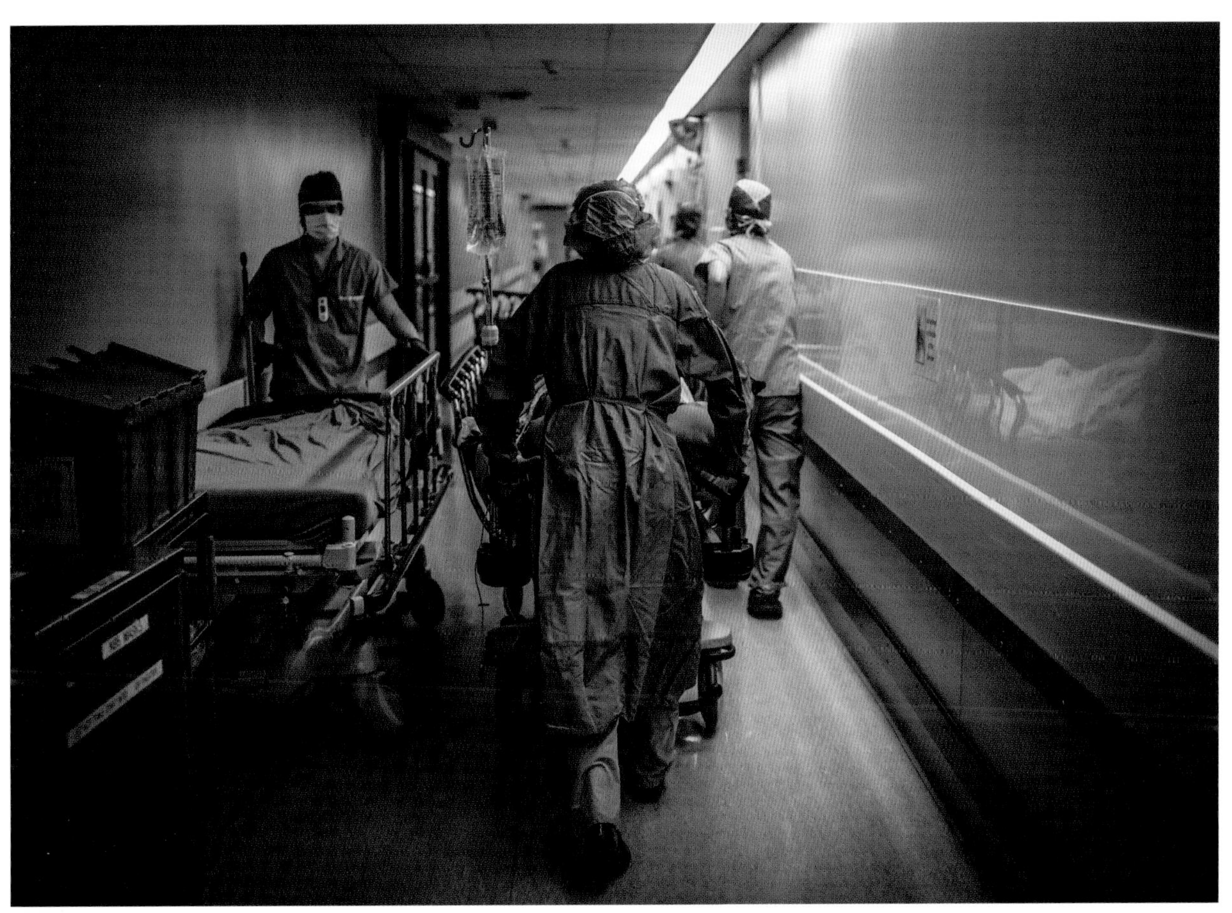

A patient is on the way to an operating
room at Peter Lougheed Centre in Calgary,
Alberta.

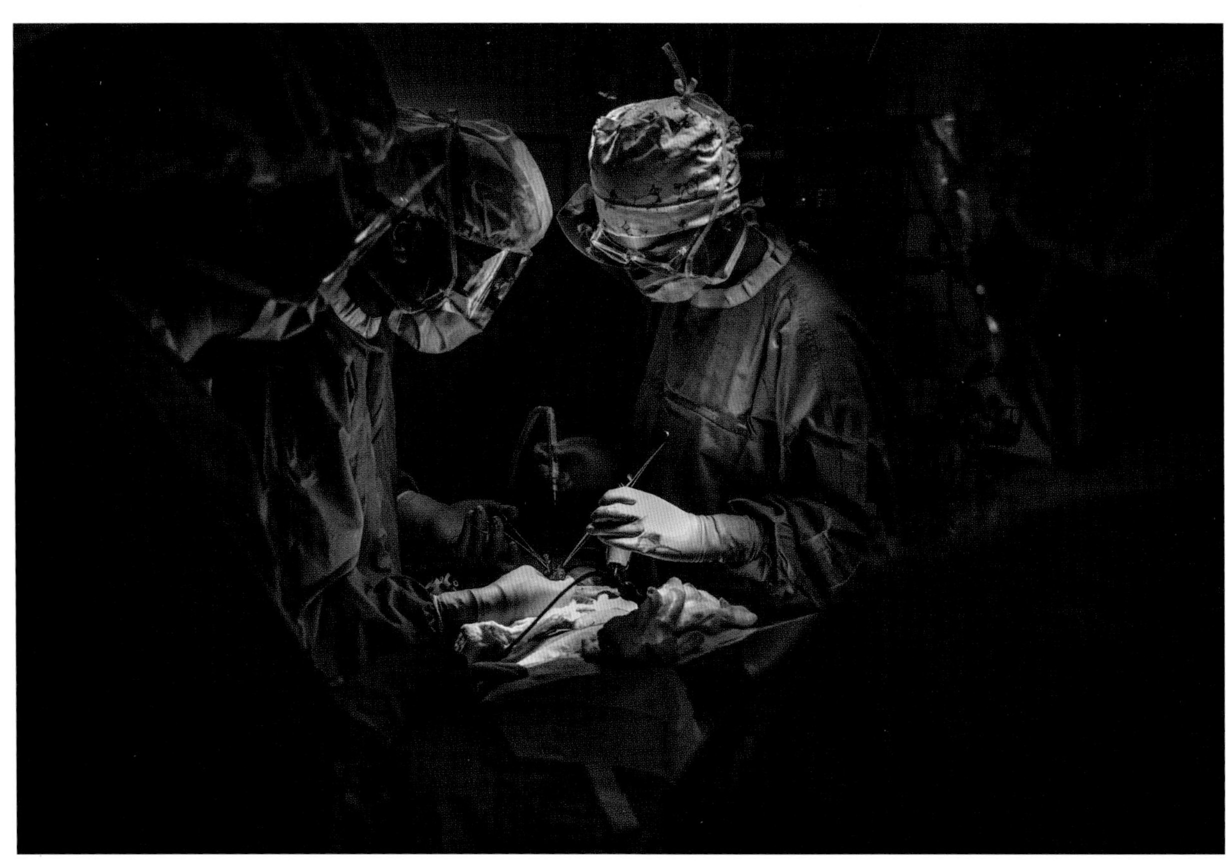

Surgeon Dr. Indraneel Datta, left, and general surgery resident Dr. Carolyn Graham perform surgery in the operating room at Peter Lougheed Centre in Calgary, Alberta.

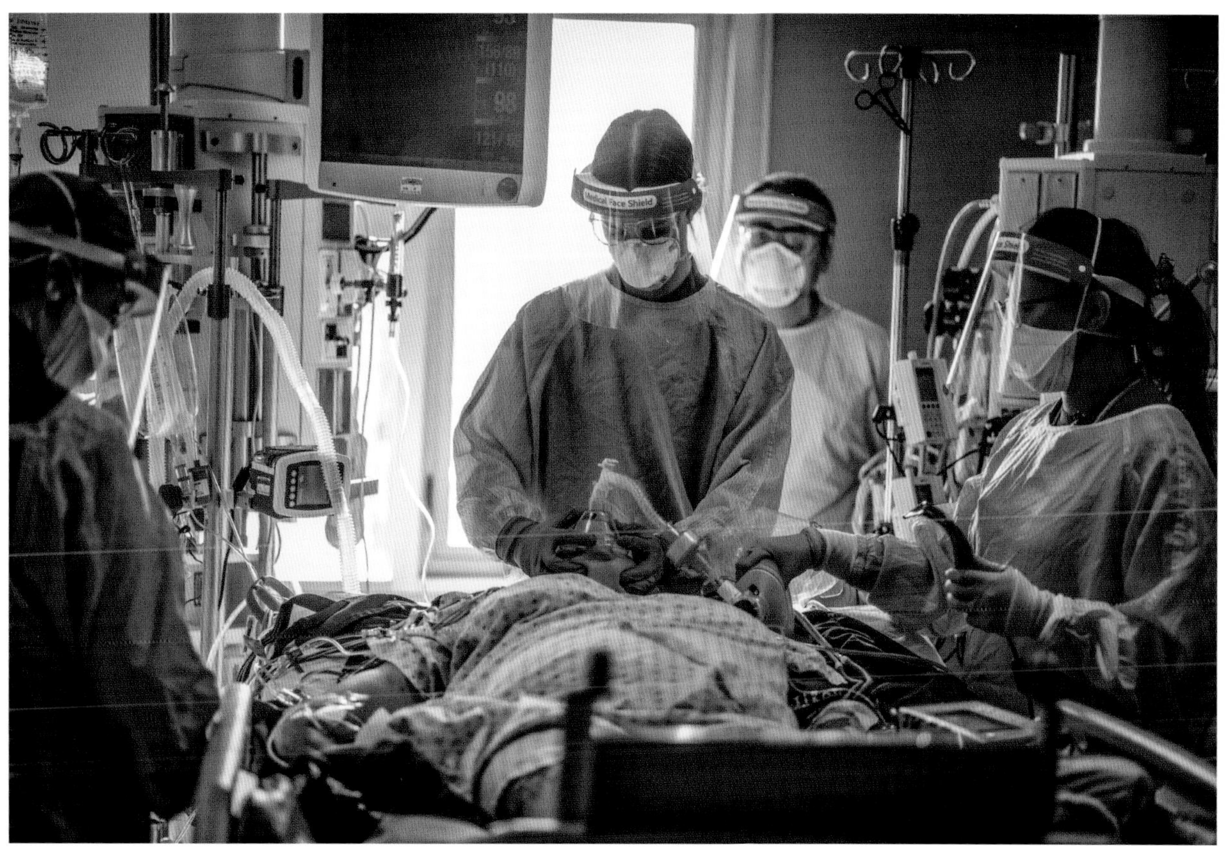

Dr. Natasha Goumeniouk, resident, prepares COVID-19 patient Christine Wesley
for intubation in the intensive care unit at
Peter Lougheed Centre in Calgary, Alberta.

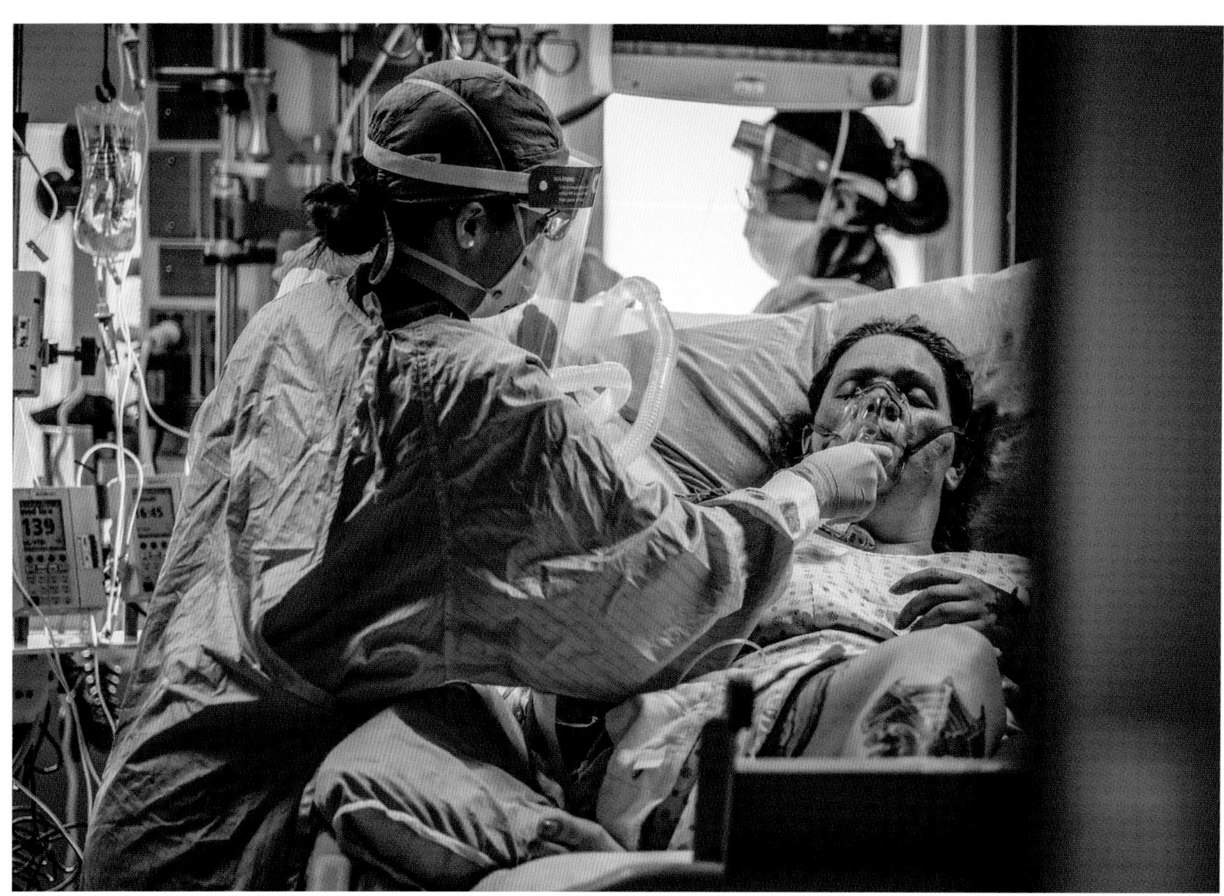

"I was hallucinating. I don't think I've ever been that mentally low, ever, in my life, where I felt so helpless and unable to do anything," says Christine Wesley, a 36-year-old new mother recovering from COVID-19 in Calgary.

She tested positive while pregnant and thinks her family likely was exposed at her daughter's school. Everyone in their family – Christine, her partner and daughter – all got sick with the virus.

Within a few days, Christine – the hardest hit – was struggling to breathe. She was hospitalized and ended up in the intensive care unit.

Oscar, her new baby, was born via emergency C-section while she was intubated. For the first few days, she could only visit remotely via tablet.

"I remember them pulling the gas mask on me…and that's the last thing I remember. And then I woke up in the ICU no longer pregnant, and no longer remembering what had happened."

She wishes people would understand just how serious COVID-19 is. "I might be leaving the hospital after three weeks," she says. "But I still have a really long recovery."

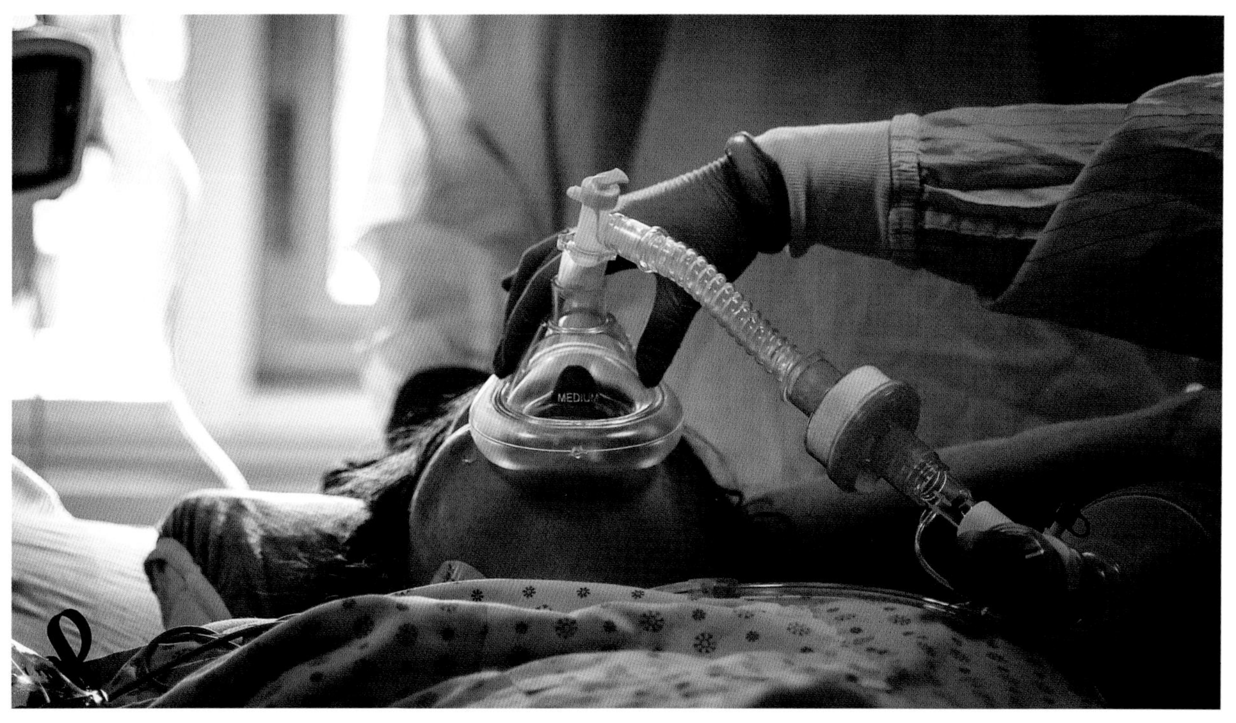

Dr. Natasha Goumeniouk, resident, prepares COVID-19 patient Christine Wesley for intubation in the intensive care unit at Peter Lougheed Centre in Calgary, Alberta.

Dr. Natasha Goumeniouk, resident, intubates COVID-19 patient Christine Wesley.

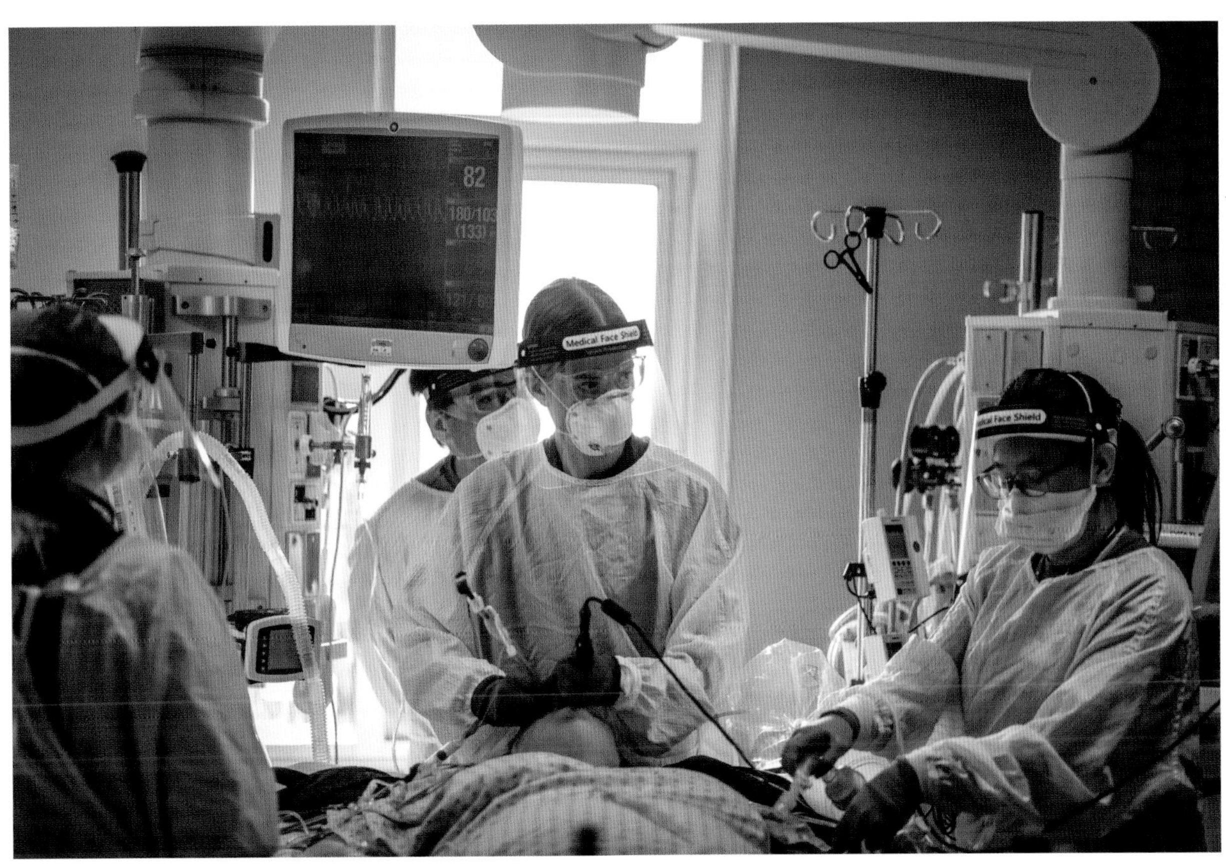
82
180/103
(133)
Medical Face Shield
Medical Face Shield

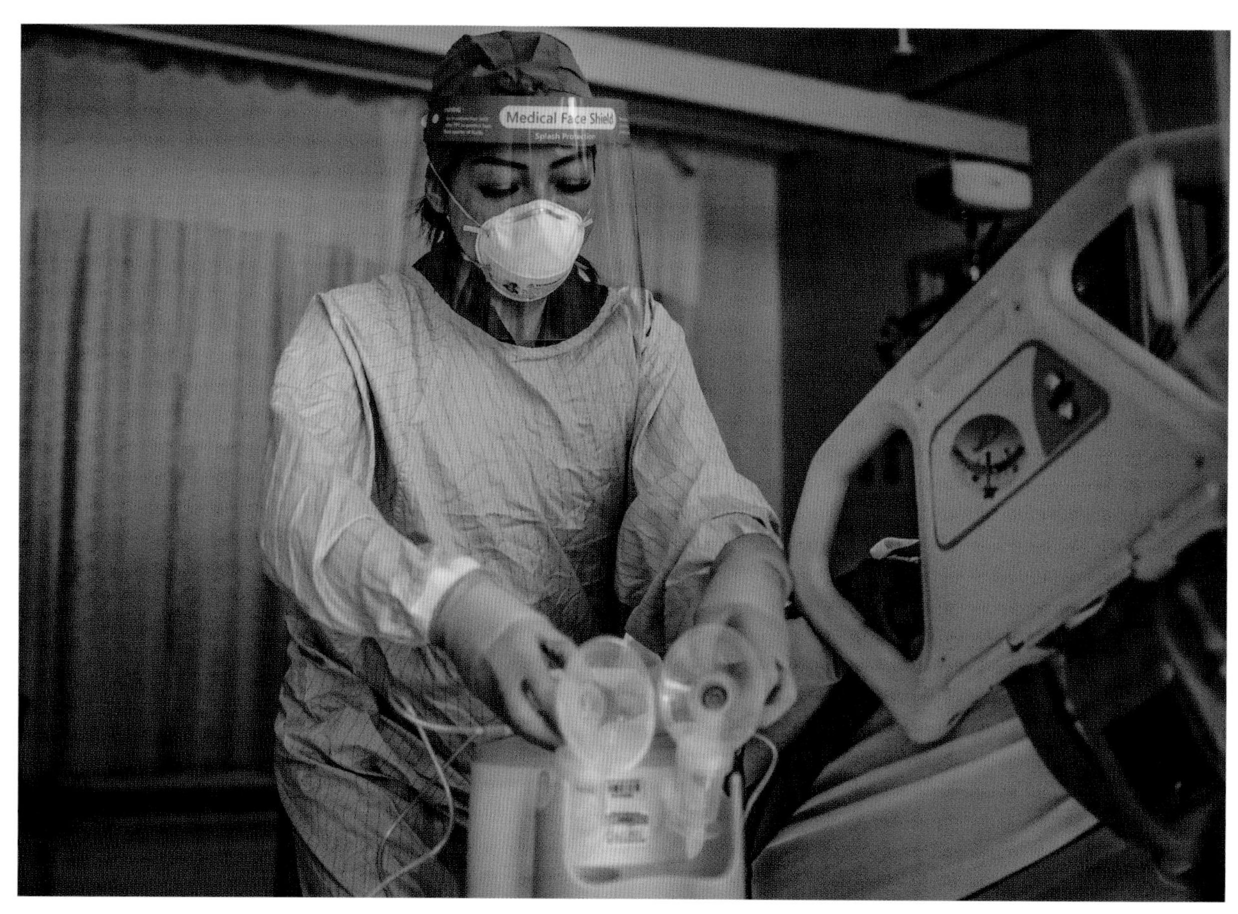

A registered nurse prepares a breast pump for a
COVID-19 patient.

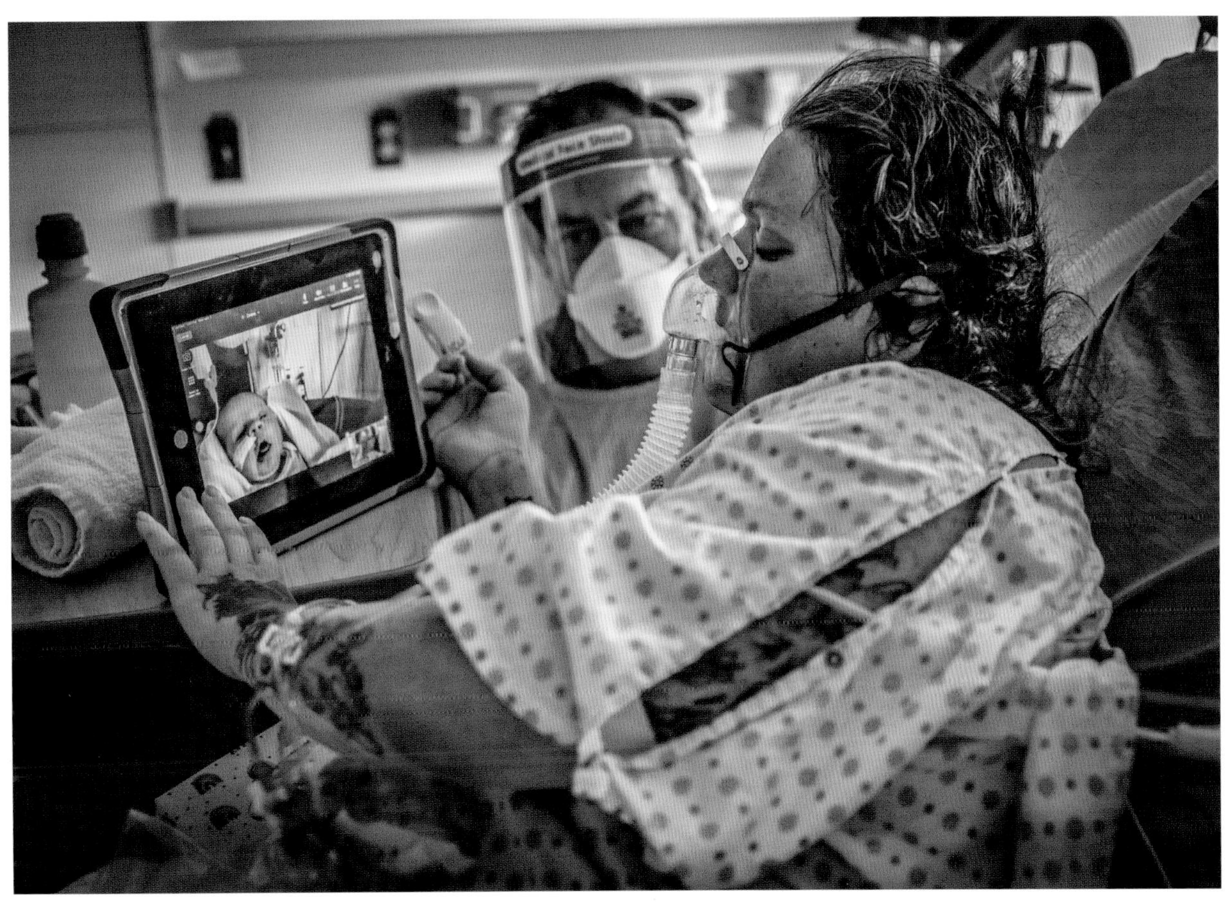

COVID-19 patient Christine Wesley, a 36-year-old
new mother, looks at her son Oscar on an iPad from
her room in the intensive care unit at Peter Lougheed
Centre. With her is volunteer Daniel Hughes.

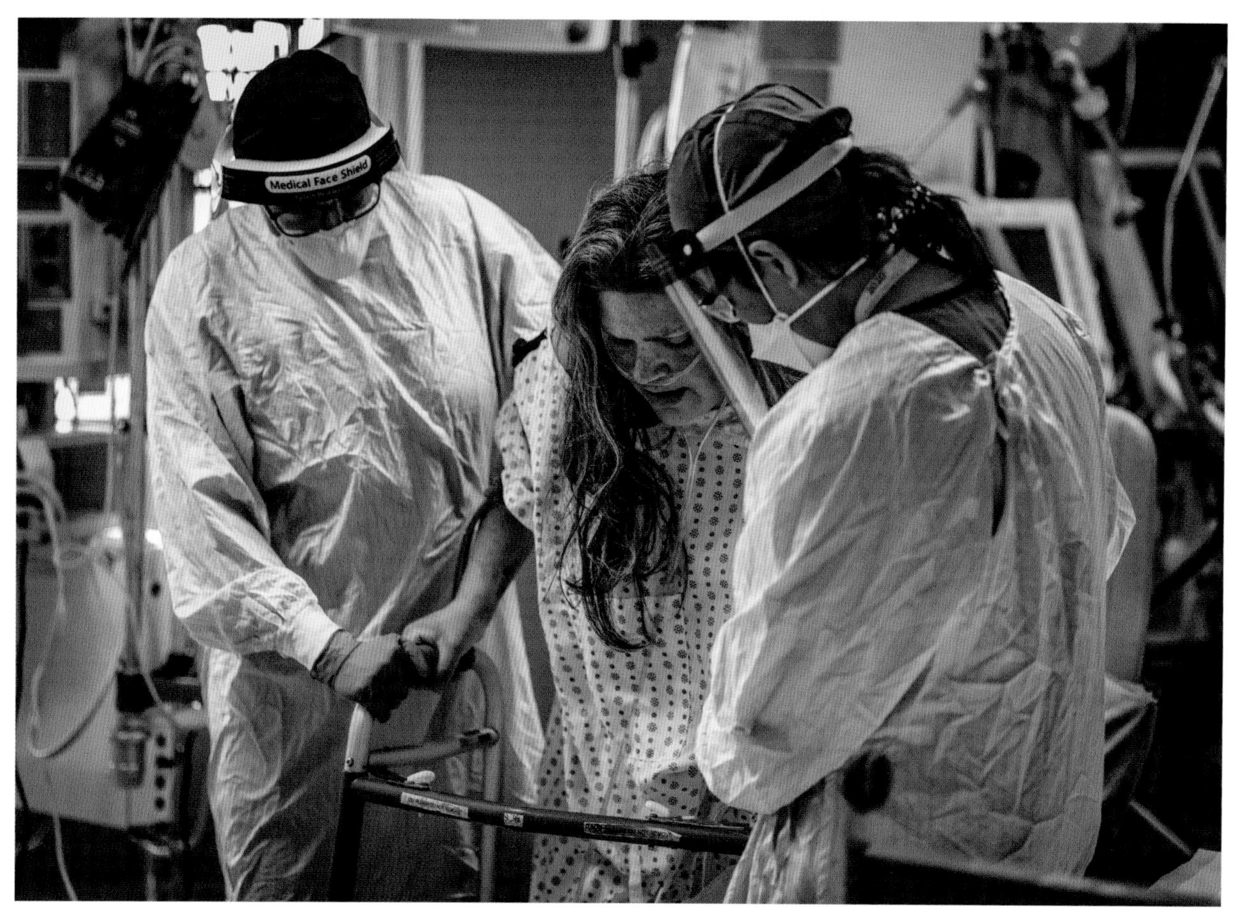

Christine Wesley, a new mother and a
COVID-19 patient, gets help from the
healthcare team.

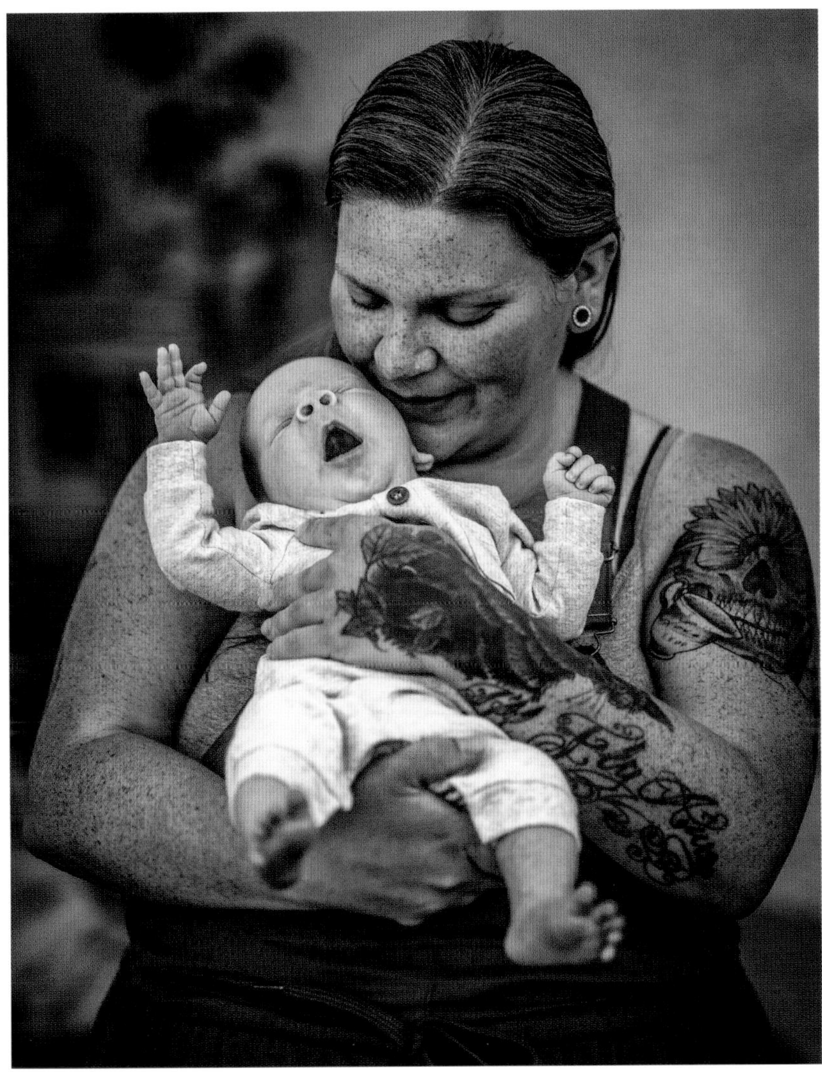

Christine Wesley, a 36-year-old new mother recovering from COVID-19, cuddles with her baby boy Oscar at her Calgary home in May 2021.

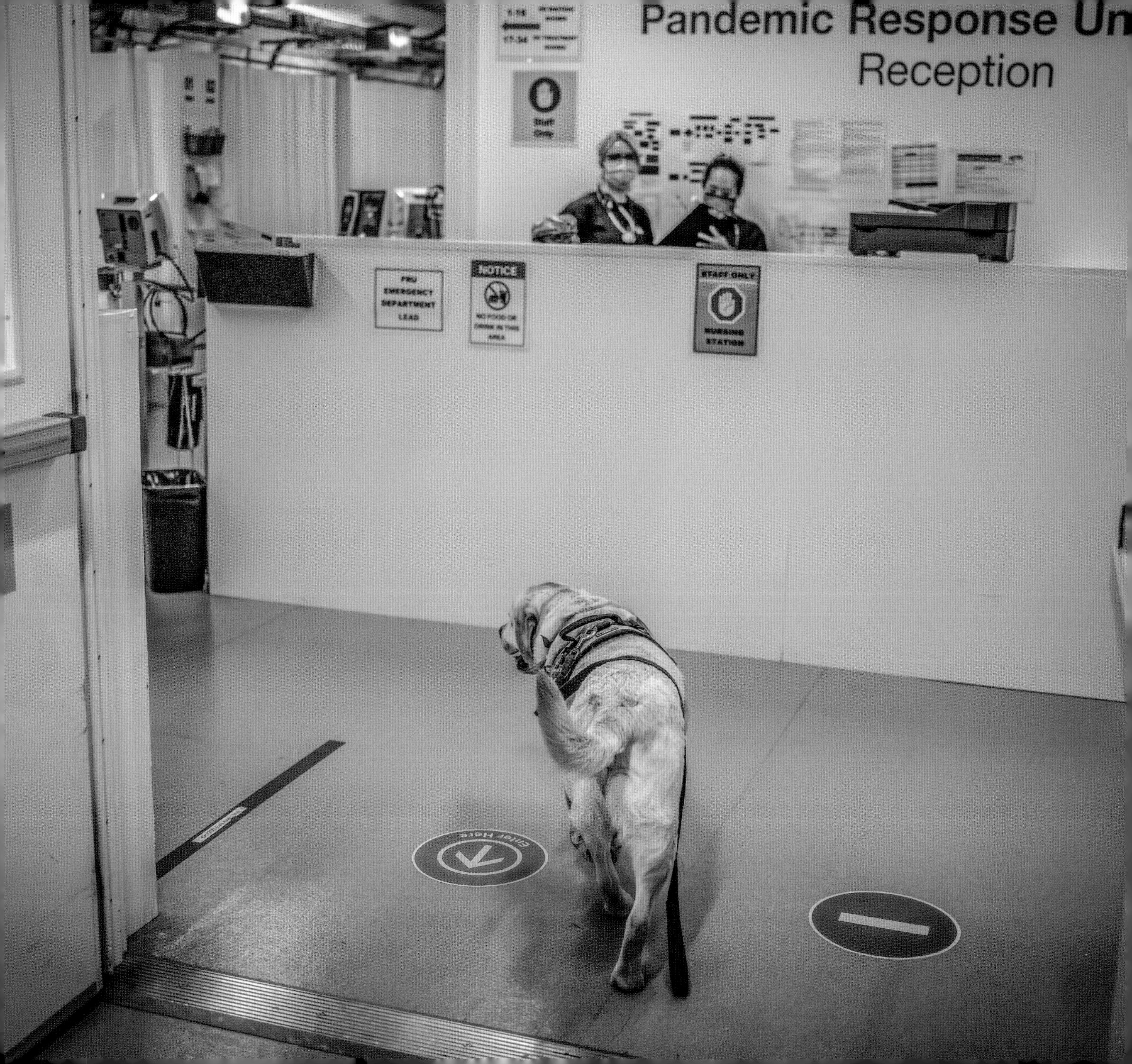

Pandemic Response Un
Reception
Staff Only
PRU
EMERGENCY
DEPARTMENT
LEAD
NOTICE
NO FOOD OR
DRINK IN THIS
AREA
STAFF ONLY
NURSING
STATION
Enter Here

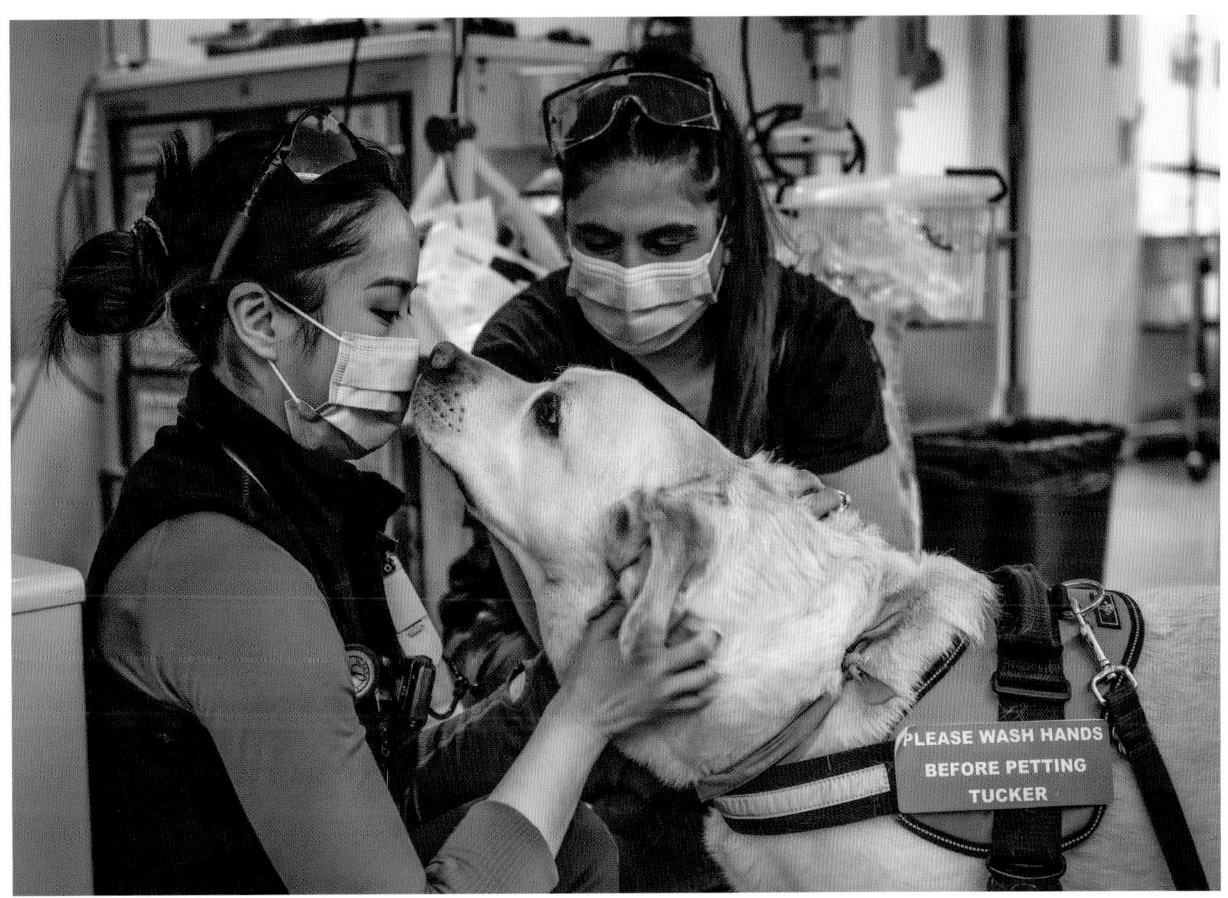

Tucker, a 6-year-old English Labrador retriever, visits staff in the Sprung Pandemic Response Unit at Peter Lougheed Centre in May 2021.

Tucker visits respiratory therapists Vanessa Sim, left, and Anisha Kumar in the emergency department at Peter Lougheed Centre in May 2021.

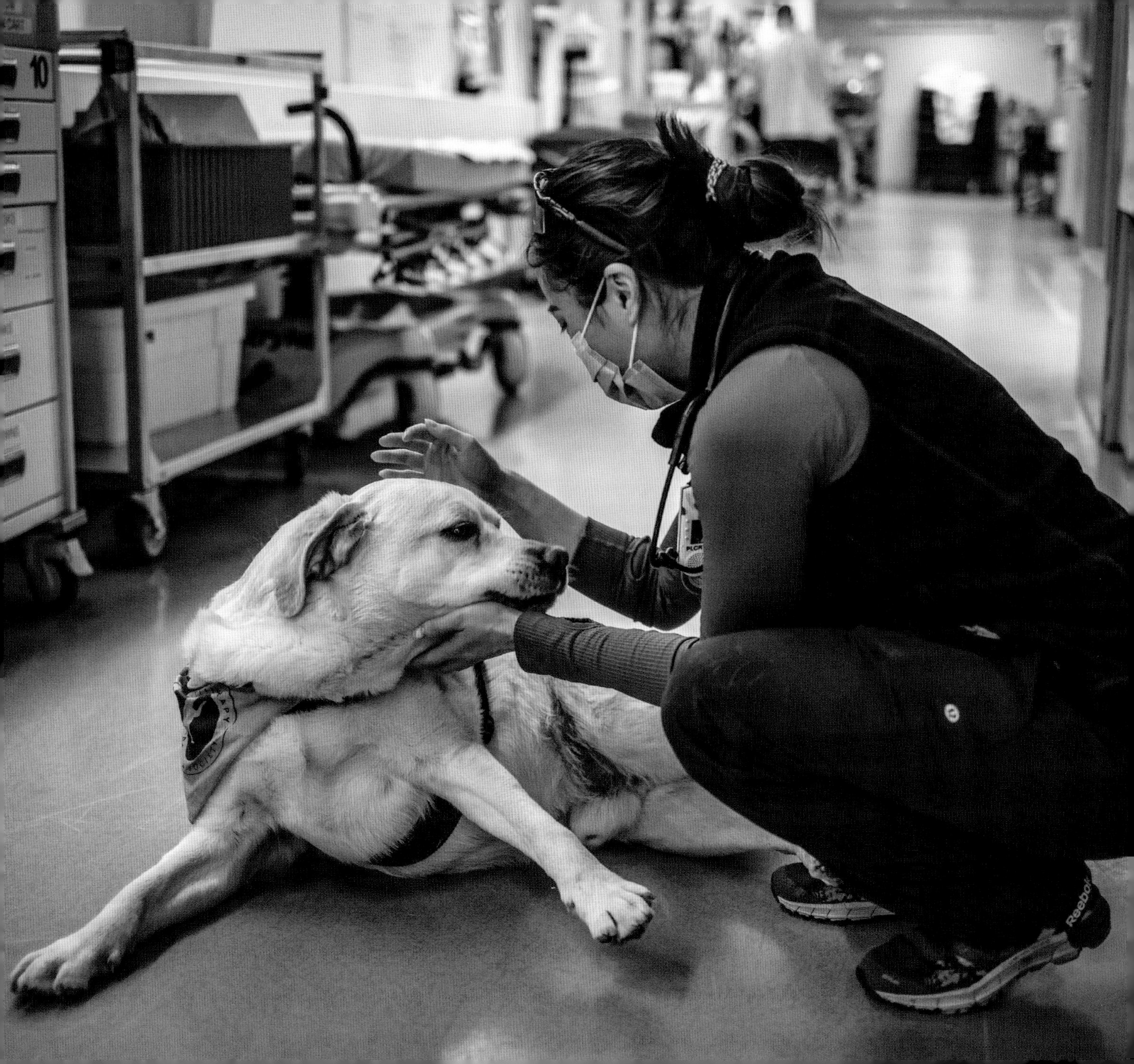

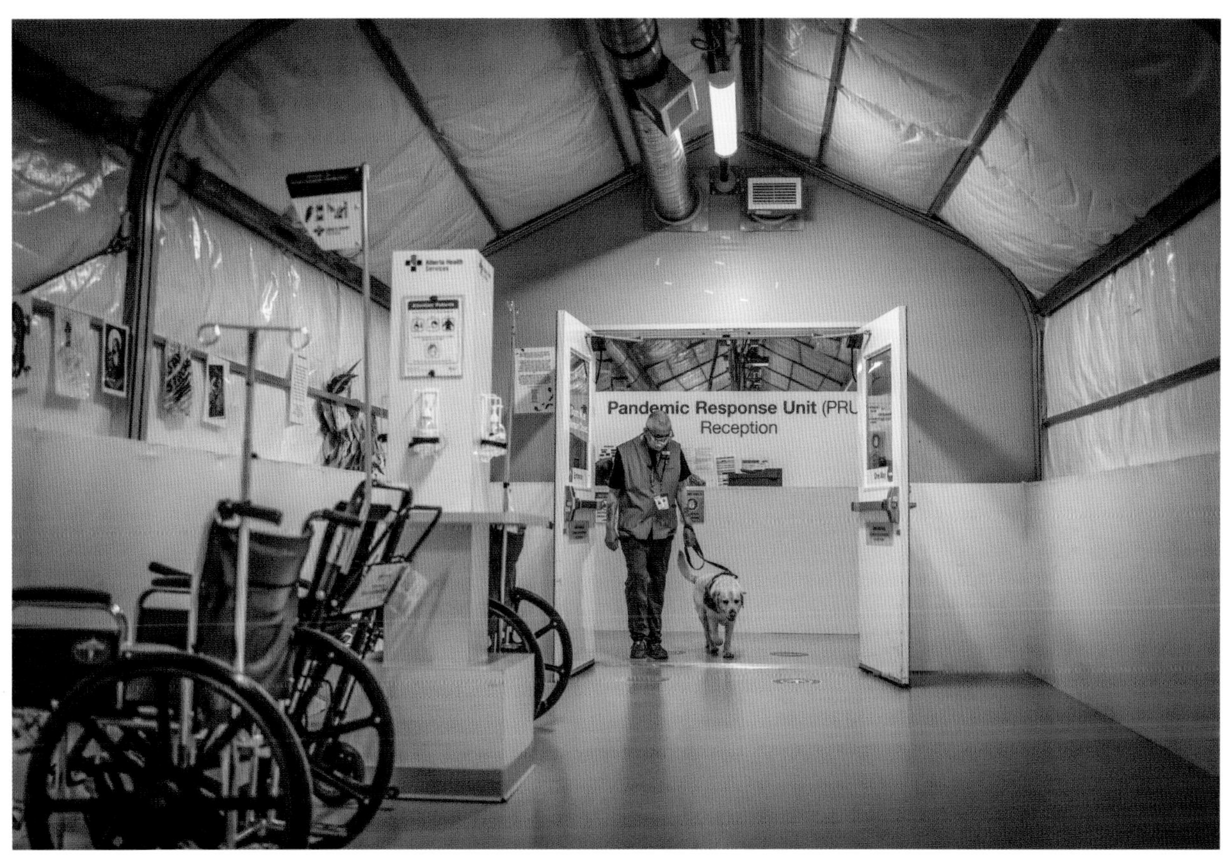

Tucker, a 6-year-old English Labrador retriever, visits respiratory therapist Vanessa Sim in the emergency department at Peter Lougheed Centre in May 2021.

Volunteer Larry Goertzen and Tucker leave the Sprung Pandemic Response Unit at Peter Lougheed Centre after visiting staff in May 2021.

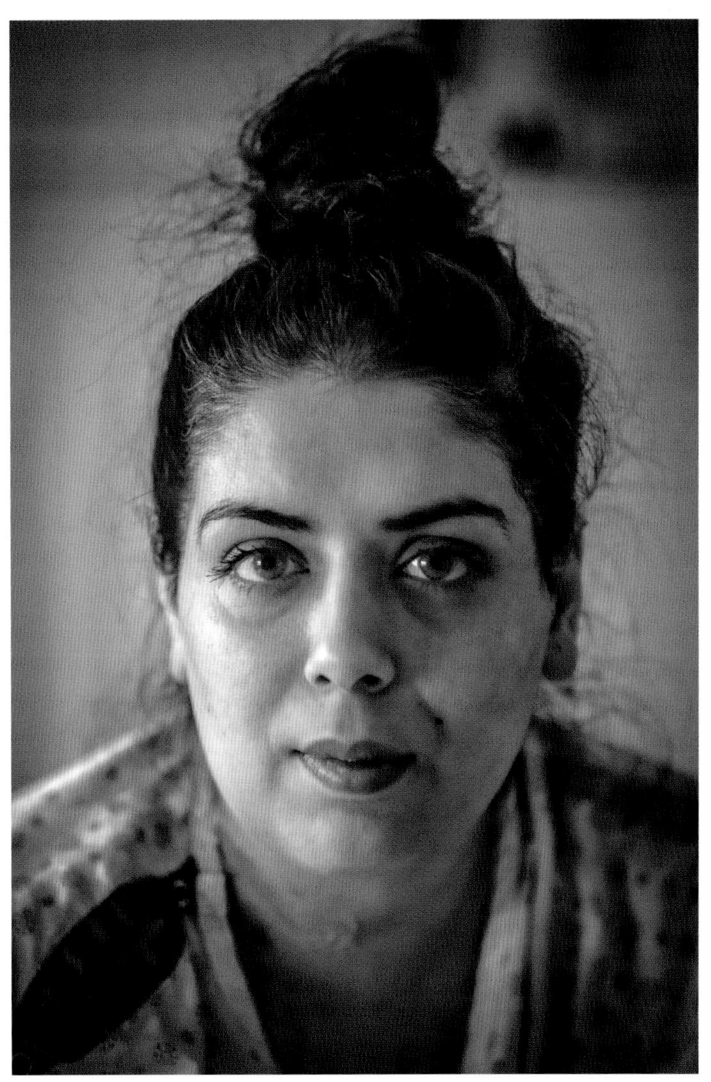

Sabbohi Asif, 29, recovered in the COVID-19 unit at Rockyview General Hospital in May 2021.

"I thought of COVID-19 as something that was stopping my life from happening. I was one of those people that did not take it seriously at all," says Asif.

Then, in early May, COVID-19 almost did stop Asif's life. She tested positive and only a couple of days later, she was in the Rockyview General Hospital's COVID-19 unit, unable to breathe. She spent two weeks on a ventilator, and she spent a long time in the hospital, recovering.

"Before coming here, what mattered the most was my career, my education, that kind of stuff," she says. "Now my entire purpose in life has changed completely. I'm going to spend the rest of my life serving humanity."

"I owe my second life to these guys," she says, gesturing toward the frontline healthcare workers who have been taking care of her. "I'm going to do what they do."

"They didn't just provide free healthcare. They gave me emotional support. They provided my husband with emotional support. They are like family to us."

Asif does an oxygen level test with registered nurse Diana Huynh.

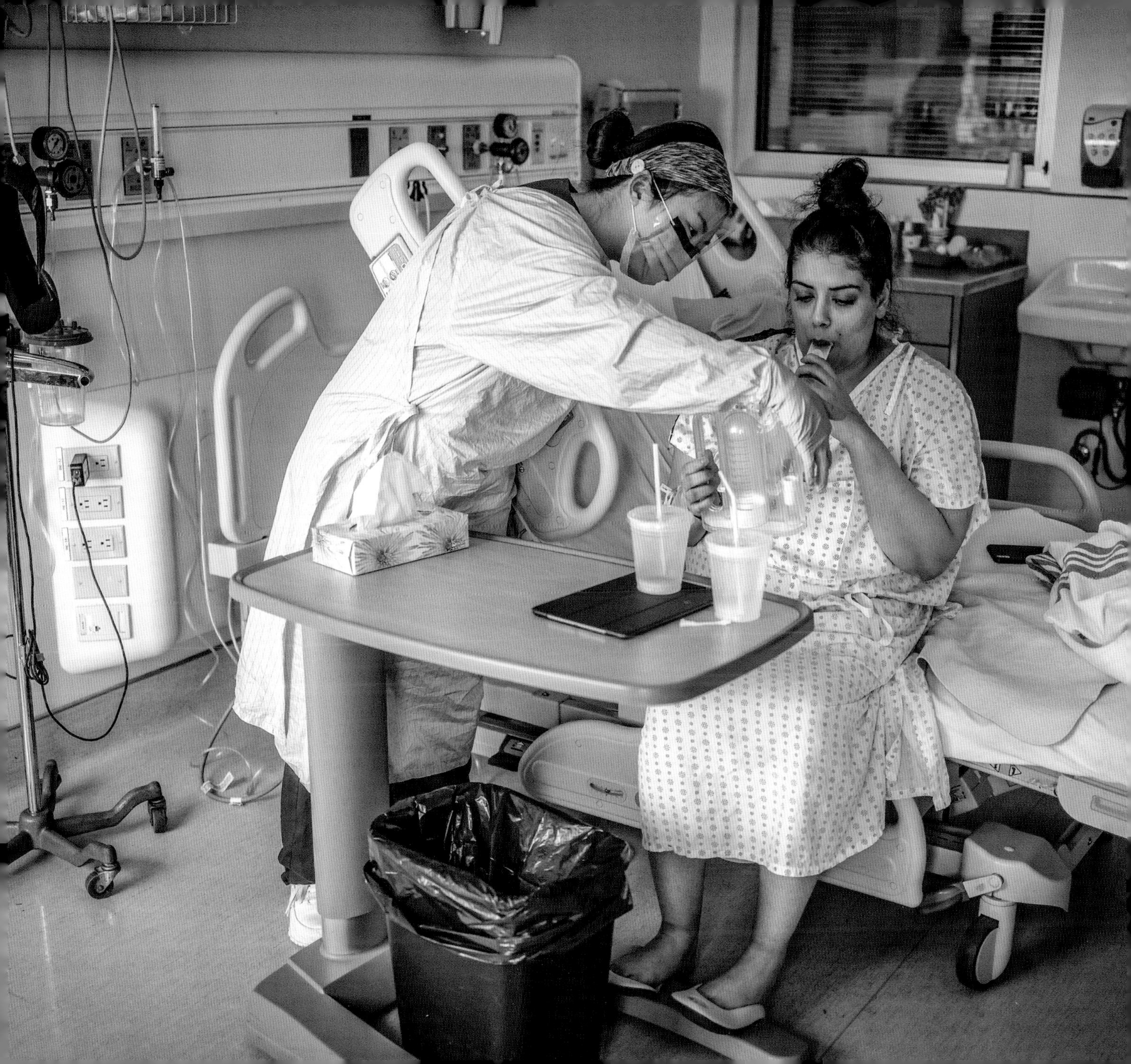

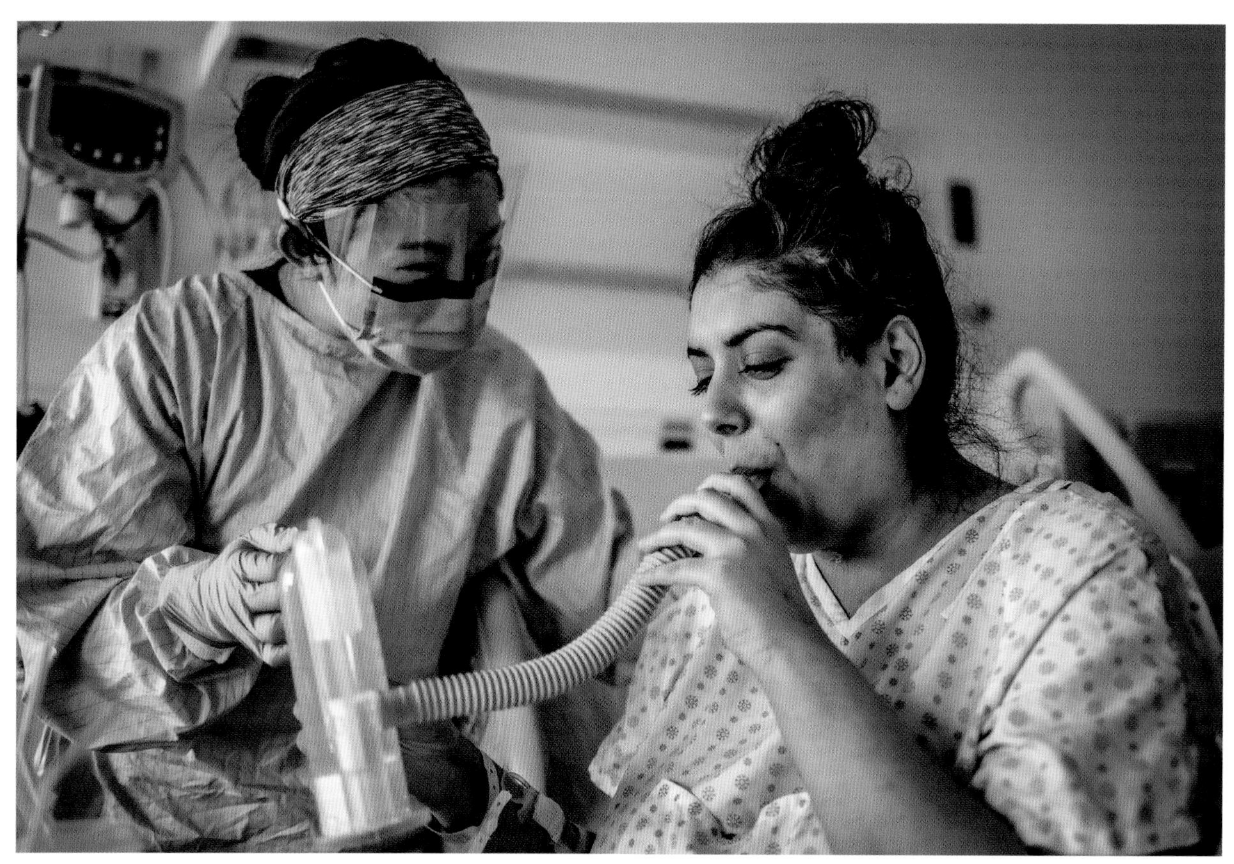

Sabbohi Asif, 29, recovering from COVID-19,
does an oxygen level test with registered
nurse Diana Huynh at Rockyview General
Hospital in May 2021.

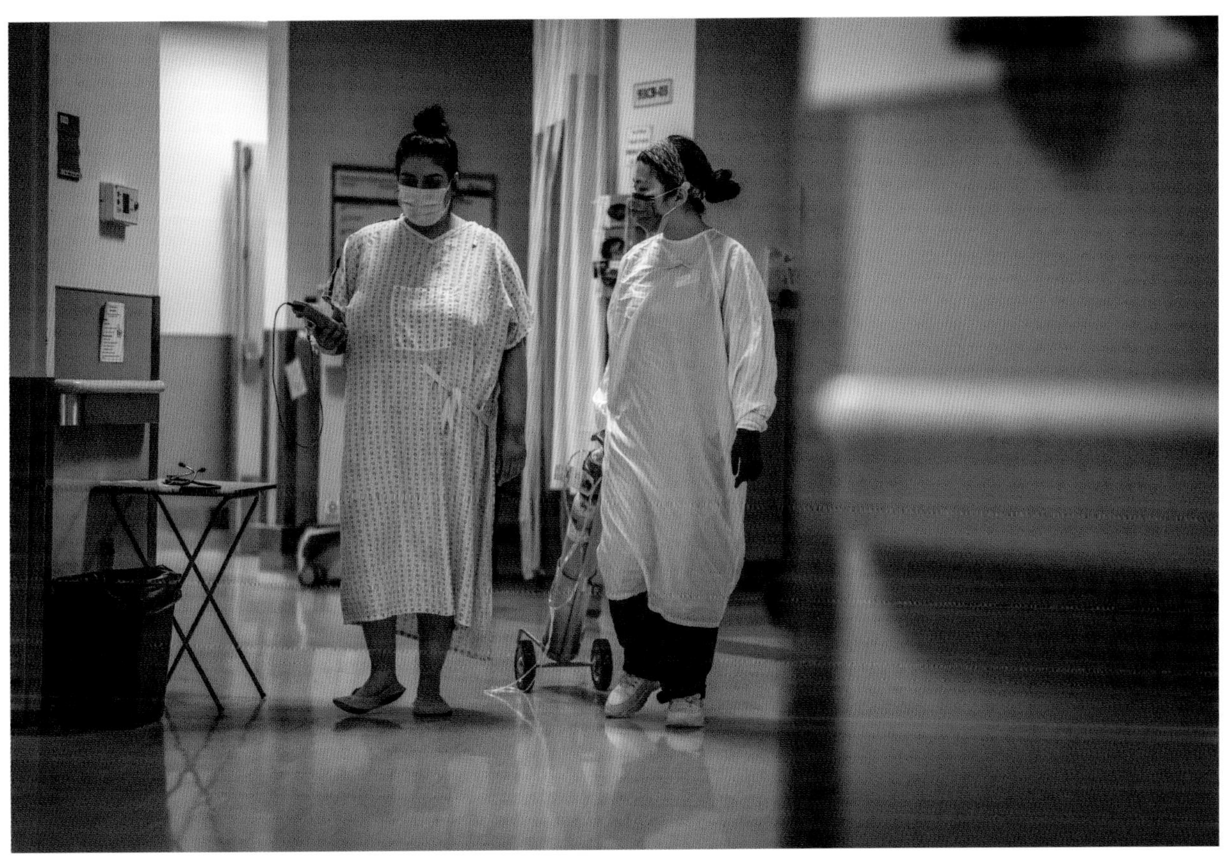

Sabbohi Asif, 29, recovering from COVID-19,
walks with registered nurse Diana Huynh at
Rockyview General Hospital on May 27, 2021.

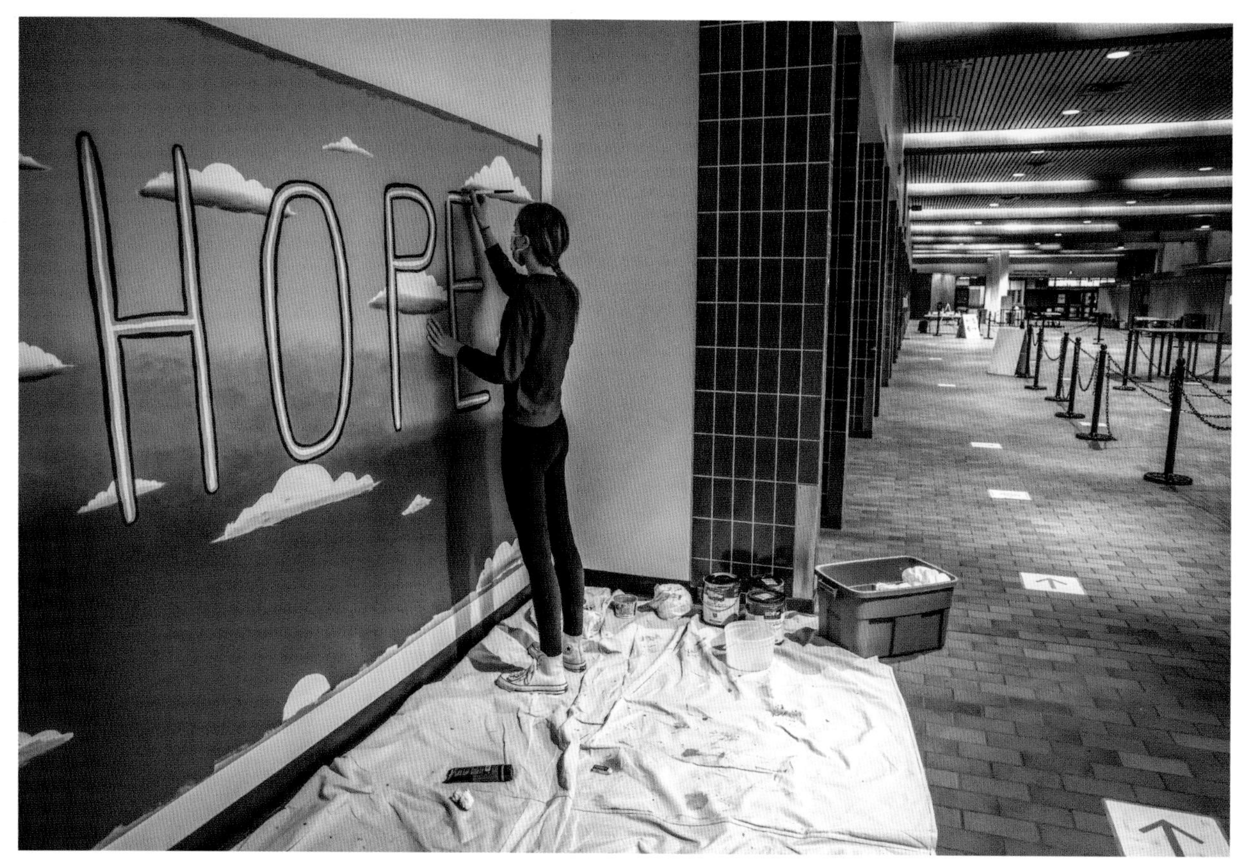

Muriel Charlebois, 14, paints her mural of hope inside the Alberta Health Services COVID-19 testing facility in the former Greyhound bus station in Calgary, Alberta, in 2021.

"It's mainly focused on spreading positivity in the community," says Charlebois.

Nalvia Recabarren, an intensive care unit clinician at Peter Lougheed Centre, shows her excitement as she waits in line to get her COVID-19 vaccine in Calgary, Alberta, in December 2020.

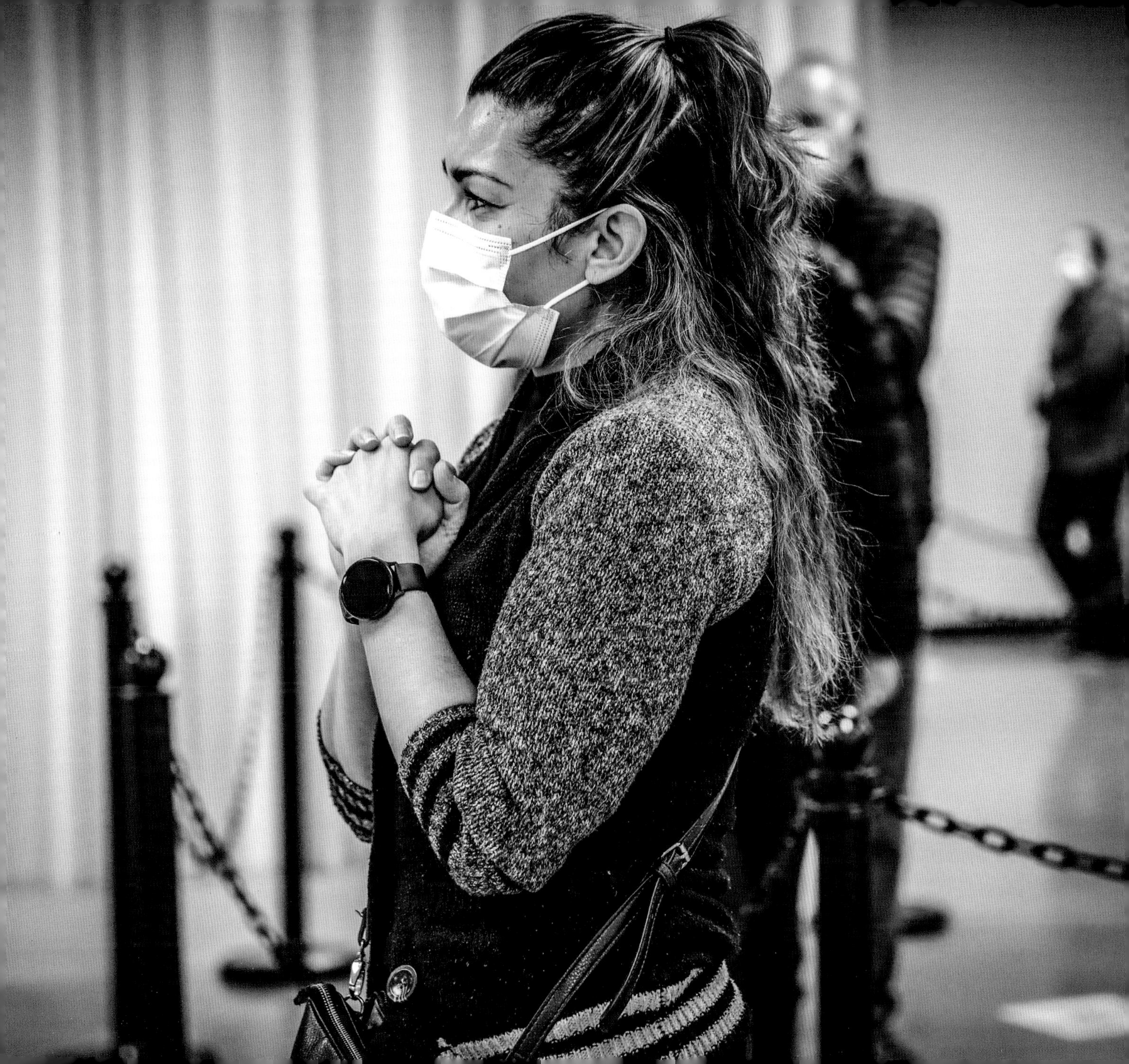

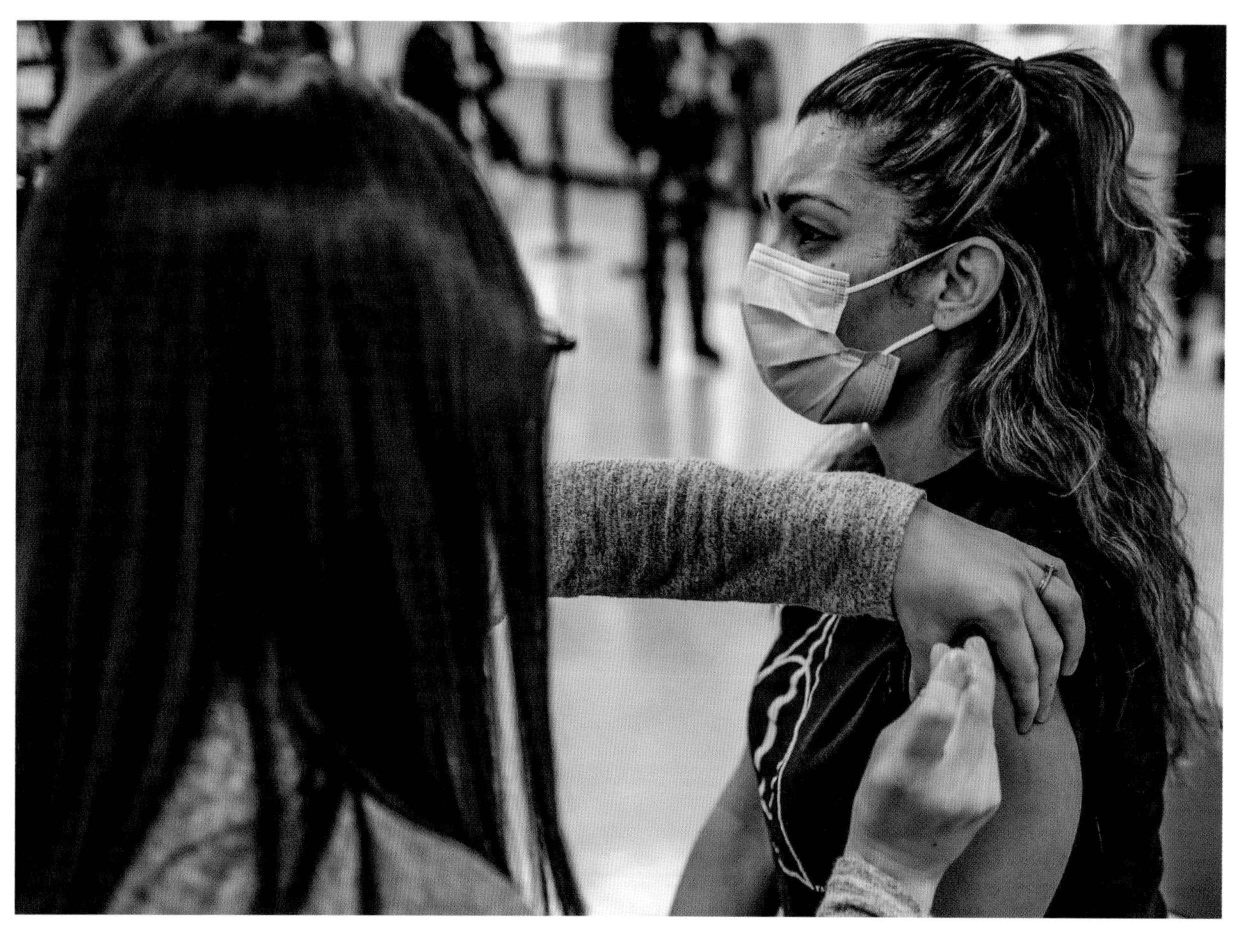

Nalvia Recabarren, an intensive care unit
clinician at Peter Lougheed Centre, is emotional as she receives her COVID-19 vaccine
in Calgary, Alberta, in December 2020.

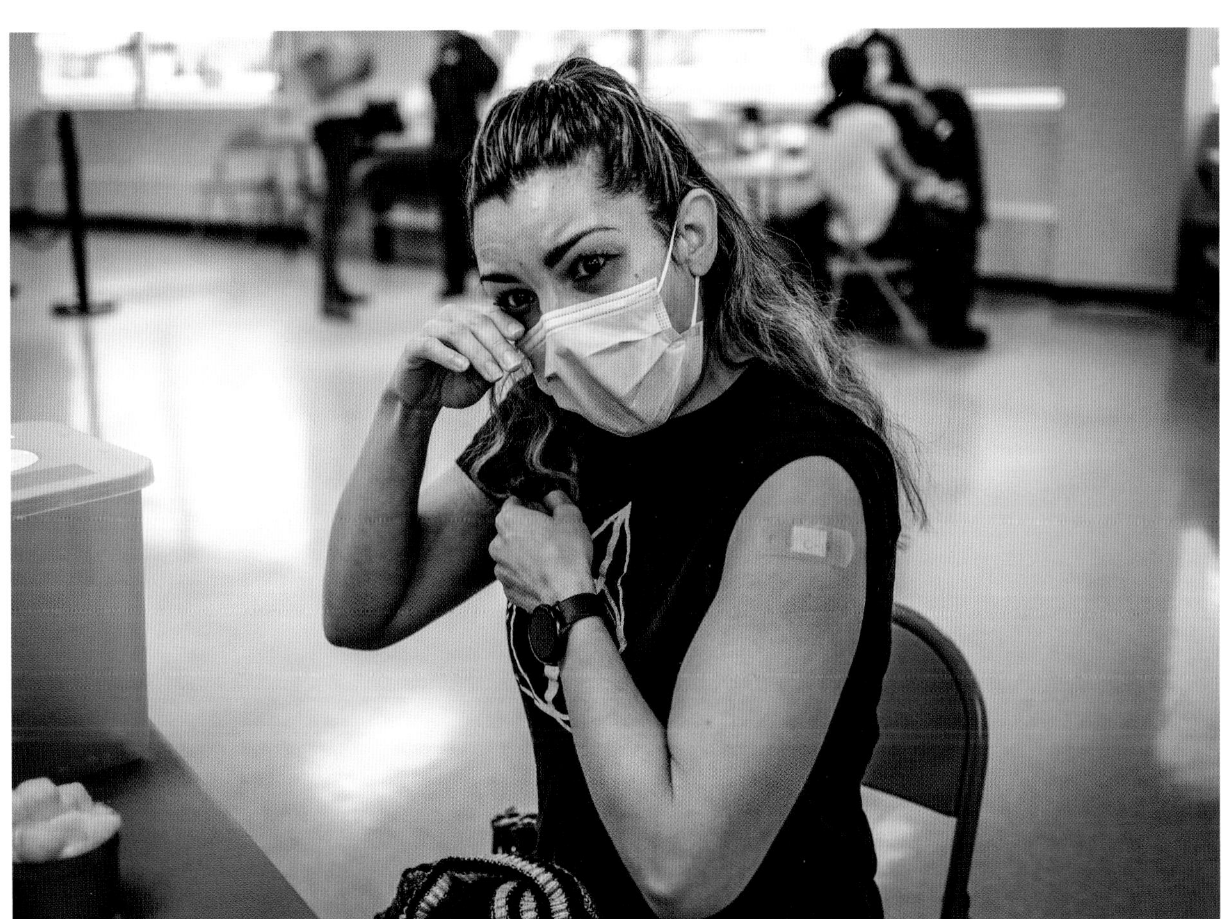

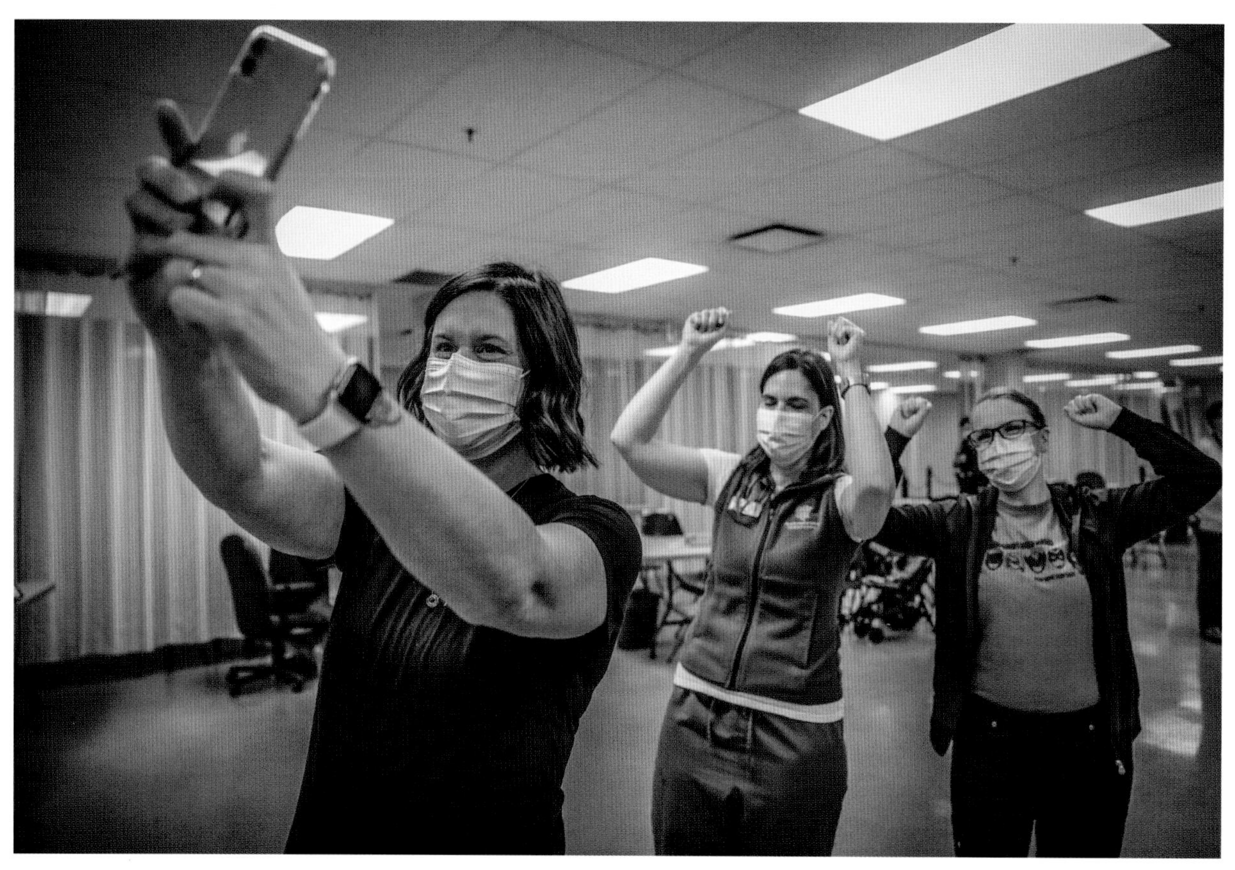

Intensive care registered nurse Tanya Harvey, left, takes
a selfie with fellow nurses Shannon Kralka and Jennifer
McKnight after all three received their COVID-19
vaccines in Calgary, Alberta, on December 15, 2020.
Harvey was the first person in Calgary to get the shot.

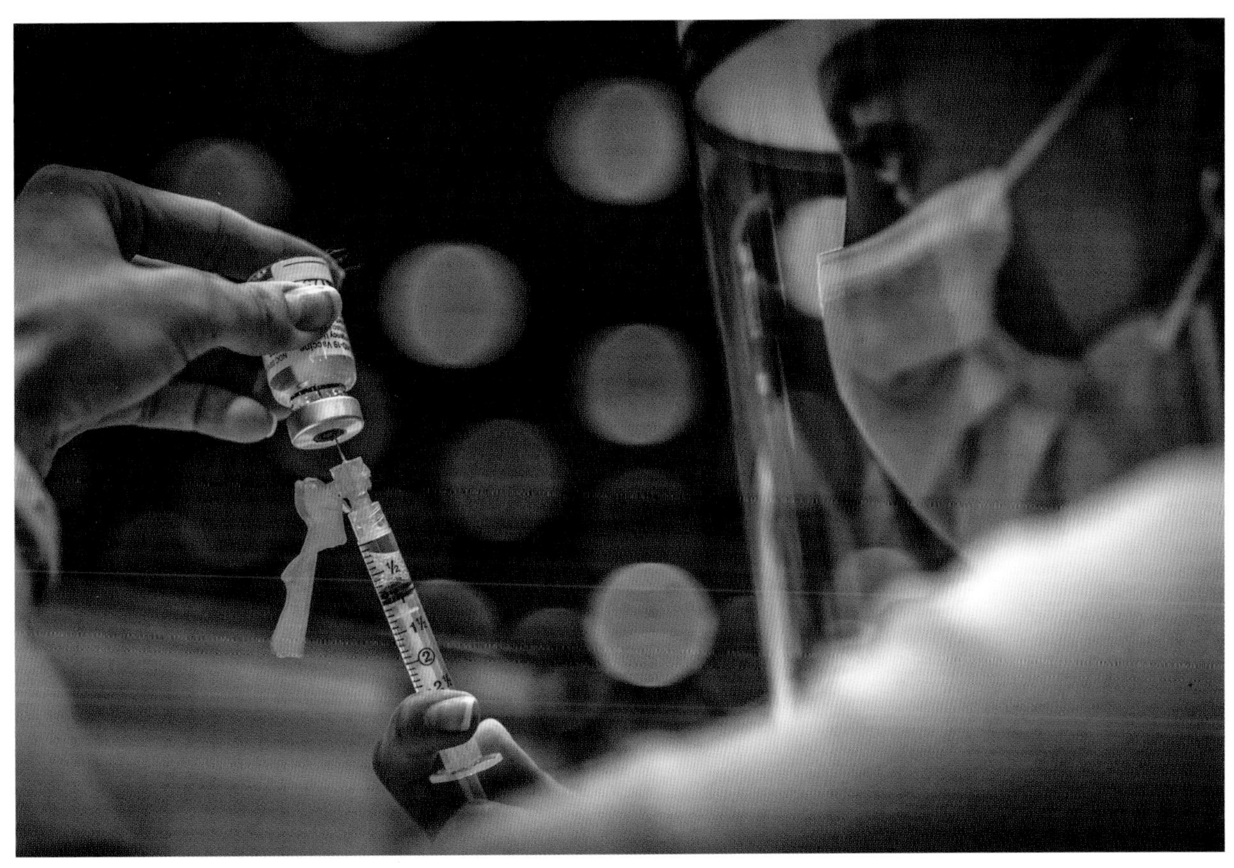

A nurse preps a COVID-19 vaccine.

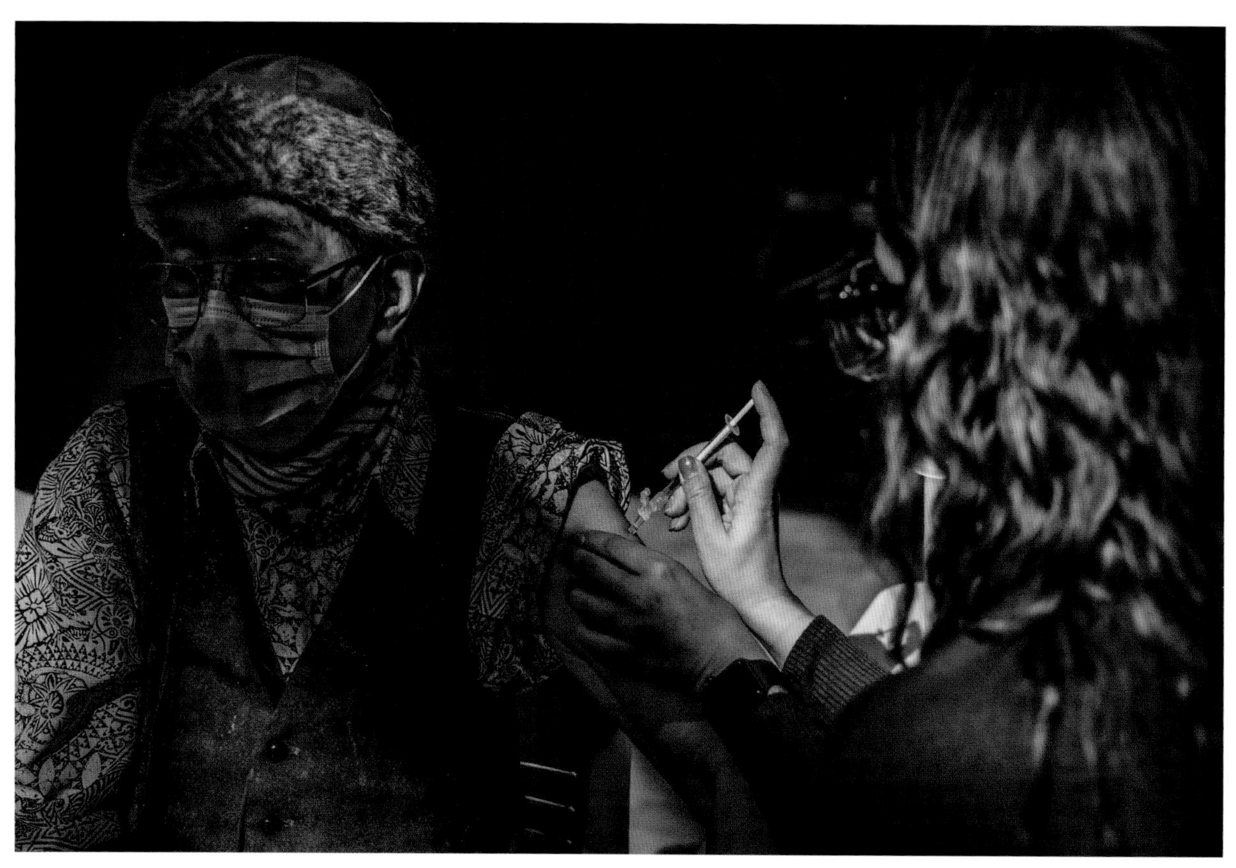

Mark Pun, 92, receives the COVID-19
vaccine from registered nurse
Shanaya Aujla in March 2021.

Sister Margaret Nadeau, 85, receives
her COVID-19 vaccine in Calgary,
Alberta, in February 2021.

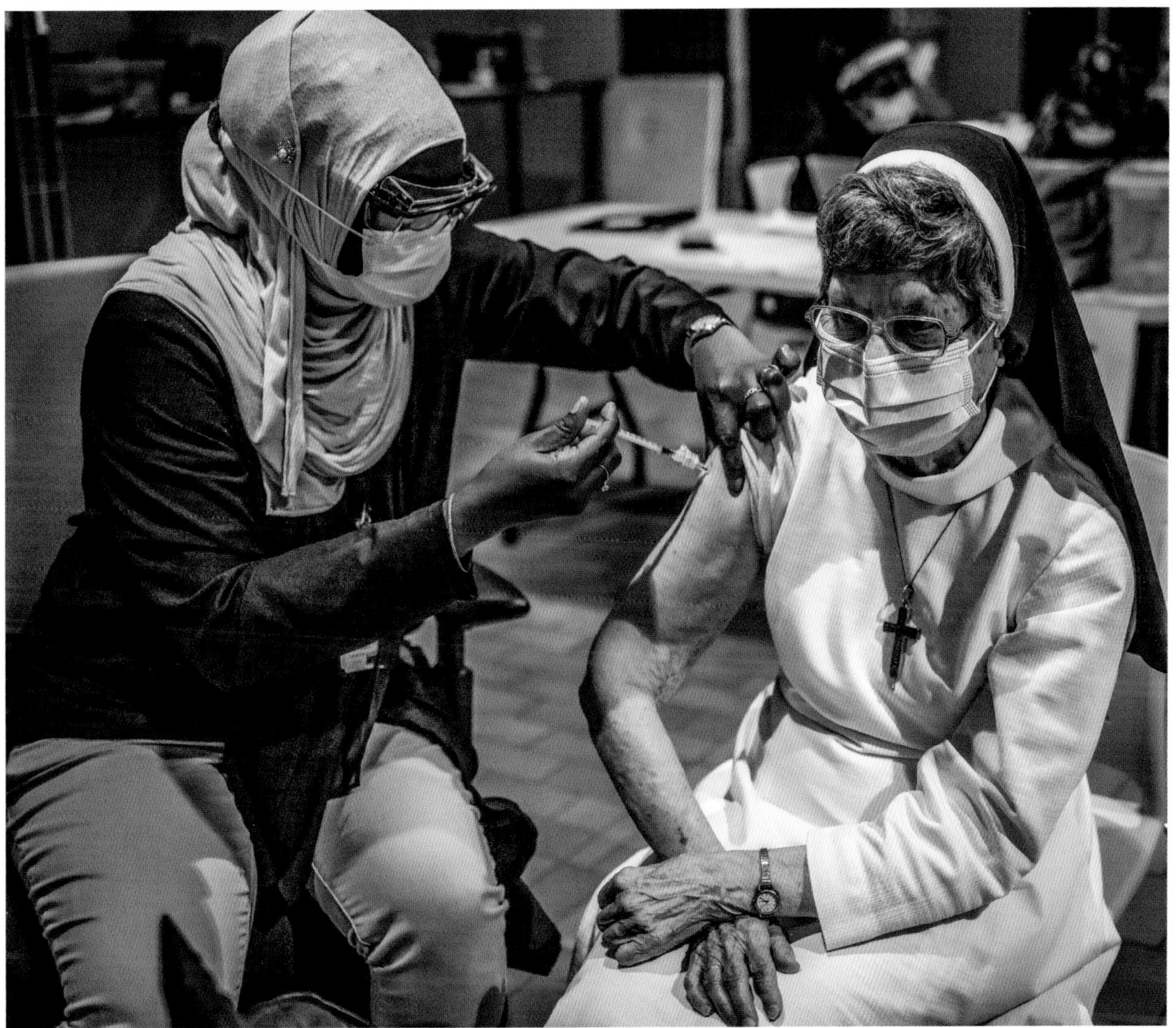

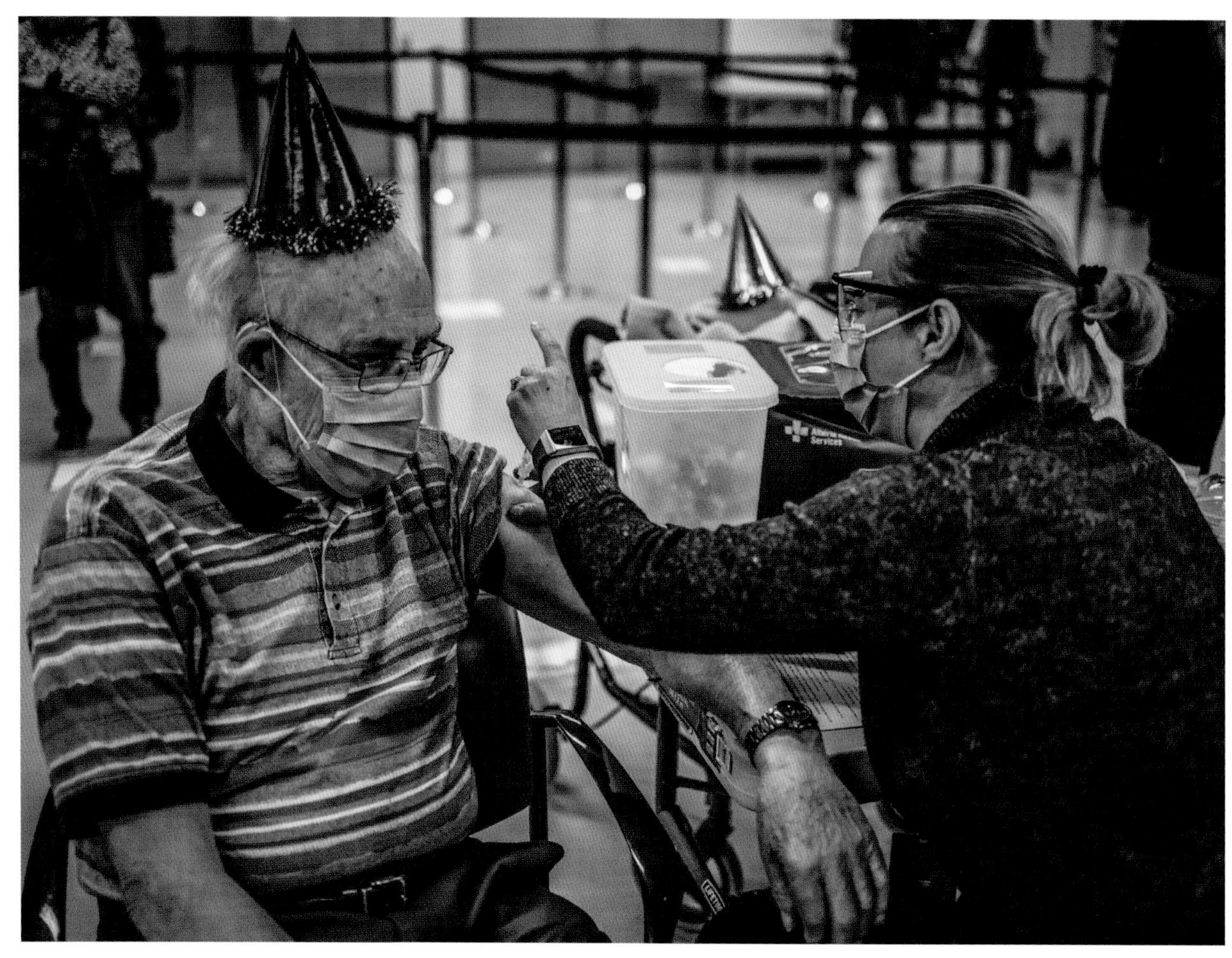

Karl Kuhnlein, 90, wears a party hat to celebrate
his COVID-19 vaccination in February 2021.

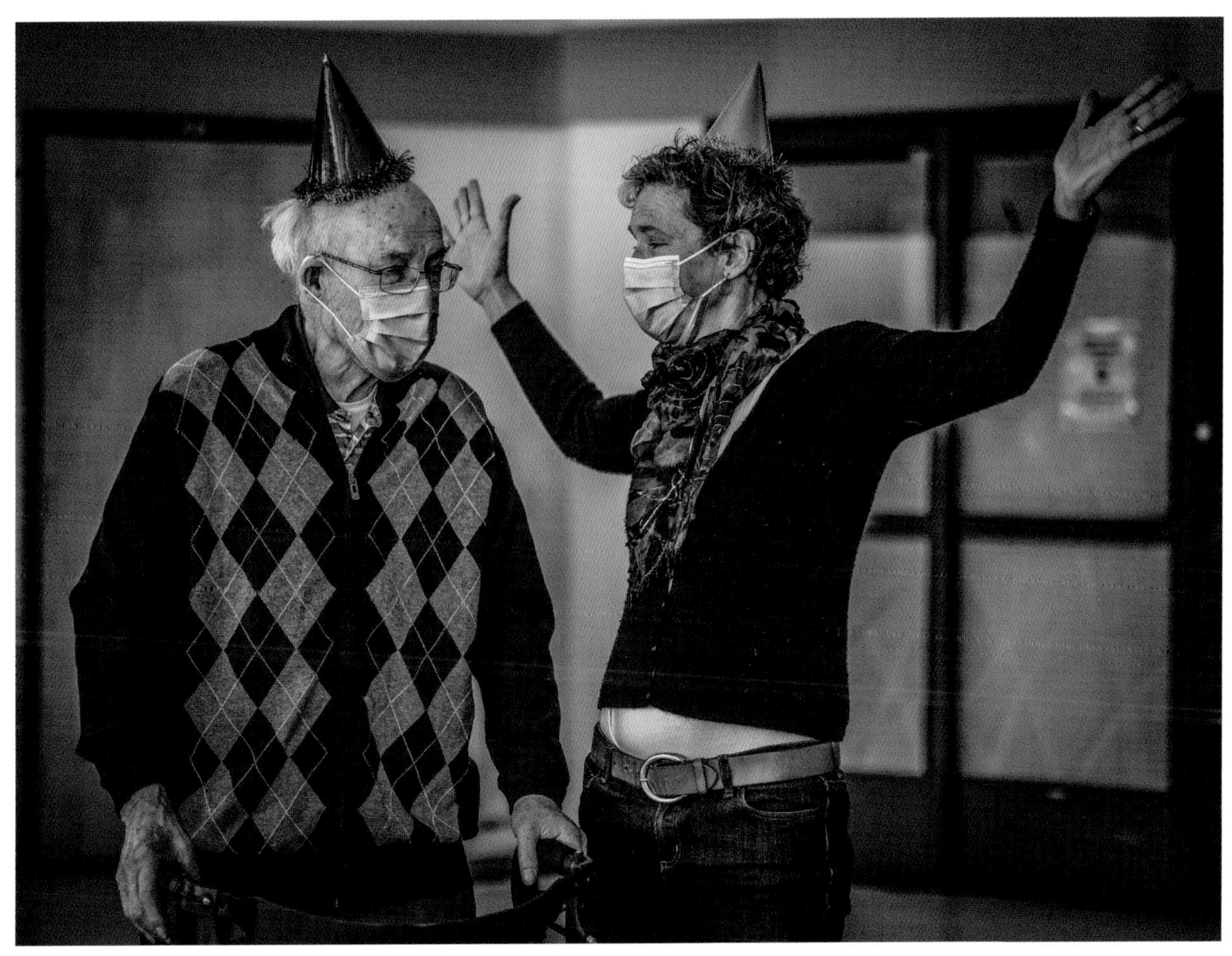

Karl Kuhnlein, 90, and his daughter-in-law Betty
Ann Lough wear party hats to celebrate Karl's
COVID-19 vaccination.

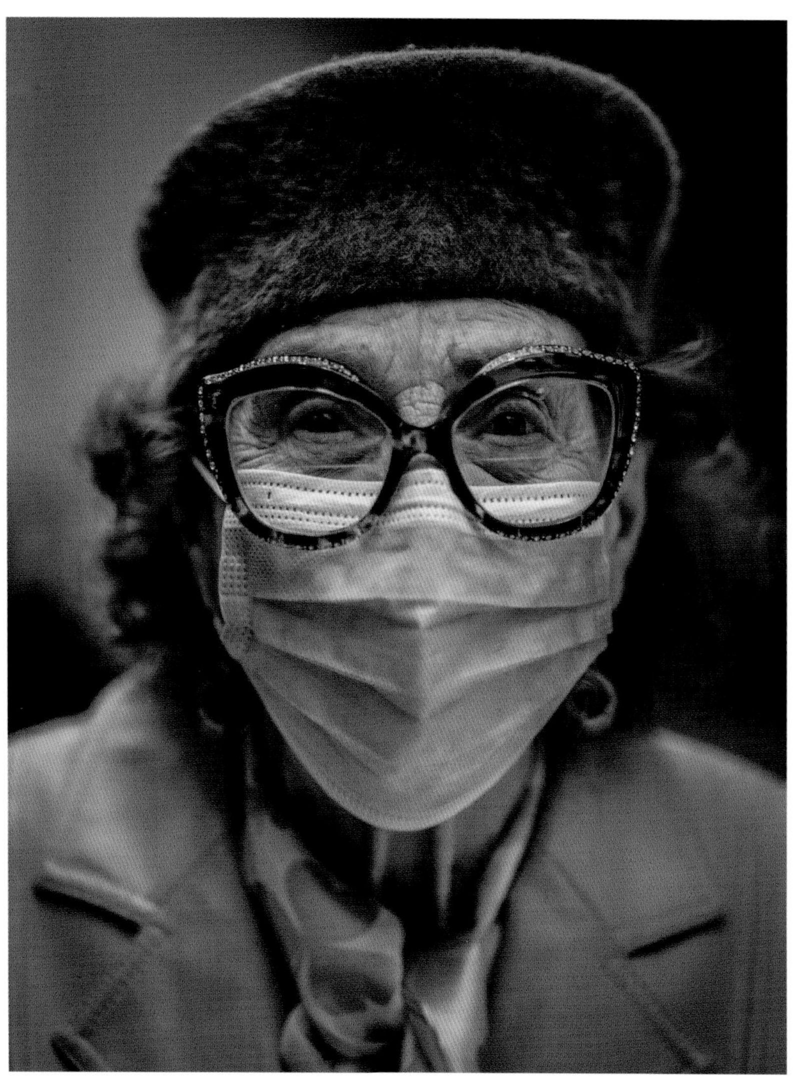

A portrait of Louise Smyth, 97, during the pandemic.

Smyth receives her second Pfizer vaccine from nurse Suzanne Pajot-Phipps in Calgary, Alberta, on April 23, 2021.

Over the years, Smyth has travelled to England, France, Germany, Italy, Japan, New Zealand and Australia. And now, after receiving her second COVID-19 vaccine, she's travelled to the grocery store. "My family provided all my food supplies during the pandemic," she says.

She's looking forward to eventually really travelling again: "I have sisters, nieces, nephews all over Canada. My best friend, she's 103. Having the FaceTime is great, because you get to see them...but we'll be able to go back to visiting people, and hugging. Some normalcy."

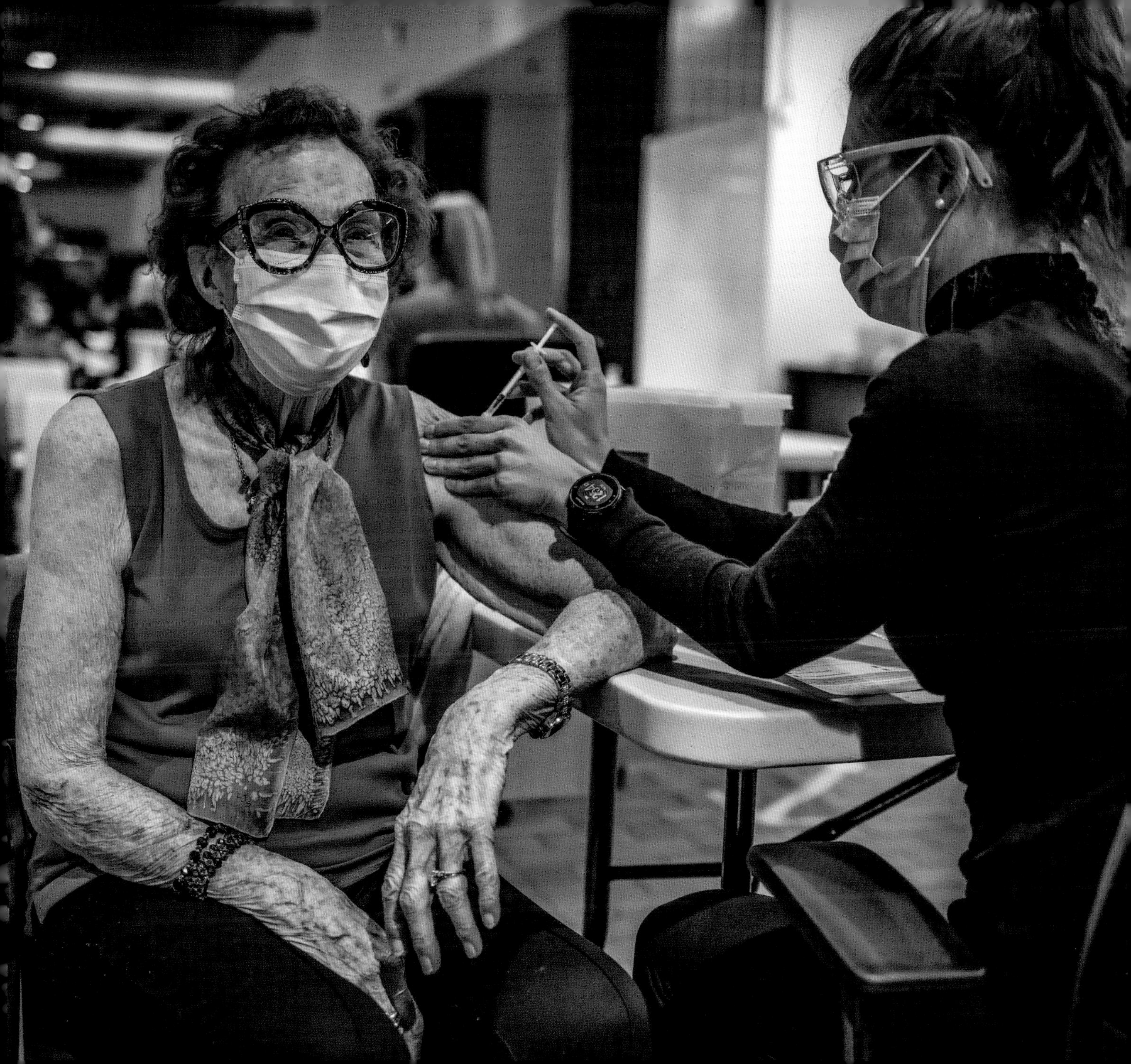

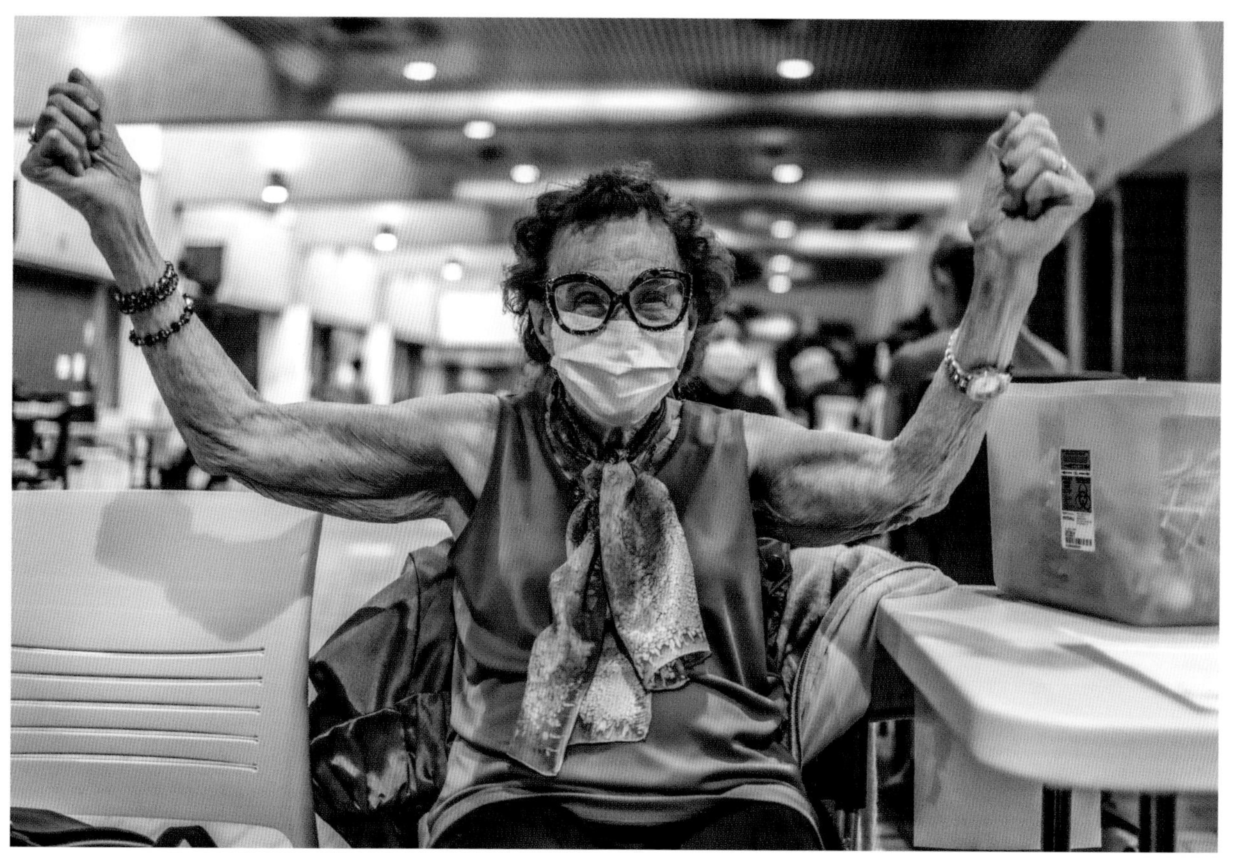

Louise Smyth, 97, is excited after receiving her second Pfizer vaccine in April 2021.

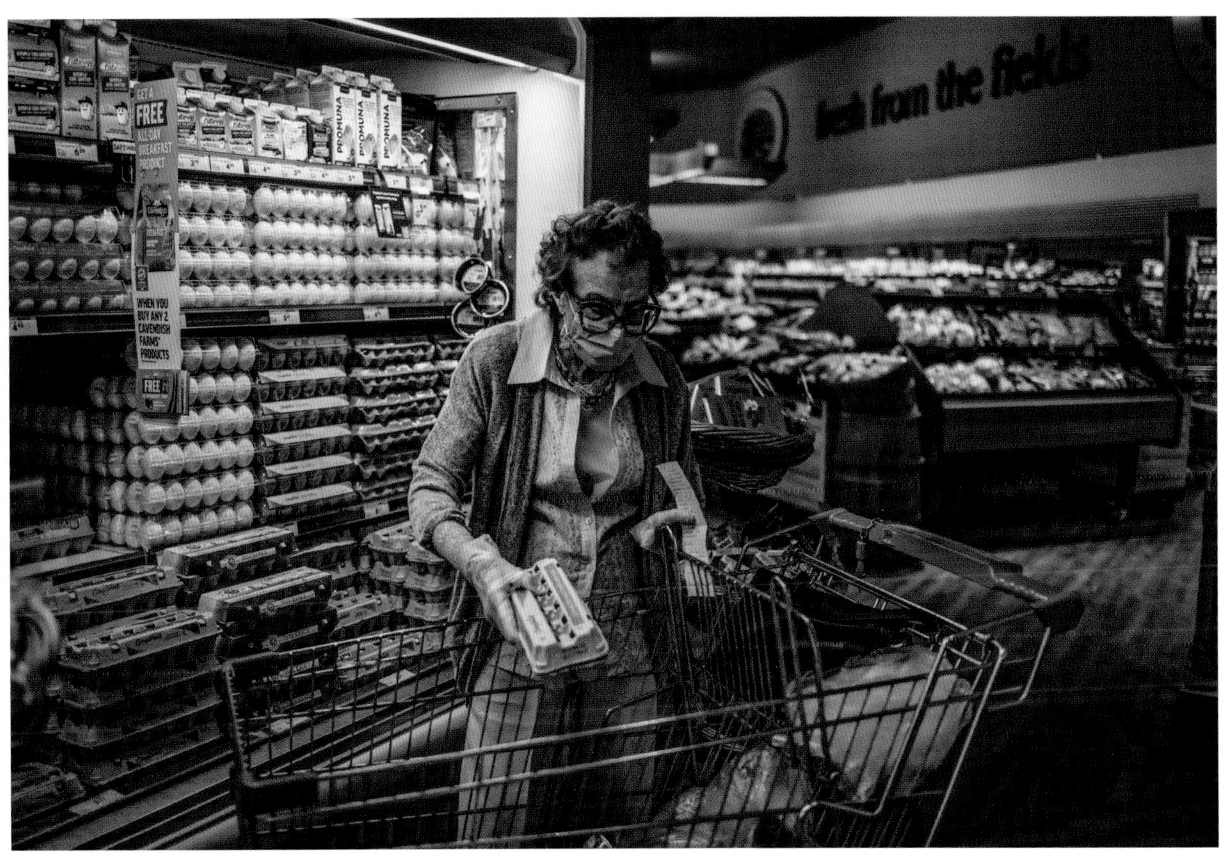

Louise Smyth, wearing gloves and mask,
does her grocery shopping.

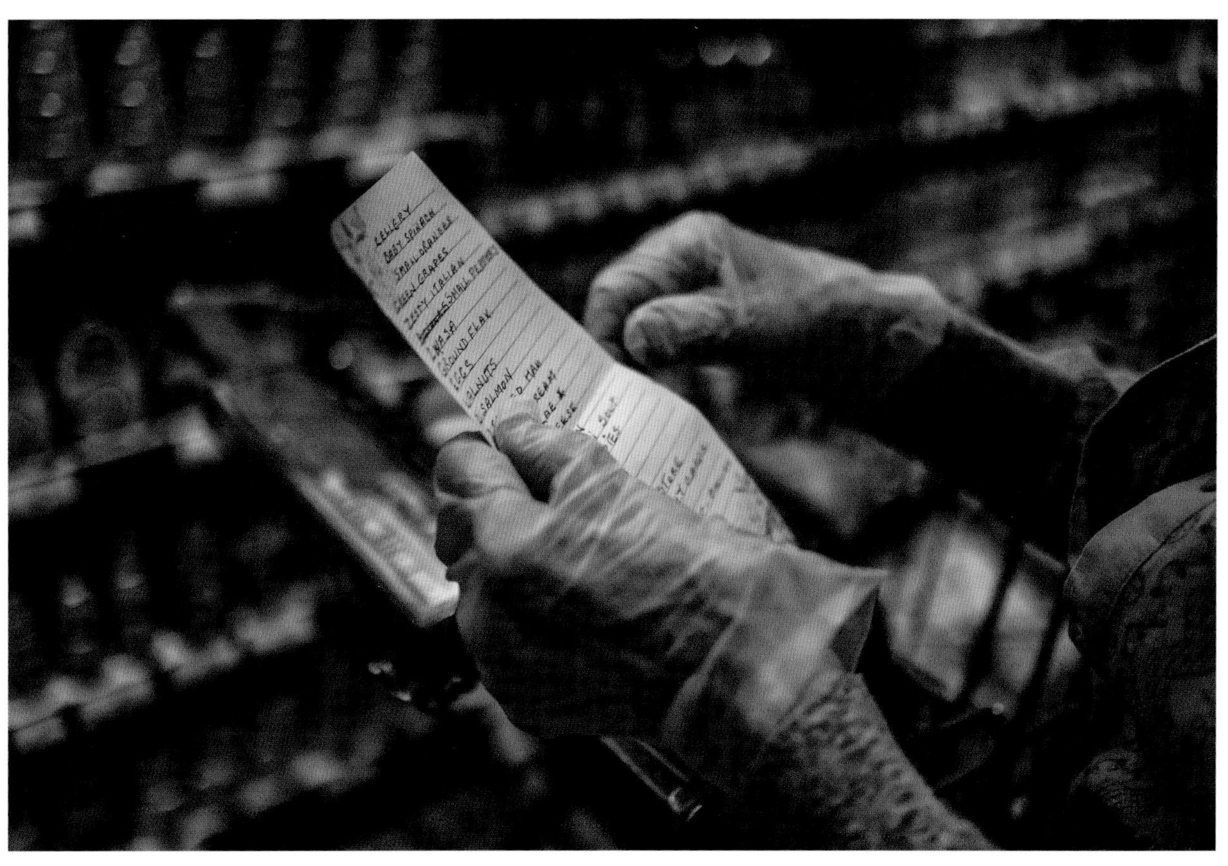

Louise Smyth, wearing gloves and mask,
does her grocery shopping.

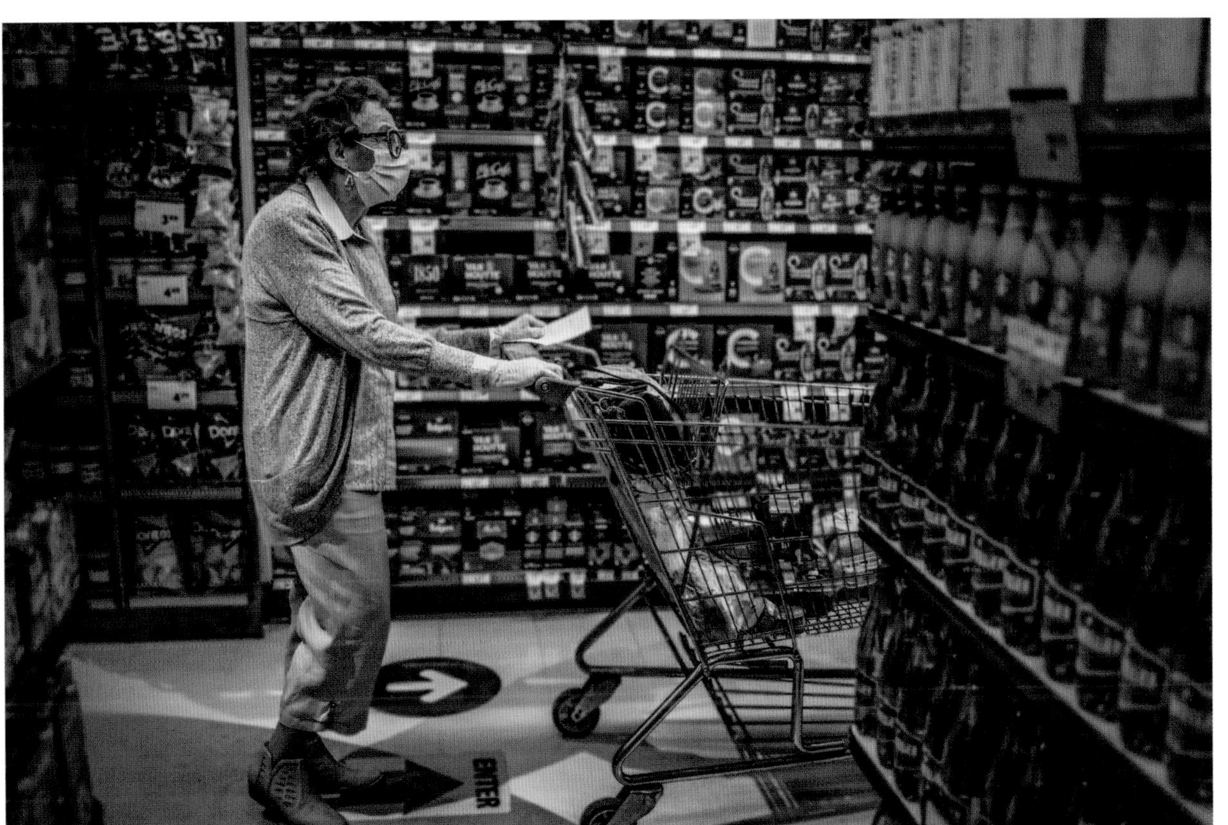

ENTER

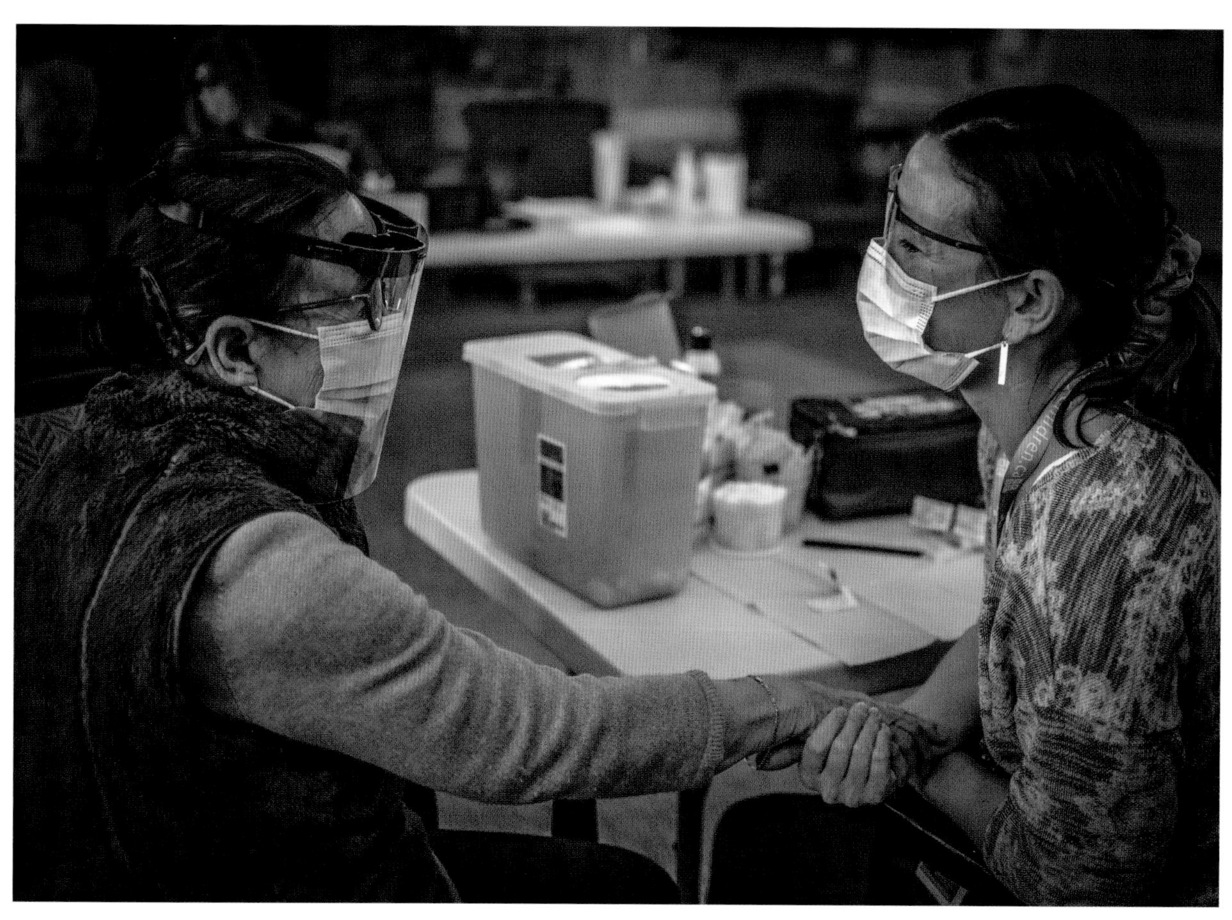

Ingeborg Kalder, left, holds hands with registered
nurse Rachel Reid after receiving her COVID-19
Pfizer vaccine at Aspen Ridge Lodge seniors'
housing in Didsbury, Alberta, in January 2021.

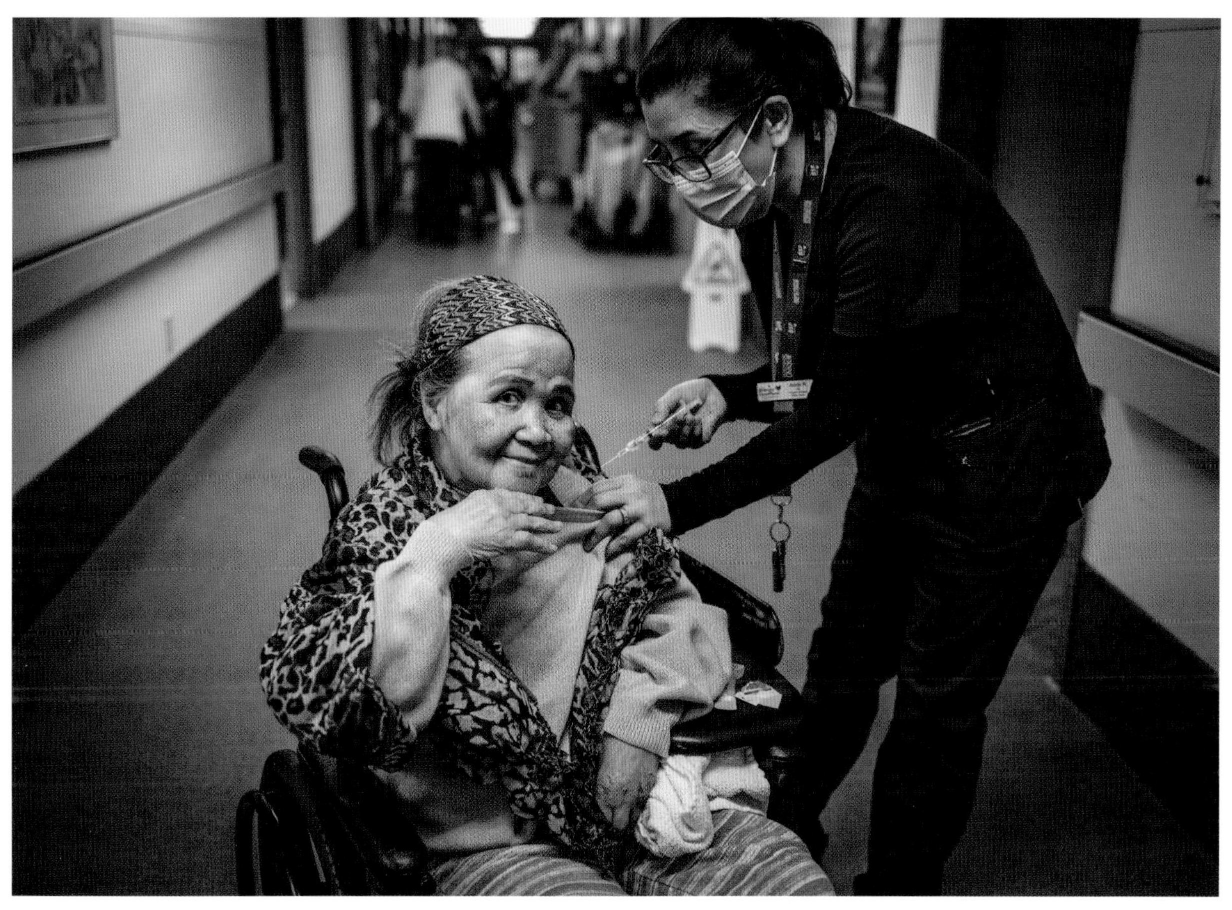

Registered nurse Abida Rehman gives Ligaya
Rudio, 80, her COVID-19 vaccine at Clifton Manor
in Calgary, Alberta.

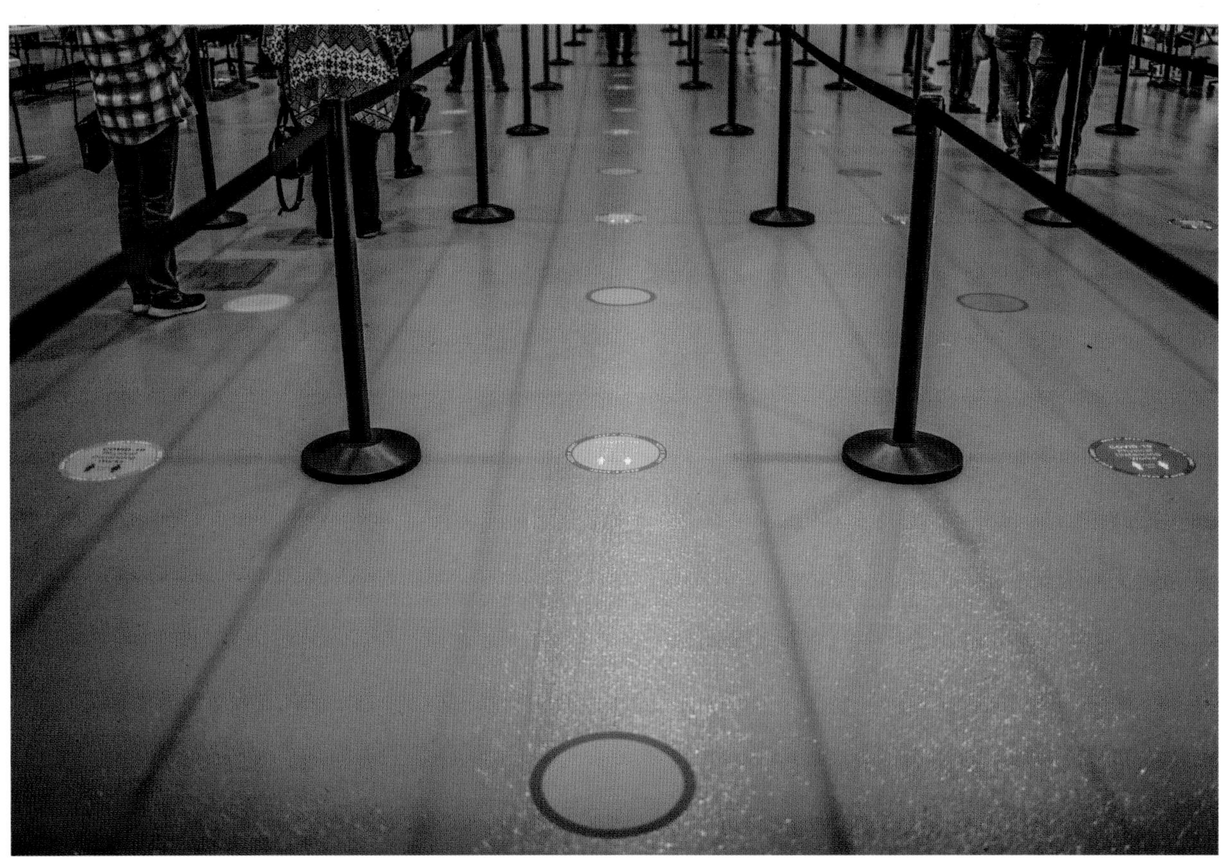

Socially distancing prompts at the COVID-19
vaccine site at the Telus Convention Centre
in Calgary, Alberta, in 2021.

Patience Ndumbi, licensed practical nurse,
gives a COVID-19 vaccine at the Telus
Convention Centre in Calgary, Alberta, in
April 2021.

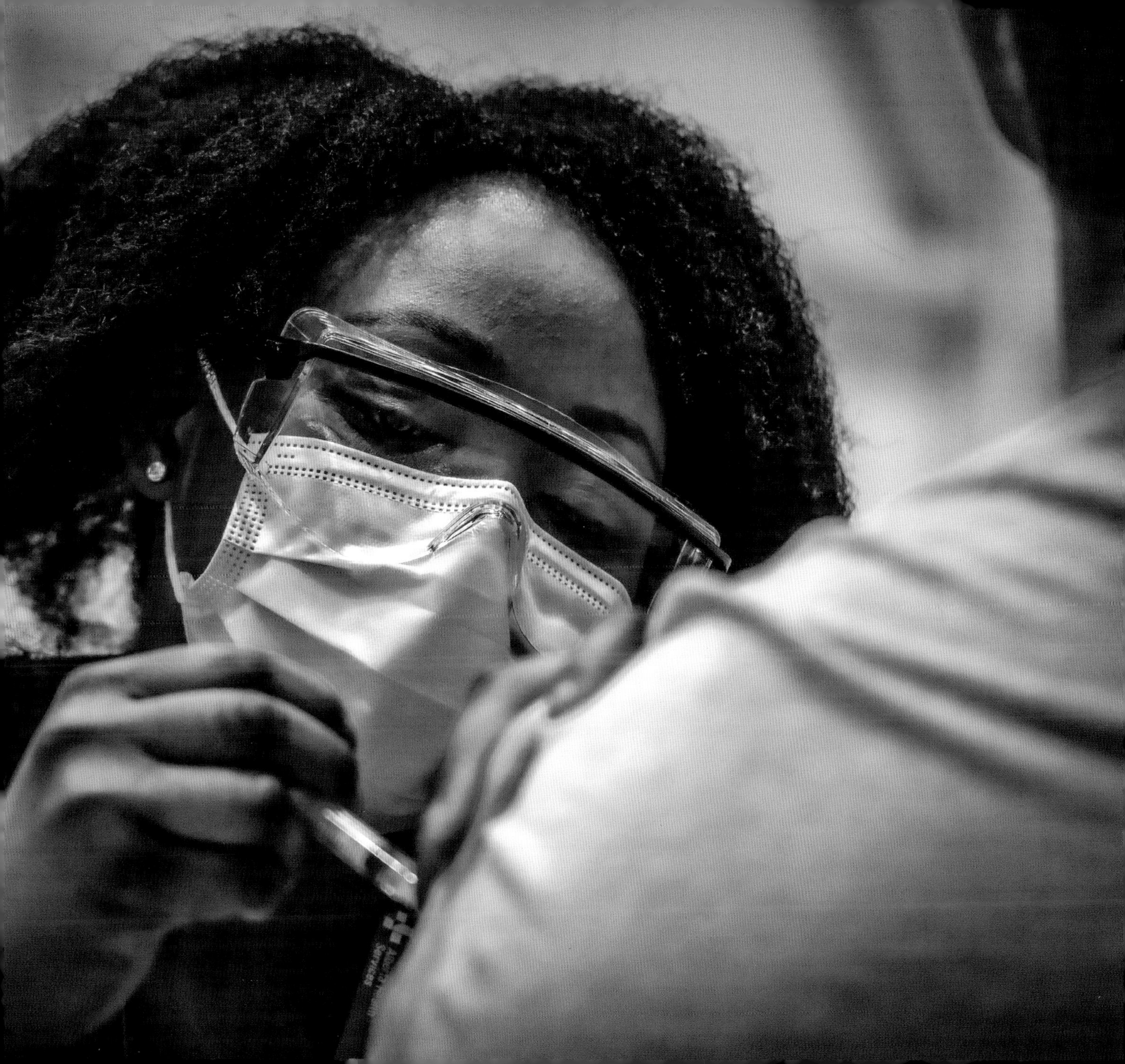

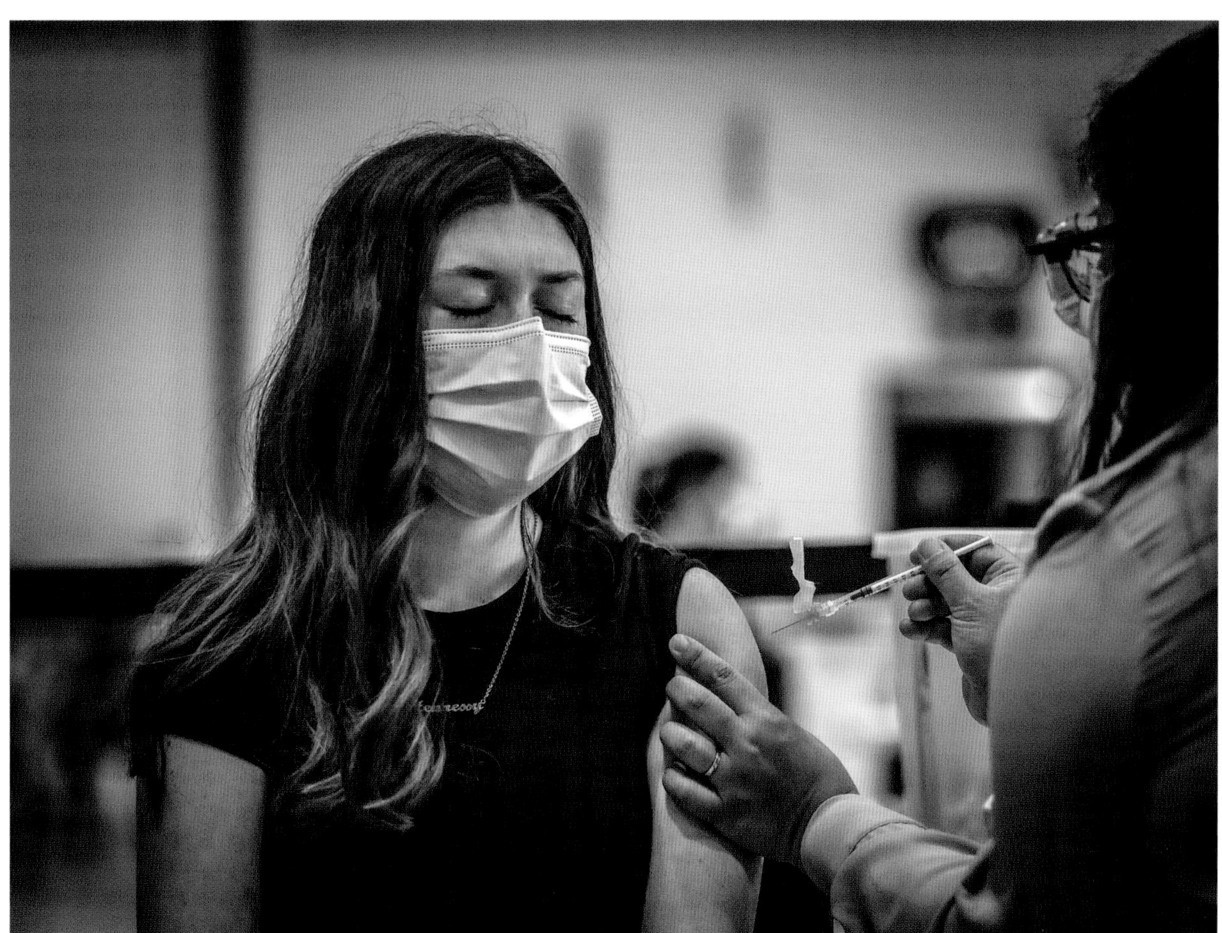

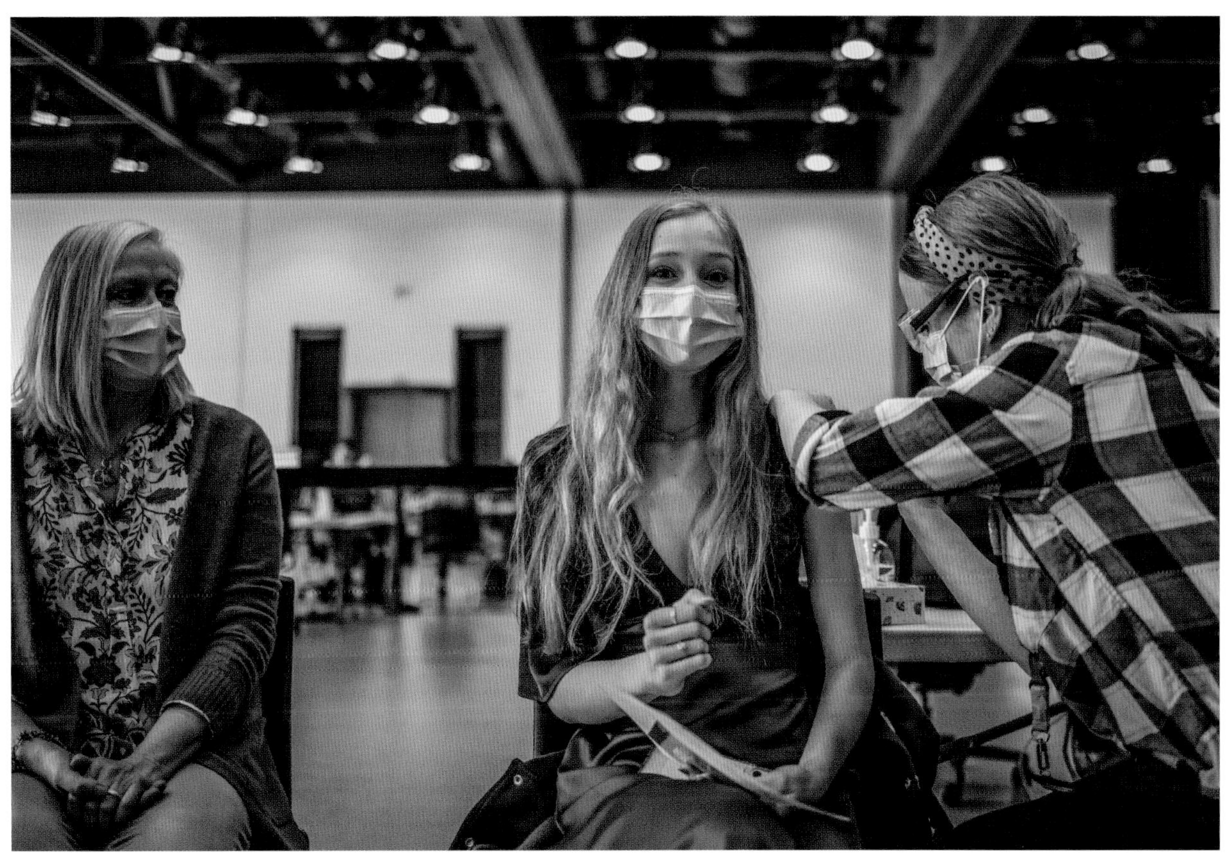

Hennessy Silvaggio, 15, receives a COVID-19
vaccine from registered nurse Rachel Lacebal
at the Telus Convention Centre, May 2021.

Muriel Charlebois, 15, wears her Grade 9 grad
dress to get her COVID-19 vaccine at Telus
Convention Centre on May 12, 2021.

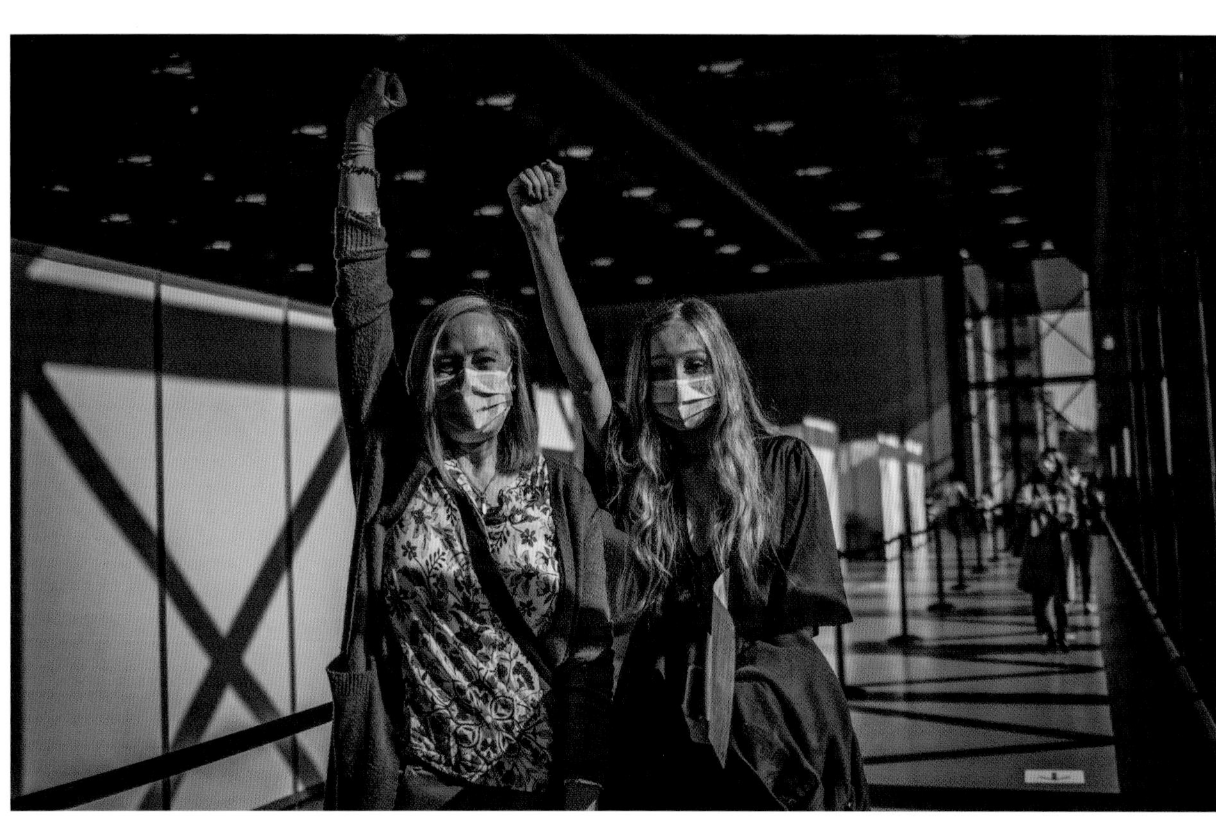

Muriel Charlebois, 15, wears her Grade 9 graduation gown to get her COVID-19 vaccine with her mom Karen Thomas at Telus Convention Centre on May 12, 2021.

"It meant a lot to me. I was really excited," says Charlebois about receiving her first COVID-19 vaccine.

"I'm wearing my grad dress for Grade 9 because I thought it's a special occasion. I have the dress. I might as well wear it out somewhere."

She says the past year has been difficult for her and her friends. "I think it's been hard on everyone, but especially people our age because we're still figuring things out. We're still discovering who we are," she says.

"I think we're going to be stronger afterward."

Her mom, Karen Thomas, echoes her words. "It's been a rough time. As a parent you just want your child to have the best growing-up experience, and this has been a tough one," Thomas says. "We're so grateful to AHS and for where we live. We're just super grateful."

Charlebois says she is looking forward to going to high school, meeting new people and going to events again.

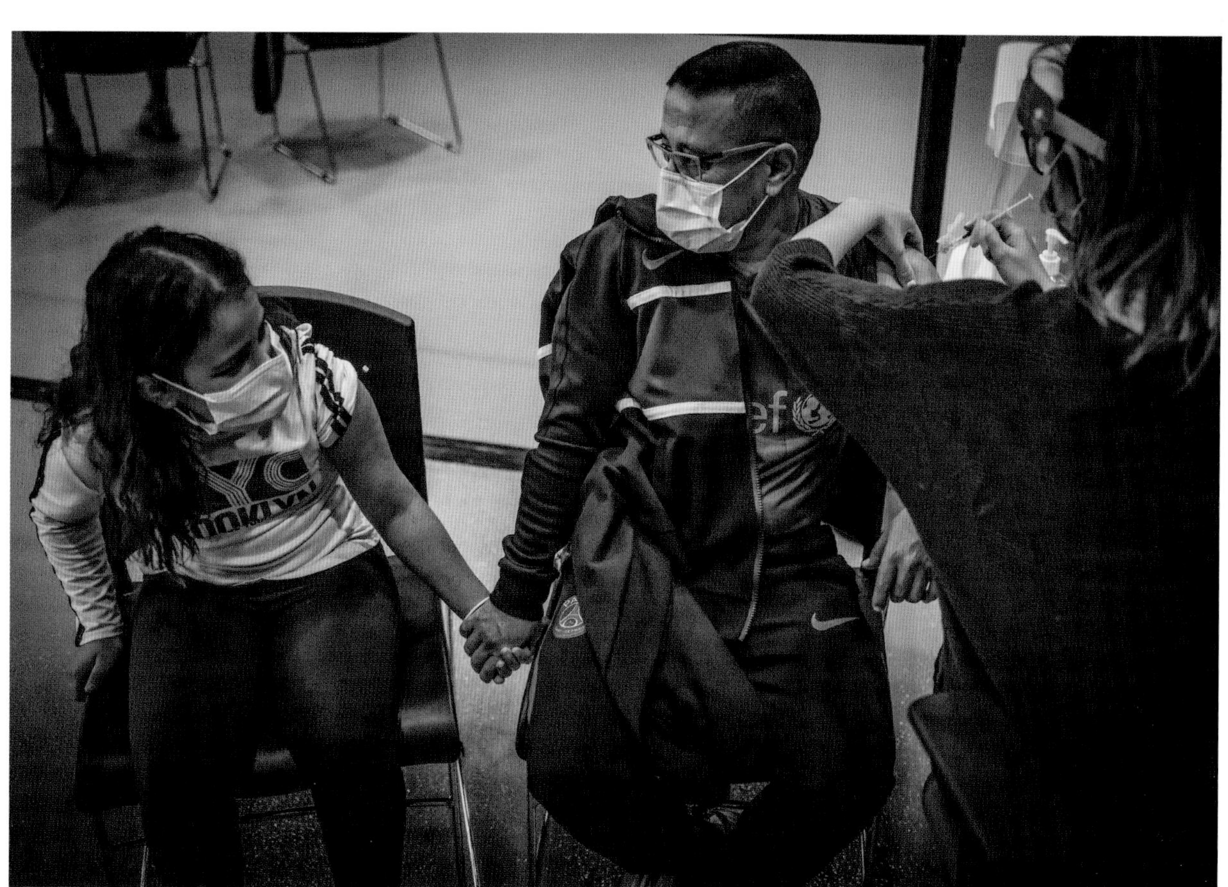

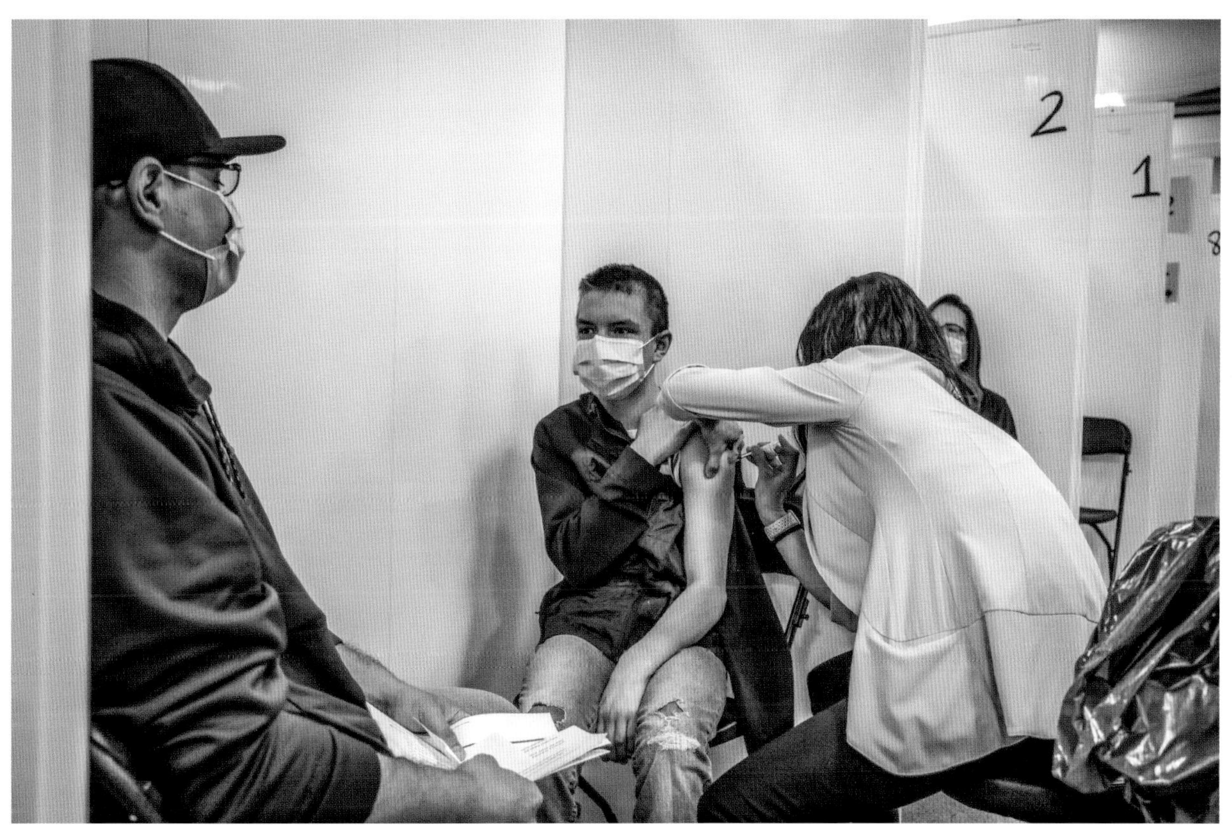

Zakaria Loukili holds the hand of his daughter Ruqayyah, 11, as he receives his COVID-19 vaccine.

Ben Krysa, 12, receives a COVID-19 vaccine from registered nurse Michelle Magnan as his dad Adam watches at the Exhibition Park West Pavilion, in Lethbridge, Alberta, on May 10, 2021.

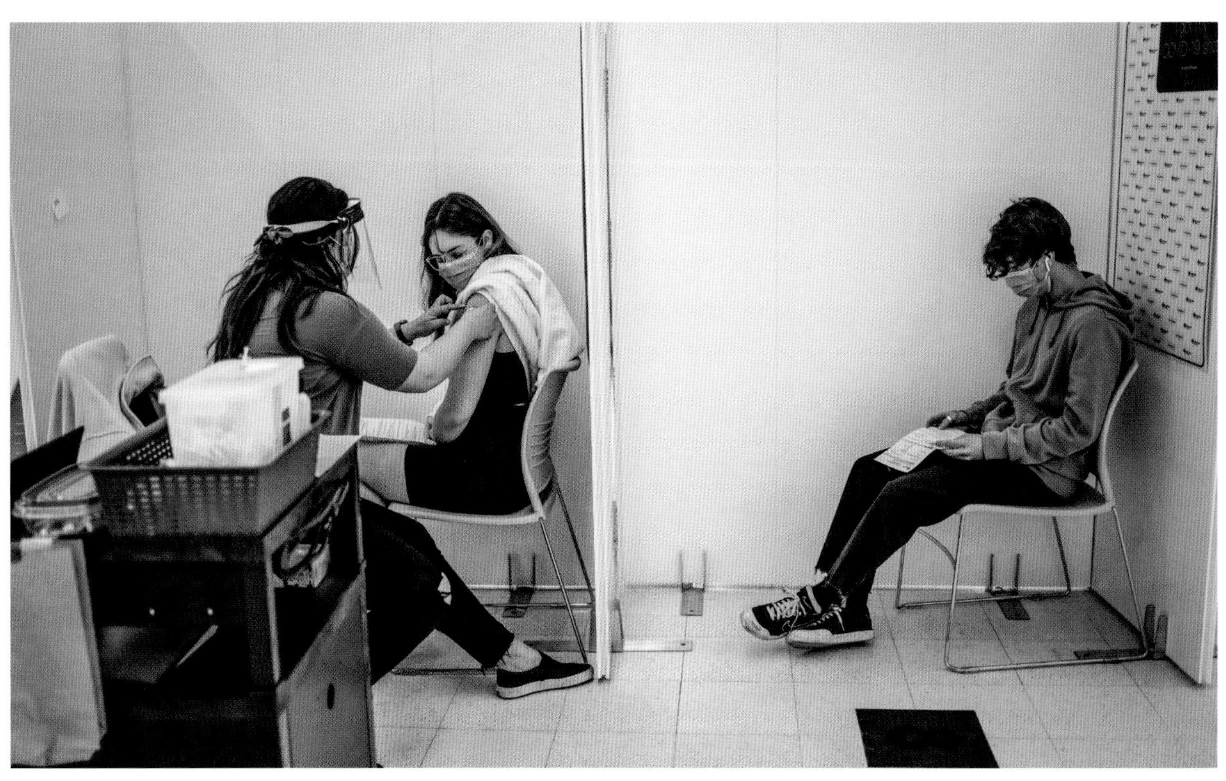

Hailey Slocombe, 21, receives a COVID-19 vaccine as Hisham Arafat, 15, awaits his turn in Calgary, Alberta, on May 11, 2021.

Sean Morin, 10, takes a photo of his mom Joanna Morin and his sister Vianna, 12, after the two received their COVID-19 vaccines at the Bannister Road clinic in Calgary, Alberta.

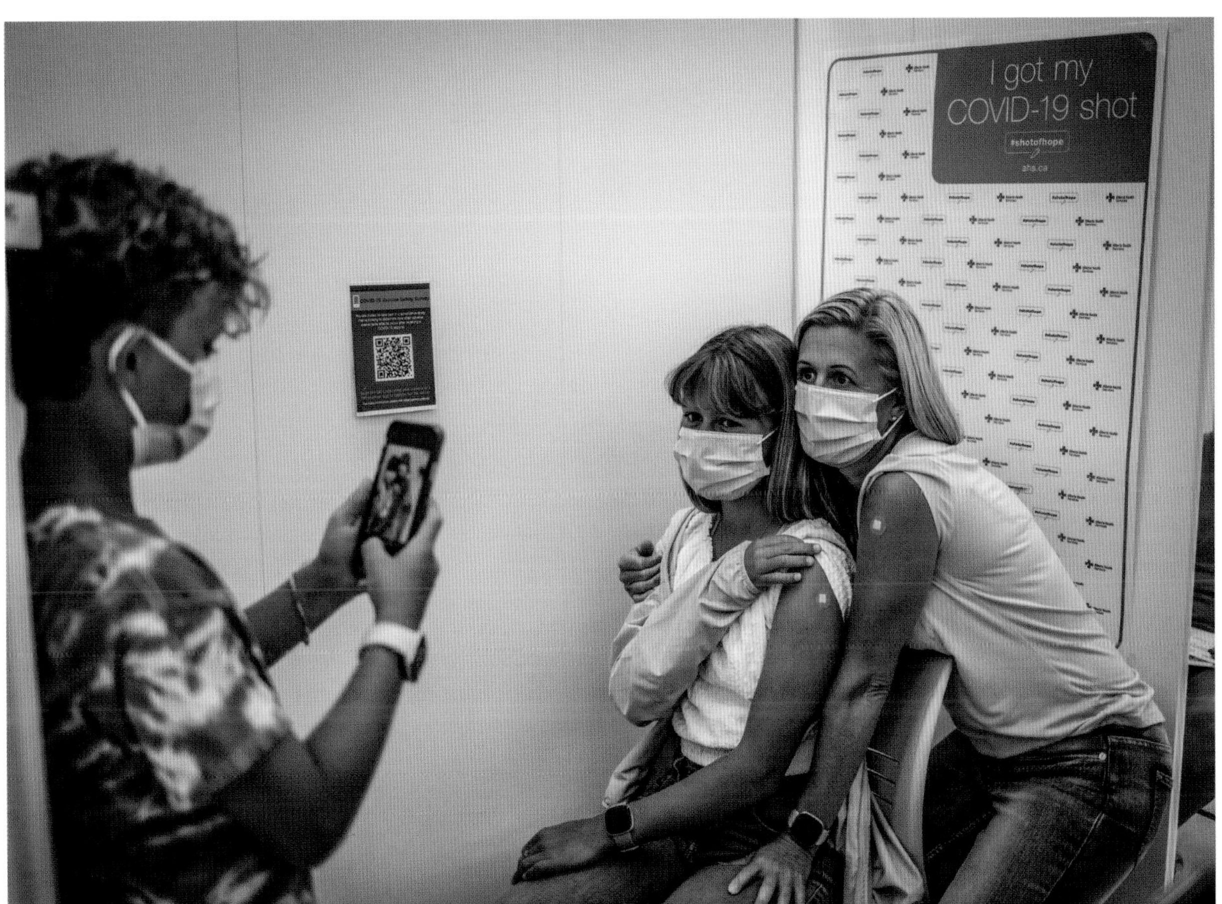

I got my
COVID-19 shot
#shotofhope
ahs.ca

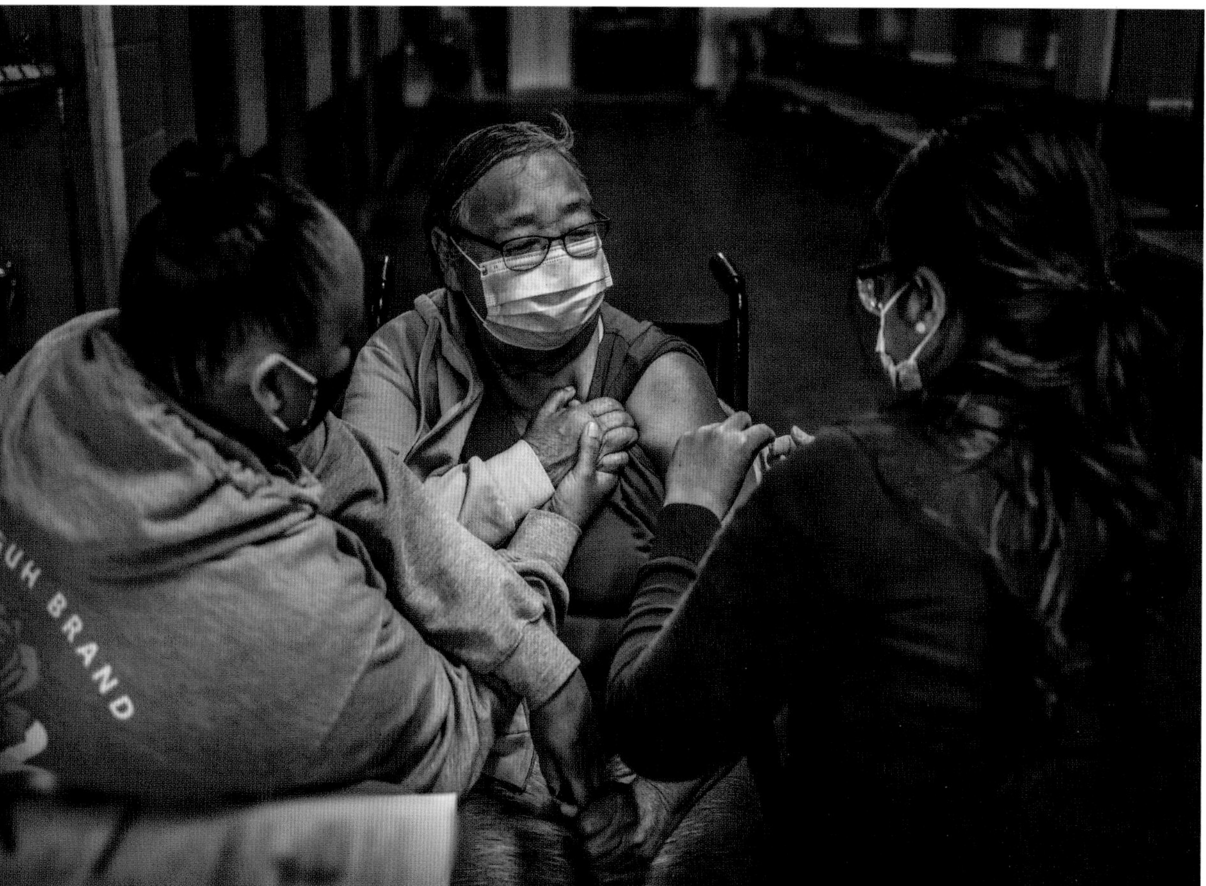

Kathy Calf Robe, left, holds the hand of her mother Victoria Calf Robe as Josie Dahl, community care paramedic with Siksika Health Services and intensive care nurse with AHS, gives her a vaccine during the Siksika Nation Rural COVID-19 Immunization Clinic at the Deerfoot Sportsplex in May 2021.

In January 2021, Victoria, 72, ended up in the intensive care unit with COVID-19. Six months later, she received her COVID-19 vaccine at the Siksika Nation Rural COVID-19 Immunization Clinic. "COVID-19 is real," Victoria says. "I'm trying to get my strength back."

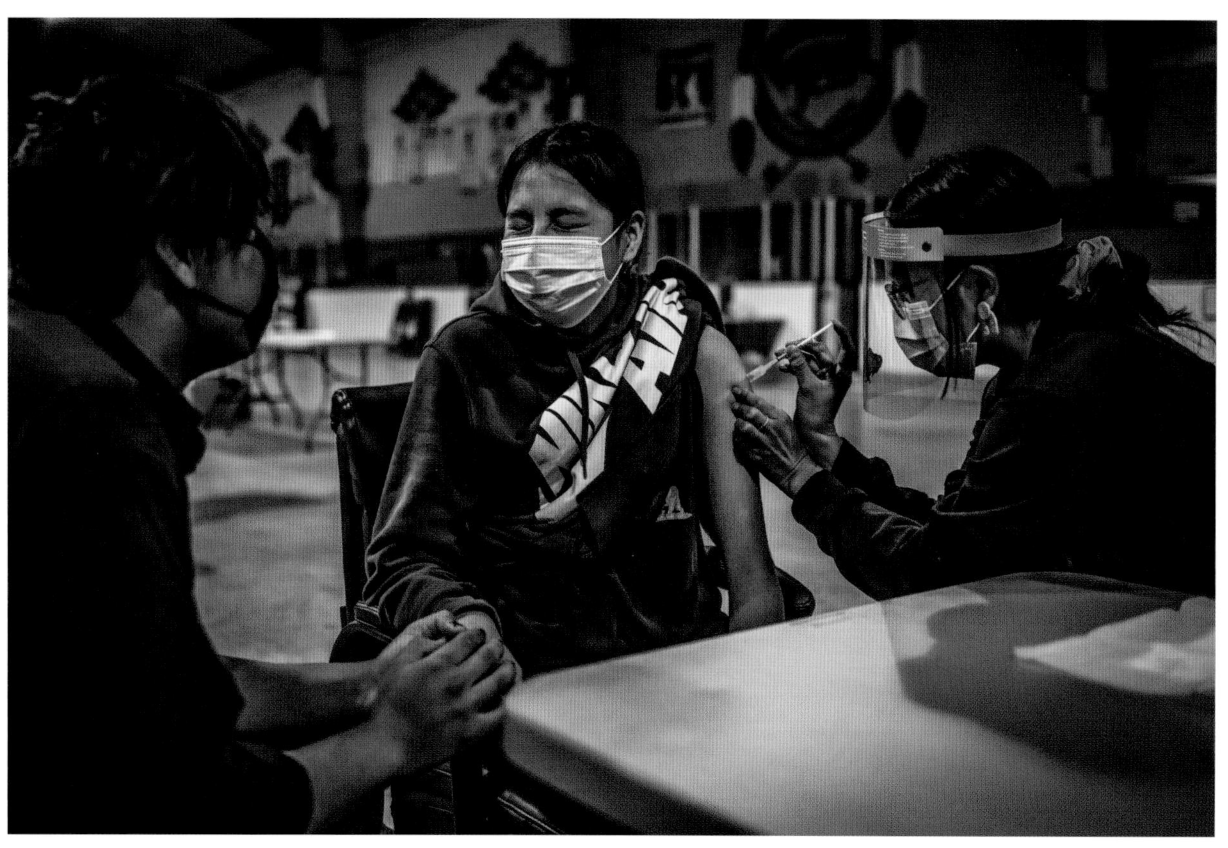

Sadie Calf Robe, 15, holds the hand of brother Joziah, 17, while getting a vaccine from Jacey Solway, a registered nurse with Siksika Health Services, during the Siksika Nation Rural COVID-19 Immunization Clinic at the Deerfoot Sportsplex on May 25, 2021.

Jaclynn Haney, 15, receives a COVID-19 vaccine from Don Sharpe, an advanced care paramedic, at the Telus Convention Centre in Calgary, Alberta, in May 2021.

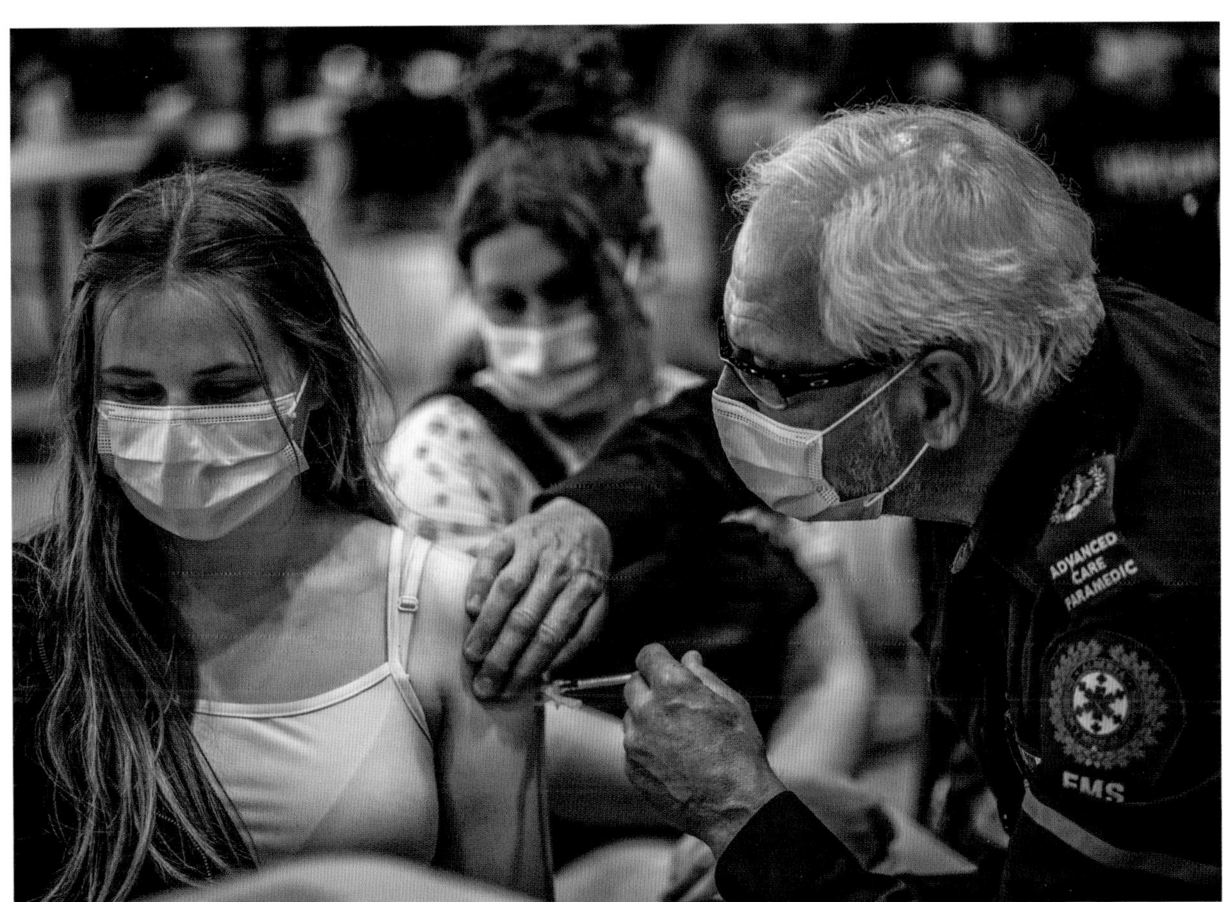

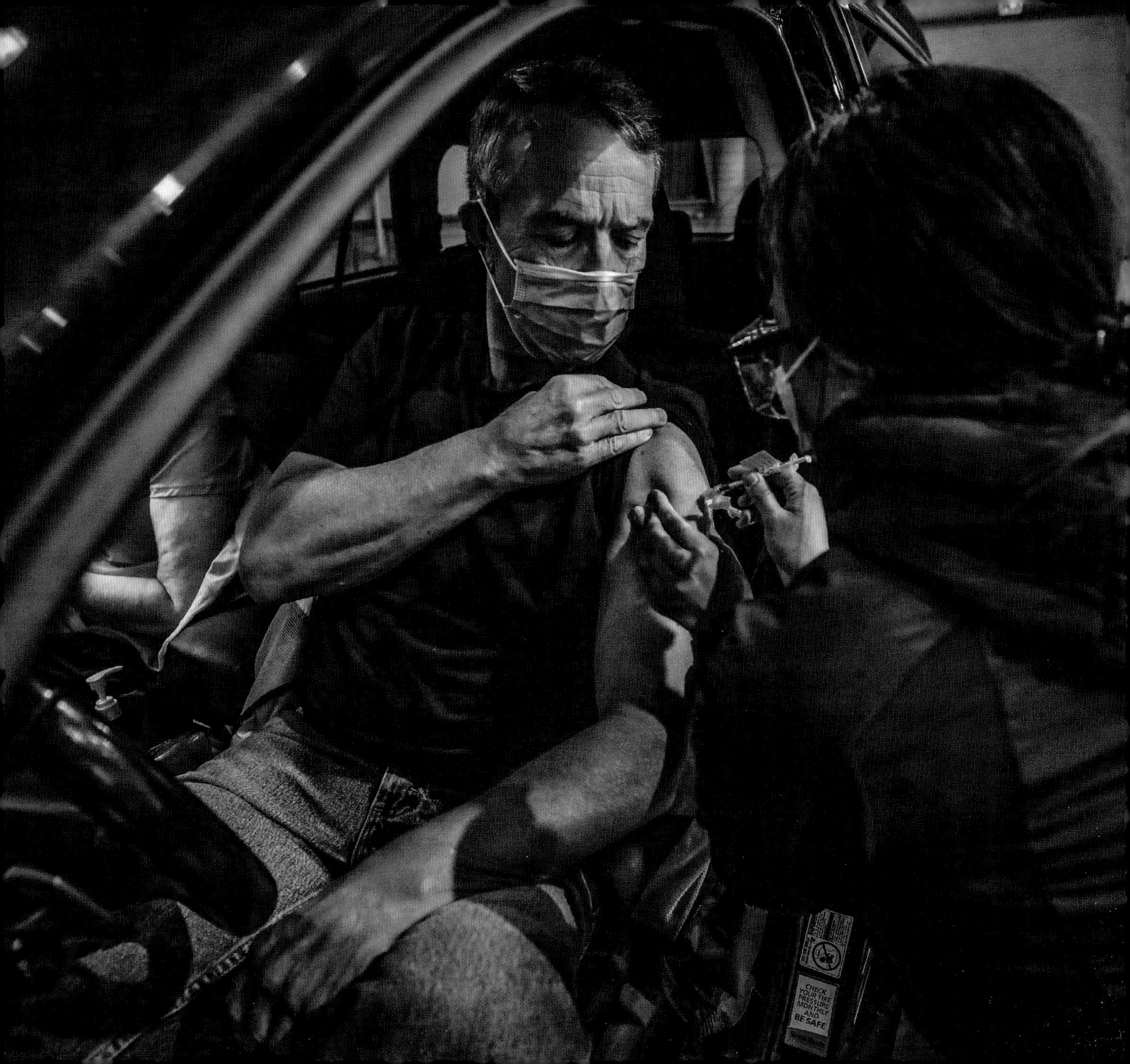
CHECK
YOUR TIRE
PRESSURE
MONTHLY
AND
BE SAFE

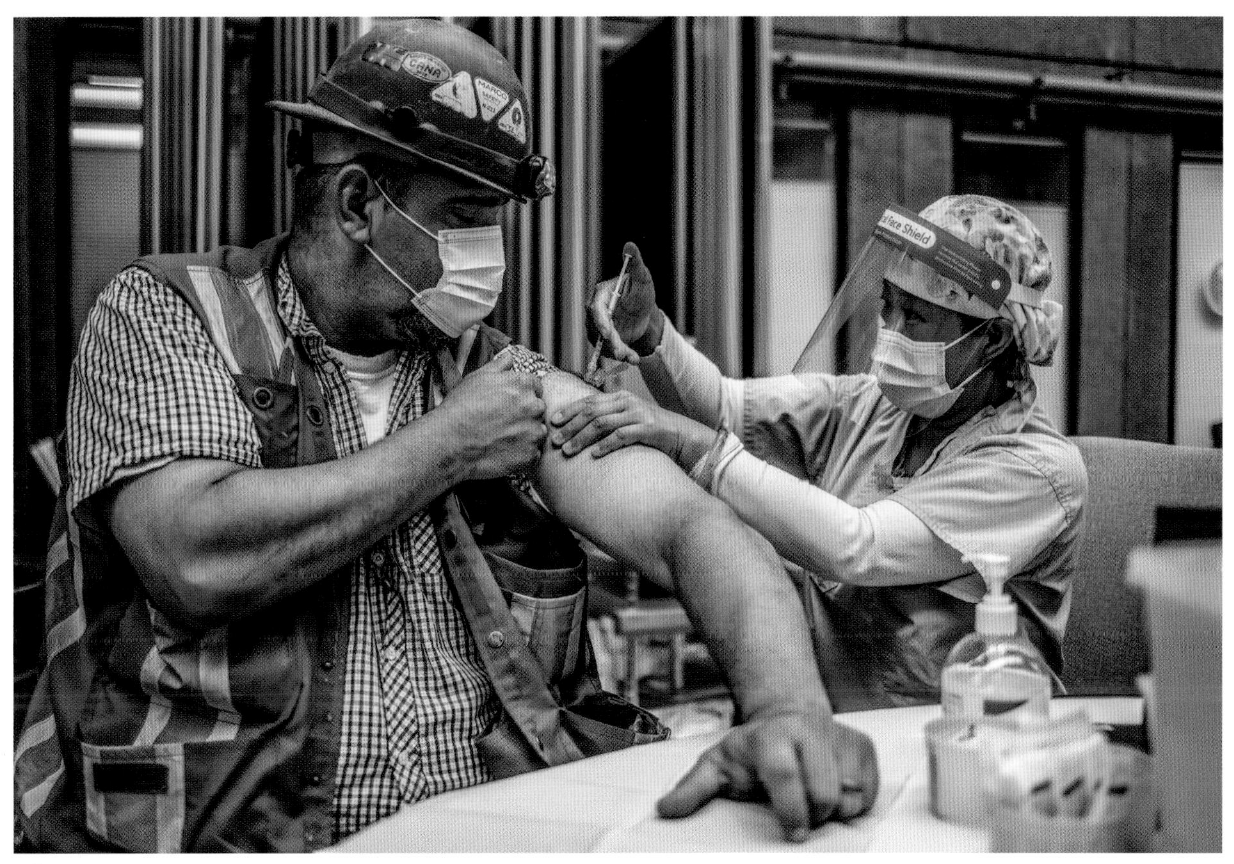

Darrell Jefferies receives a COVID-19 vaccine from licensed practical nurse Shekinah Balisong at the drive-through immunization clinic in Calgary, Alberta, on June 7, 2021.

Construction worker Cory Olson, left, receives a COVID-19 vaccine from registered nurse Mei Chu at the Health Sciences Centre at Foothills Medical Centre in Calgary, Alberta, on June 4, 2021.

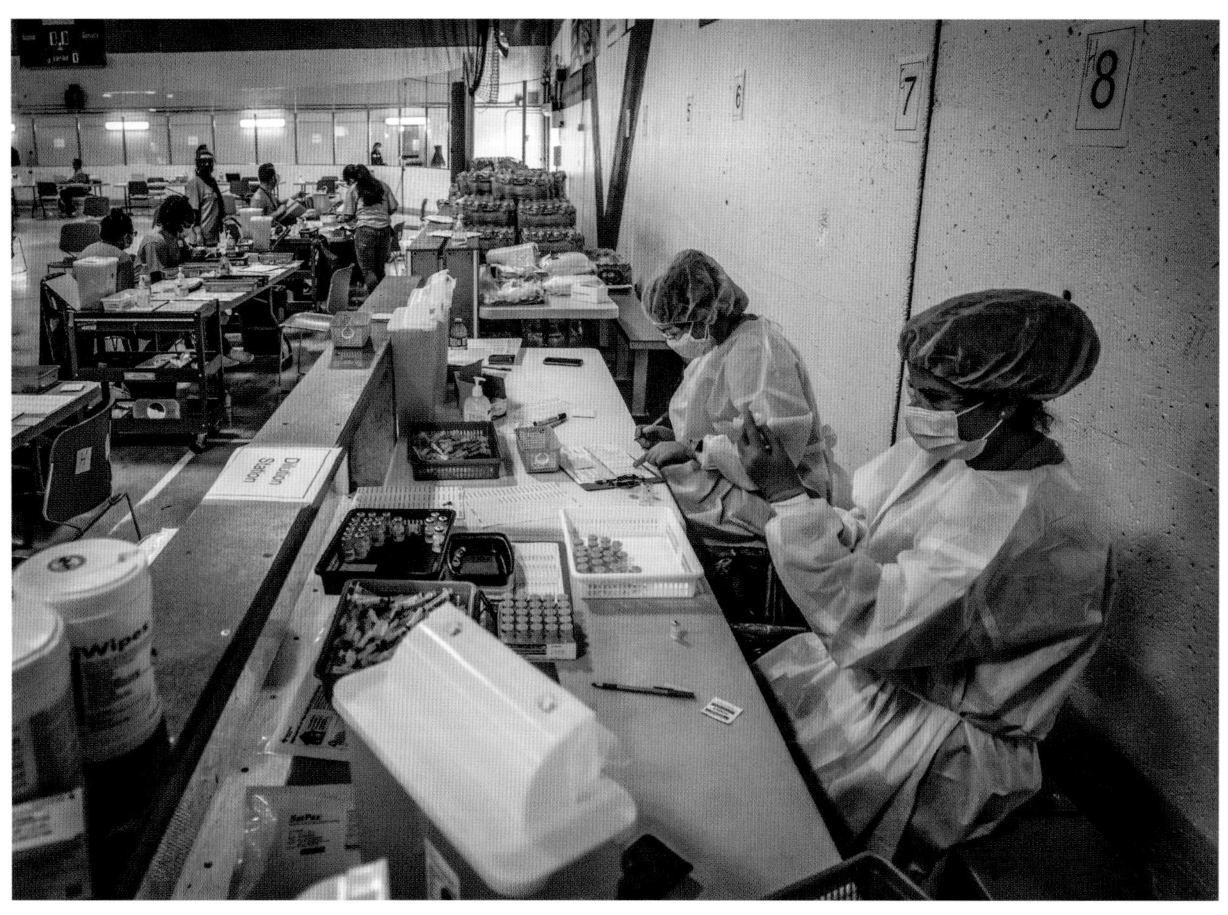

Staff at the COVID-19 vaccine pop-up clinic
at Village Square Leisure Centre in Calgary,
Alberta, on June 5, 2021.

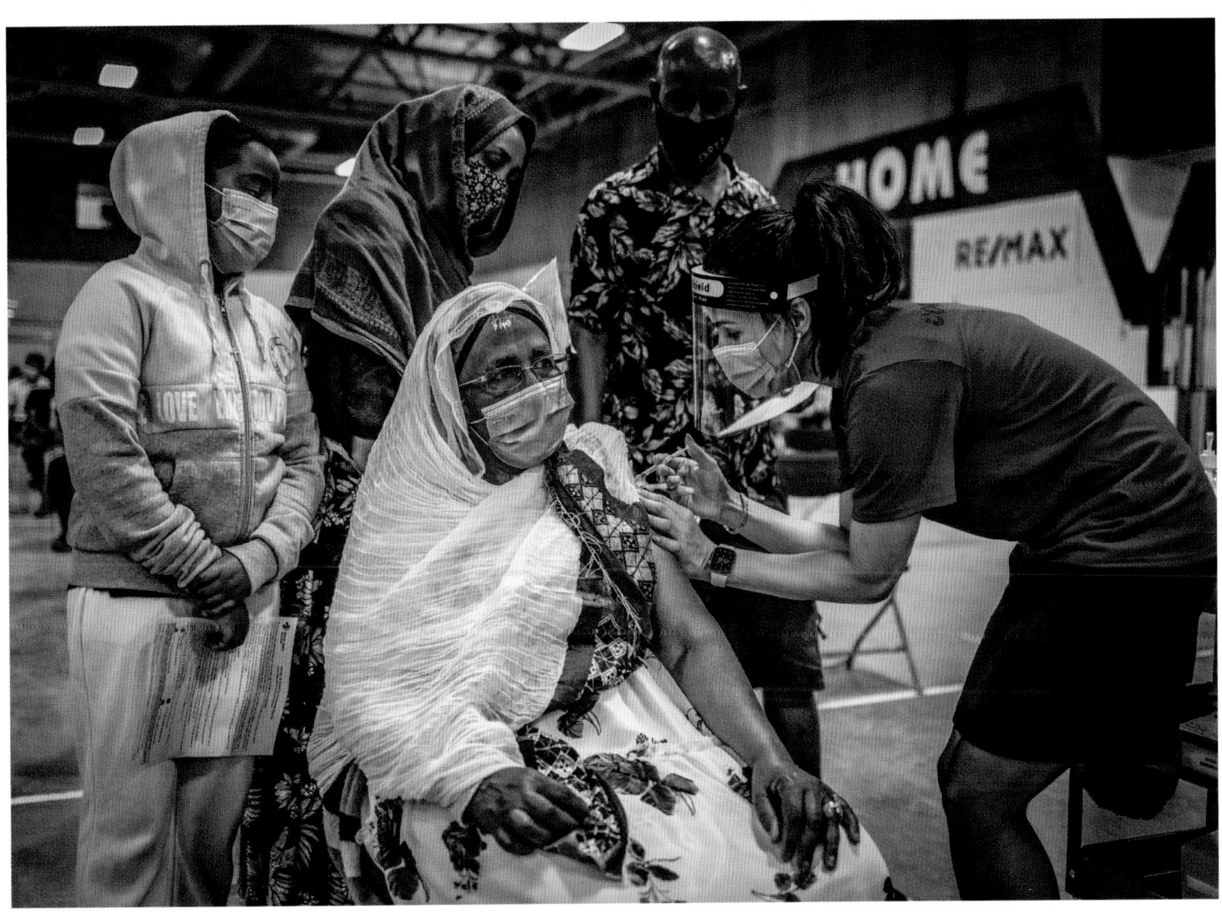

Dr. Gaganjot Sandhu gives a COVID-19
vaccine to Elsa Tesfu at the pop-up clinic at
Village Square Leisure Centre on June 5, 2021.

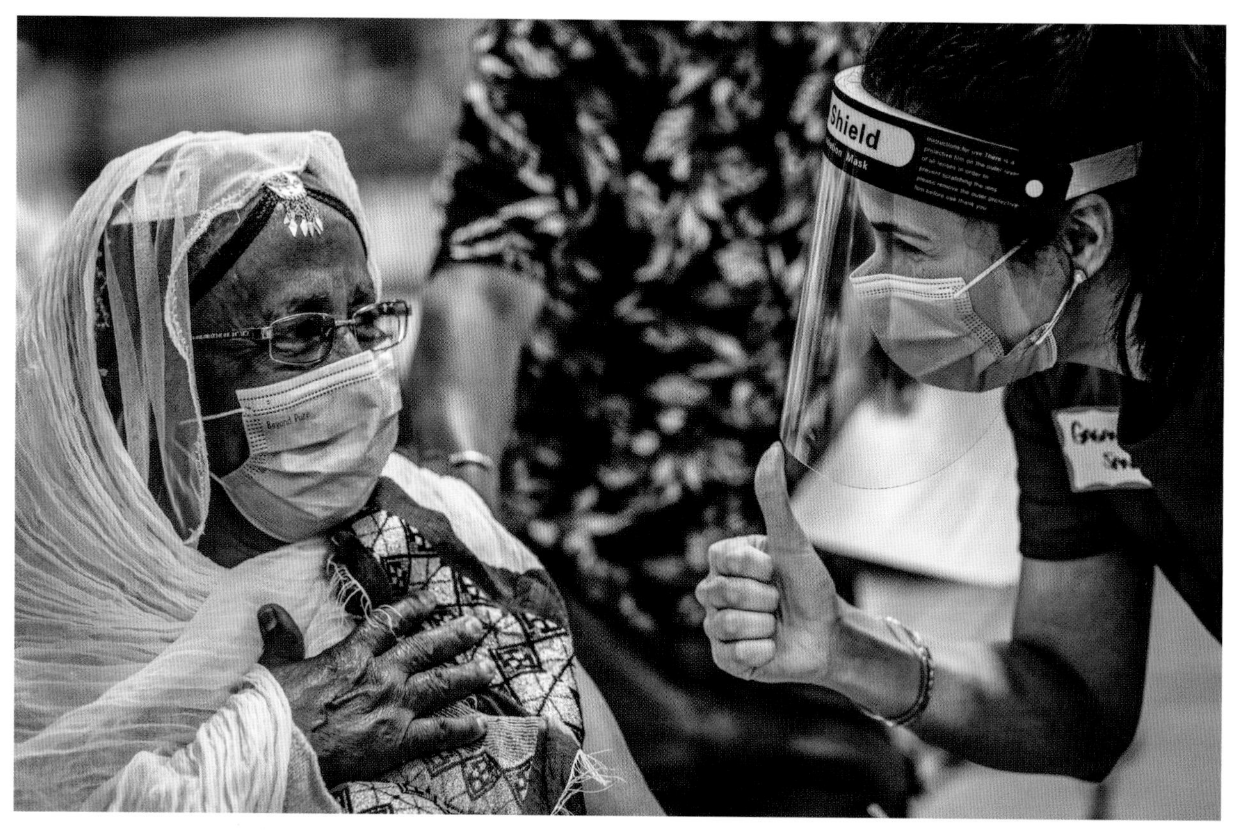

Dr. Gaganjot Sandhu gives a COVID-19
vaccine to Elsa Tesfu at the pop-up clinic at
Village Square Leisure Centre on June 5, 2021.

Maria Bol, left, watches her daughter Nyibol
Aciek, 13, receive her COVID-19 vaccine from
Dr. Gloria Mazloum at the pop-up clinic at
Village Square Leisure Centre on June 6, 2021.

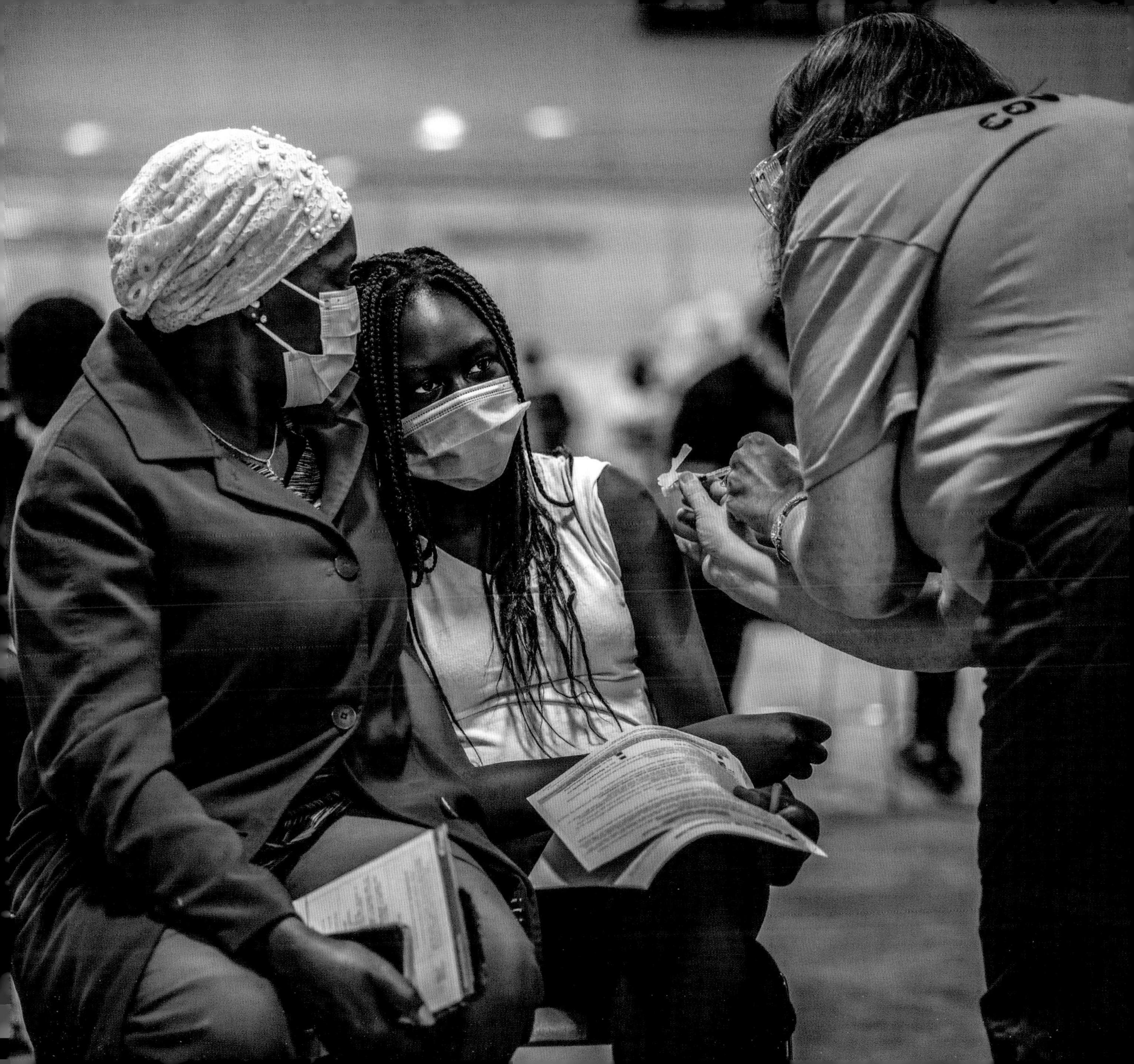

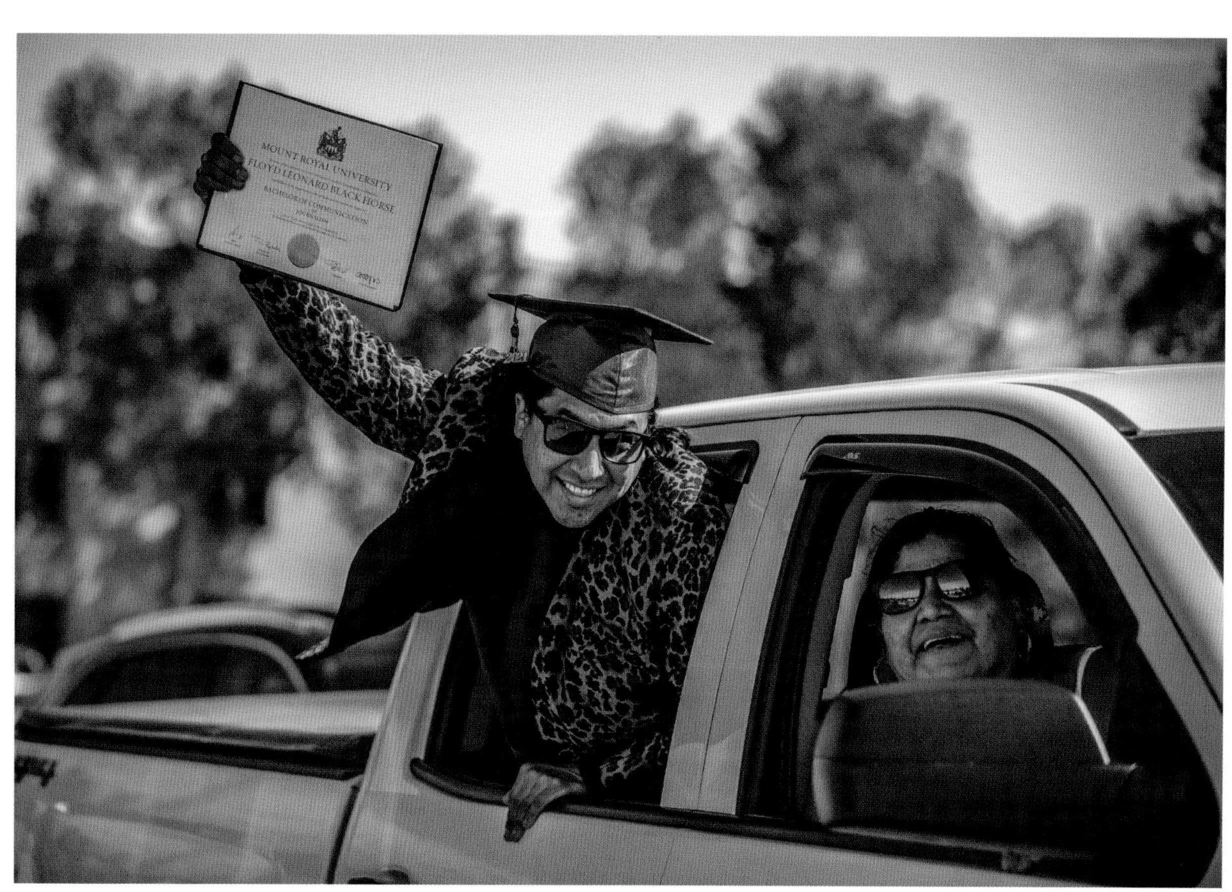

MOUNT ROYAL UNIVERSITY
FLOYD LEONARD BLACK HORSE
BACHELOR OF COMMUNICATION
JOURNALISM

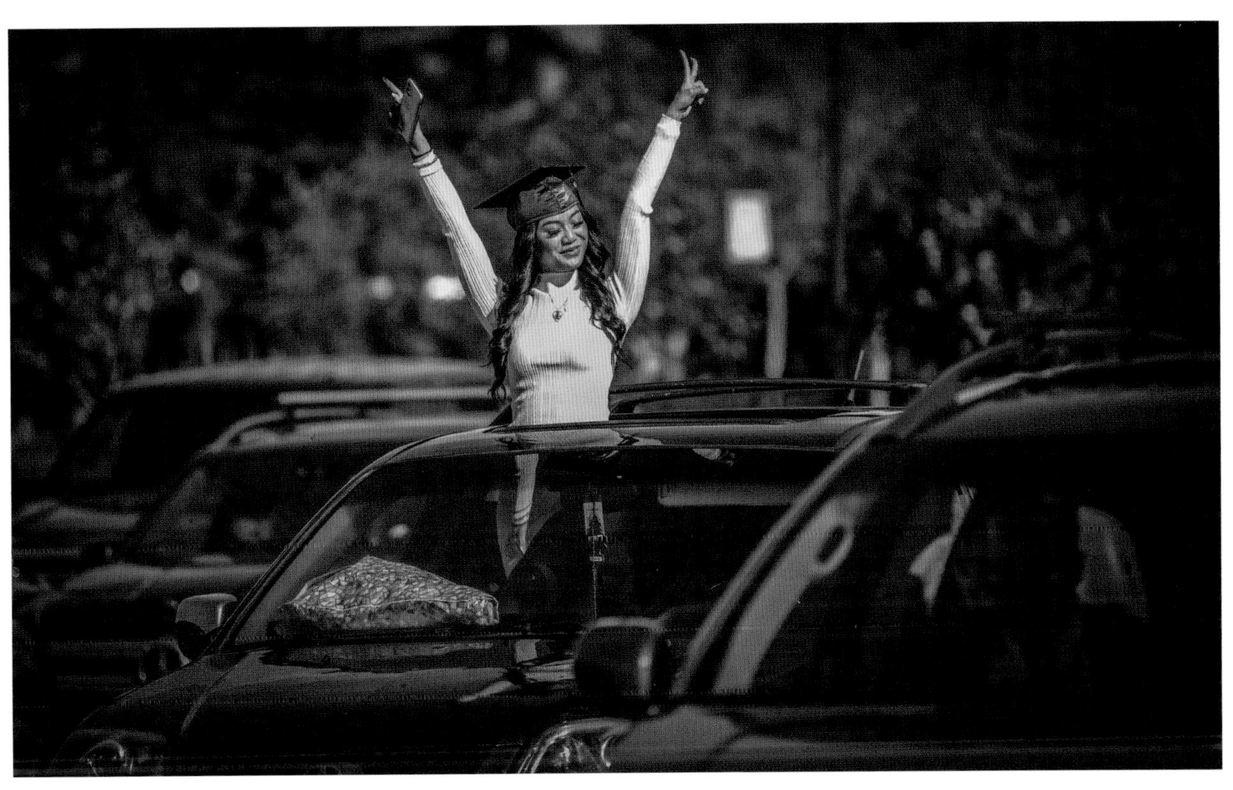

Floyd Black Horse celebrates during the drive-in graduation ceremony at Mount Royal University on June 7, 2021.

Mount Royal University graduates celebrate during the drive-in graduation ceremony on June 7, 2021.

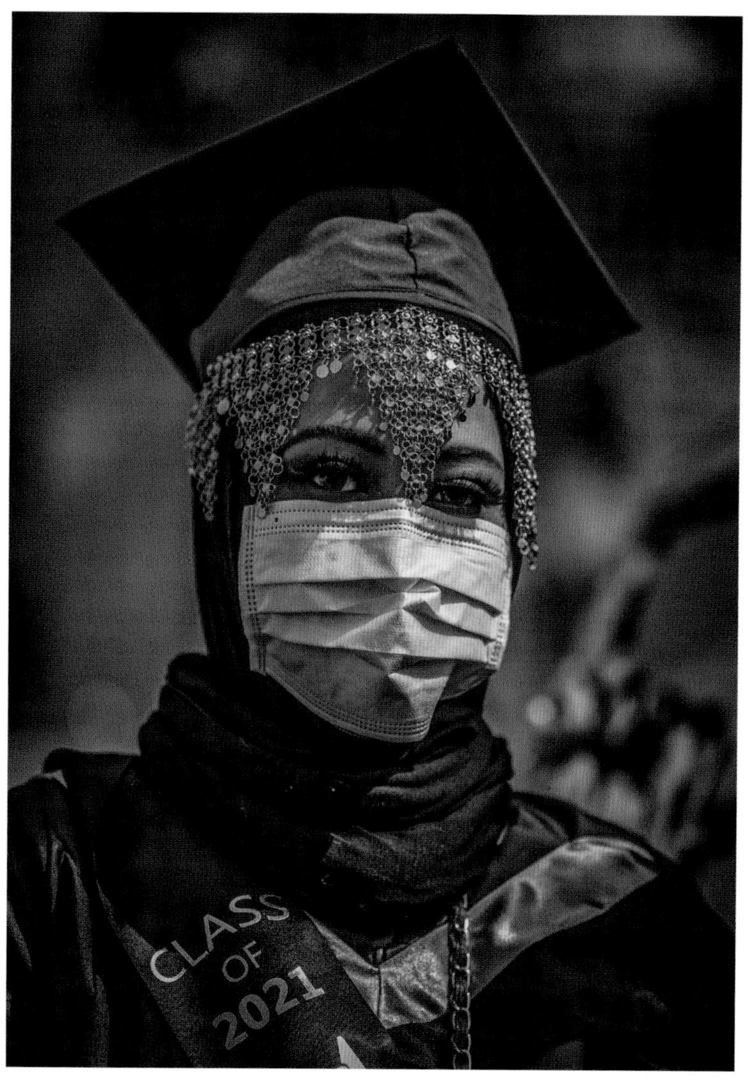

Timaj Gato during the drive-in graduation ceremony at Mount Royal University on June 7, 2021.

From left to right, Isabella Swaita, Marie Walker, Madeleine Harvey and Alessia DiMarzo pose during a socially distanced Grad 2020 photo.

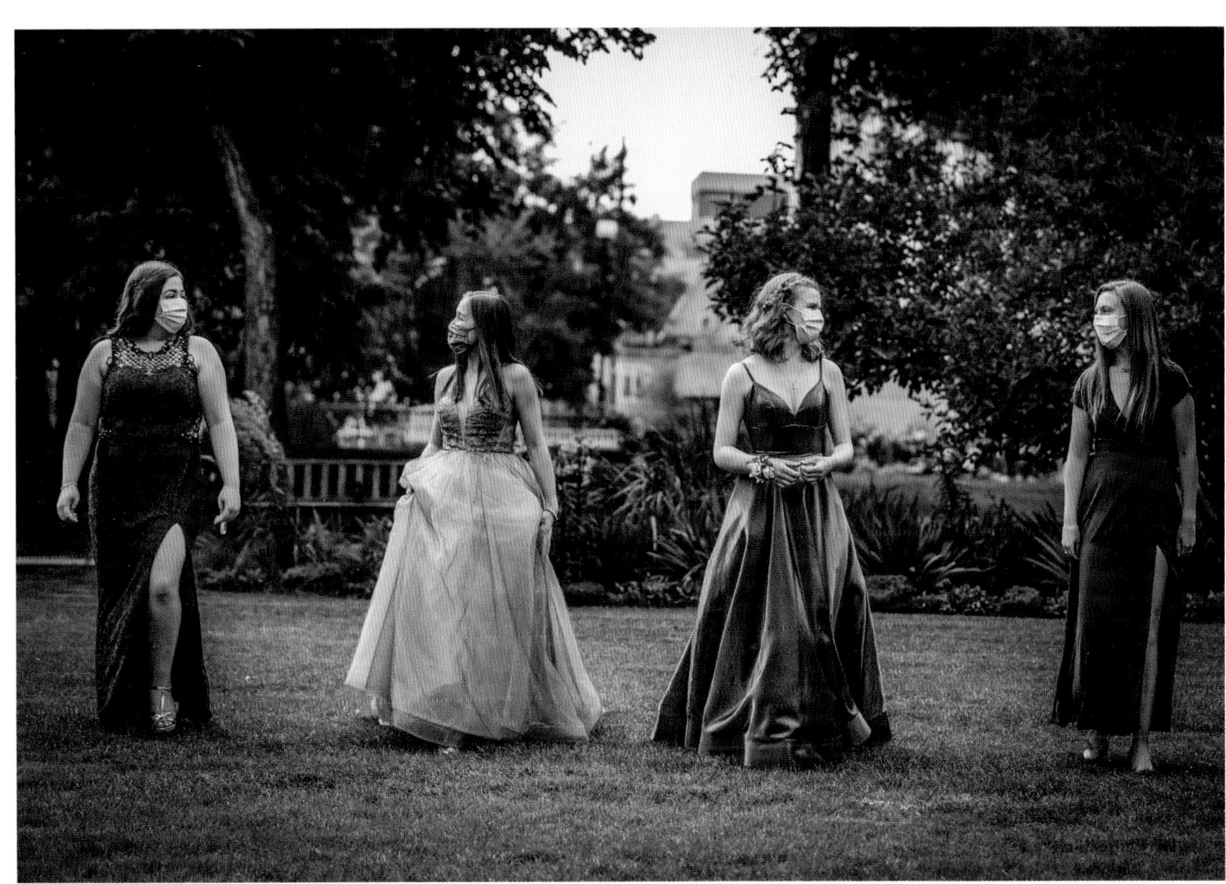

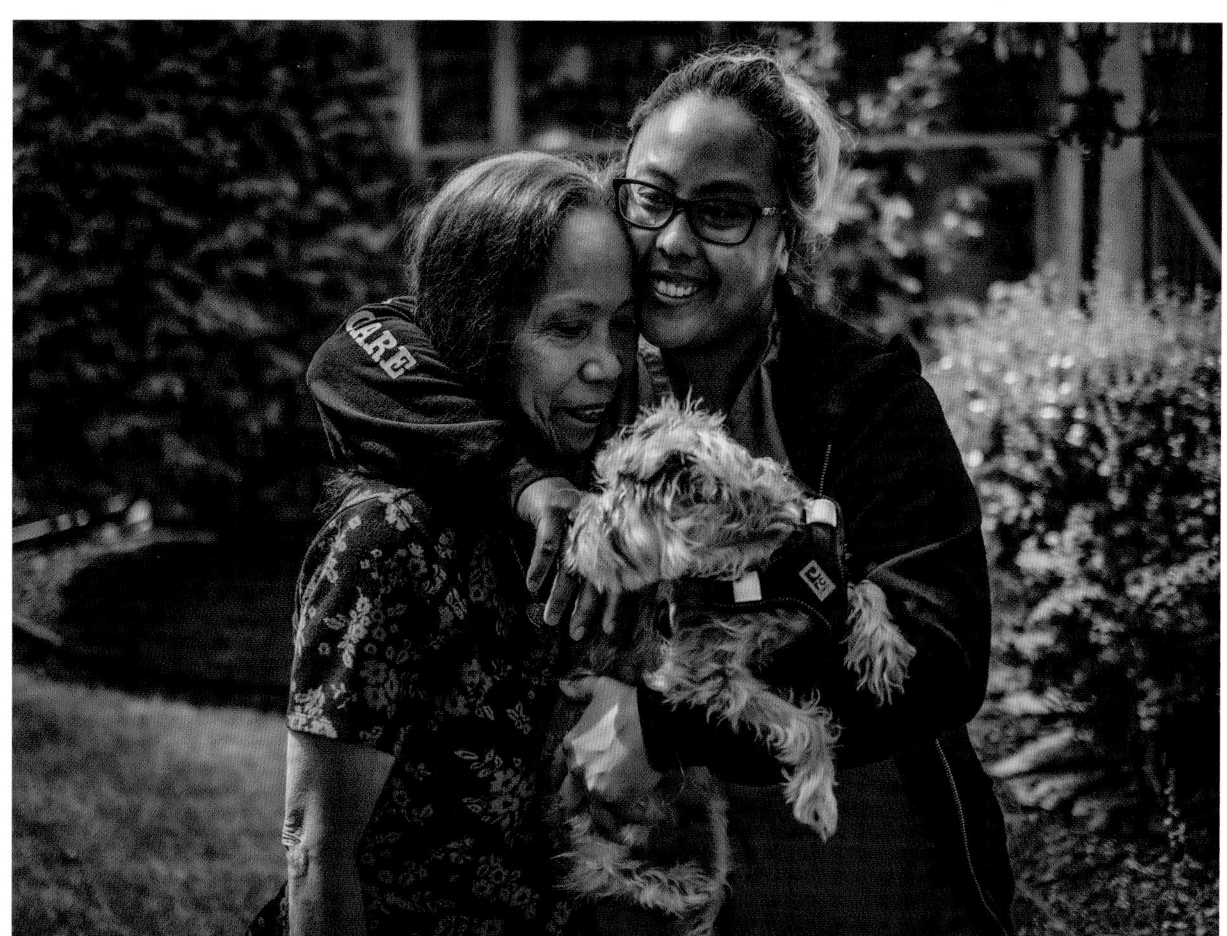

Intensive care unit nurse Mia Torres hugs her grandma Lourdes Abulencia for the first time in more than a year on July 9, 2021.

"It was really hard to not see her face to face," says Torres, who cared for patients in the intensive care unit at Peter Lougheed Centre.

"But I was scared that if I did come and see her without being vaccinated, she would get sick. I would've never wanted to deal with the fact that my grandma ever got COVID-19 from me."

For Torres, the hardest part of working in the intensive care unit was seeing entire families sick, especially grandparents ill with COVID-19.

"I remember seeing a young grandma, her grandkids brought her and I thought 'This could've been my grandma. This could've been me'. I will never forget it," she says.

Now, Torres and her grandmother are looking forward to going for lunch together.

"I am very proud of her," says Abulencia of her granddaughter.

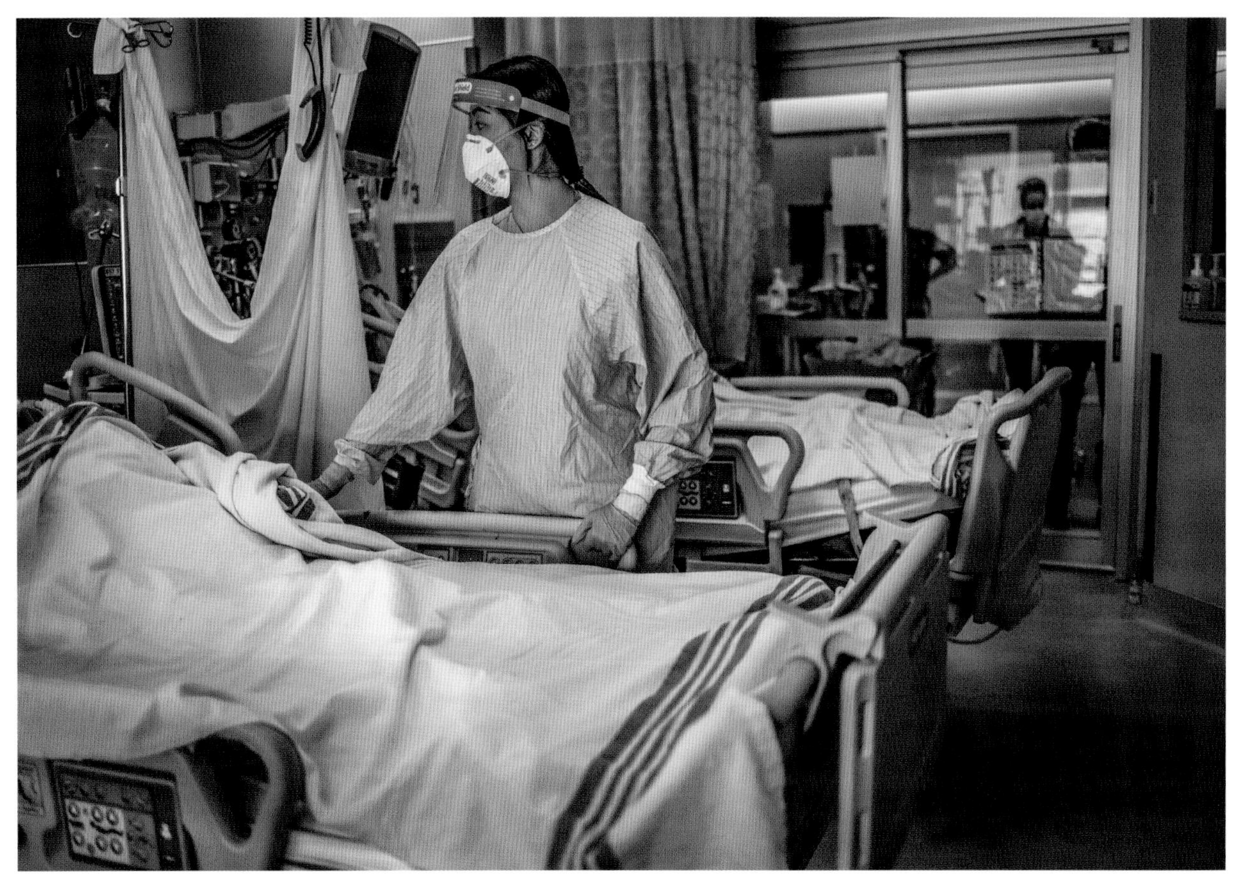

Registered nurse Tamara with two COVID-19 patients
in a single room in the intensive care unit at Foothills
Medical Centre during the fourth wave.

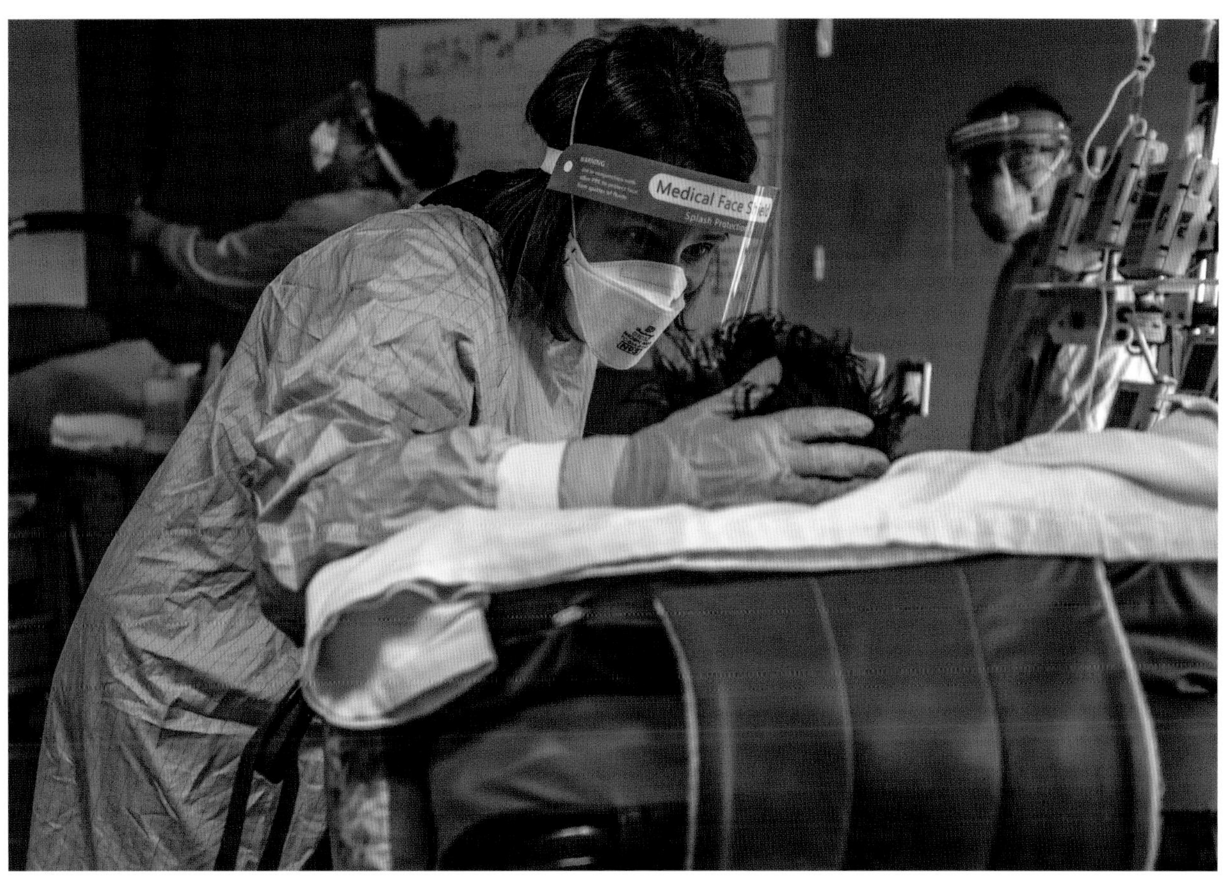

Physiotherapist Maureen Tosh, left, works with a
COVID-19 patient at Peter Lougheed Centre in the
intensive care unit in September 2021.

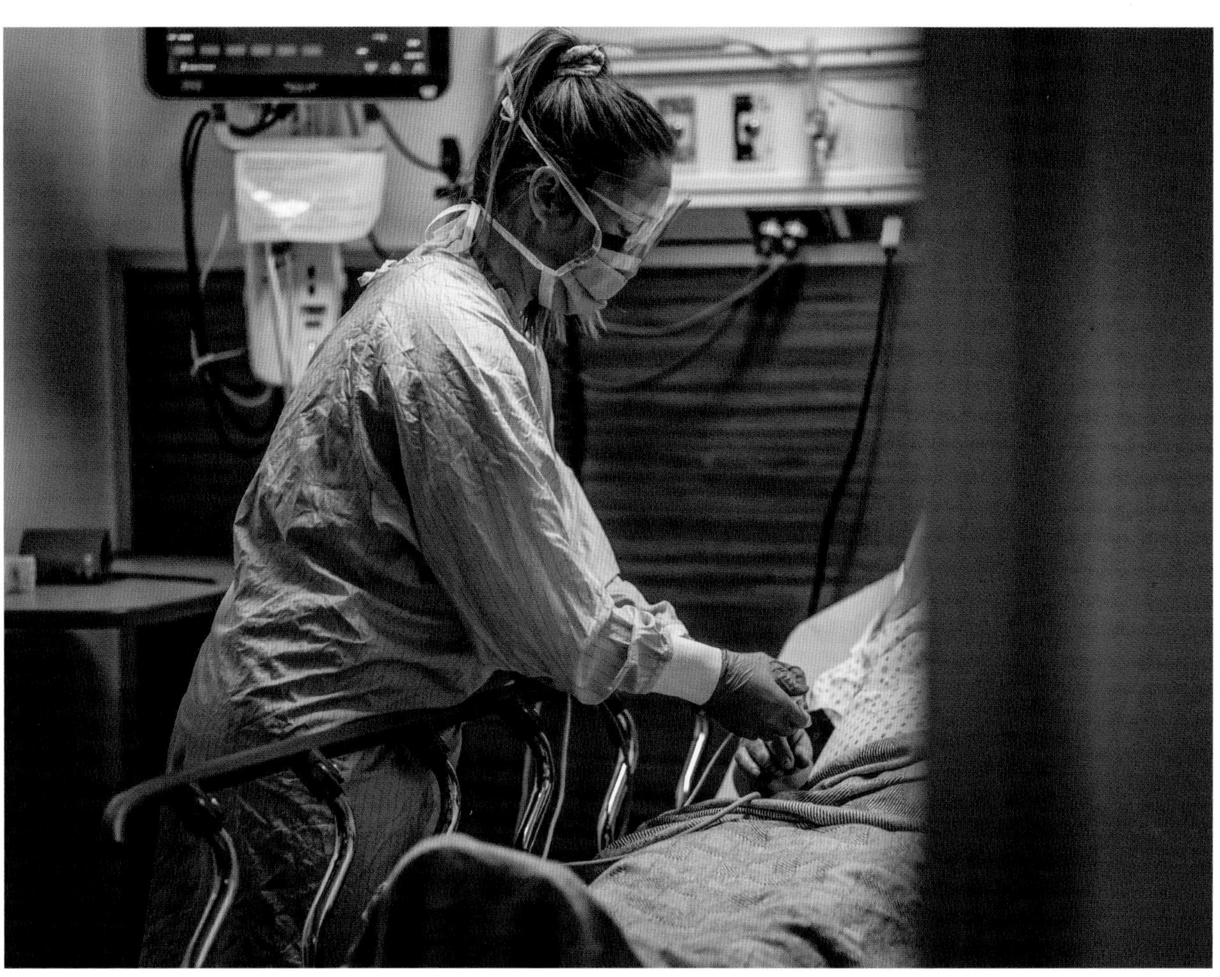

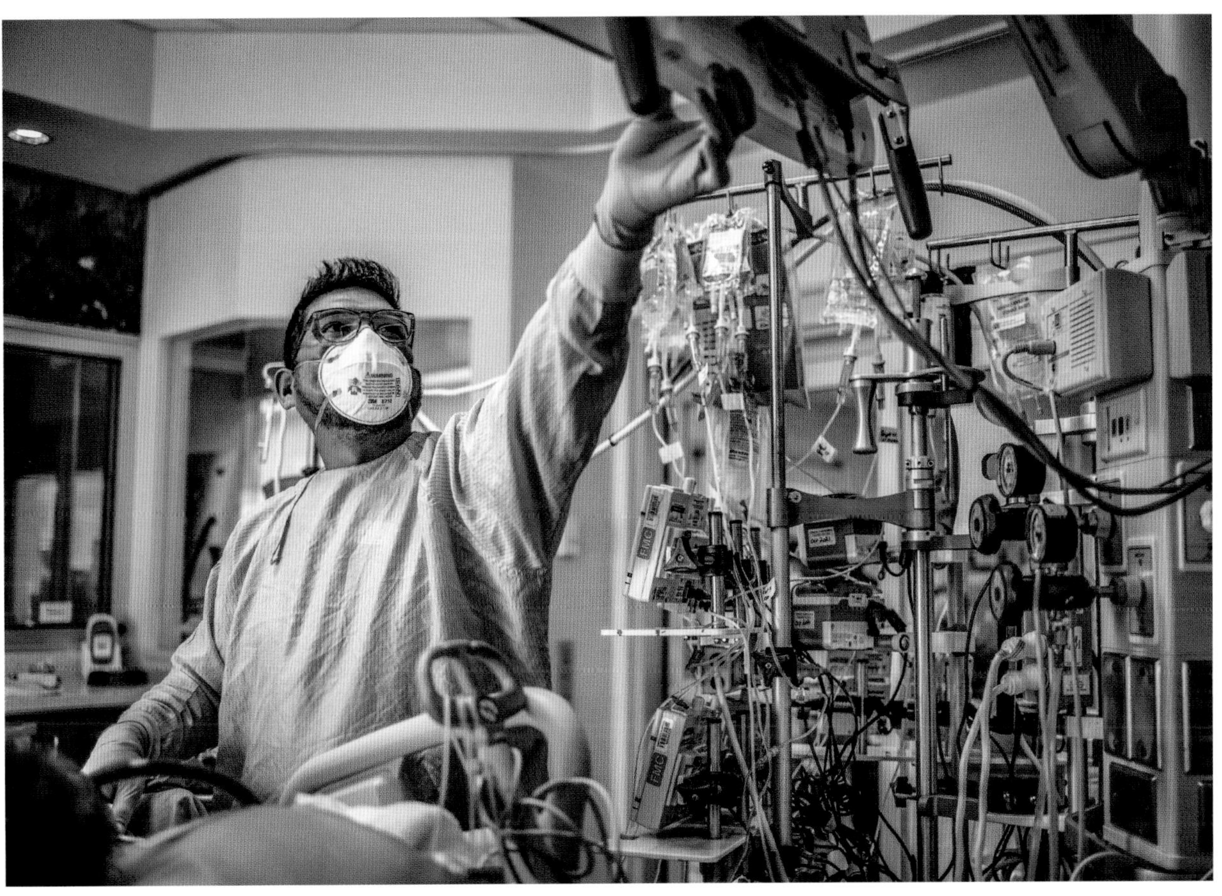

Registered nurse Renae Nedza in the emergency room at Chinook Regional Hospital in Lethbridge, Alberta.

Registered nurse Richard Tamon monitors the vitals of a patient with COVID-19 at Foothills Medical Centre.

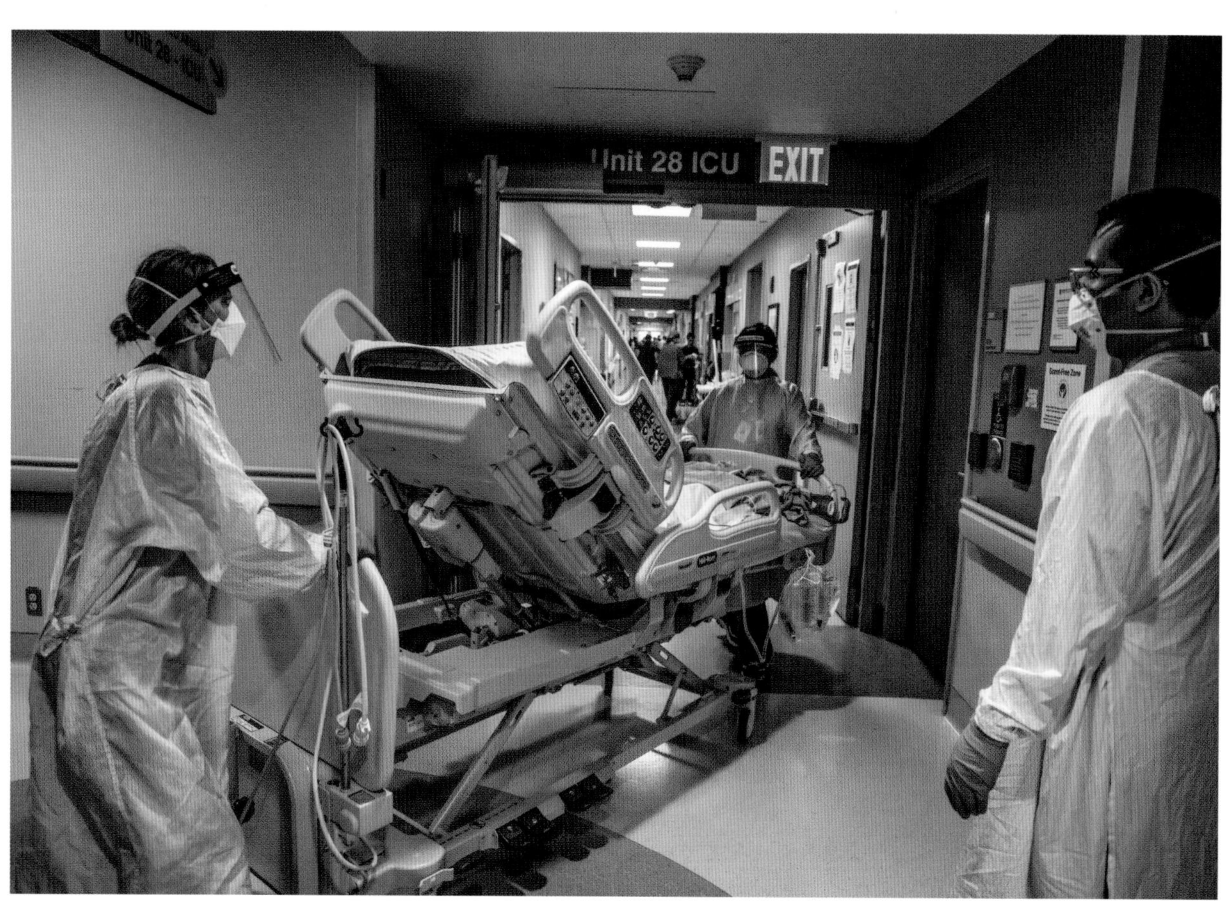

Unit 28 ICU
EXIT
Scent-Free Zone

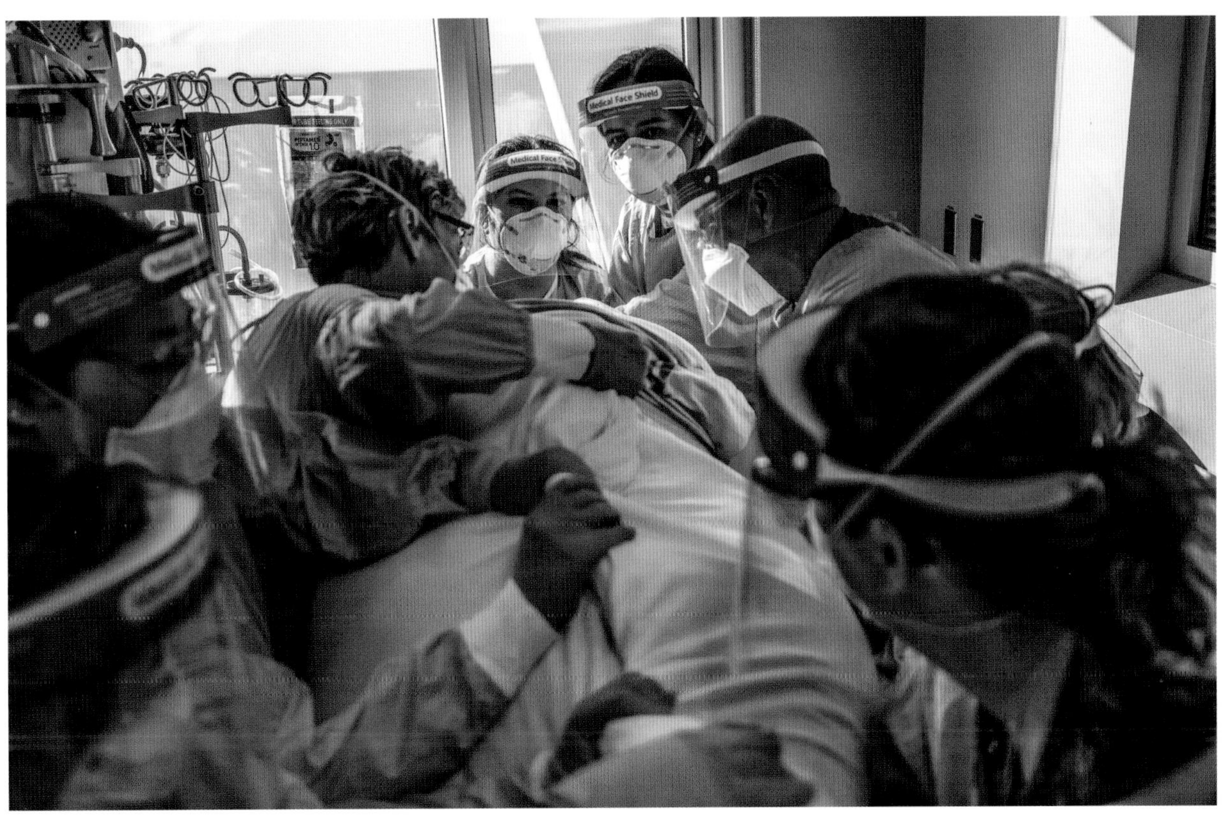

Porters and other healthcare staff bring a
COVID-19 patient from the COVID-19 unit to
the intensive care unit to be intubated at Peter
Lougheed Centre on September 15, 2021.

A healthcare team moves a patient with
COVID-19 onto their stomach, which can help
increase oxygen flow.

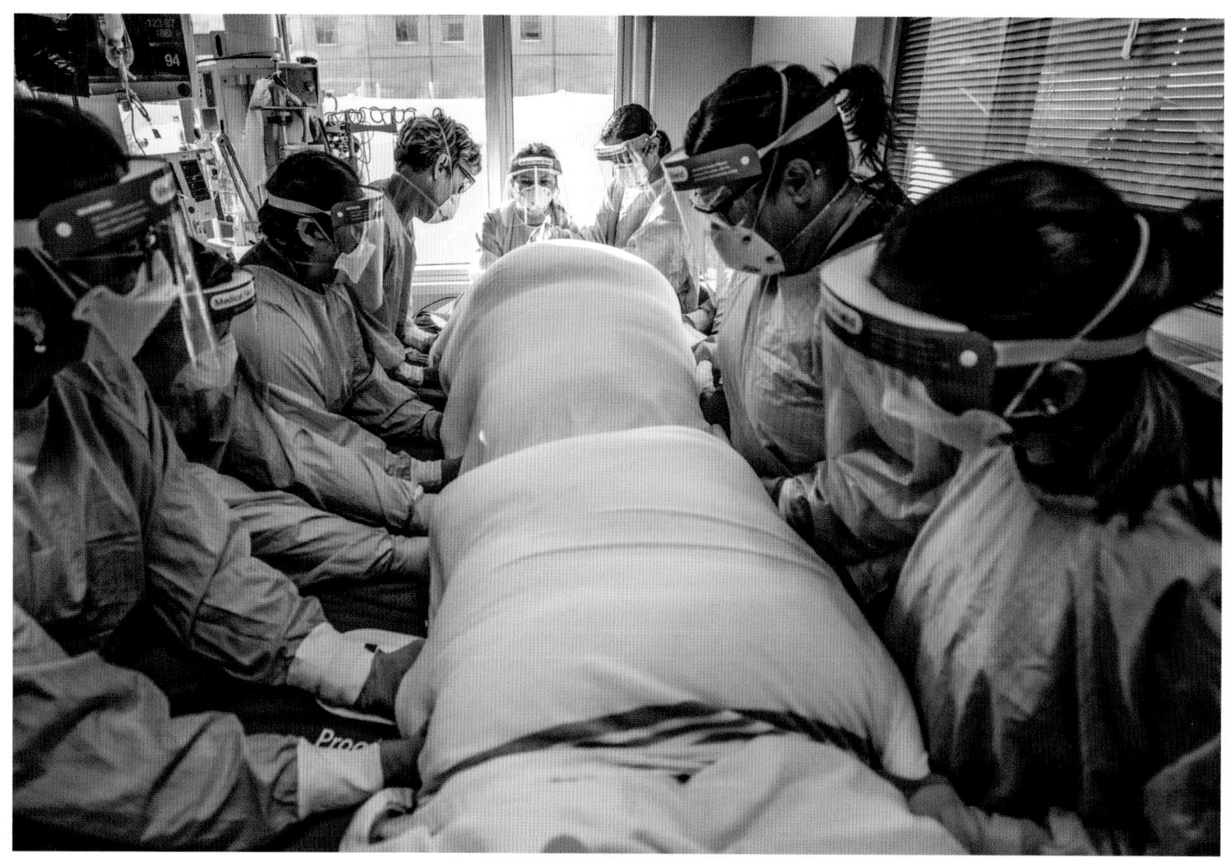

A healthcare team moves a patient with COVID-19 onto their stomach, which can help increase oxygen flow.

Respiratory therapist Jerell Mananghaya cuddles with Quincy, a 4-year-old English sheep dog, who volunteers with his owner for PALS, in the intensive care unit at Peter Lougheed Centre in September 2021.

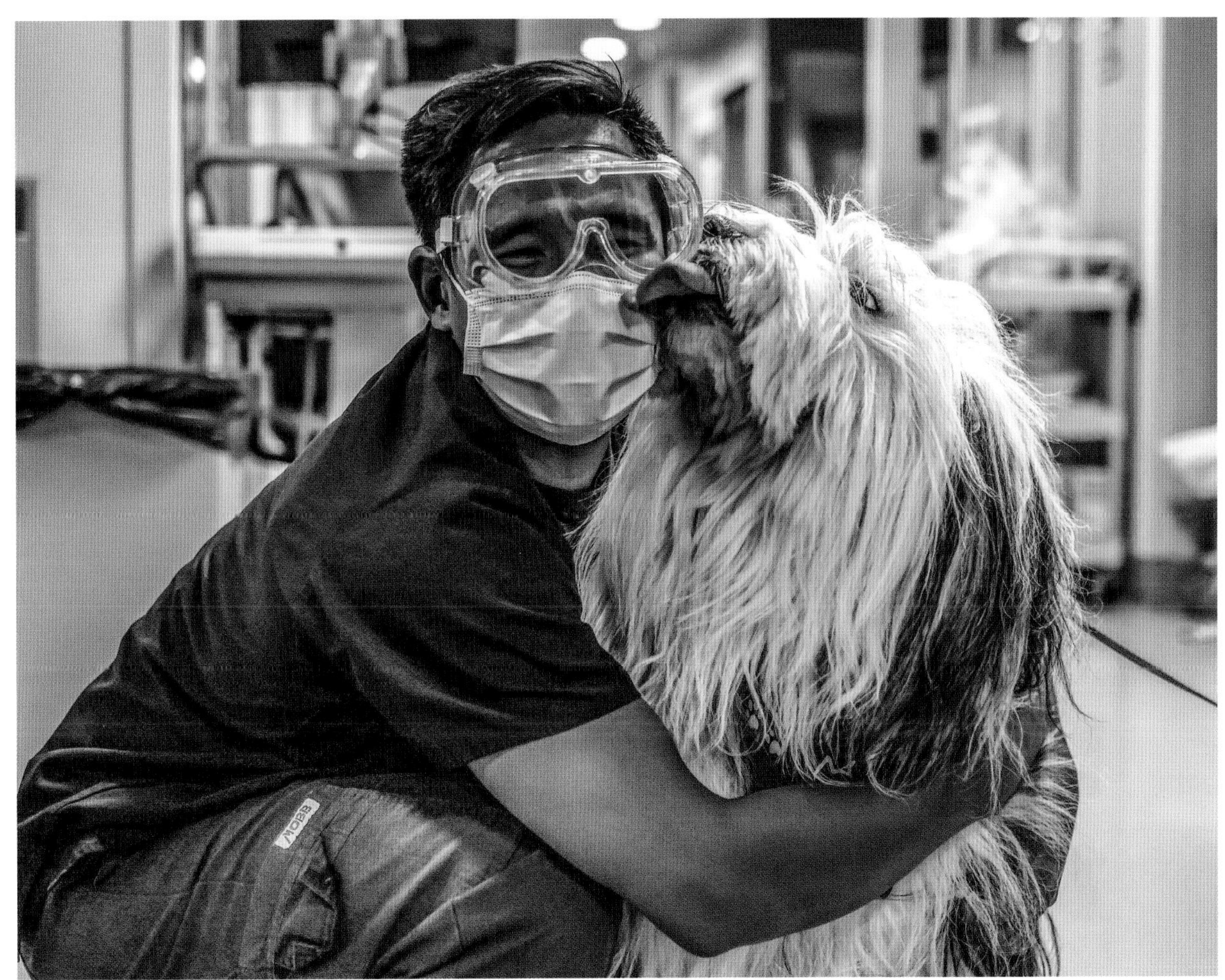

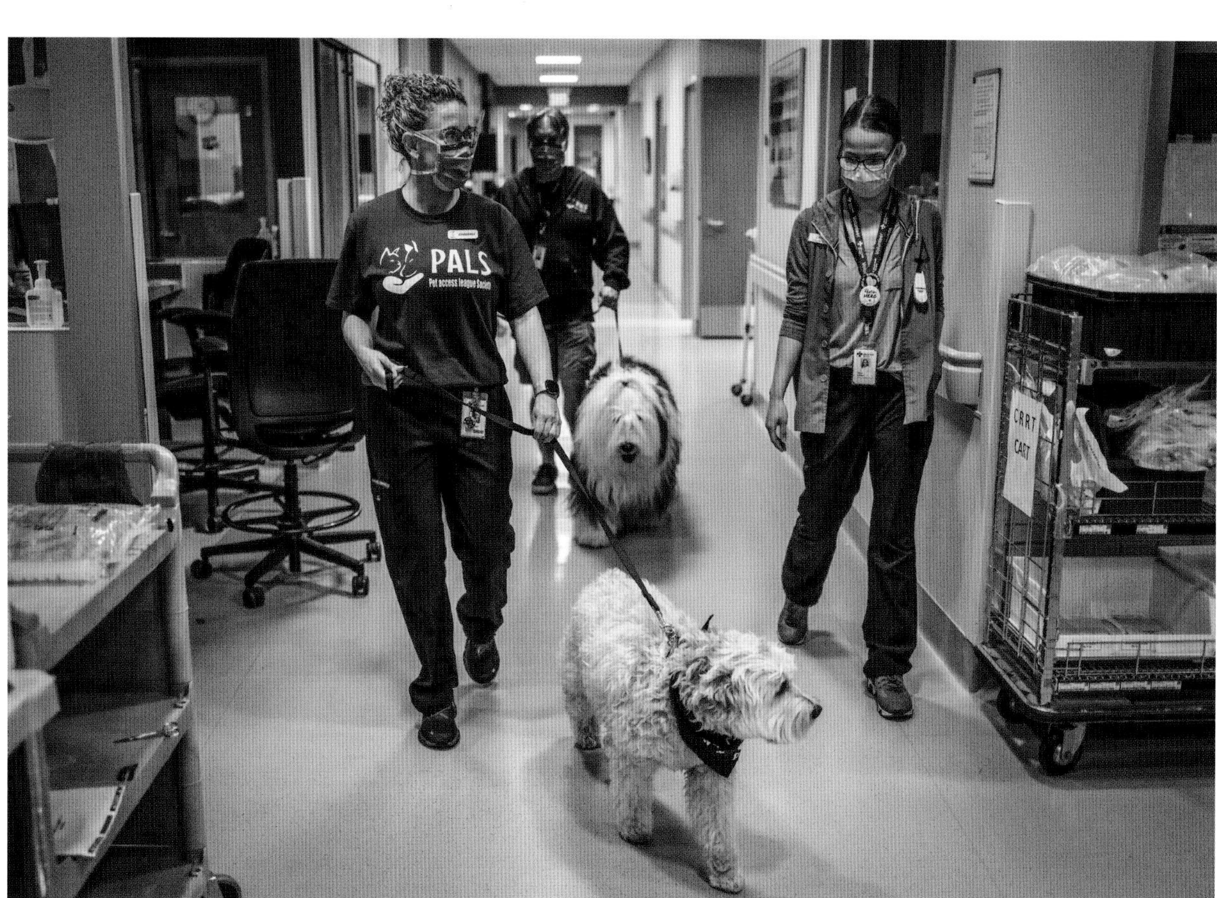
PALS
Pet access league Society
CRRT
CART

Foothills Medical Centre ICU manager Kimberly Pennell and her dog Murphy visit the intensive care unit at Peter Lougheed Centre in September 2021.

Pennell volunteers with the Pet Access League Society (PALS).

She recently brought Murphy to meet with staff and physicians at Peter Lougheed Centre. Accompanied by Quincy, owned by fellow PALS volunteer Russell Morash, they received quite the reception.

"The staff came running to see them, exclaiming, 'This has been the best part of my day,'" Pennell says. "It definitely filled my cup."

Pet therapy has been shown to provide comfort and support for people experiencing high levels of stress. The Volunteer Resources Pet Therapy program works with groups throughout the province to provide support at sites across Alberta.

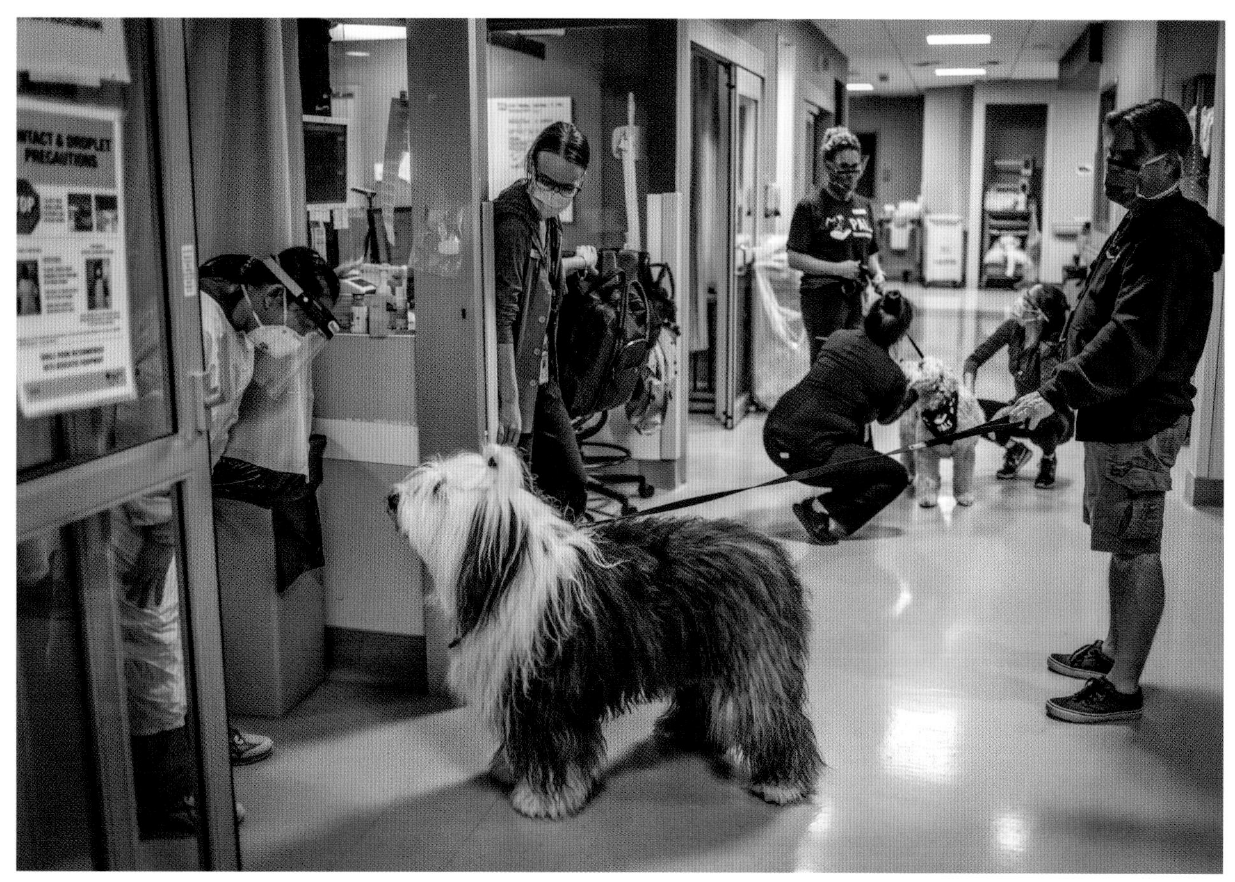

PALS volunteers visit healthcare staff in the
intensive care unit at Peter Lougheed Centre
in September 2021.

A registered nurse comforts a COVID-19
patient minutes before intubation in the
intensive care unit at Peter Lougheed Centre
in September 2021.

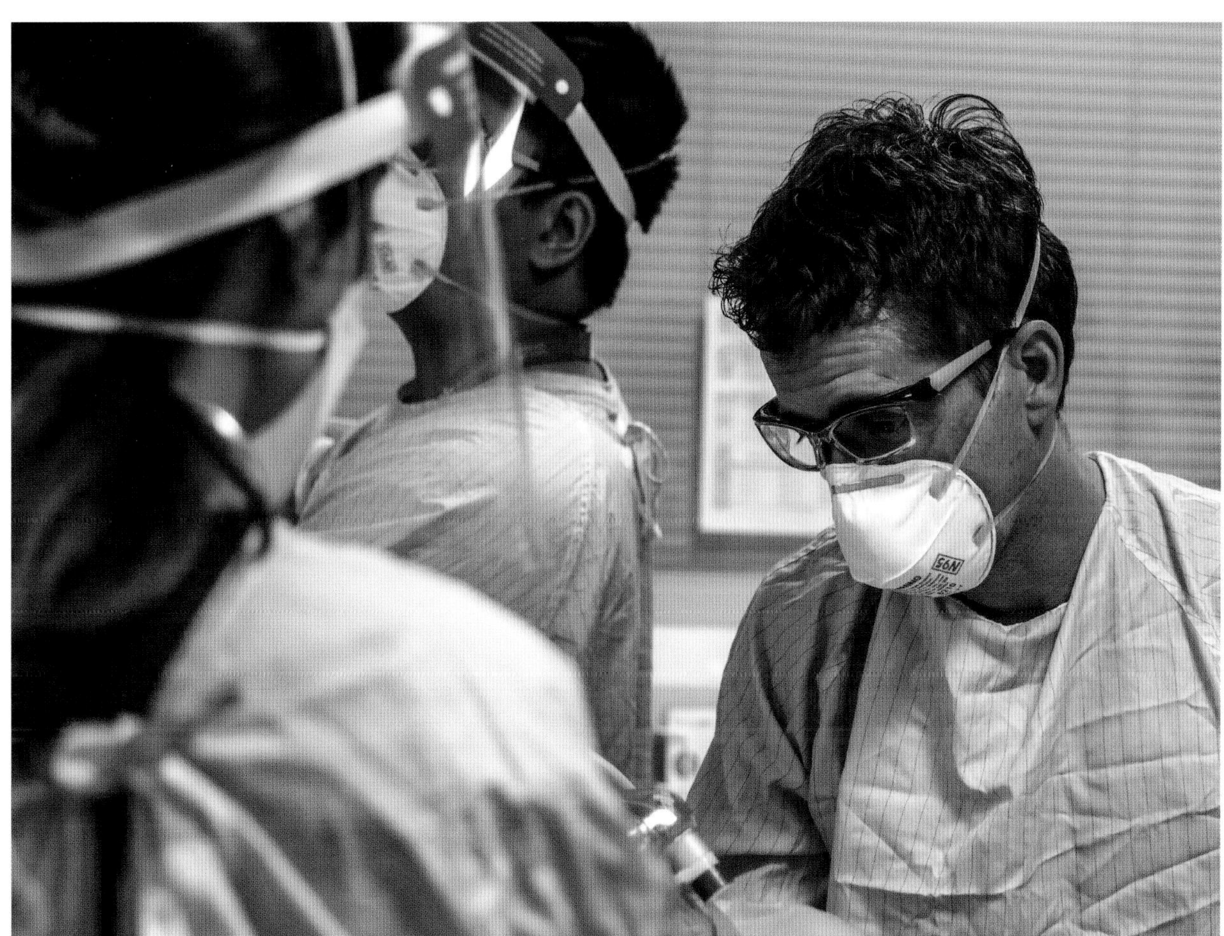

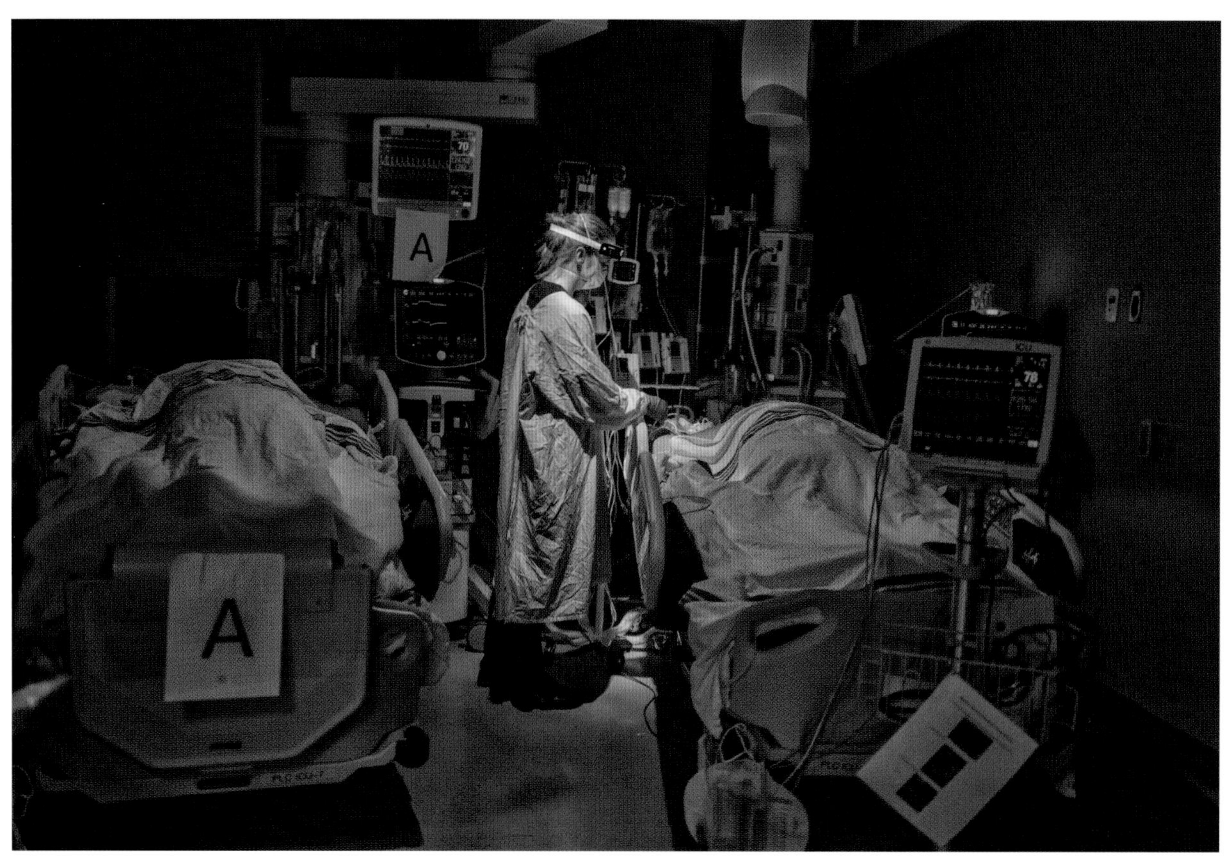

Registered nurse Jeremy Schlosser takes care
of two COVID-19 patients during the night shift
in the intensive care unit at Peter Lougheed
Centre during the fourth wave.

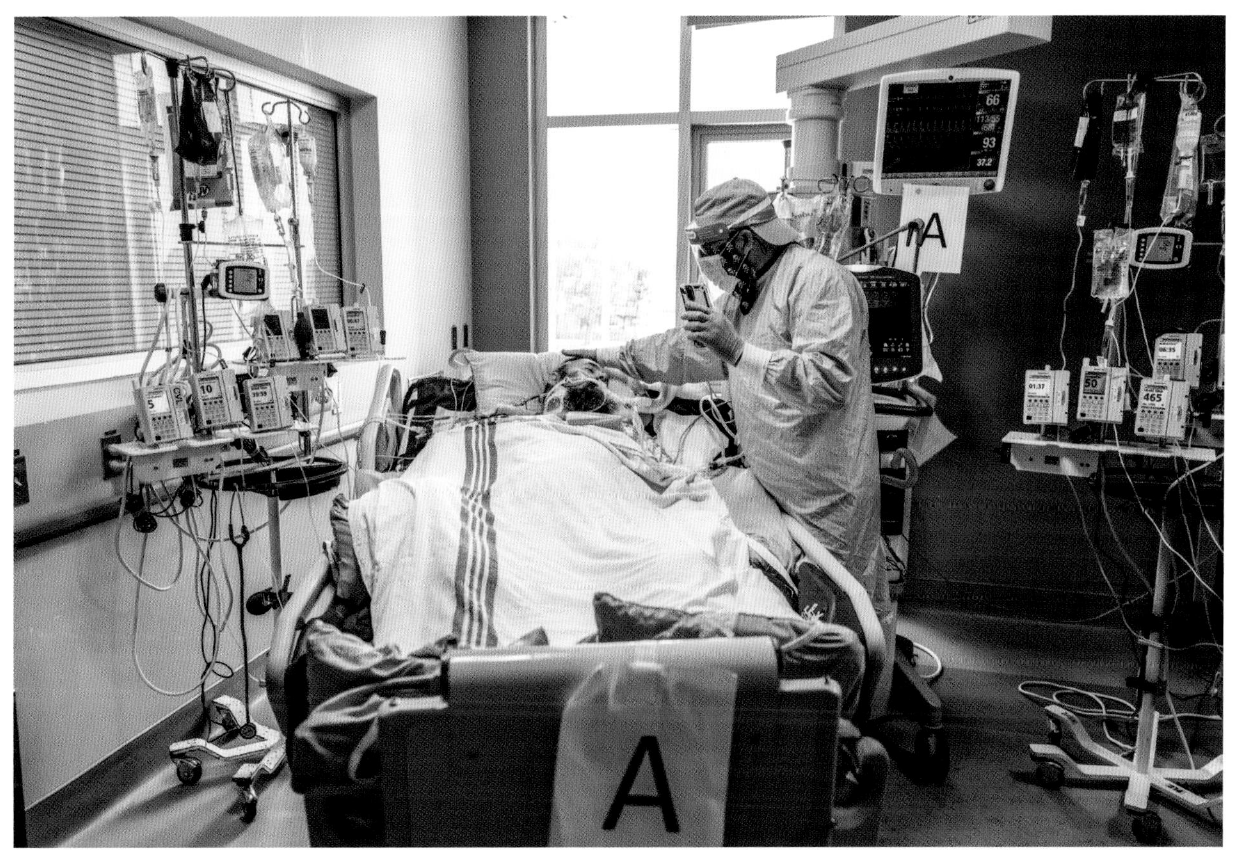

Intubated COVID-19 patient Bernie Cook gets
a visit from his brother Joseph Guimond in the
intensive care unit on September 17, 2021, at
Peter Lougheed Centre.

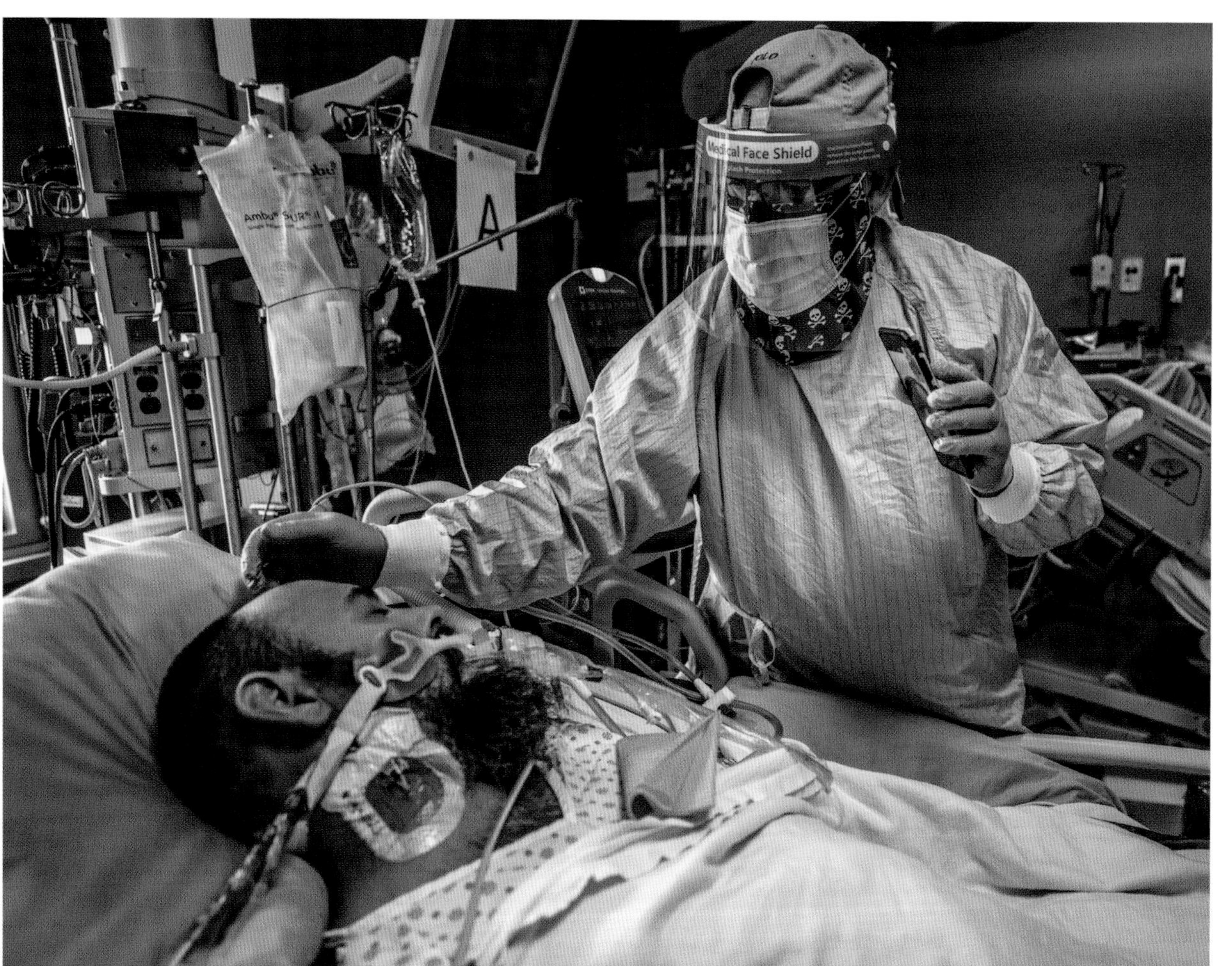

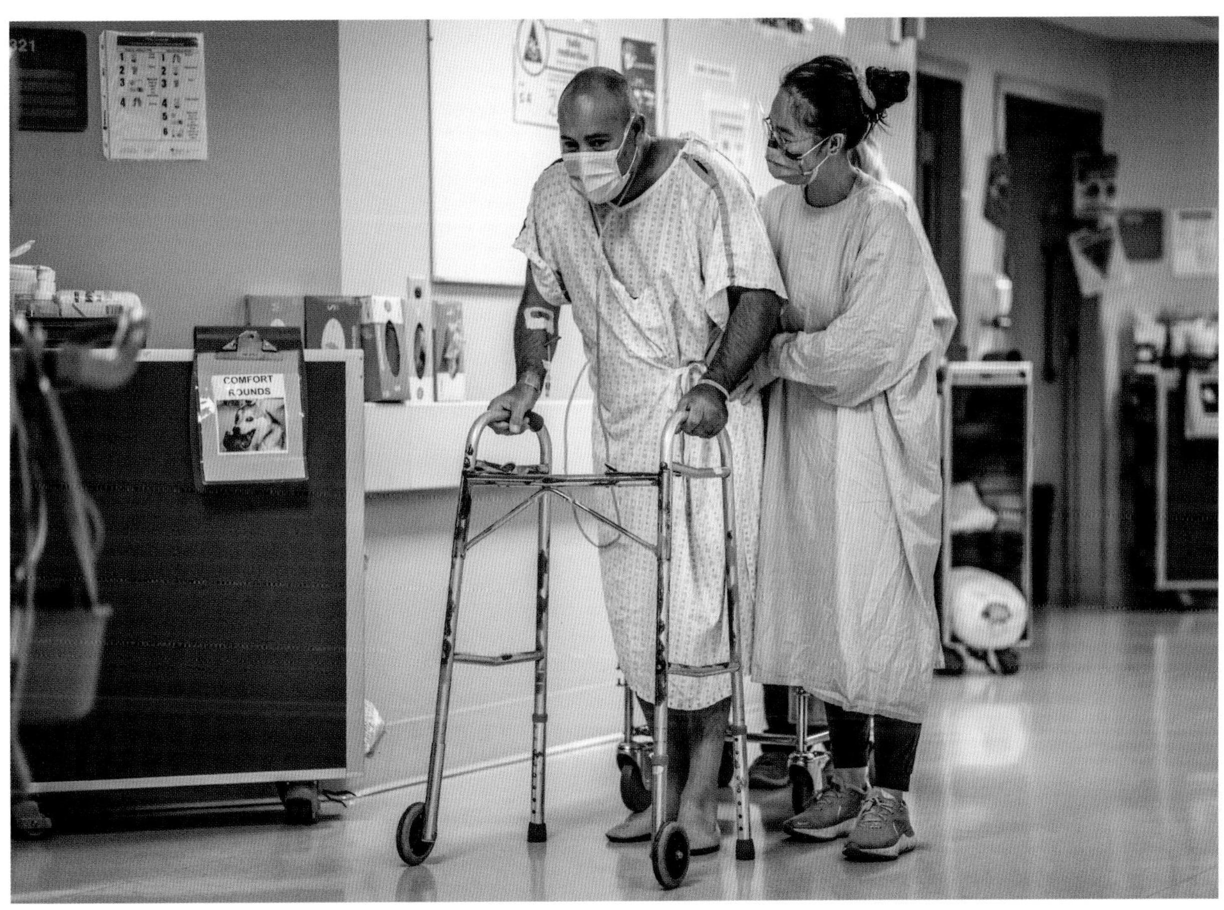

Intubated COVID-19 patient Bernie Cook gets a visit from his brother Joseph Guimond in the intensive care unit on September 17, 2021, at Peter Lougheed Centre.

Bernie Cook works through his first therapy session in the COVID-19 unit after being discharged from intensive care on September 21, 2021, at Peter Lougheed Centre.

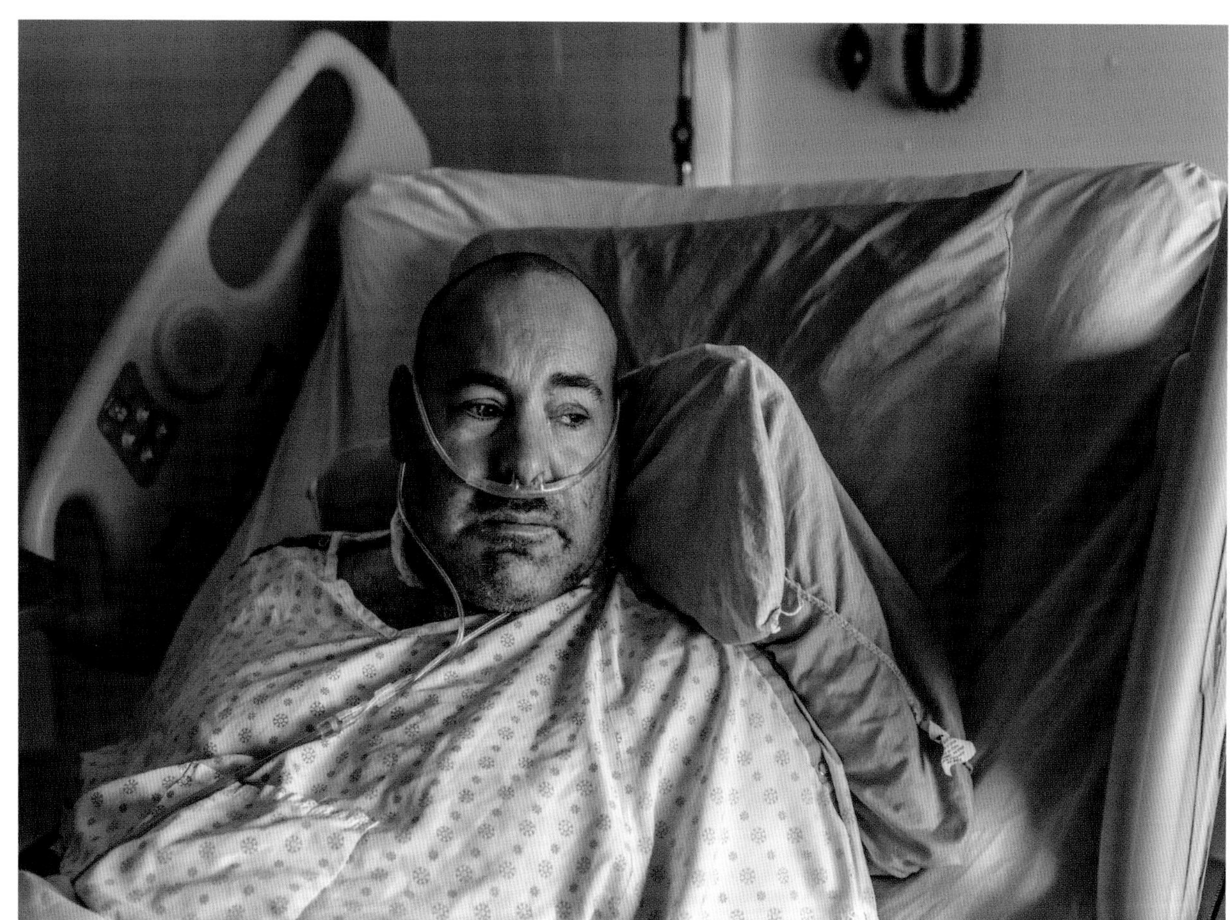

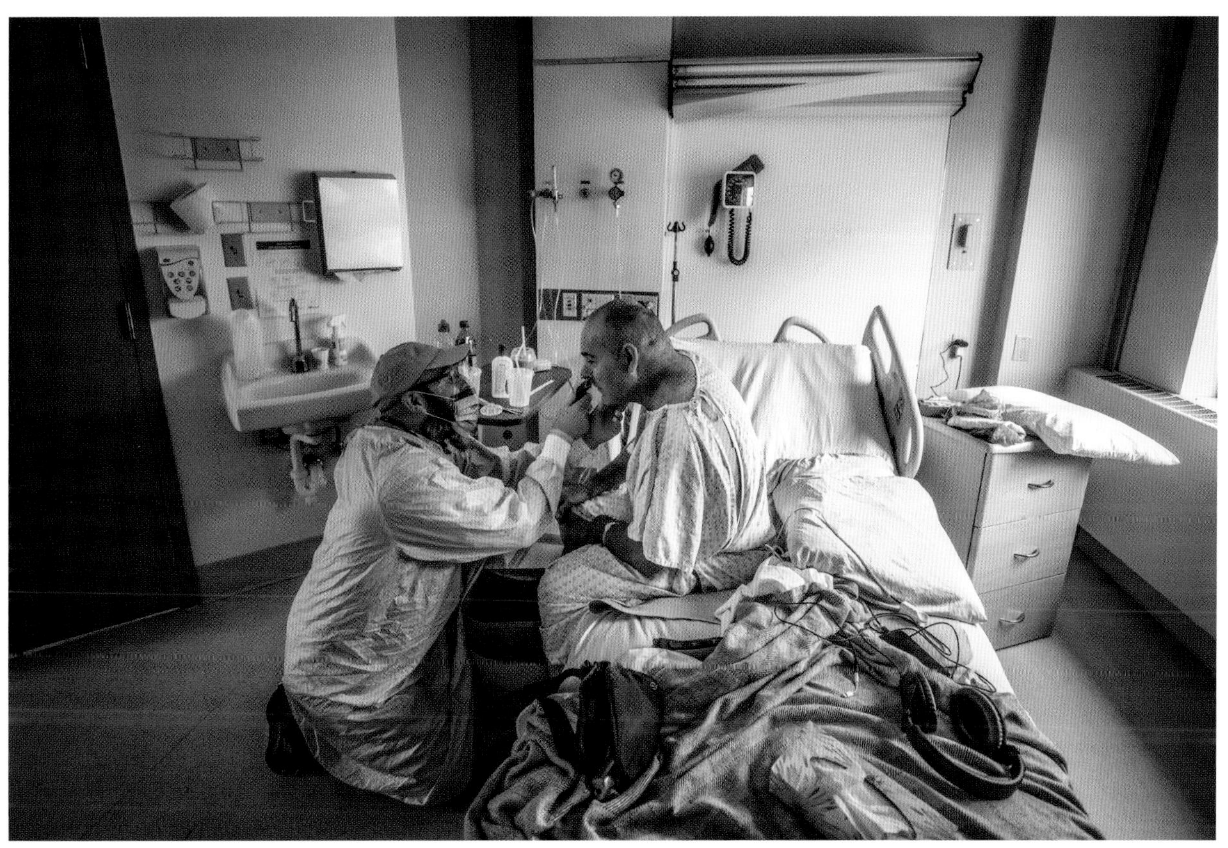

Bernie Cook, 46, in the COVID-19 unit after being discharged from intensive care on September 21, 2021, at Peter Lougheed Centre in Calgary.

Bernie Cook receives a shave from his brother Joseph Guimond in the COVID-19 unit at Peter Lougheed Centre on September 22, 2021.

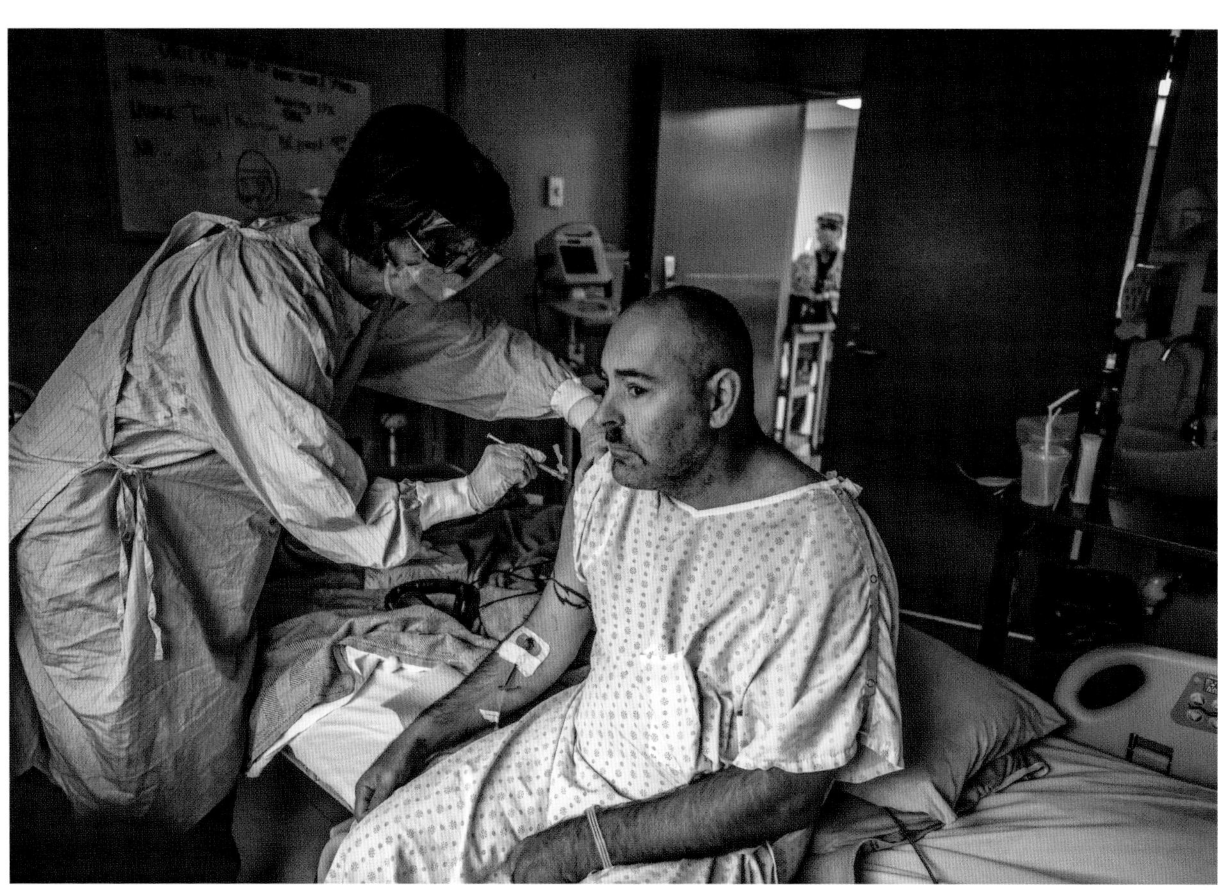

Bernie Cook receives a vaccine in his hospital room on the COVID-19 unit at Peter Lougheed Centre on September 22, 2021.

"I ended up getting COVID-19, one of the variants, and it nearly killed me," says Cook, 46. "If it wasn't for the staff here at the ICU, I'd be dead."

Bernie spent two weeks in the Peter Lougheed Centre ICU and was on a ventilator. His family did not know if he would survive.

"It was really scary," says Bernie, who credits the healthcare team for saving his life. "It's dark. I've seen desolation. COVID-19 is the scariest and darkest thing I've ever come across."

"The ICU staff paid so much care and attention. It's just remarkable, how much compassion they have."

Bernie's wife had already gone for her COVID-19 vaccine. As for Bernie, he hadn't got around to it. "Just being lazy, you know," he says. "Maybe not taking it as seriously as I could have or should have, and because of that, it nearly cost me my life."

On September 22, Bernie received his first dose of COVID-19 vaccine in hospital. "And I'm looking forward to living, really truly living."

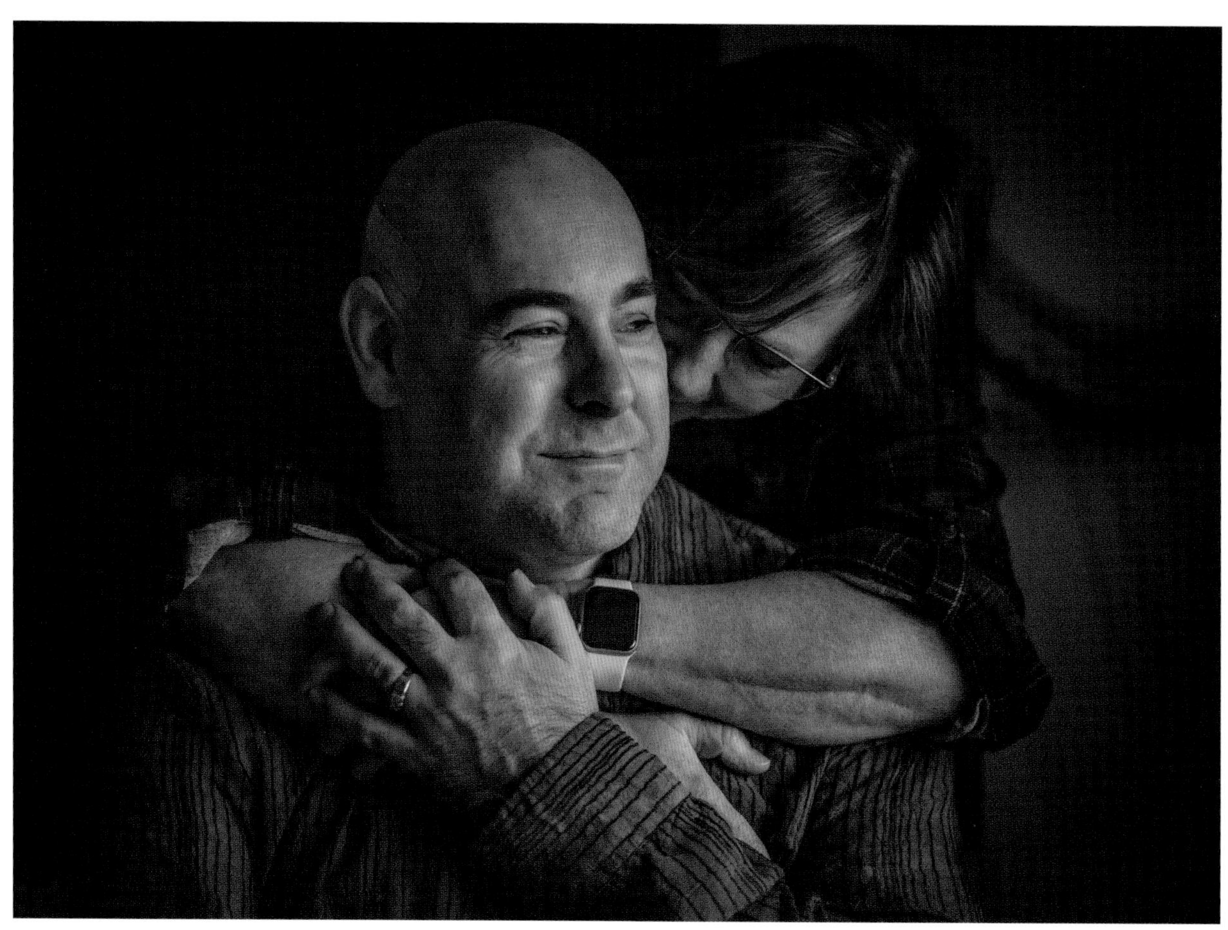

Bernie Cook — at home with his wife Susan
in Calgary, Alberta, on November 12, 2021 —
has nothing but gratitude for the healthcare
workers who helped save his life.

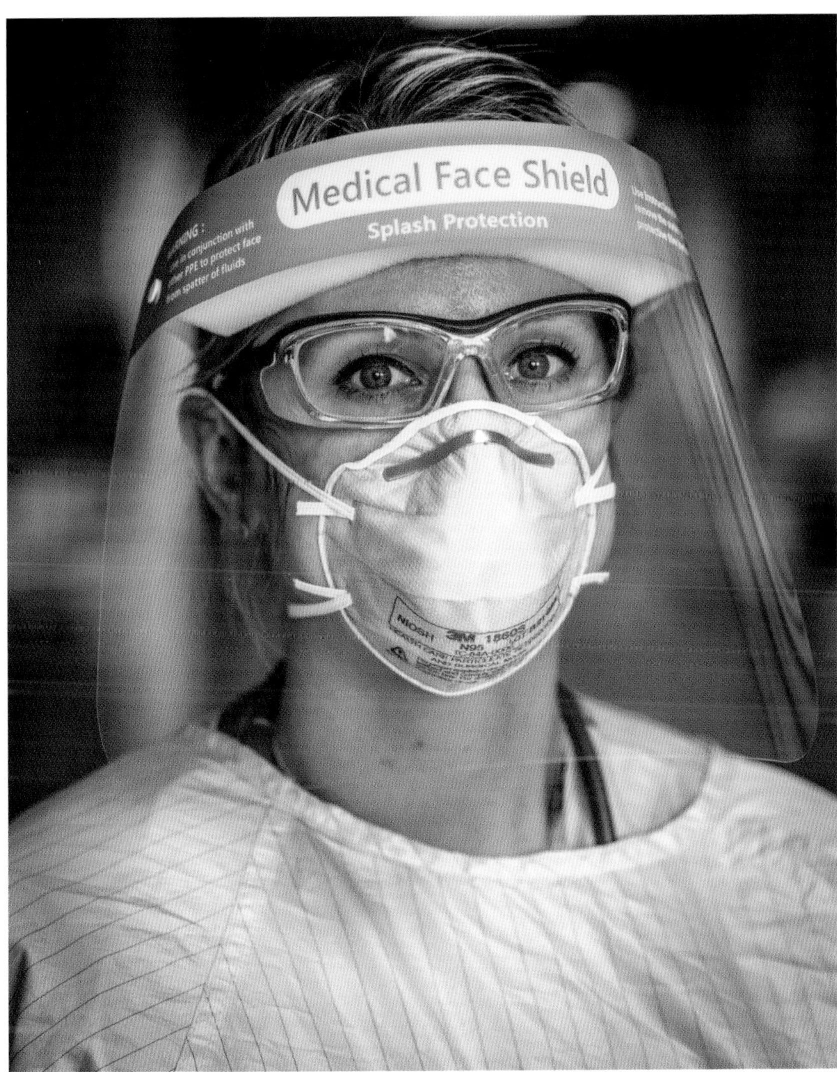

Respiratory therapist Nancy Van
Der Velden in the intensive care unit
at Peter Lougheed Centre.

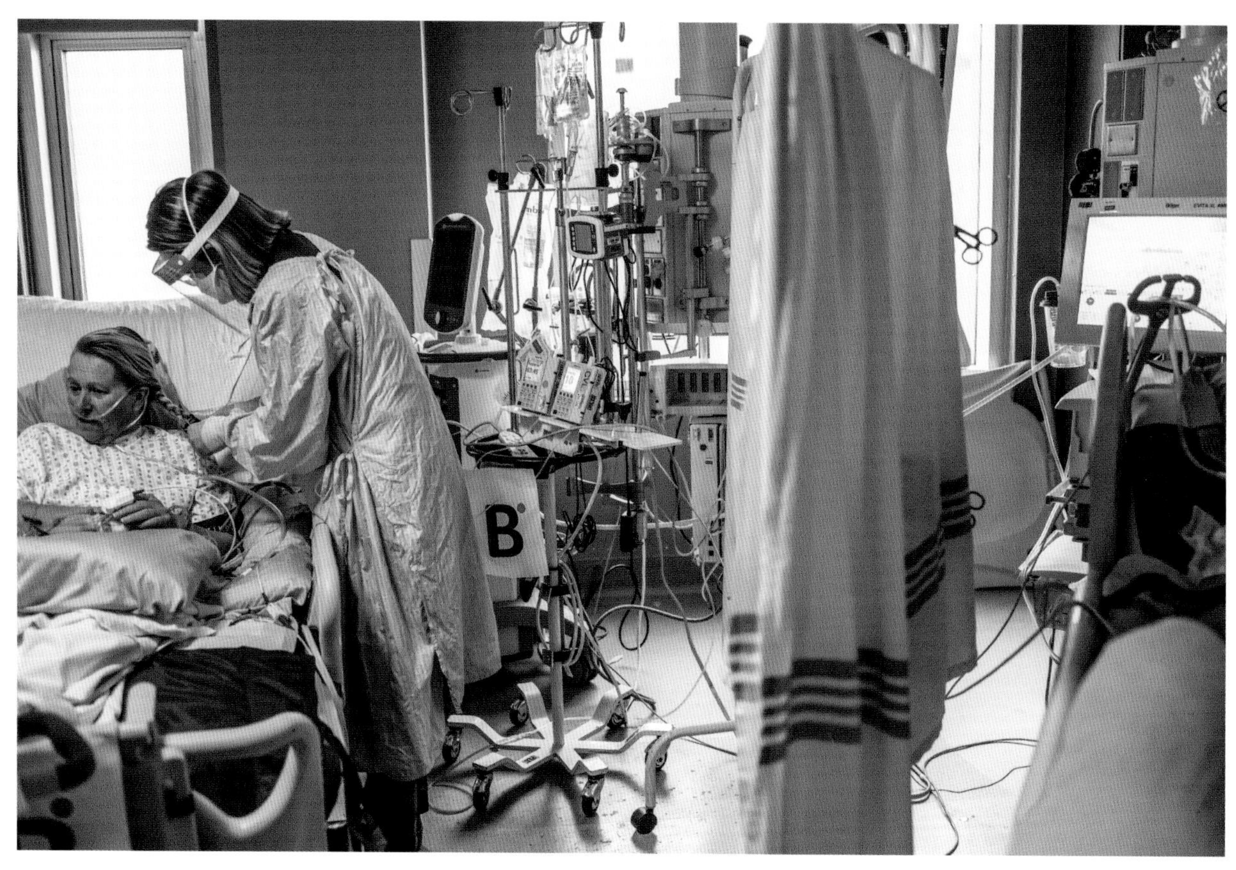

A registered nurse braids COVID-19 patient Cheryl Kopp's hair in the intensive care unit at Peter Lougheed Centre.

Reg Kopp, 61, visits his wife Cheryl in the COVID-19 unit at Peter Lougheed Centre on October 12, 2021. They both had COVID-19 but Cheryl was in the intensive care unit for ten days.

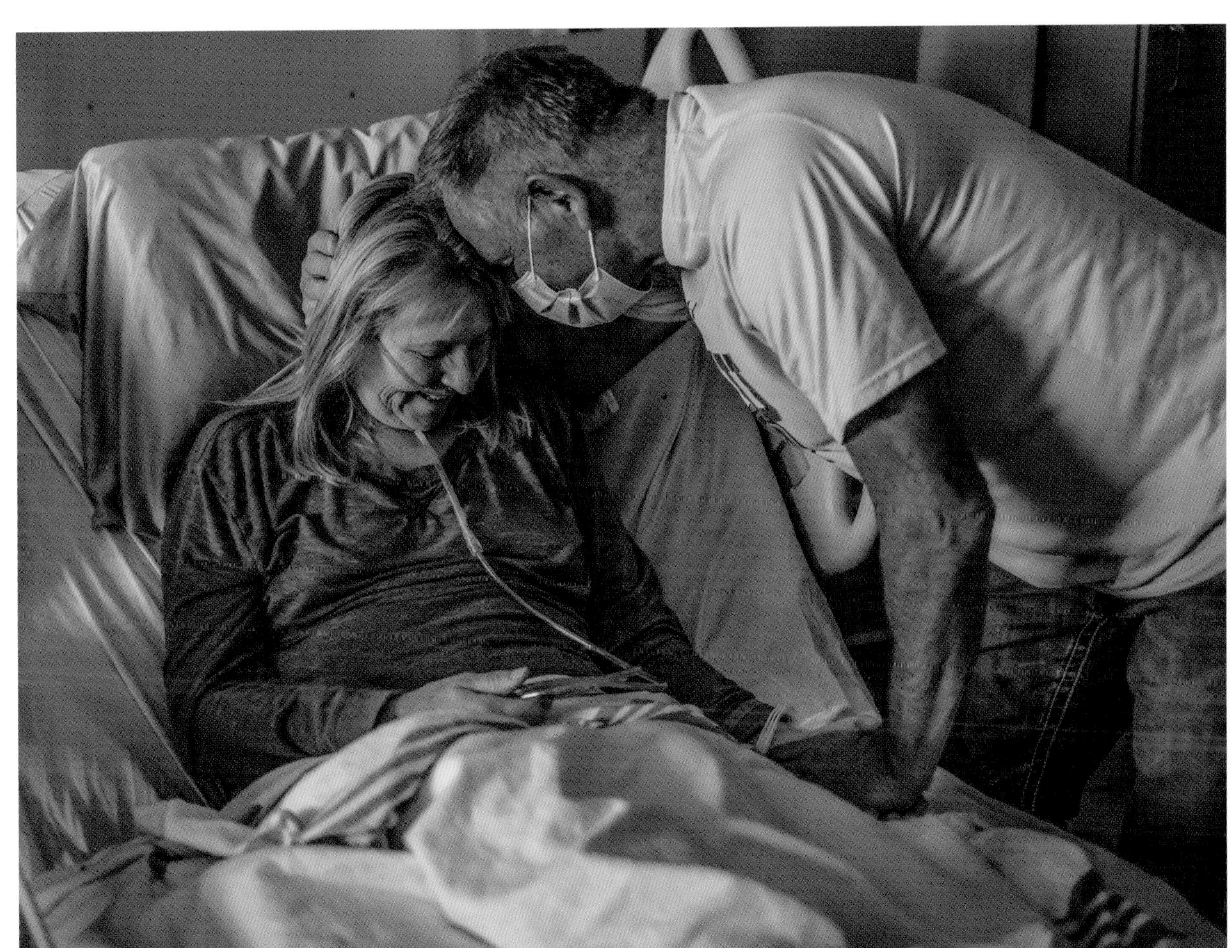

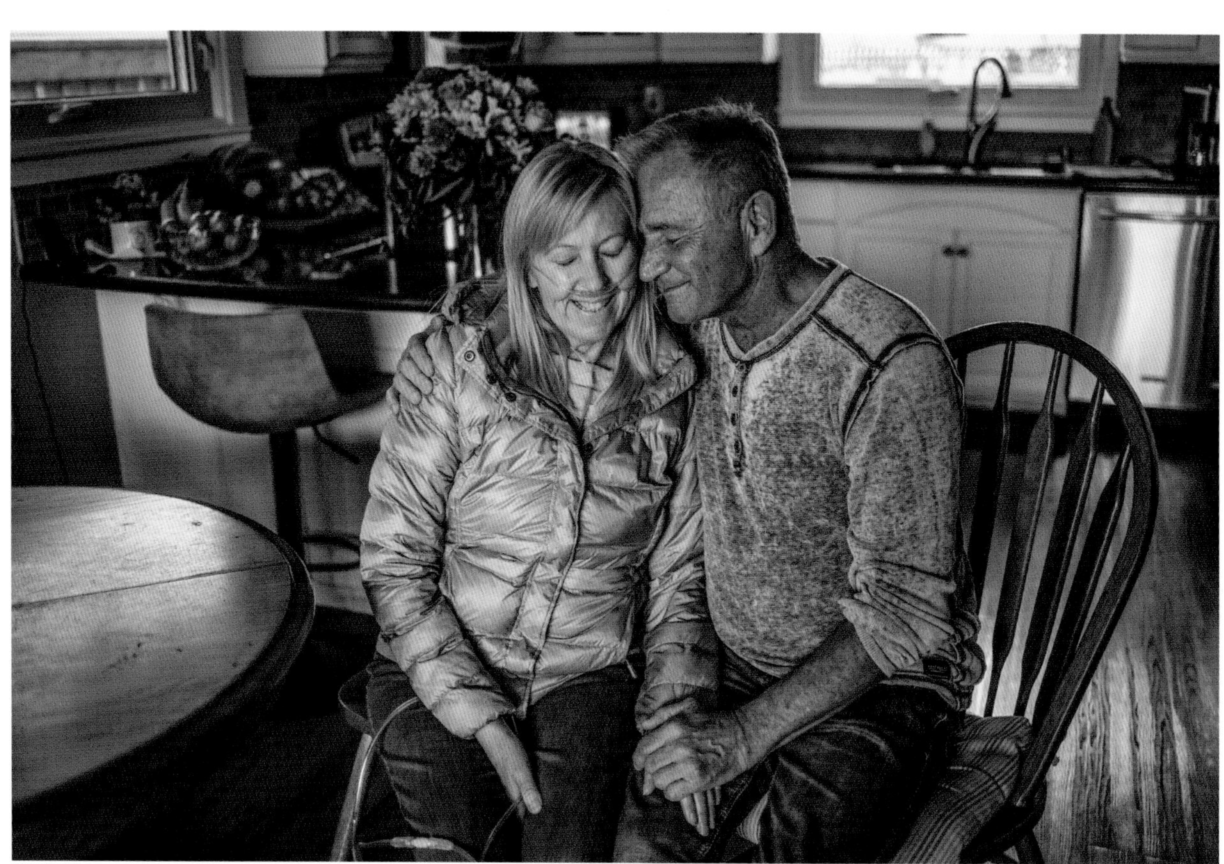

"Everything is a challenge," says Cheryl Kopp. "Everything in my life has changed. It is so challenging, from going to the bathroom to having a bath to putting socks on. Nothing is the same anymore."

Cheryl, 57, tested positive for COVID-19 in September 2021. She had developed a cough, which quickly got worse. Her husband, Reg Kopp, 61, also became sick.

"The first three days, I thought, 'This is really nothing,'" Cheryl recalls. "And then, it hit, and it hit hard.... This is not the flu. This is something entirely different."

For the first ten days, the two struggled at home. "We hurt so bad for days, and we did nothing but sleep and wake up and throw up, try to eat a little bit," Reg says. "It was horrible. We both went downhill pretty fast."

Reg started to feel a bit better after a few days, but Cheryl just became sicker. "I was watching her on the Saturday night, trying to sleep, and she was just convulsing, crying in her sleep," Reg says. "I was really worried."

The next morning, Cheryl's lips were blue and she was crying, struggling to breathe.

He took her to the hospital and by the time he returned home, a doctor called to tell him to say goodbye to his wife of 35 years.

"Just like that," Reg says. "I just said 'I love you.'"

Cheryl spent ten days on a ventilator in the ICU and developed large blood clots in her lungs. She is still on medication and oxygen.

The Kopps were not vaccinated against COVID-19, something that they now regret. Like many people, they had seen misinformation on social media, claiming that COVID-19 wasn't real and that the COVID-19 vaccines would make them sick.

"We stalled too much. We were always waiting for something better, better research to come along," Cheryl says. "And then life gets busy and so do you, and you put it on the back burner."

But both Reg and Cheryl say their opinion of vaccines has changed. They are now vaccinated against COVID-19. "We both got our shots," Reg says. "It's a real no-brainer."

As for the healthcare workers that saved his wife's life? "Beautiful people," says Reg. "I can't thank the Alberta hospital services enough. They saved my wife's life. They saved her life and they were so good to me."

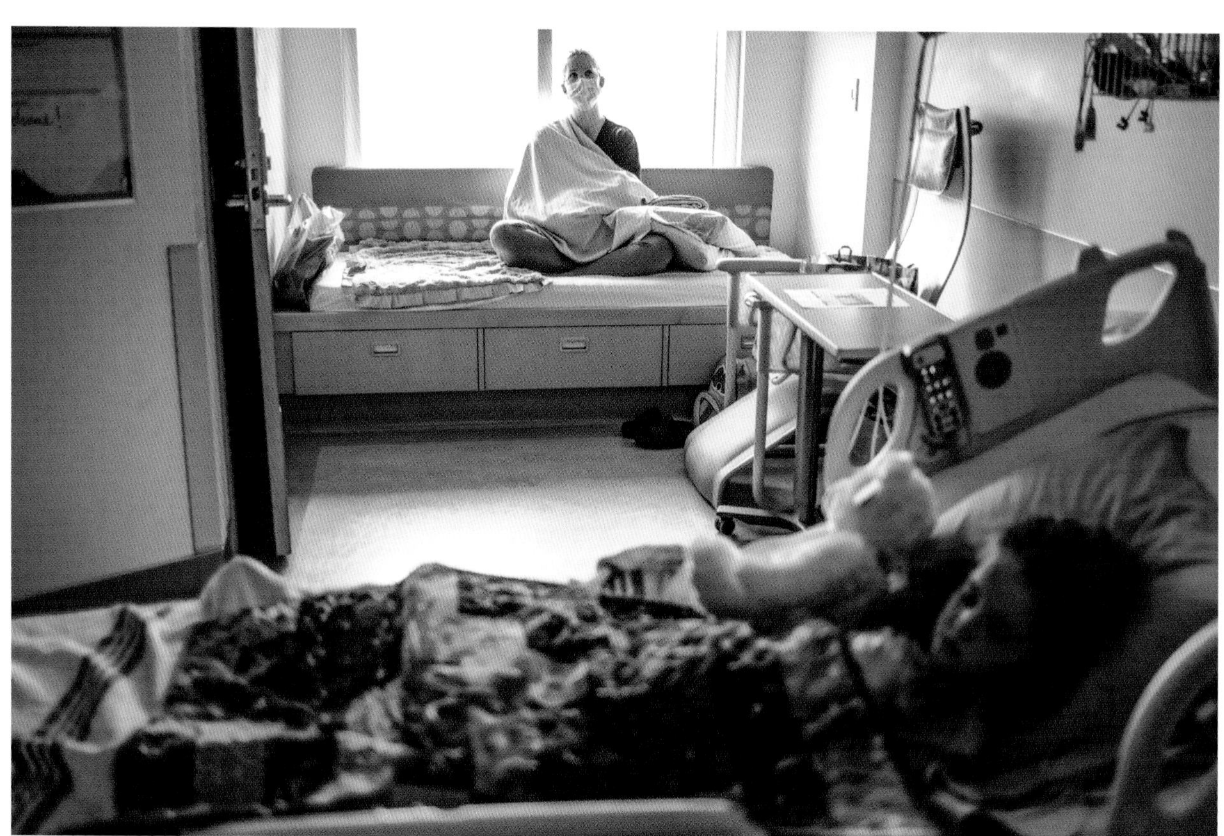

Rebecca Walker nurses her six-week-old son Ovo as her daughter Winnifred (Freddie), 6, sleeps at Alberta Children's Hospital in Calgary on October 22, 2021.

Mike and Rebecca Walker thought their daughter had a bladder infection.

But when Freddie's fever skyrocketed, they knew it was something much more serious. Mom and Dad rushed the six-year-old from their home in Raymond to the local emergency ward — then, via ambulance, to Lethbridge, then, via air ambulance, to Alberta Children's Hospital in Calgary.

Freddie was diagnosed October 19 with multi-system inflammatory syndrome in children (MIS-C), which appears to be linked to COVID-19. It is a dangerous condition that can affect the brain, lungs, kidneys or, in Freddie's case, the heart.

"It's been scary," said Mike. "That first day, it was, 'Is she going to make it? What's going to happen?' But since we've been here, it's been good. It's reassuring to know that she's in good hands. It's more about how quickly she can recover, but we know that's she going to."

Seven weeks earlier, while pregnant with the couple's fifth child, Rebecca tested positive for COVID-19. "Freddie had been in the same household as me, so she had been exposed."

Then came that frightening fever and subsequent MIS-C diagnosis, a development that shook her mother.

"It was pretty sad and kind of scary," said Rebecca. "But they took really good care of her. She's now out of the ICU and doing a lot better. She's doing much better."

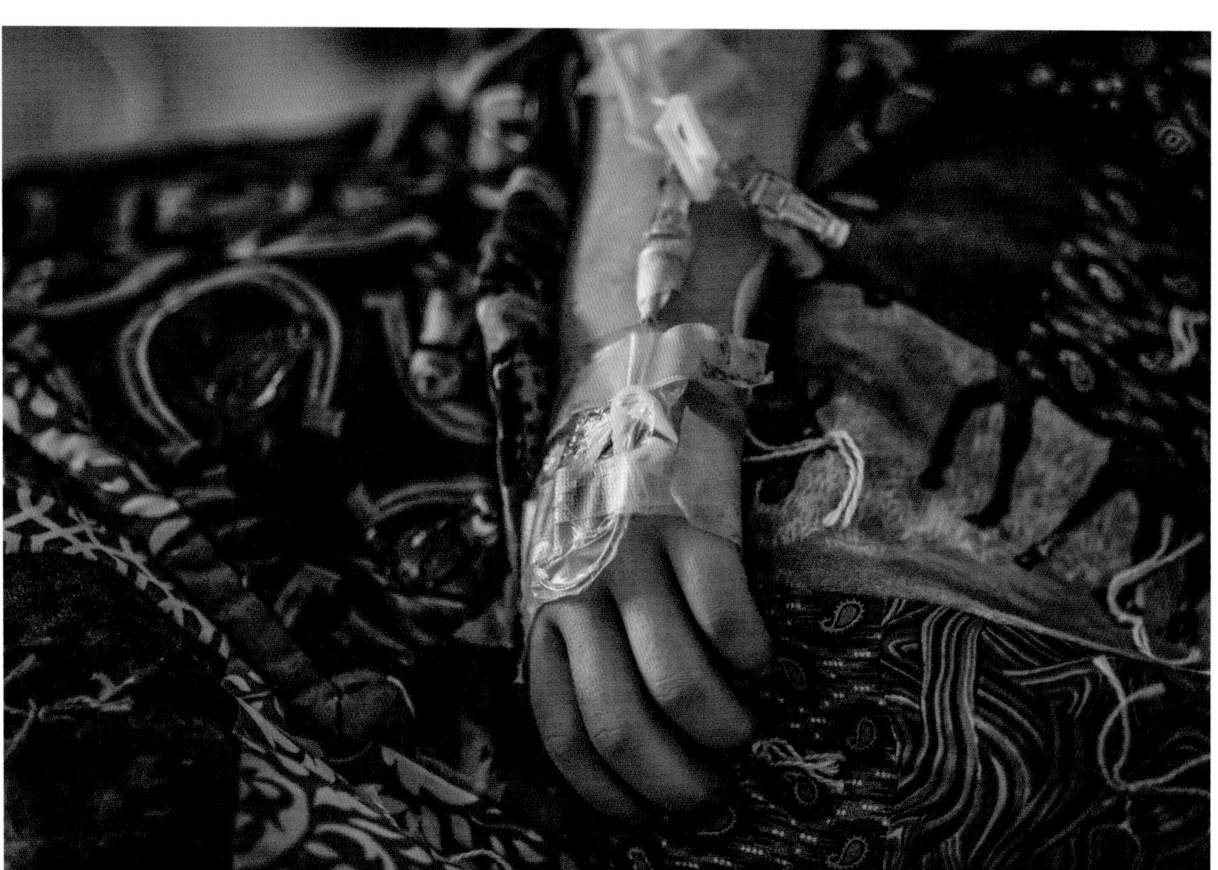

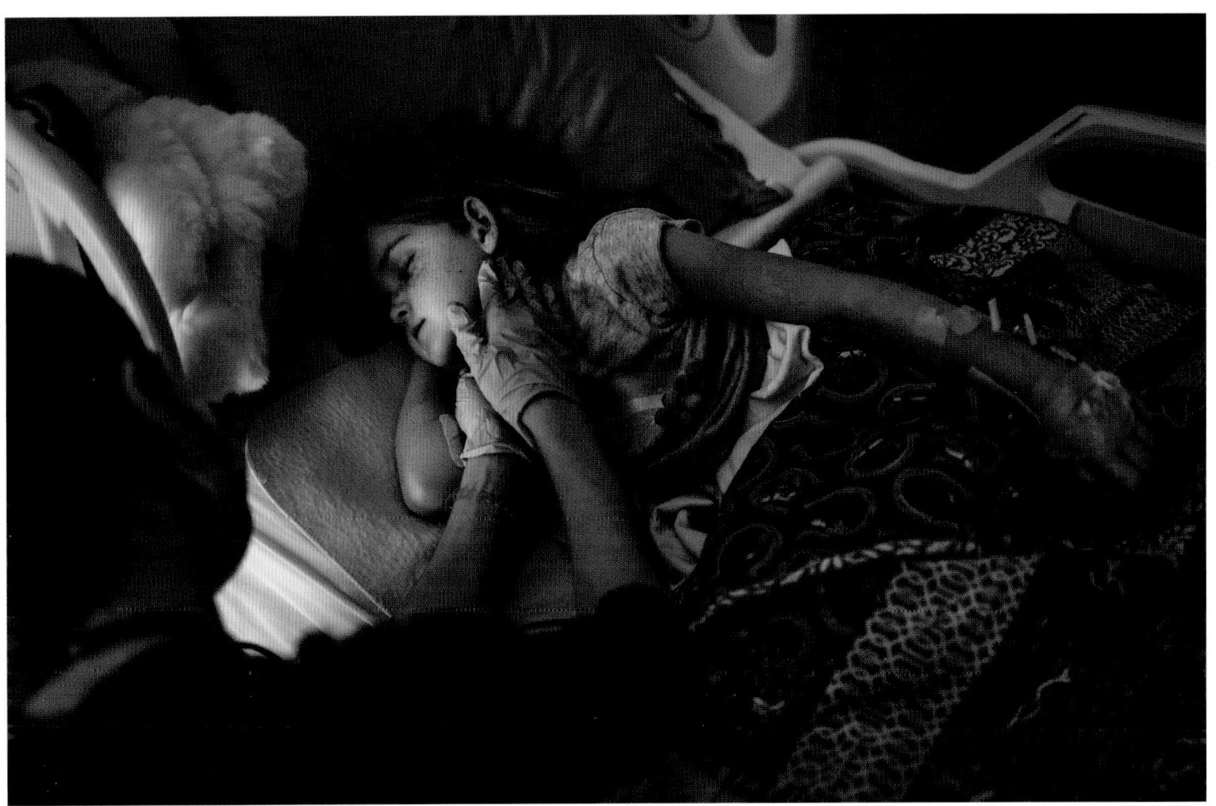

Freddie Walker, 6, at Alberta Children's Hospital in Calgary on October 22, 2021.

A doctor checks on Freddie Walker on October 22, 2021. Freddie was diagnosed with multi-system inflammatory syndrome in children (MIS-C), an illness linked to COVID-19.

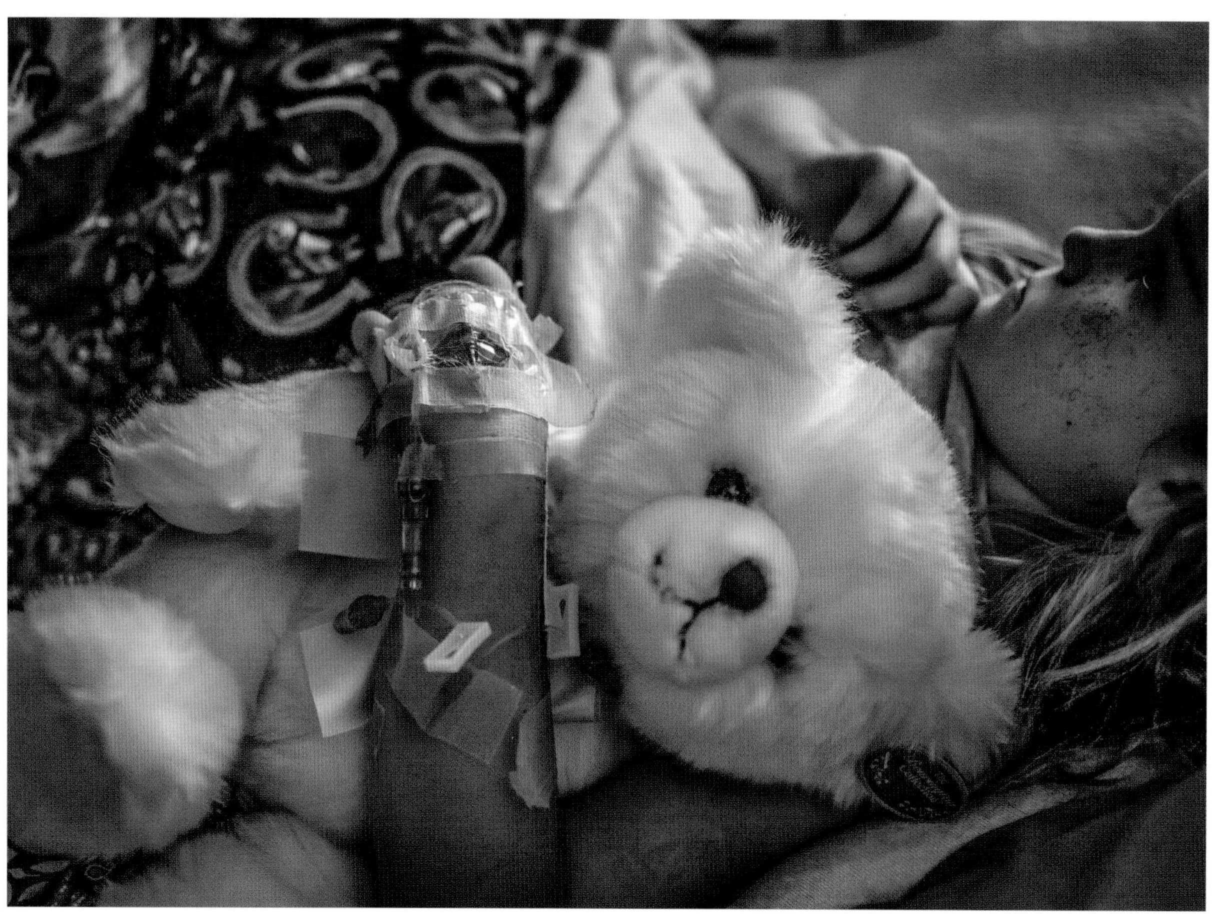

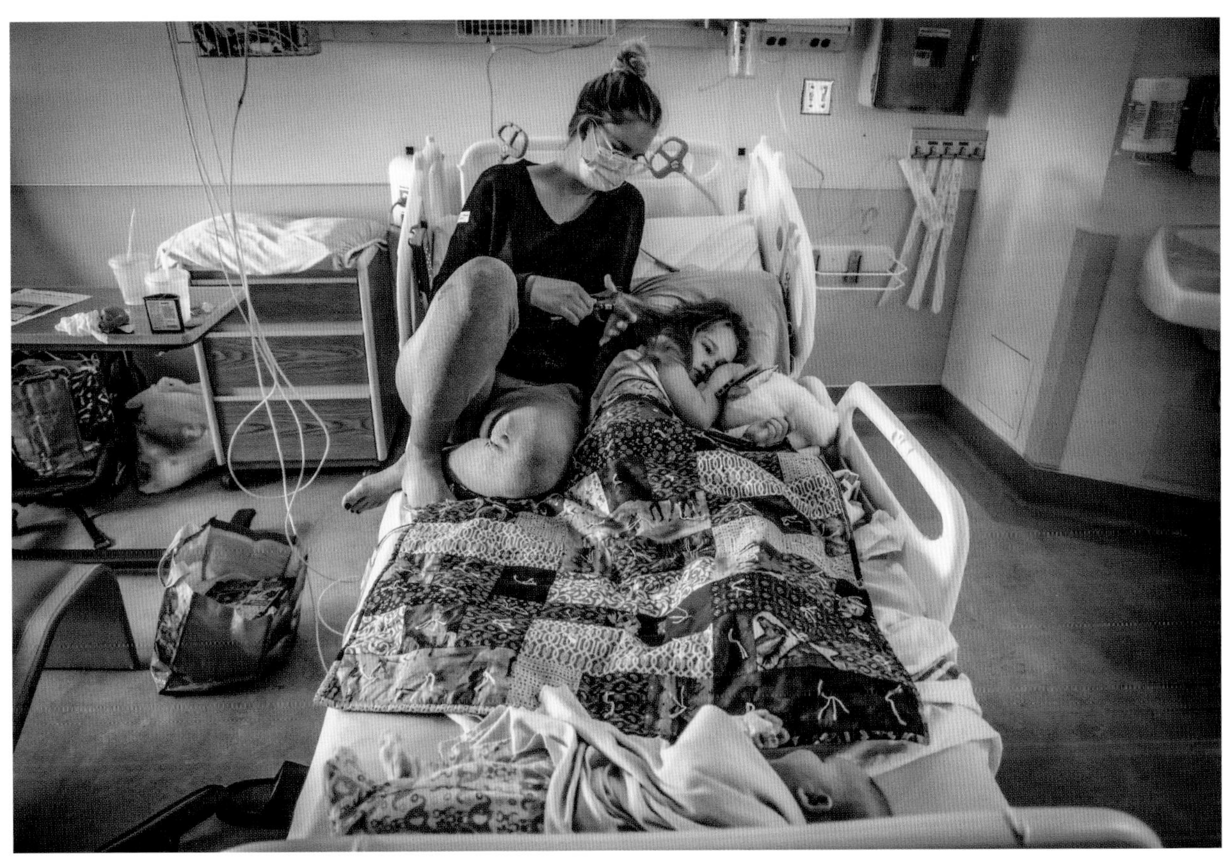

Freddie Walker, 6, cuddles a stuffie at Alberta Children's Hospital.

Rebecca Walker brushes Freddie's hair in their room at Alberta Children's Hospital in Calgary on October 22, 2021.

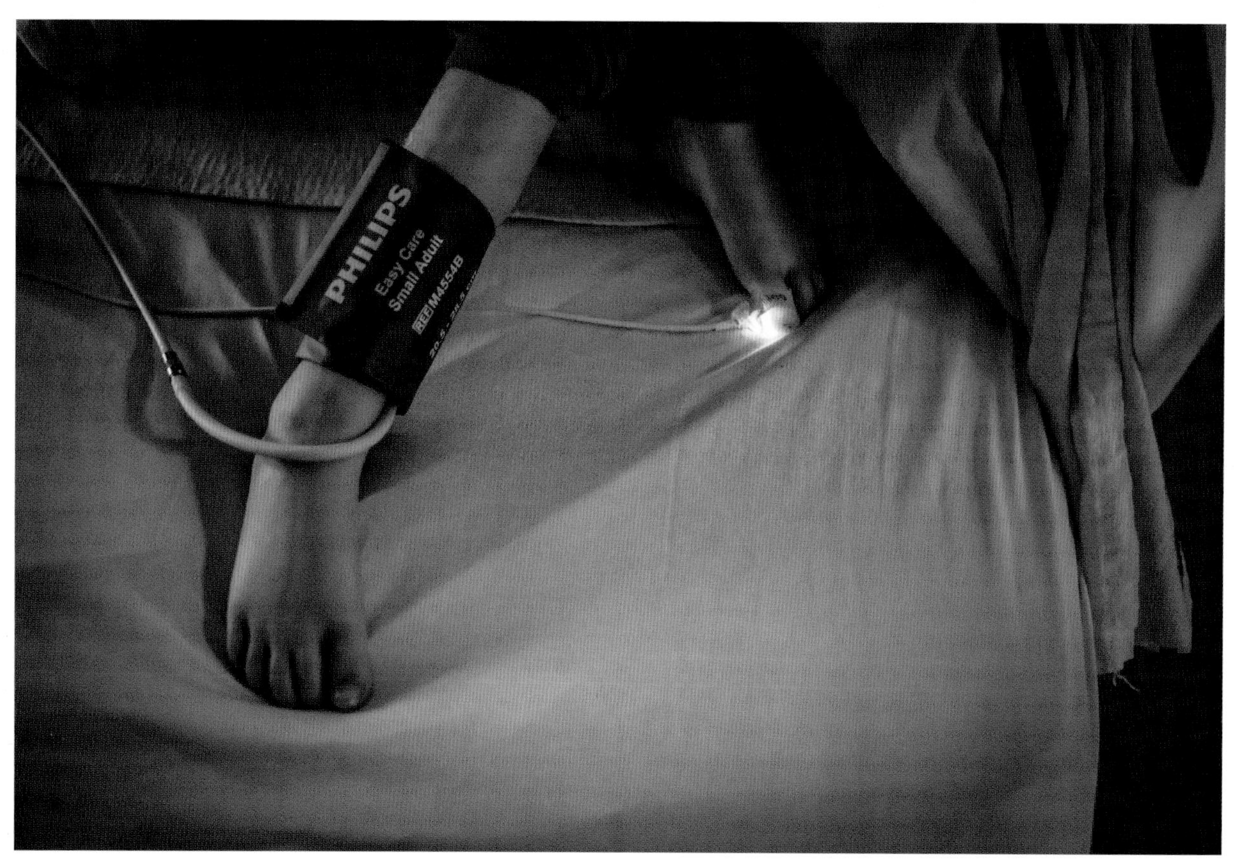

The vital signs of Freddie Walker, 6, being monitored at Alberta Children's Hospital in Calgary on October 22, 2021.

A nurse takes the temperature of Freddie Walker at Alberta Children's Hospital.

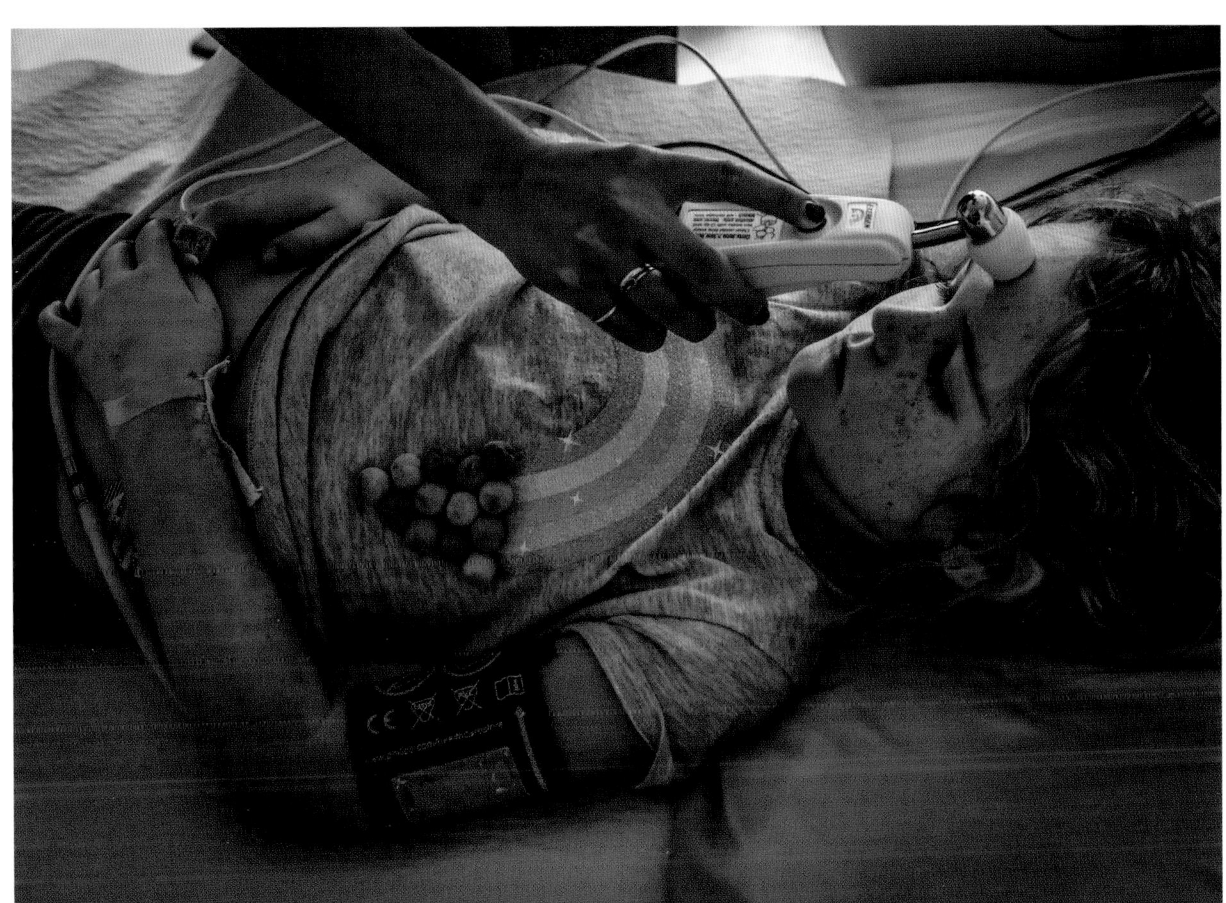

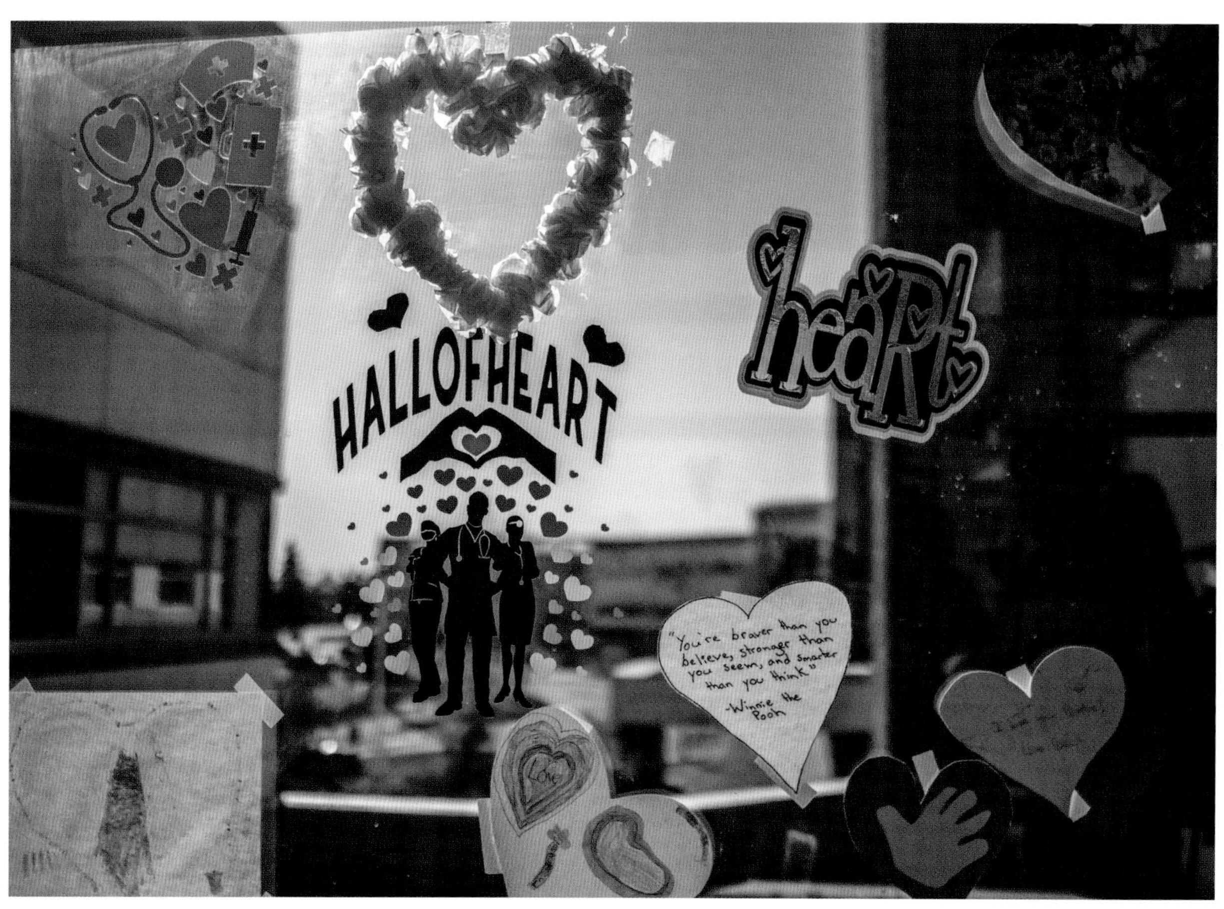

The hallway to the intensive care unit at Red Deer Regional Hospital.

A doctor comforts a COVID-19 patient at Rockyview General Hospital during the fourth wave.

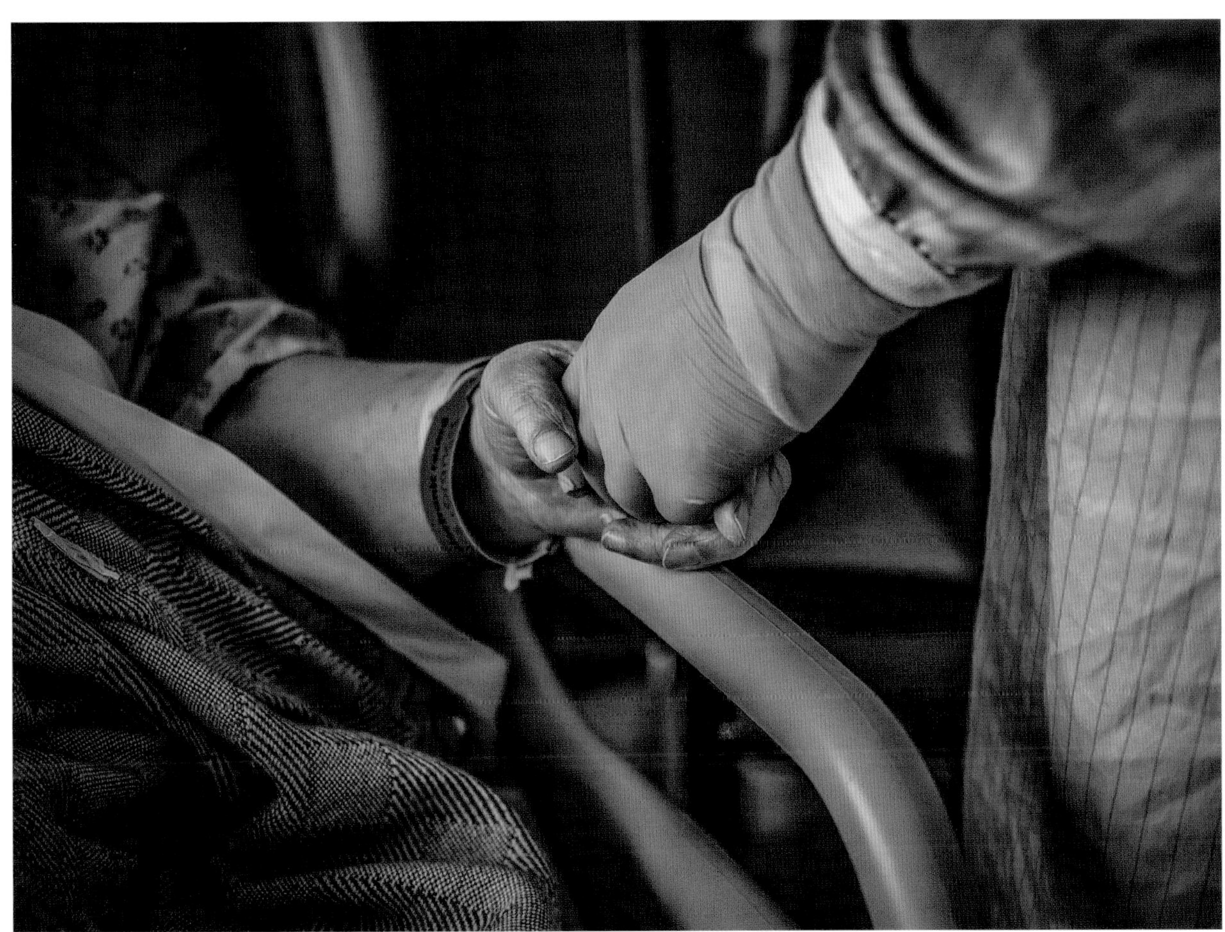

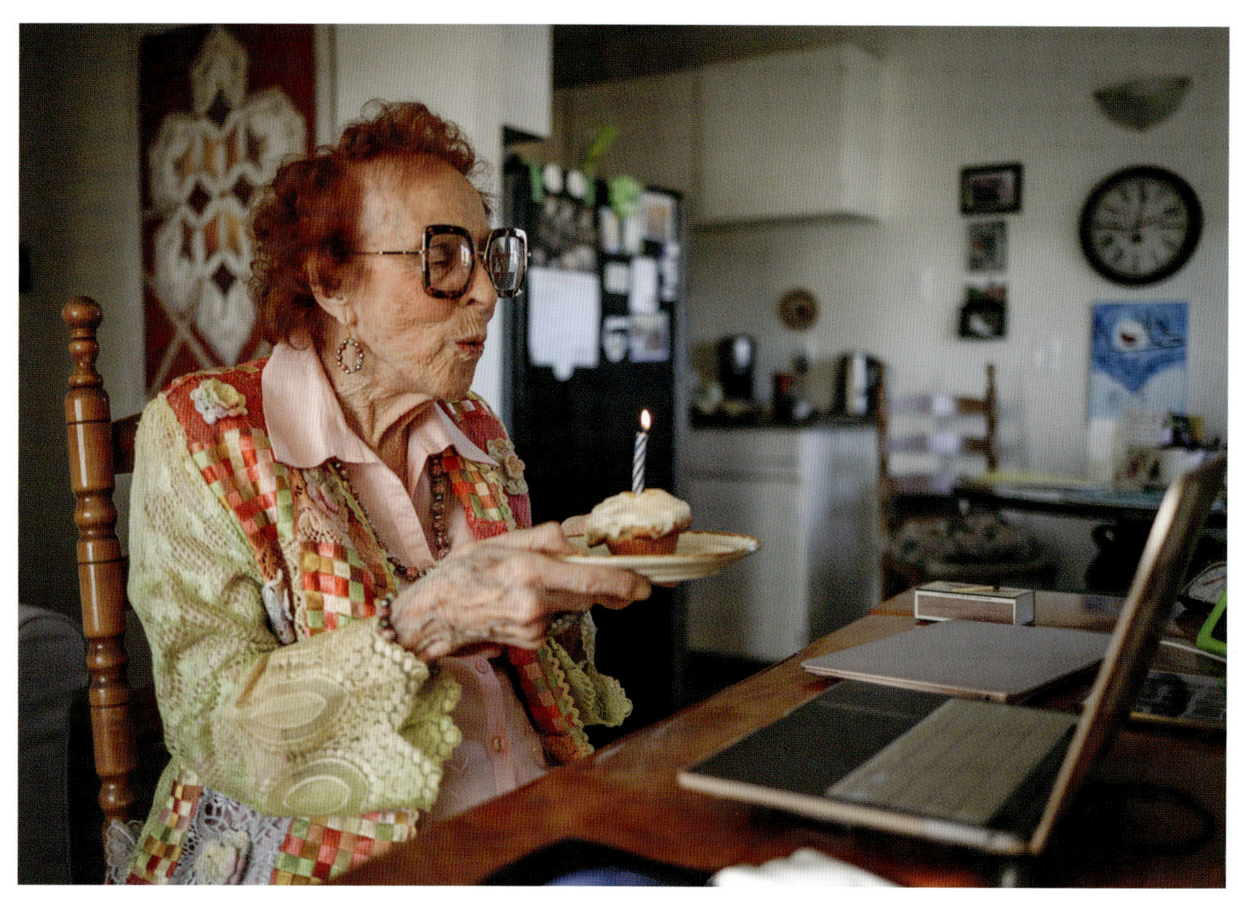

Looking to a brighter future, Louise Smyth
celebrates her 98th birthday by FaceTiming
her friends and family on November 20, 2021.

For information on purchasing bulk quantities of this book, or to obtain media excerpts or invite the author to speak at an event, please visit rmbooks.com and select the "Contact" tab.

RMB | Rocky Mountain Books Ltd.
rmbooks.com
@rmbooks
facebook.com/rmbooks

Cataloguing data available from Library and Archives Canada

ISBN 9781771605632 (softcover)

ISBN 9781771605649 (electronic)

Design by Chyla Cardinal
Cover photo: Matengey Sangarie, housekeeping, at Peter Lougheed Centre in Calgary, Alberta. April 2020.

Printed and bound in China

We would like to also take this opportunity to acknowledge the traditional territories upon which we live and work. In Calgary, Alberta, we acknowledge the Niitsítapi (Blackfoot) and the people of the Treaty 7 region in Southern Alberta, which includes the Siksika, the Piikuni, the Kainai, the Tsuut'ina, and the Stoney Nakoda First Nations, including Chiniki, Bearpaw, and Wesley First Nations. The City of Calgary is also home to Métis Nation of Alberta, Region III. In Victoria, British Columbia, we acknowledge the traditional territories of the Lkwungen (Esquimalt and Songhees), Malahat, Pacheedaht, Scia'new, T'Sou-ke, and W̱SÁNEĆ (Pauquachin, Tsartlip, Tsawout, Tseycum) peoples.

We acknowledge the financial support of the Government of Canada through the Canada Book Fund and the Canada Council for the Arts, and of the province of British Columbia through the British Columbia Arts Council and the Book Publishing Tax Credit.

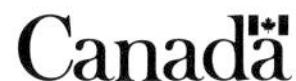
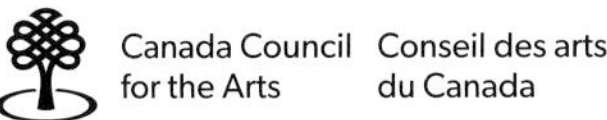
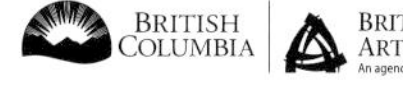
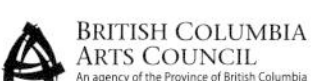